ISLAMIC BIOMORPHIC PATTERNS

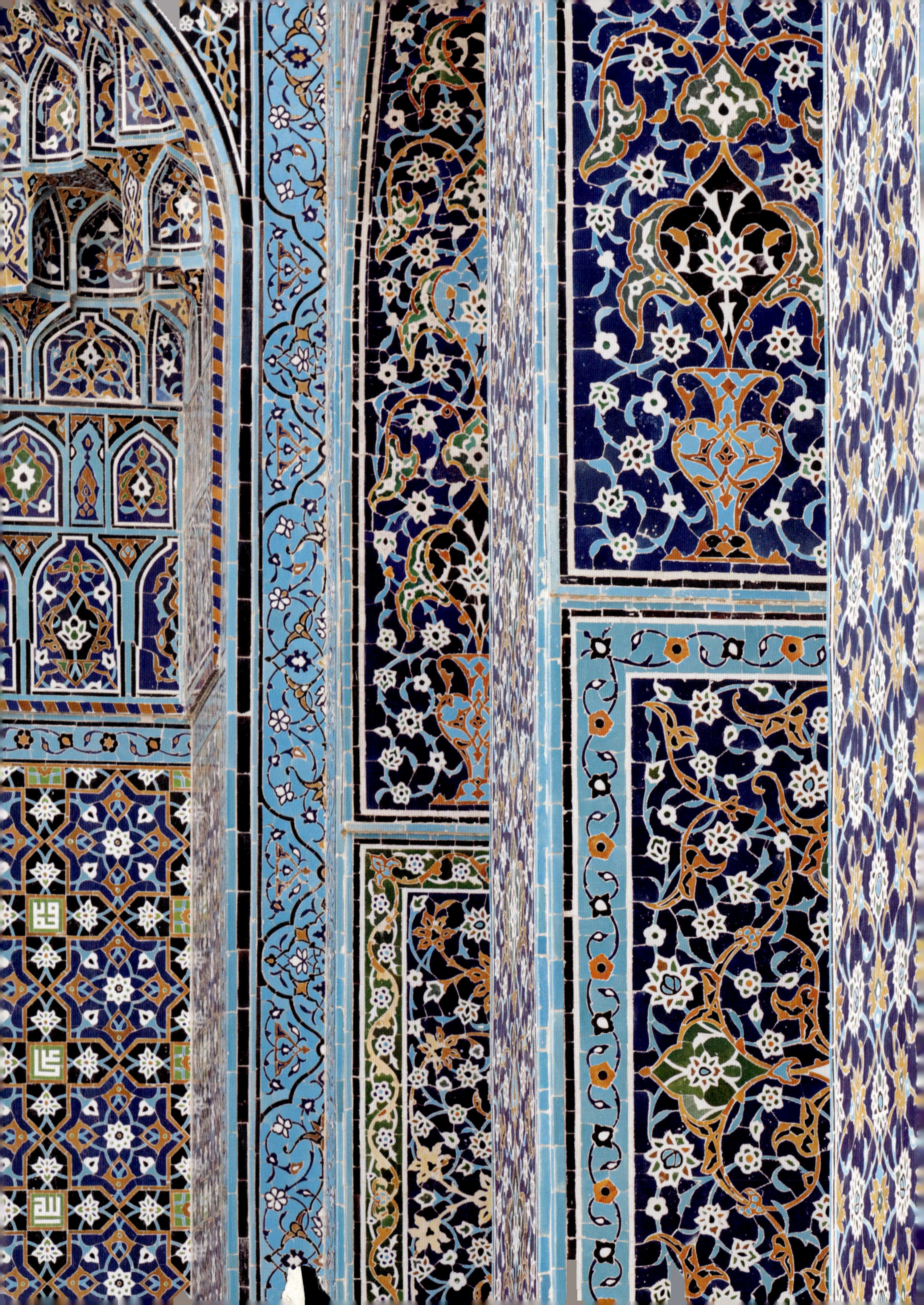

ISLAMIC BIOMORPHIC PATTERNS

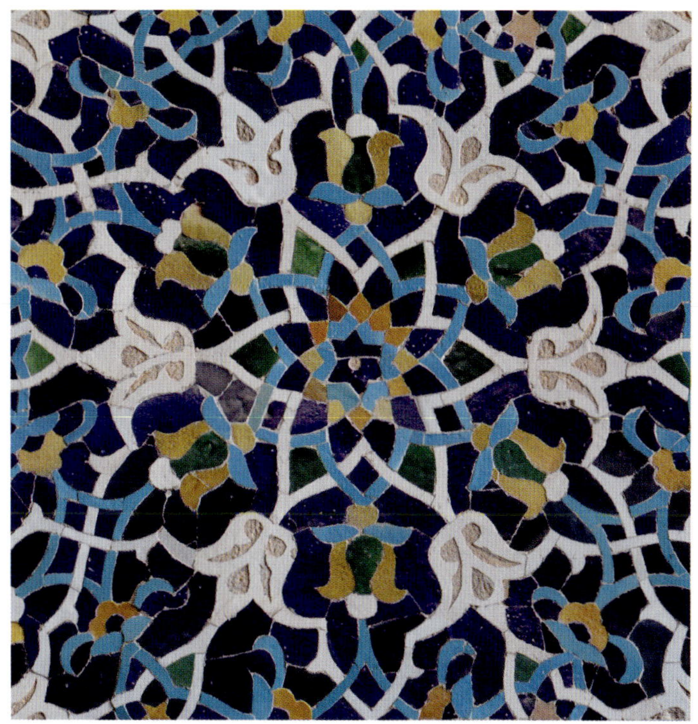

Creating Motifs Inspired by the Natural World

ESRA ALHAMAL

HERBERT PRESS

LONDON · OXFORD · NEW YORK · NEW DELHI · SYDNEY

HERBERT PRESS
Bloomsbury Publishing Plc
50 Bedford Square, London, WC1B 3DP, UK
29 Earlsfort Terrace, Dublin 2, Ireland

BLOOMSBURY, HERBERT PRESS and the Herbert Press logo are trademarks of Bloomsbury Publishing Plc

First published in Great Britain in 2025

A catalogue record for this book is available from the British Library
Library of Congress Cataloguing-in-Publication data has been applied for

ISBN: 978-1-7899-4174-6; eBook: 978-1-7899-4176-0

1 3 5 7 9 10 8 6 4 2

Designed and typeset by Laura Woussen Design
Printed and bound in China by RR Donnelley Asia Printing Solutions Limited

To find out more about our authors and books visit www.bloomsbury.com and sign up for our newsletters

Frontispiece: Floral tilework on the facade of Sheikh Safi-al-din Ardabili Mausoleum, Ardabil, Northern
Iran

CONVERSION CHART

Metric		Imperial
2.5 centimetres (cm)	=	1 inch (in)
90 centimetres	=	1 yard (yd)
1 metre (m)	=	39 inches

To my grandfather, Naji.
May you rest in peace. Your love and support made me what I am today.
I wish you were here to see all the beautiful patterns around us.

To my son, Laith-Naji.
Follow your passion and fill this world with wonders.

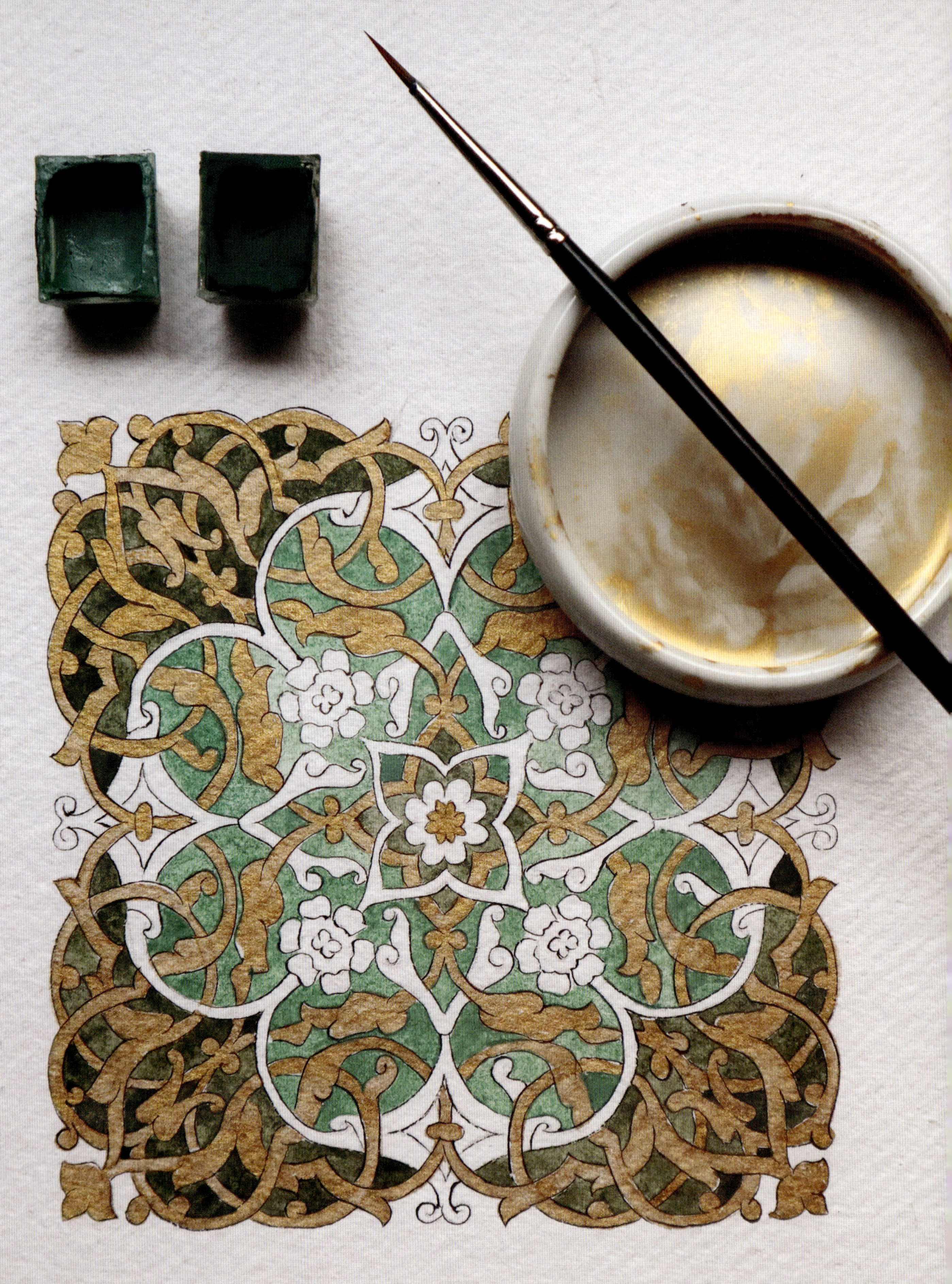

CONTENTS

INTRODUCTION

PERSONAL PATTERN EXPLORATION

Studying, drawing and painting patterns were never part of my plan. The path I was paving was to be a university lecturer, just like my mother – the logical way to go. I knew I enjoyed teaching, and a lecturing job would give me a solid and secure future. My grandfather insisted that I further my education into a PhD, which I did. My plan remained the same for my future, but it all changed during the five years of my doctorate.

It is funny how we think we are destined for one path and work towards it for years, but in reality plans rarely stay the same. Every prediction I had for myself changed for the better and led me to beautiful patterns that spoke to my soul more than anything I had encountered before.

Curiosity was the initial motivation that led me to my first pattern workshop with the Art of Islamic Pattern in East London in 2014. Here I realised that all my previous design education was purely Western. I barely knew the names of Arab architects and I had no clue how to draw patterns from scratch using a compass and a straight edge.

A new window of creative ideas opened up after that first class, which led me to many more workshops and art trips of pattern exploration. With each one, I felt more peaceful from within. When I started painting the patterns I was drawing, I felt that I was allowed to think without boundaries; that my thoughts were free from constraints and I could go deep within my own mind. I had not felt those emotions when practising any other type of art.

My state of mind shifted and I found myself enjoying the slowness and the opportunity for silence and reflection. The constant repetition is a place for contemplation and patience rather than frustration. To achieve the symmetrical qualities inherent in patterns requires plenty of repetition, and as David Cranswick told me in a workshop I completed with him: 'Repetitive tasks lead to a meditative state of mind.'

There are many words to describe the state of mind that occurs while you silently, slowly work on a task: meditation, contemplation, mindfulness, thoughtfulness … however, the name of it is irrelevant; it is the outcome of calm that matters. I hope you too can feel this sense of peace while studying and painting the patterns.

Patterns surround us wherever we go. My favourite patterns are those that come from the Islamic world, especially from the sixteenth century. I loved them so much that I made them the subject of my PhD, which I feel privileged to have completed in 2022. Having the time and opportunity to study any aspect of art and design is such a luxury and a joy. The academic process was difficult, but the beauty of the patterns kept me going. Additionally, the creative community of Instagram and my circle of talented friends in London encouraged me and lifted my spirit each time I shared my patterns with the wider world.

My pattern journey started in London and I thought I would be there forever, but again life changed and I now find myself as the Managing Director of The School of Calligraphy and Ornamentation in Fujairah, UAE. Even after a decade of studying patterns there remains so much to learn and paint that I know I will be kept busy for at least the next ten years. So, the new plan is to not a solid one, but rather to trust the process and to keep on exploring patterns.

THE WORLD OF PATTERNS

The world of patterns is expansive. In a sense, we live within endless patterns, from the formulations of clouds in the sky, to the arrangements of rocks and plants on the ground, to the shapes of flowers around us. Nature itself is an arrangement of patterns, and for centuries artists and designers have been inspired to incorporate them within our lived spaces to the extent that they cover our walls, ceilings and floors. The desire to decorate with patterns has been a human instinct from the beginning of time, as is evident from the development of patterns and motifs found in cave drawings to those we have today.

Every civilisation brought with it a new taste for patterns and a fresh way of seeing the world that later turned into decorative elements. Islamic civilisations continued with their own visual culture in the production and practice of calligraphic, geometric, figurative and biomorphic patterns. The latter will be the subject of this book and will be defined below.

DEFINING 'ISLAMIC'

The word 'Islamic' is conveniently used to describe all artistic expressions and architectural creations, from the seventh to the seventeenth centuries, under any ruler or dynasty that identified as Muslim. However, using the word 'Islamic' can be misleading, since it could inaccurately describe a pattern as a religious symbol, or the maker of the pattern as a strictly practising devout Muslim, which may or may not be the case. Additionally, using one word to describe ten centuries of art, craft and architecture will undoubtedly fall short.

In fact, in the Arabic language and other native languages of the Islamic world, such as Urdu, Persian, Turkish and so on, it is uncommon to use the word 'Islamic' outside of a religious context, especially in reference to art. In Arabic literature before the twentieth century, the word 'Islamic' was not used in the context of art, but instead more specific titles were referenced, for example, the name of the exact dynasty that the art comes from: Andalusian, Ottoman, Mamluk, Safavid, Seljuk and so on. Therefore, we have to be aware of the presence of many more classifications and categorisations within the catch-all 'Islamic' description.

In some instances, the word 'Islamic' is used to describe the unifying quality of art, crafts and architecture that is usually found in the Islamic world. This is a valid point because there is almost a brand-like outcome in the types of shapes, motifs and styles that have been produced to beautify buildings, books and objects.

In the Western world, the use of the word 'Islamic' has become common, to the point that not using it can be confusing to readers who are seeking these patterns – hence the use of the word in this book's title. However, I would like to highlight that using the word 'Islamic' here does not carry religious connotations; instead, it refers to the Islamic countries where these patterns populate surfaces.

PATTERN TYPES

Patterns from the Islamic world have been categorised into four main types: calligraphic, geometric, biomorphic and figurative. Even though these are the four most common types of pattern, this should not negate the fact there are other types of pattern that are not usually mentioned or studied.

Calligraphic is the first pattern type since it was the first visual expression and written format to record the word of God: the Quran. The second type is geometric, which is extremely important as it was used as the basis of many major monuments. As the name suggests, the patterns are based on geometry and mathematical rules that are created from a series of circles and lines forming star-like arrangements. Geometry is the ground, structure and skeleton of other decorative patterns such as the third type, known as biomorphic (or *Nabati*) patterns. The fourth pattern type, figurative, is less common than the first three but there are many examples of it, especially on tiles in palaces, schools and story manuscripts.

The focus of this book is on the third type: biomorphic /*Nabati* patterns. The word 'biomorph' means derived from plants and elements of living organisms, and is used to refer to curved, circular, free-flowing shapes and motifs. Some of these shapes resemble flowers that have been stylised and taken from nature, while others are abstract forms without an identical natural source. This style of pattern has been referred to previously as 'arabesque', meaning Arab style, which is an inaccurate description since the most popular examples of biomorphic patterns originate from non-Arabic speaking countries such as Turkey, Iran and India.

Biomorphic patterns are known by other names, depending on which language you use. For example, in the Arabic language, it is referred to as *Nabati*, which literally means from plants or plant based. In Farsi, there are two main words: *Islimi*, which refers to any organic form, and *Khatai*, which refers specifically to floral motifs. In Turkish, the same word, *Khatai*, is also used to describe floral motifs, and the word *Rumi* – in reference to patterns drawn by the Romans – describes other non-floral organic shapes. It is noticeable that both Farsi and Turkish have more vocabulary in the field of patterns

since both nations are still teaching and practising this
art form. For example, in Turkish, the word *Yaprak*
is used for leaves and *Penc* refers to circular flowers.
Another example is that in Farsi, the word *Toranj* is used
to describe certain inorganic shapes. There are many
other words that can give us a deeper understanding of
motifs that we do not have in the English language.

For a long time, Islamic biomorphic patterns have not
been considered a worthy subject of study in academia,
hence the minimal resources. However, interest is
growing, which is evidenced by the number of students
that have been attending workshops in London and
worldwide.

HOW TO USE THIS BOOK

This book is divided into three parts to help you
understand Islamic biomorphic patterns better. The
first part will give you a brief historic overview of
their development. In the second part, you will study
12 historic patterns from the basic grid to the motif
arrangement. The third part explains how to paint these
patterns using two styles: the contemporary approach
and the classic, more traditional illumination style.

Be reassured that you do not need previous drawing
or painting experience to excel in this art form; this
drawing style is systematic and does not require you
to imagine things that you have not seen before. In
fact, the practice of drawing biomorphic patterns relies
heavily on using historic references to understand
the visual language of the Islamic countries. You are
welcome to innovate with motifs and styles later on, but
this should not be a concern when starting out.

The purpose of this book is to familiarise you with the
visual language and teach you to see the patterns in a
more analytical way. It should serve as a starting point
into the world of pattern exploration. Learning from
the masters of this art is always the first step. Before
even thinking about creating your own designs, you
should understand what came before you and how
the motifs worked in harmony together. Think of the
motifs as words of a foreign language; you would not
be able to speak a new language, create sentences and
communicate without learning the words first.

This is an art book that includes practical guides to
drawing the patterns, but it contains more than steps
to follow. The practice of drawing and painting patterns
is meditative and thoughtful; it is an abstract way of
connecting more deeply with our creative thoughts and
the divine inspiration behind them.

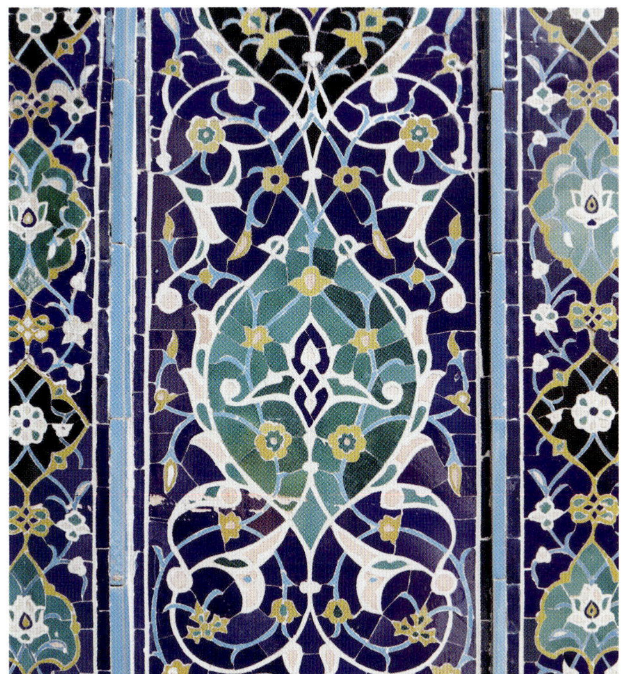

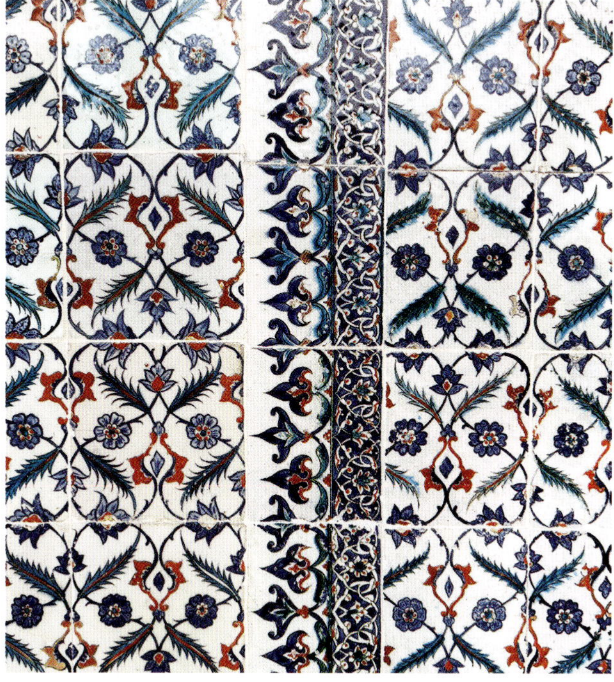

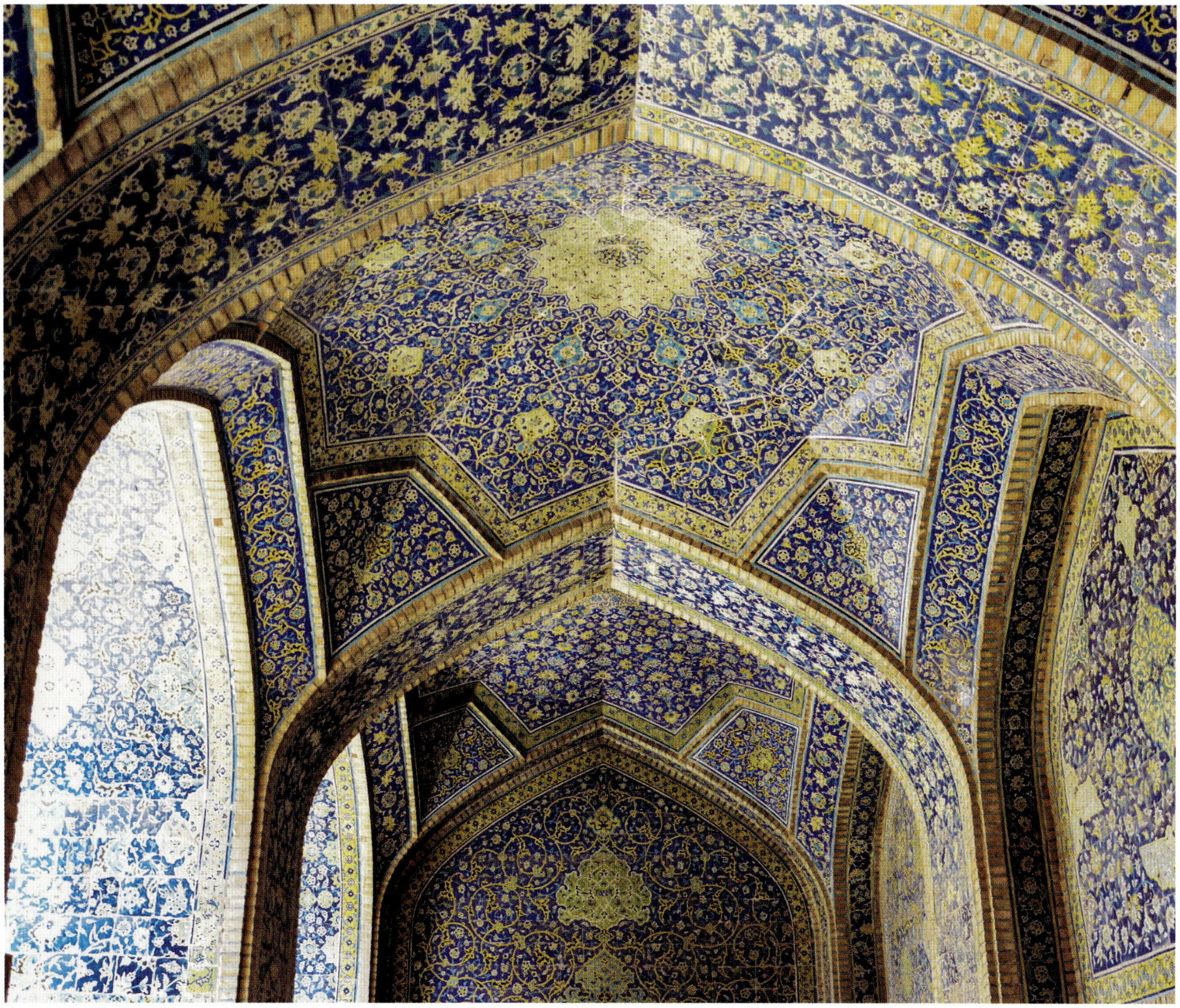

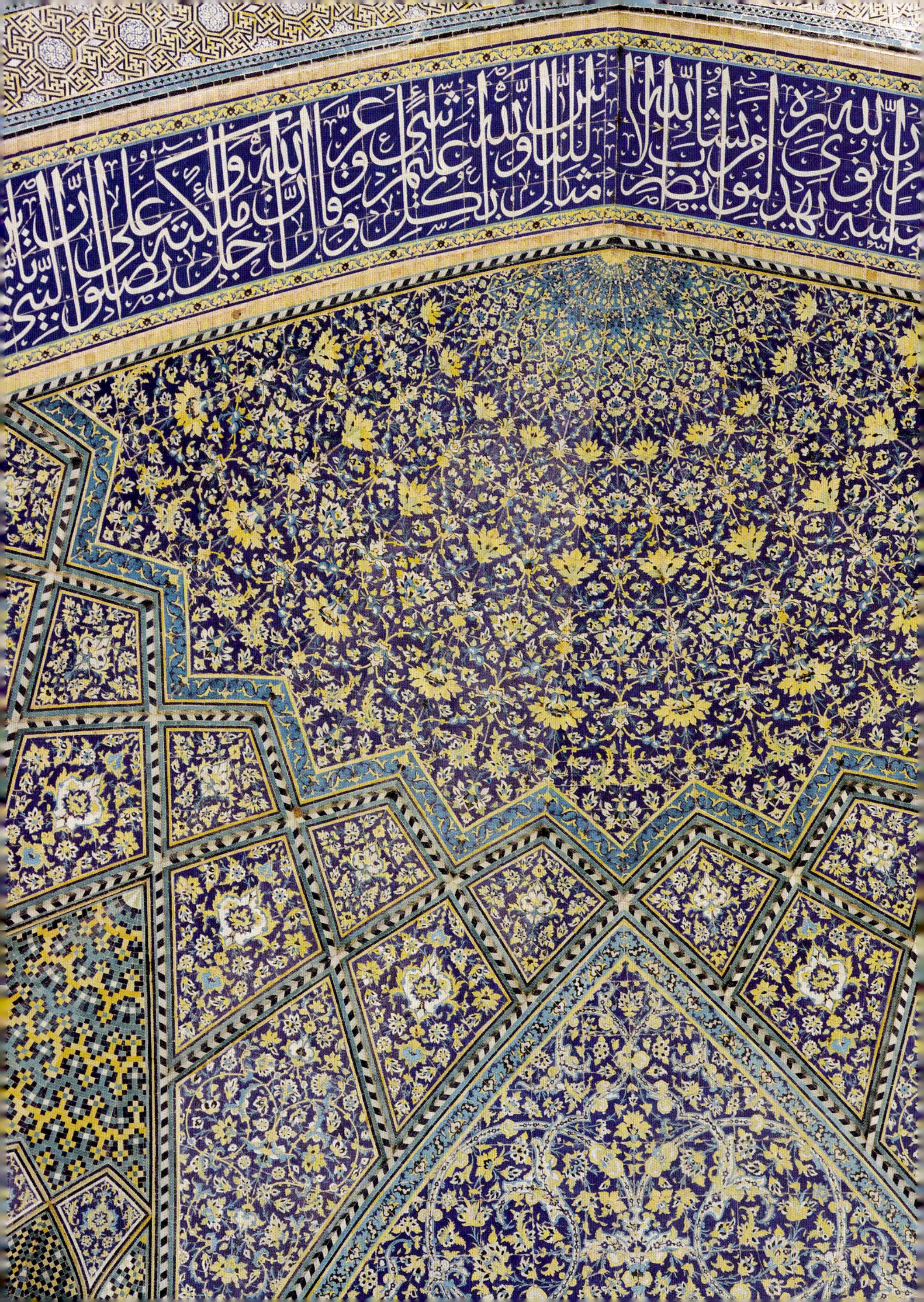

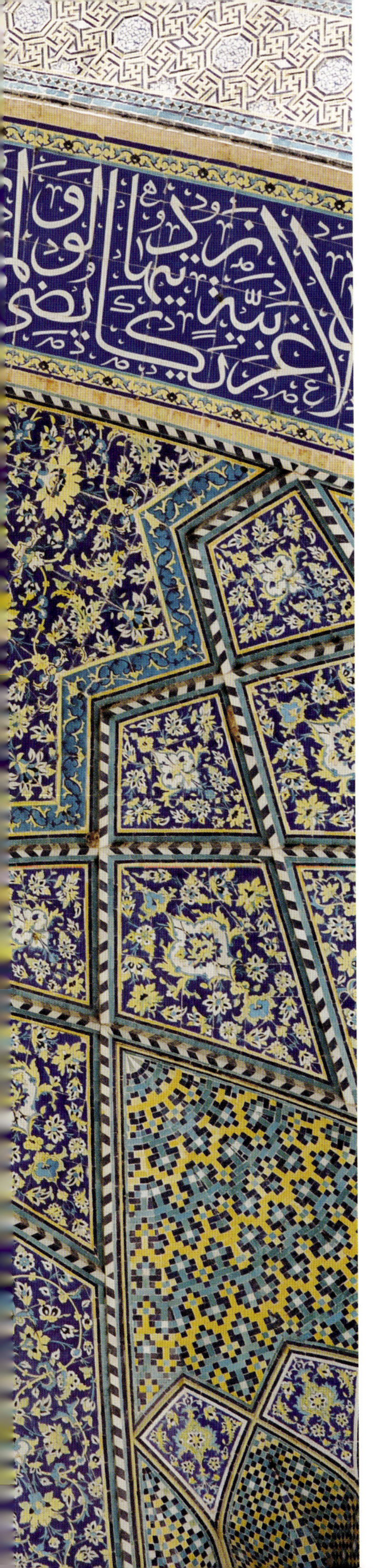

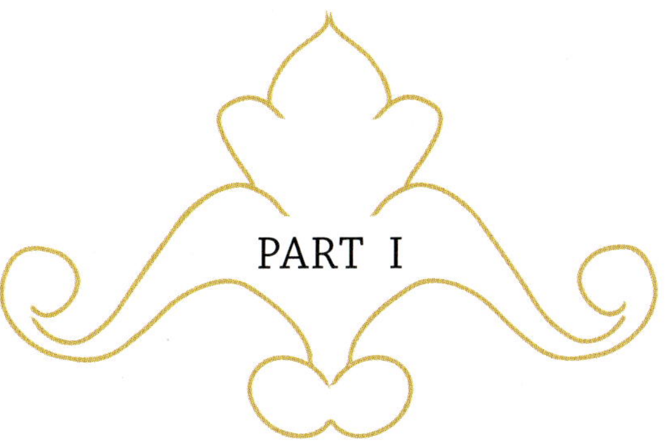

PART I

PATTERN DEVELOPMENT & HISTORY

THE ISLAMIC WORLD

The Islamic world is a rich, varied and non-homogeneous world that started in the seventh century and continues to thrive today. It is impossible to pinpoint one geographical area or time period where patterns originated because of all the variations, and the events that took place across the centuries.

The Islamic world used to extend from India and Indonesia to Andalucía (Spain). That expansion started in the seventh century when Prophet Muhammad – peace be upon him – received the message of Islam and started spreading it. It continued after his death through the dynasties that ruled that region, so when we read about the Islamic world we are faced with many possibilities, timelines, creative efforts and so on.

It is important to note that the Islamic world and its creative output is not a thing of the past. Islamic art is a living practice. Some of the styles, media and practices have changed through time, but that should be considered normal. The art is impacted by each person's culture, lived experiences and the state of the world they inhabit. Muslims and residents of the Islamic world continue to produce artworks, but these works are not considered 'Islamic'. They fall under many different categories and it seems that regional names are used for these, such as Arab art, Middle Eastern art, North African art and so on. It is an interesting comparison that art produced in America or Europe is not categorised in this way, but is instead grouped by media.

THE INFLUENCE OF HISTORY

To track the development of patterns, we need to take a brief look at the historical context in which these patterns were developed to compare their influences and style. Art, patterns and other objects cannot be studied in isolation, independent of their origins, surroundings and influences.

The first dynasty after Prophet Muhammad and his four successors was the Umayyad dynasty (AD 661–750), which later moved to Andalucía (AD 711–1031). They were followed by the Abbasids (AD 750–1258), whose focus was on establishing the Islamic rules and building an important architectural infrastructure of mosques and palaces across the lands they absorbed into their kingdoms. Pattern development was still considered very new at that stage.

The Islamic world consisted of two main geographical areas on either side of the Arabian Peninsula: the eastern part – the Sasanian Empire – and the western part – the Byzantine Empire. It is interesting to track pattern development in both the eastern and western Islamic worlds, especially since the ruling powers had different visual styles. Although the development and changes were parallel, the style of patterns, colour palettes and calligraphy were different.

To track and pinpoint the origin of the patterns is a challenge, especially as there are access restrictions to certain sites and their images, and other sites have been destroyed or naturally deteriorated over time. There are various ways to approach this, such as by going to areas that allow access or by collecting digital imagery available through online collections. Since the Islamic world is very large with many important locations, I have chosen to focus on historic patterns from Turkey, Persia and parts of Central Asia. These patterns were created over a span of seven centuries that saw countless power struggles.

SIXTH- AND SEVENTH-CENTURY PATTERNS

Before Islamic rule extended to Iran and Central Asia in AD 642, the Sasanians (AD 224–651), whose state religion was Zoroastrianism, were the dominant ruling power. The patterns that were used during that time showcase the visual language that was present. The most developed artistic pattern styles date from the sixth century, and these patterns included clear shapes and defined motifs. Sometimes there are disputes about whether these patterns were remnants of the Sasanians or the early Muslims. Generally, patterns borrow and repurpose elements from ruling periods and geographical locations.

The examples opposite, from the Metropolitan Museum's collection in New York, show some of the stucco work that was created in the sixth century, during the Sasanian period. The quality is simple and it includes natural elements of leaves and animals with a basic geometric shapes around the borders.

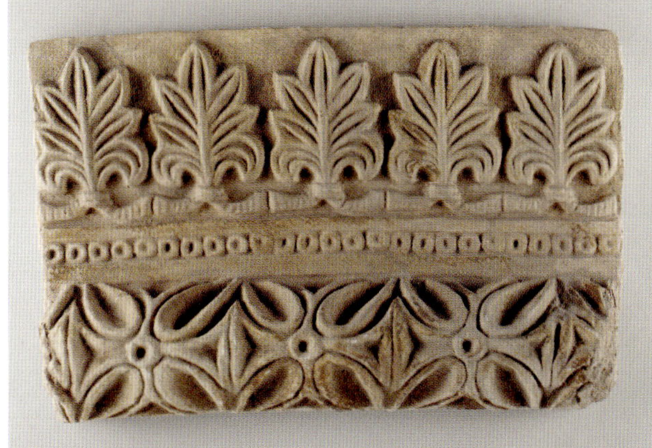

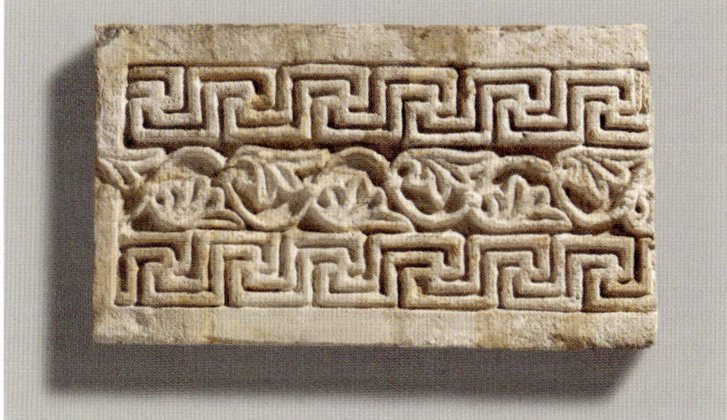

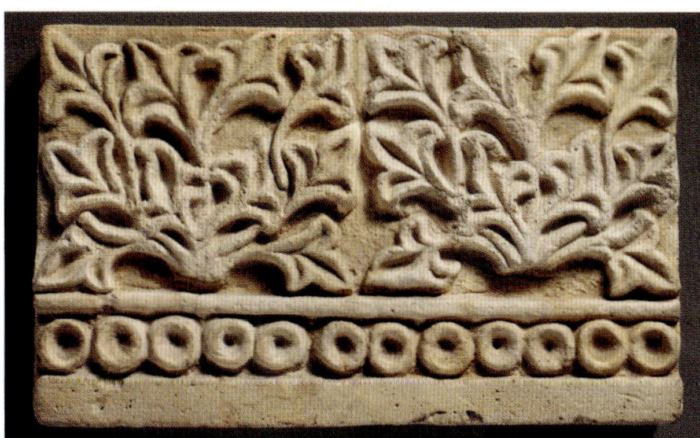

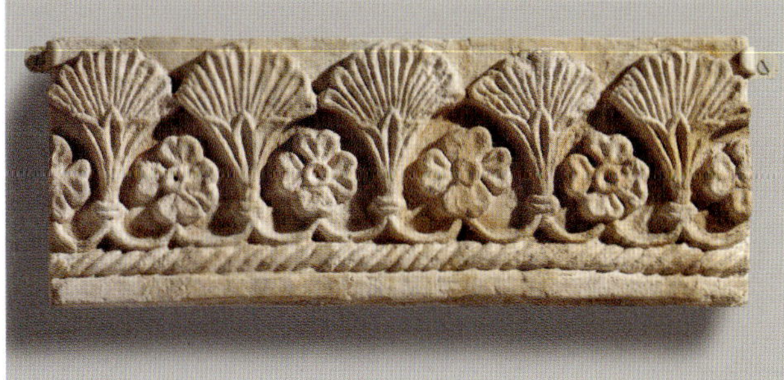

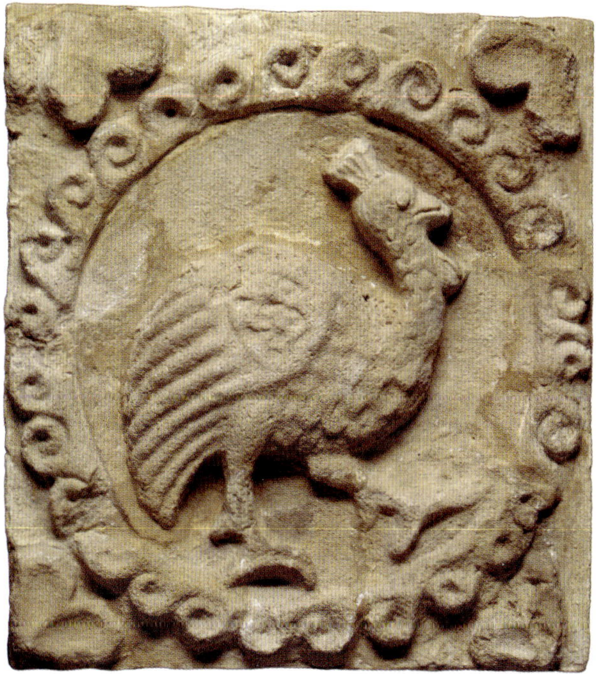

From the seventh century onwards, the religion in parts
of Iran and Central Asia changed when the Muslim Arabs
of the Umayyad and Abbasid dynasties took control of
the region. This change was responsible for a shift in the
visual language. After the Abbasids, a series of short-
term dynasties ruled, including the Tahirids, Saffarids,
Samanids and Buyids. They had power struggles with
each other, but managed to rule one after the other from
the ninth to the eleventh century. The Seljuks of Iran
ruled from the mid-eleventh century until the end of the
twelfth century.

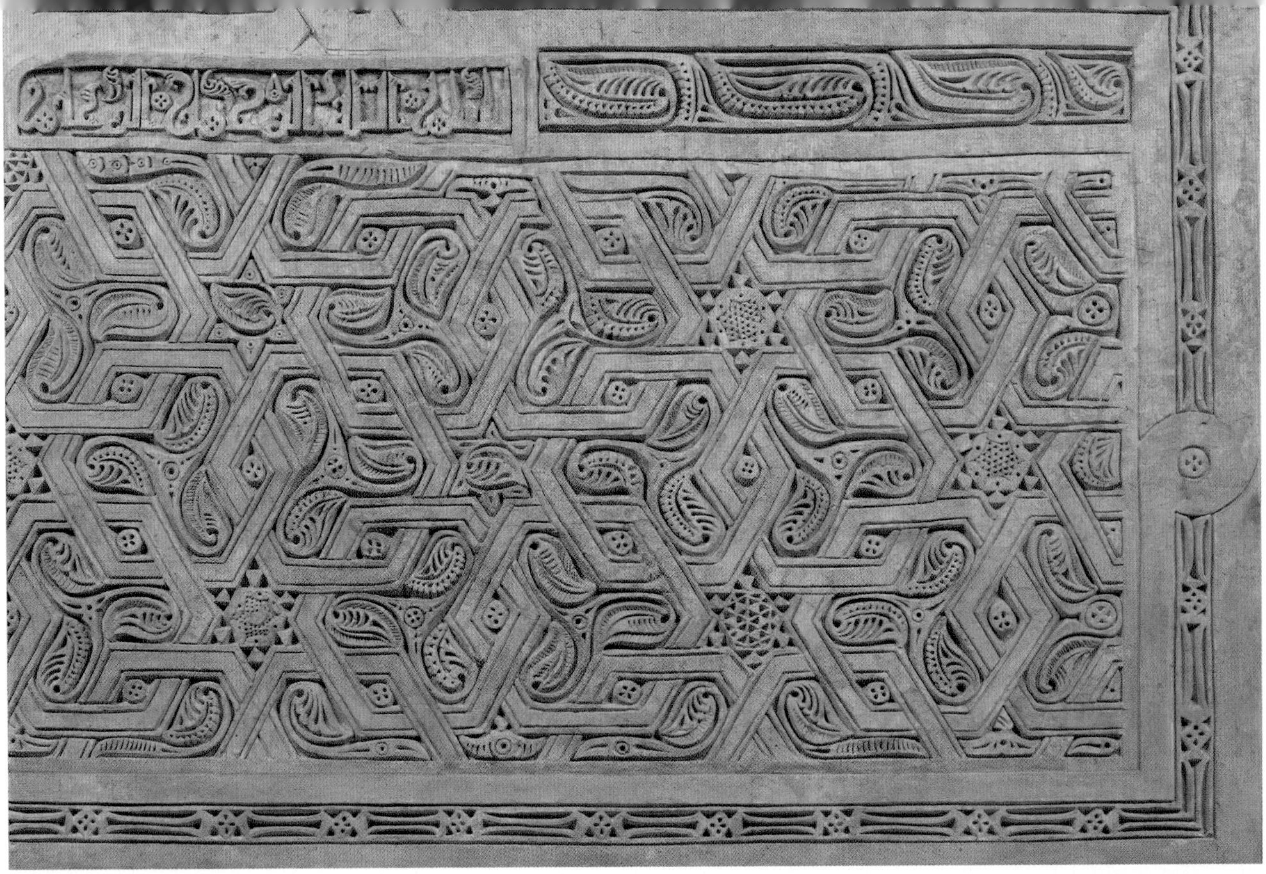

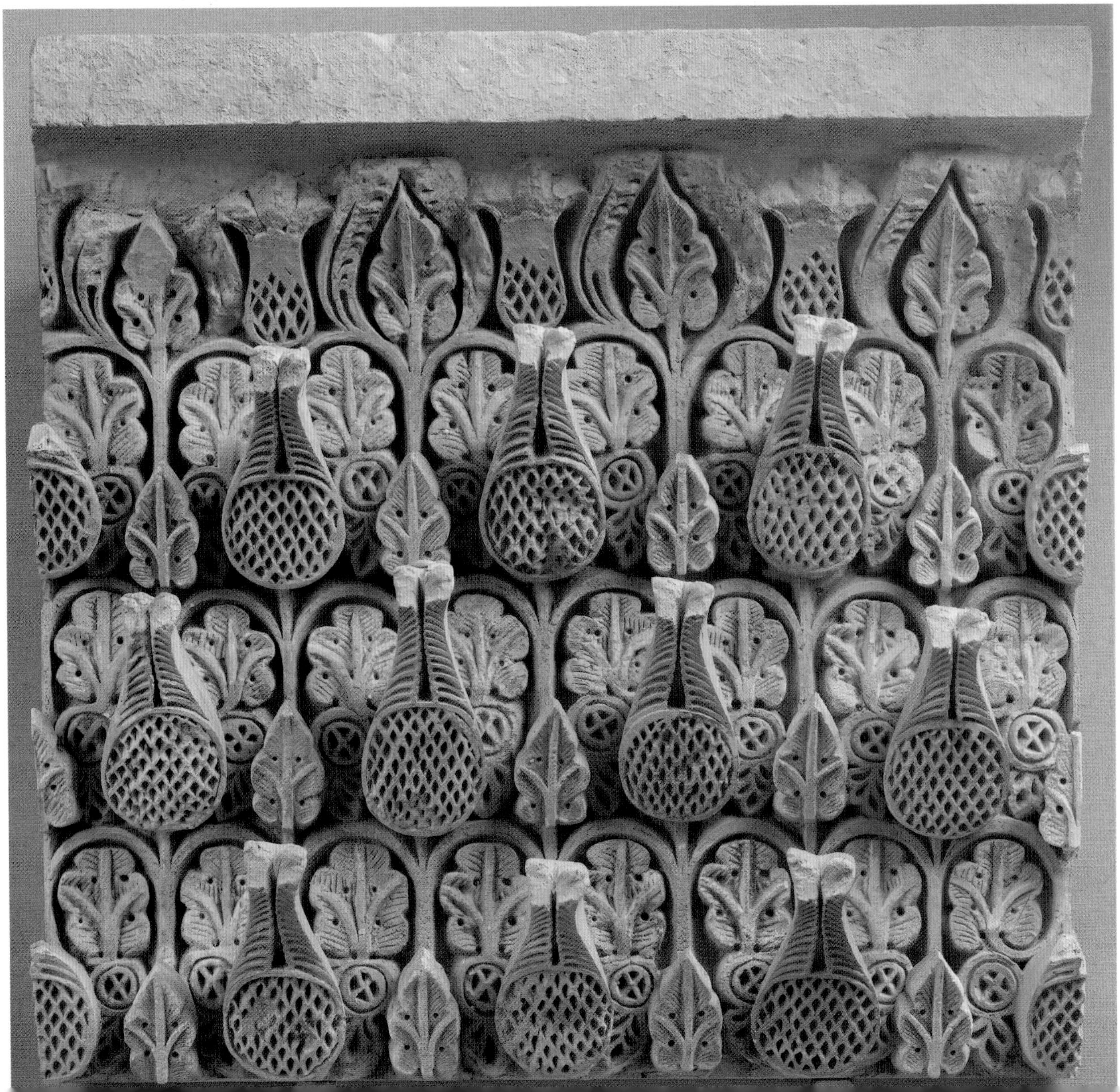

TENTH-CENTURY PATTERNS

The top left panel, from the tenth century, showcases the use of biomorphic patterns with geometry and Arabic calligraphy. It is thought that this pattern could have been part of a mosque or a residence in Nishapur, Iran.

A great architectural example that is dated to the tenth century and combines contributions from the short-term dynasties is the Tepe Madrasa in Nishapur, Iran. One of the stucco panels (bottom left) acquired by the Metropolitan Museum's collection in New York shows us the connection to the Sasanians and the improvement to the details and symmetry.

ELEVENTH- AND TWELFTH-CENTURY PATTERNS

The rule of the Seljuks of Iran extended to larger areas, from the Hindu Kush mountains to Eastern Anatolia, and from Central Asia to the Persian Gulf. There are many visual examples that illustrate the huge level of detail and care given to the patterns during this period. Additionally, there is a clear inclusion of calligraphy and geometry in objects, which is a style that seldom appeared during the Abbasid dynasty. Examples of the use of geometry and detail are shown in the eleventh-century golden roundel and twelfth-century brass mirror cover.

← Dado panel, tenth century, excavated in Iran, Nishapur, 174.3 × 235.6 cm. Metropolitan Museum of Art, New York.

← Fragment of a cornice panel, tenth century, Tepe Madrasa in Nishapur, Iran, tenth century, 74.5 × 17.5 cm. Metropolitan Museum of Art, New York.

↙ Mirror, twelfth century, made in Iran, 2.5 × 19.4 cm. Metropolitan Museum of Art, New York.

↓ Roundel, eleventh century, Iran, 0.5 × 7.1 cm. Metropolitan Museum of Art, New York.

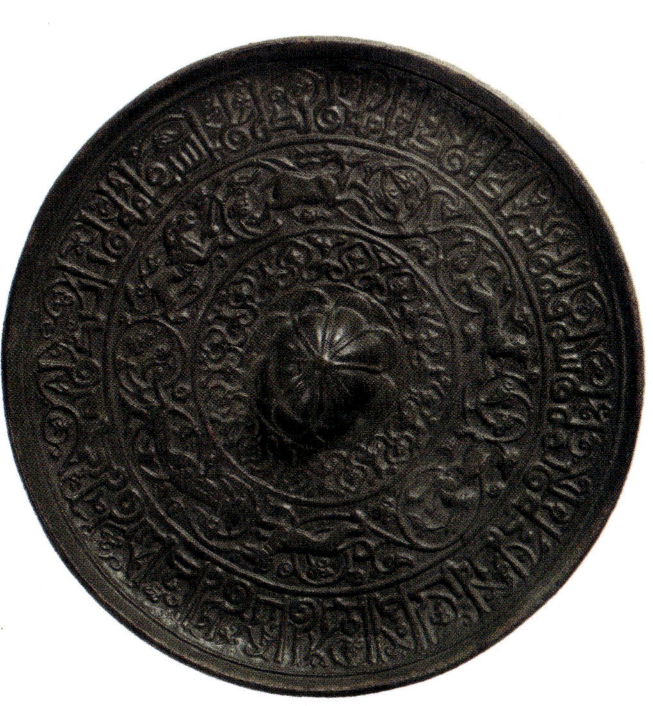

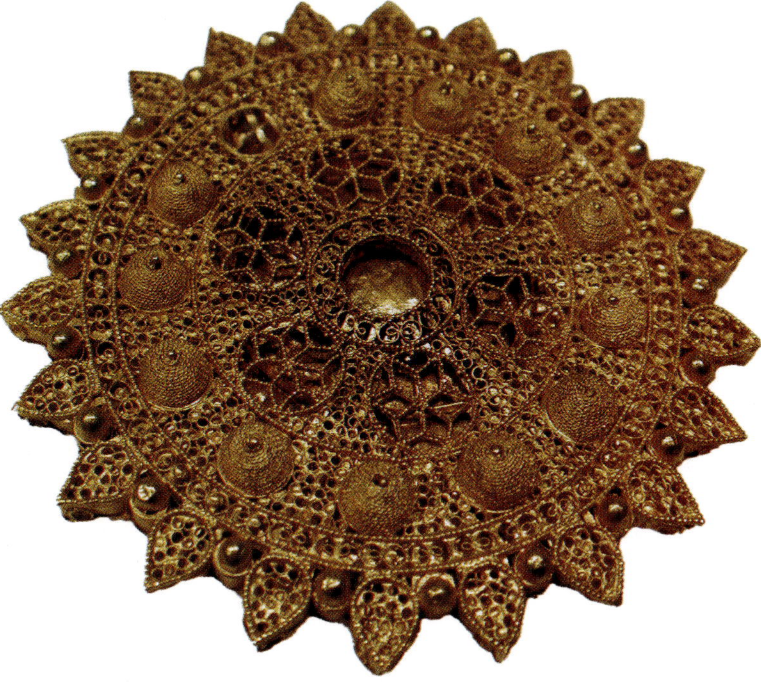

The patterns were not limited to architecture and objects; they were also found in religious and secular manuscripts. The examples below are from a book of Munajat, or 'confidential talks' of Prophet Muhammad's cousin and son-in-law, 'Ali ibn Abu-Talib, which are in the form of prayers to God. The style of the leaves within the calligraphy is similar to that of leaves found within the patterns adorning objects.

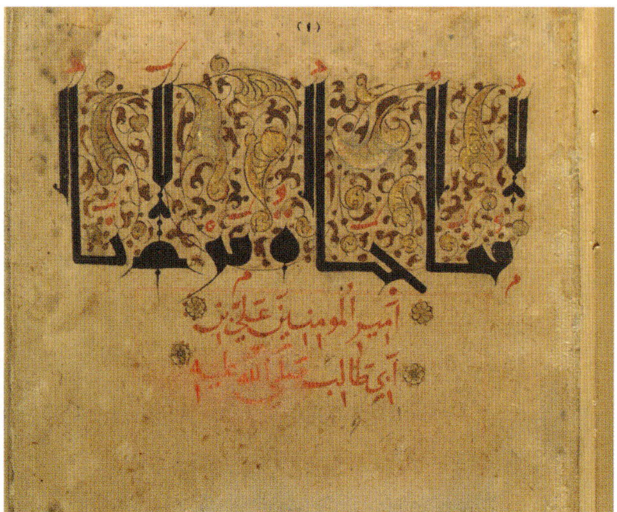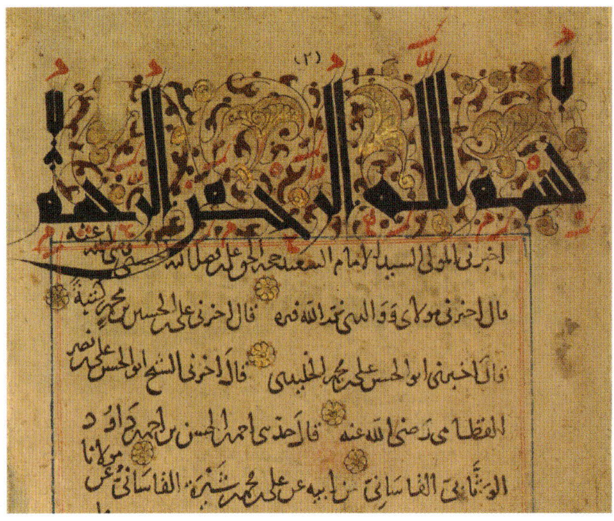

↑ Munajat (Confidential Talks) of 'Ali ibn Abu-Talib, c.1200, attributed to Iraq, possibly Mosul, 17.4 × 13.1 cm. Metropolitan Museum of Art, New York.

FURTHER DYNASTIES

By the end of the twelfth century, a new development in the world of Islamic art occurred that changed the course of pattern design. The Ilkhanid dynasty (1256–1353) made great contributions to the Islamic world by producing coloured, shimmery tiles, known as 'Kashan' tiles in reference to their city of production, that had not been seen before. The patterns seen in the example opposite (top) combine plants, animals and calligraphy. These biomorphic shapes were then used in the coming centuries in a more defined way.

The most significant pattern developments occurred over three consecutive periods in Iran and Central Asia: the Timurid (1307–1507), Safavid (1501–1722) and Mughal (1526–1858) dynasties. Parallel to them were the Ottomans in Turkey (1300–1923). The art of these four dynasties shares many techniques and motifs. Additionally, the simple shapes used in previous centuries became more advanced, and the architectural sites showed huge power and wealth.

THE TIMURID DYNASTY

The Timurid dynasty advanced many arts and crafts. Their work transformed brass-work, tiles and manuscripts, as you can see in the examples opposite (bottom) and on pp.20–1.

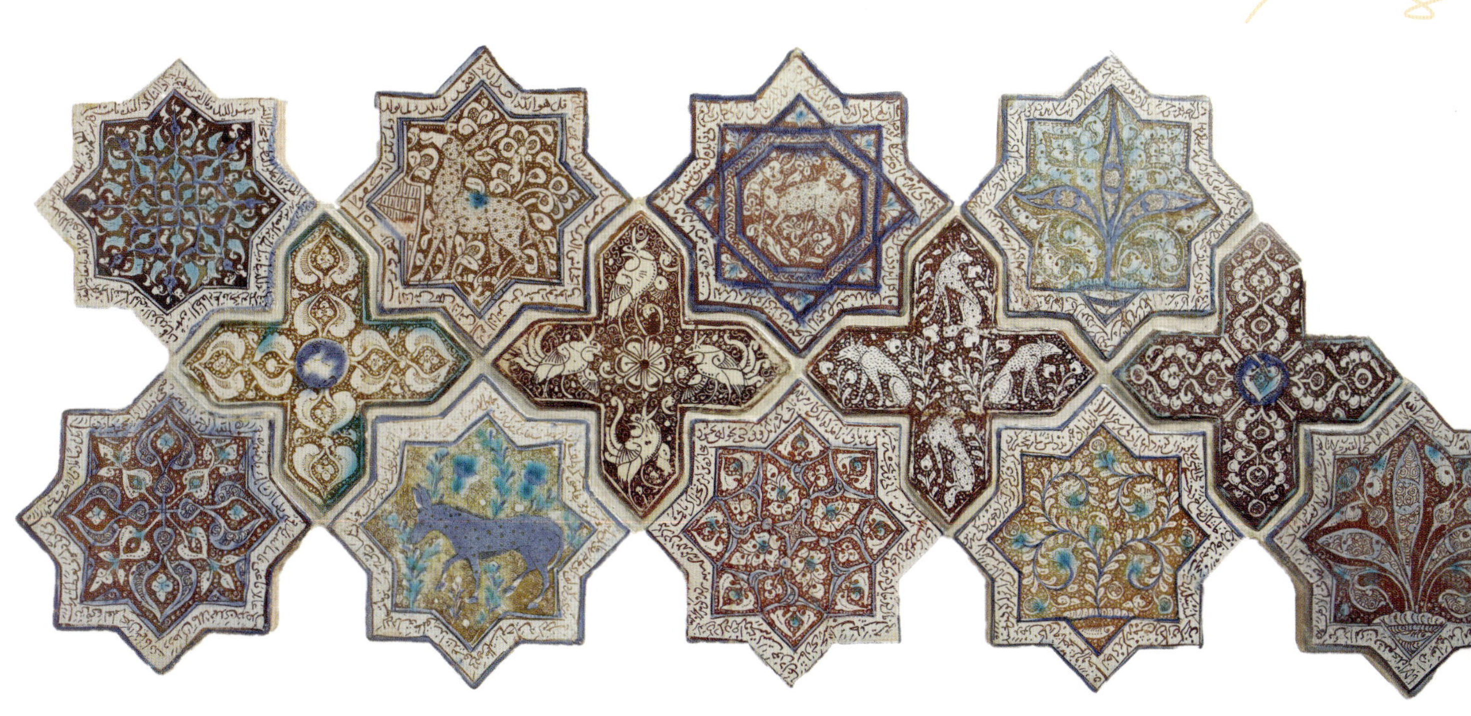

↑ Star-shaped tiles, thirteenth century, made in Iran, probably Kashan, 20.3 × 20.3 cm. Metropolitan Museum of Art, New York.

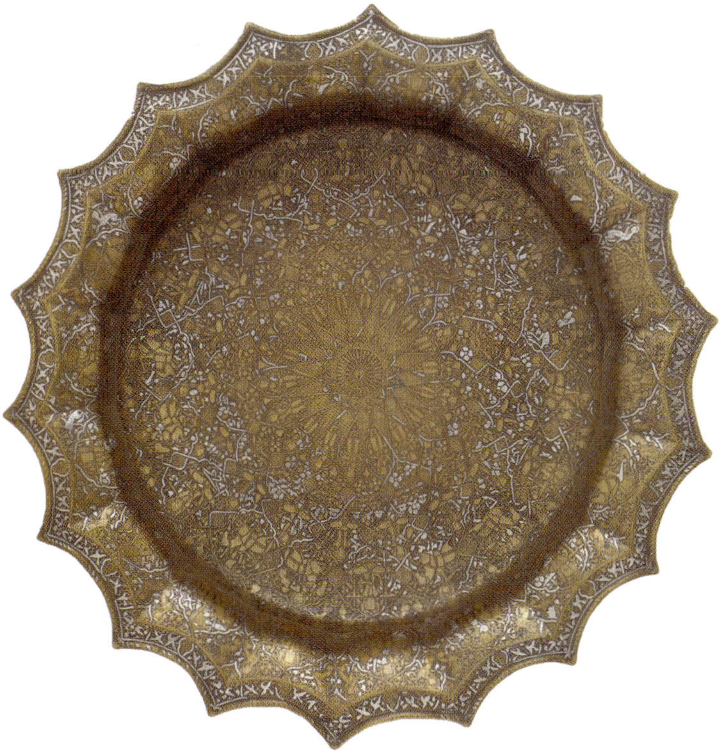

↑ Basin with figural imagery, early fourteenth century, attributed to Iran, 13 × 51.1 cm. Metropolitan Museum of Art, New York.

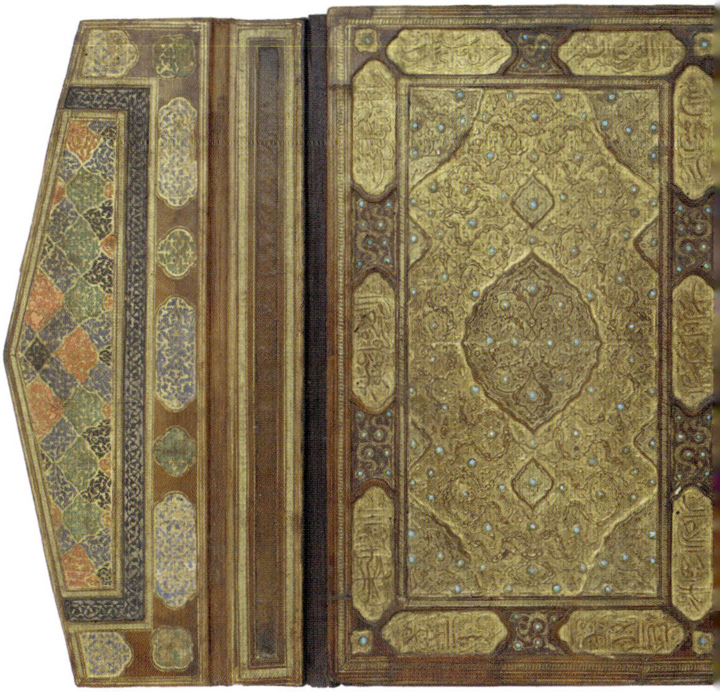

↑ Qur'an bookbinding inset with turquoise, sixteenth century, made in Iran. Open: 35.6 × 68.6 × 3.8 cm. Metropolitan Museum of Art, New York.

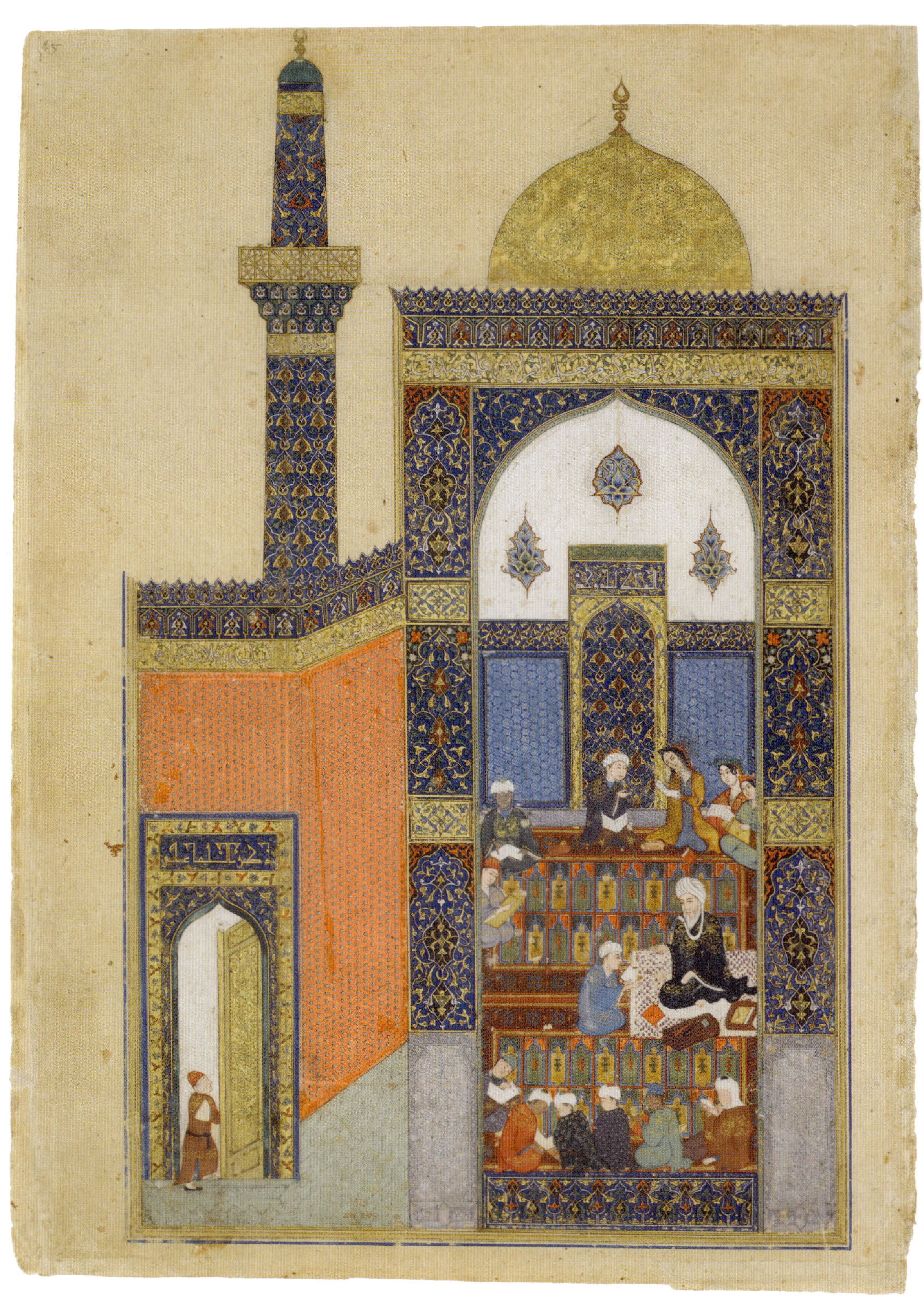

↑ 'Laila and Majnun at School', folio from a Khamsa (Quintet) of Nizami
of Ganja, fifteenth century, made in Herat, present-day Afghanistan.
Page: 31.3 × 22.9 cm. Metropolitan Museum of Art, New York.

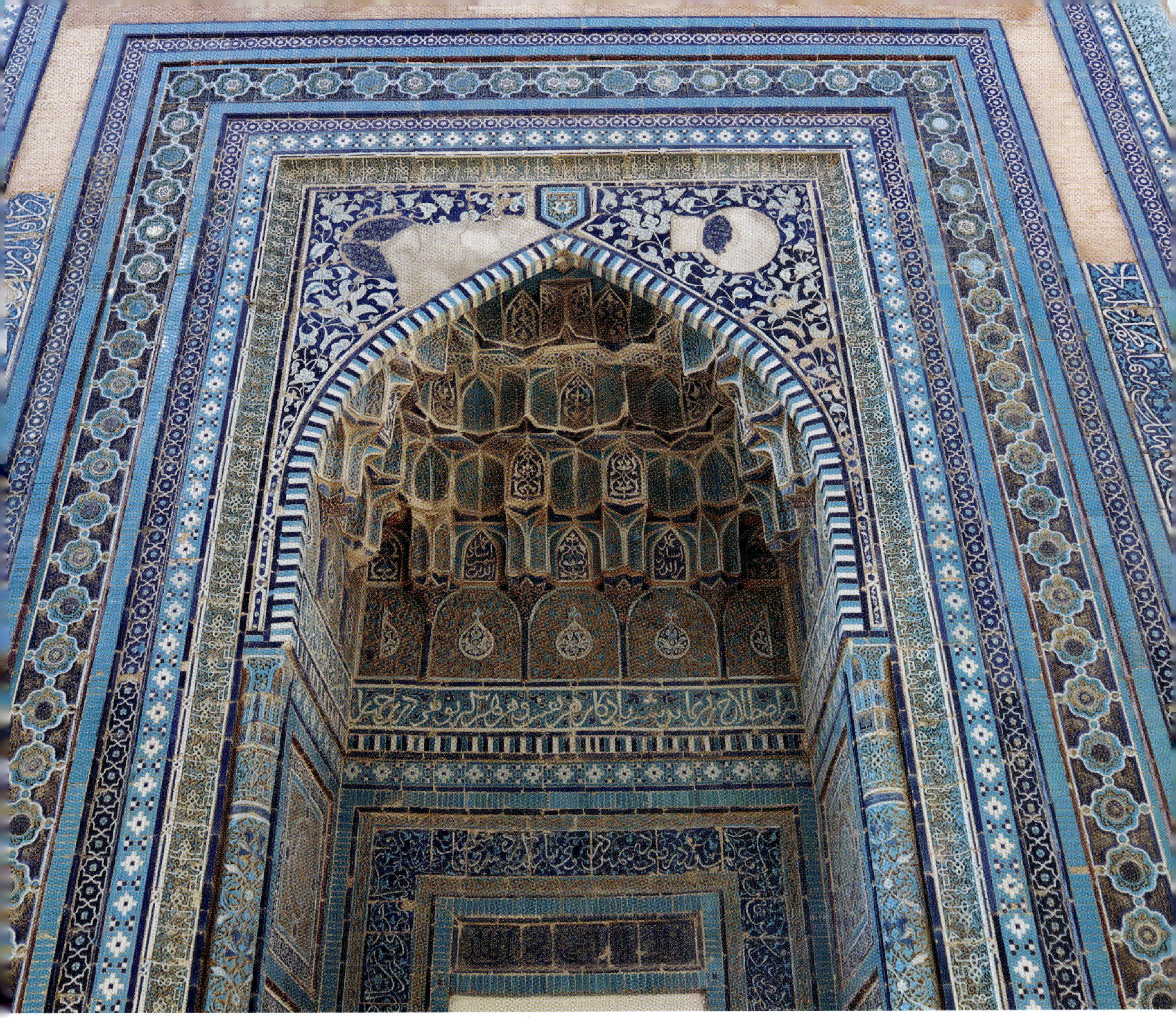

The blue Timurid tiles in Bukhara, Uzbekistan.

A close look at the fifteenth century Timurid ornamental patterns in Bukhara, Uzbekistan.

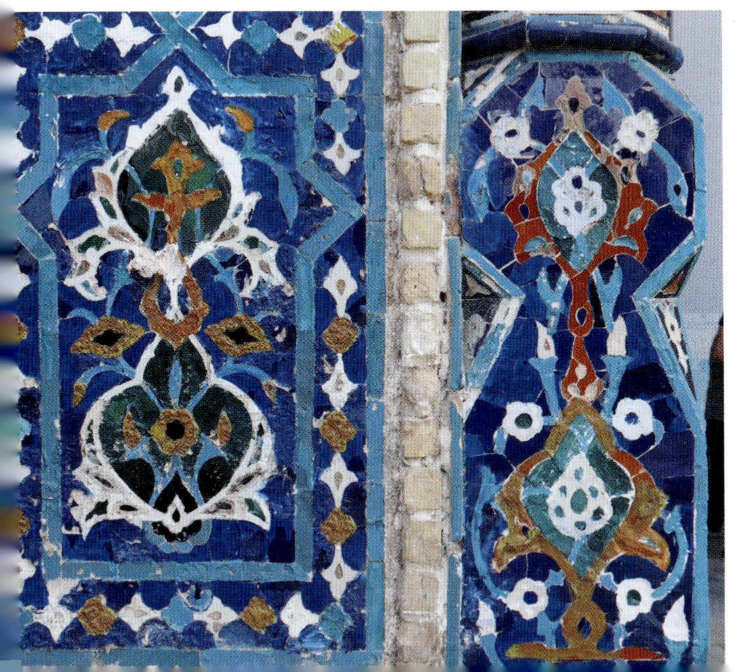

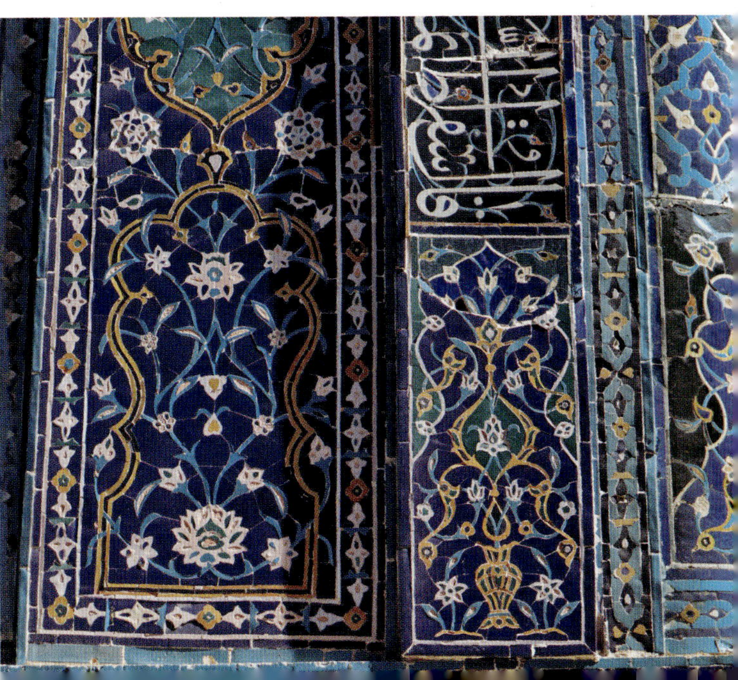

THE SAFAVID DYNASTY

The Safavid dynasty built on what the Timurids created and developed the Islamic tiles further. Instead of creating them as small pieces to be assembled like mosaics, as was done during the Timurid period, they introduced the seven-glaze technique known as 'Haft Rang' – a tile glazing technique that produces beautiful, colourful tiles.

↓ Courtyard inside the Imami Mosque, Isfahan, Iran.

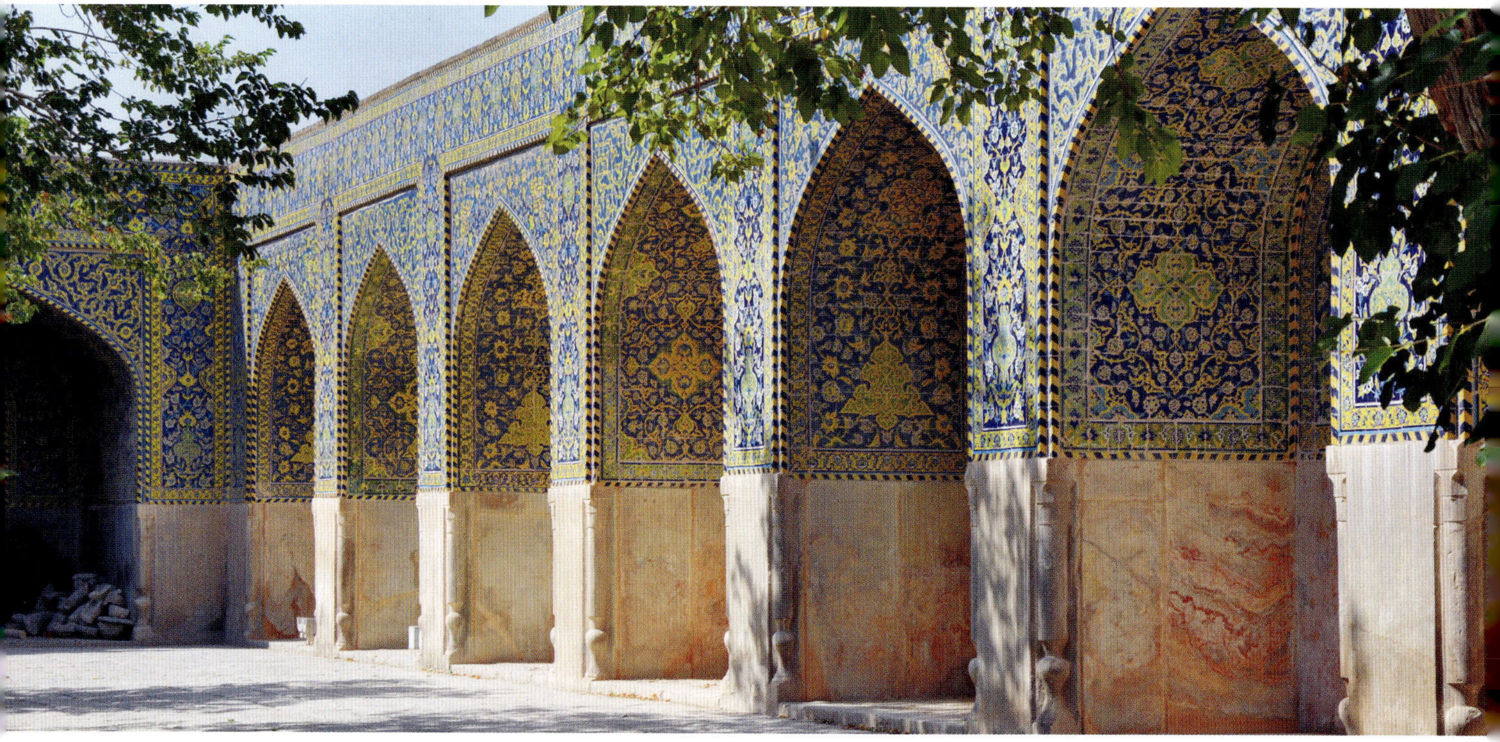

↓ Muqarnas and blue tiles of Iran.

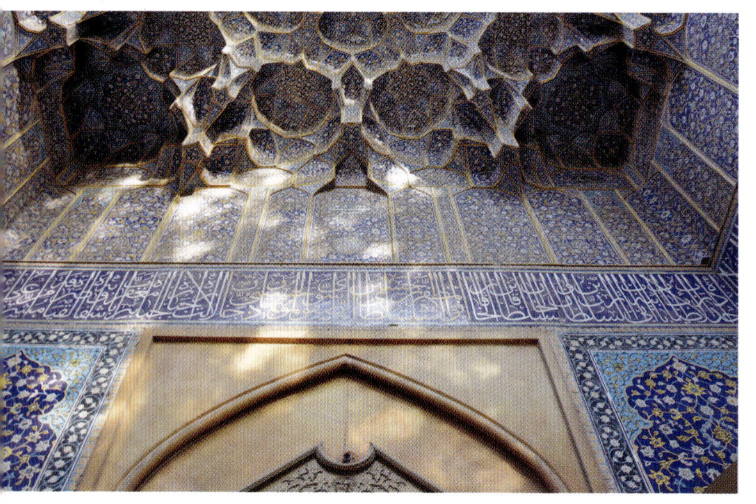

↓ The ceiling of the prayer room in Sheikh Lotfollah Mosque in Isfahan, Iran.

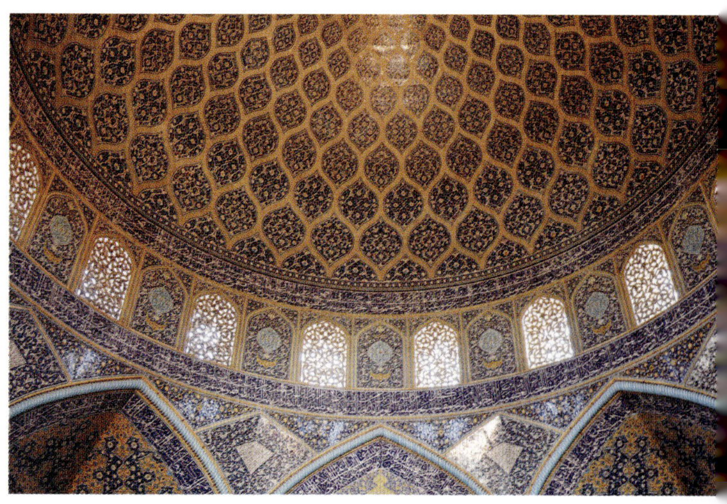

The Safavids also made many contributions to
manuscripts and textiles, which likewise incorporated
biomorphic patterns.

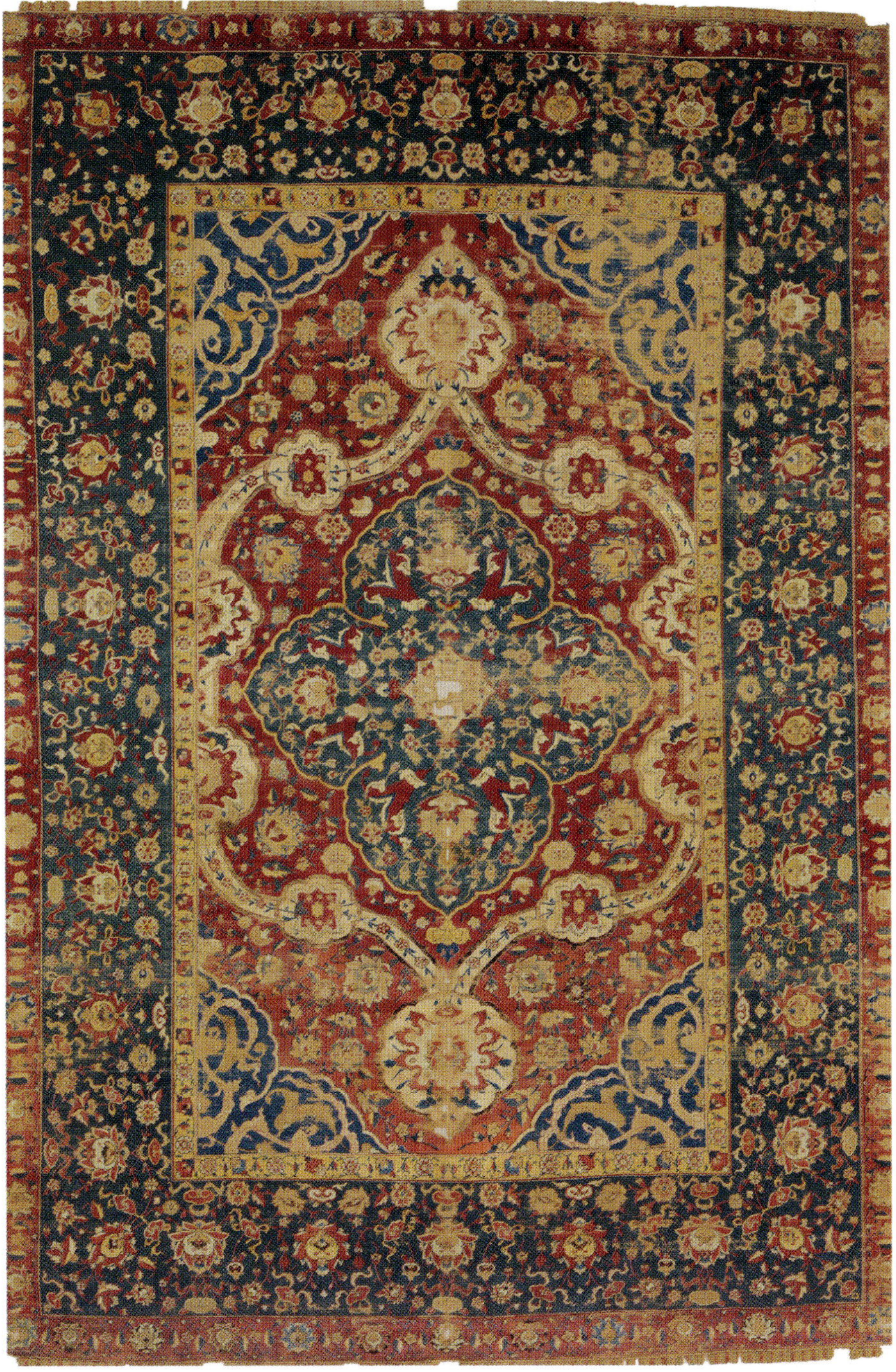

← Silk Kashan carpet, sixteenth
century, made in Iran, probably
Kashan. Rug: 243.8 × 165.1 cm.
Metropolitan Museum of Art,
New York.

POINTS TO STUDY FURTHER

The Mughals also contributed significantly and created
an empire of great beauty, but their geographical
location and beautiful patterns are beyond the scope of
this book. Here I have focused on the main dynasties
that had the biggest impact in the eastern part of the
Islamic world. There are other dynasties that I have not
explored that also contributed in various ways to the
overall development of patterns; these are all fascinating
subjects that are worth investigating separately. There
are so many schools of thought on what took place, and
each academic or historian could have a slightly different
perspective to my own, so make sure to research
patterns and histories from various sources to gain a
more holistic understanding.

I hope that the patterns in this chapter will have
inspired you to learn more about how they are drawn
and painted. As you have seen, there is a huge variety
and selecting 12 patterns to study was challenging, but
this is only the beginning. The patterns I have selected
in the next part of the book are from various parts of
Turkey, Iran and Central Asia and they are an excellent
starting point.

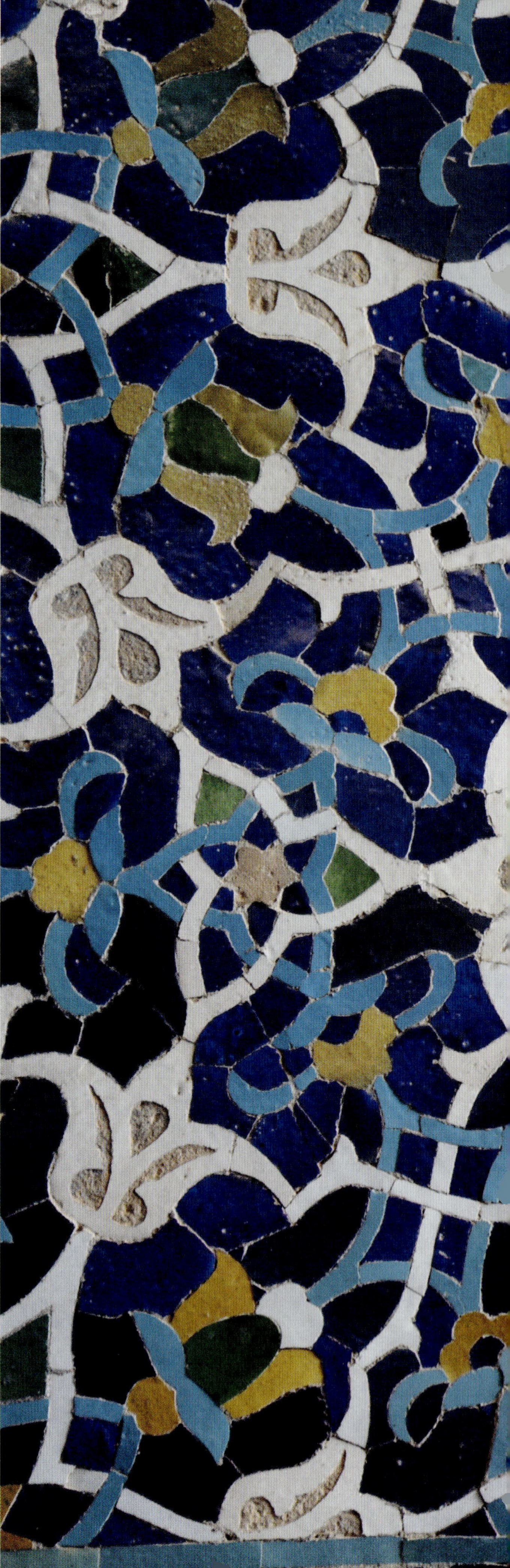

→ A close look at the fourteenth-
century ornamental patterns in
Yazd, Iran.

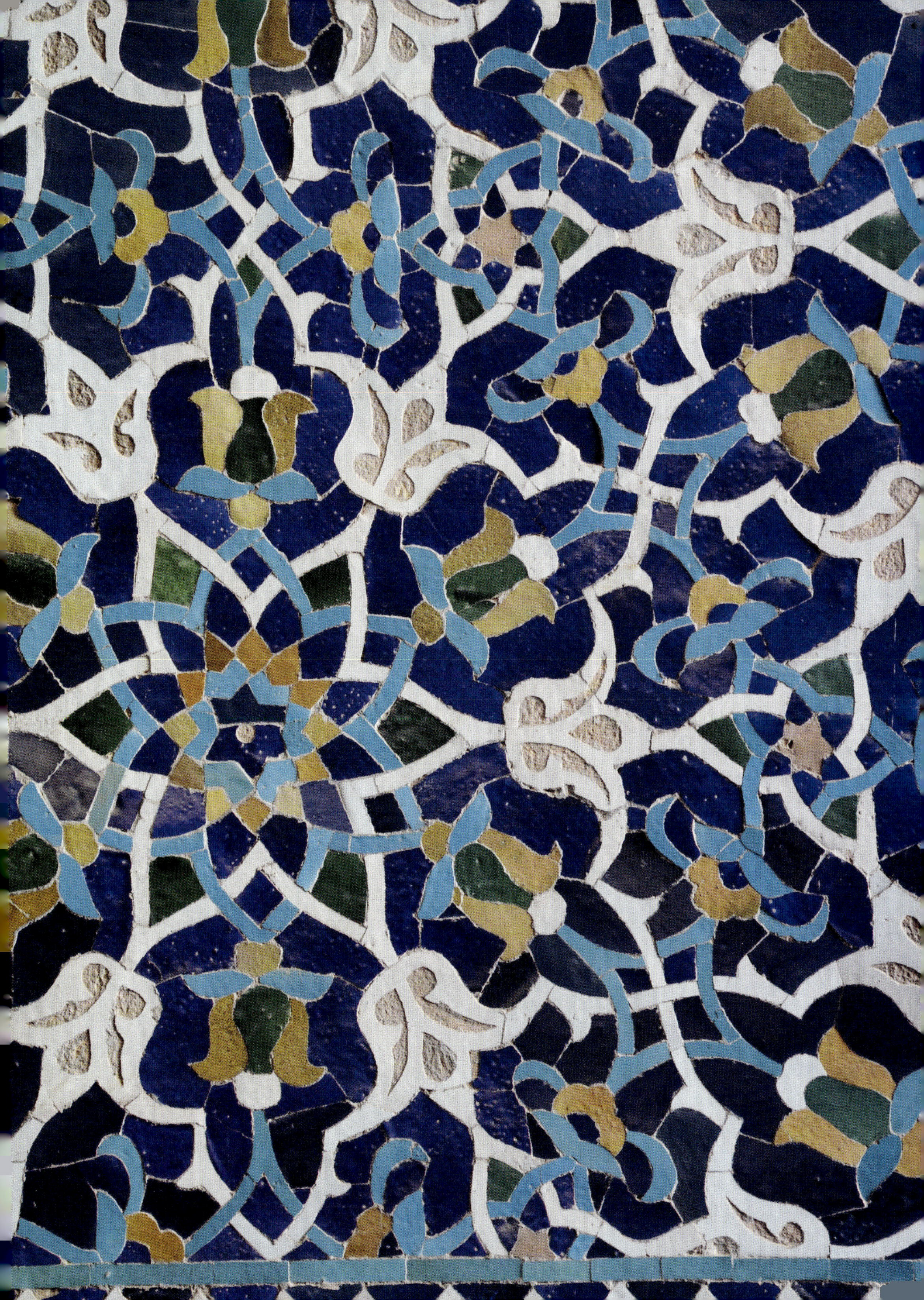

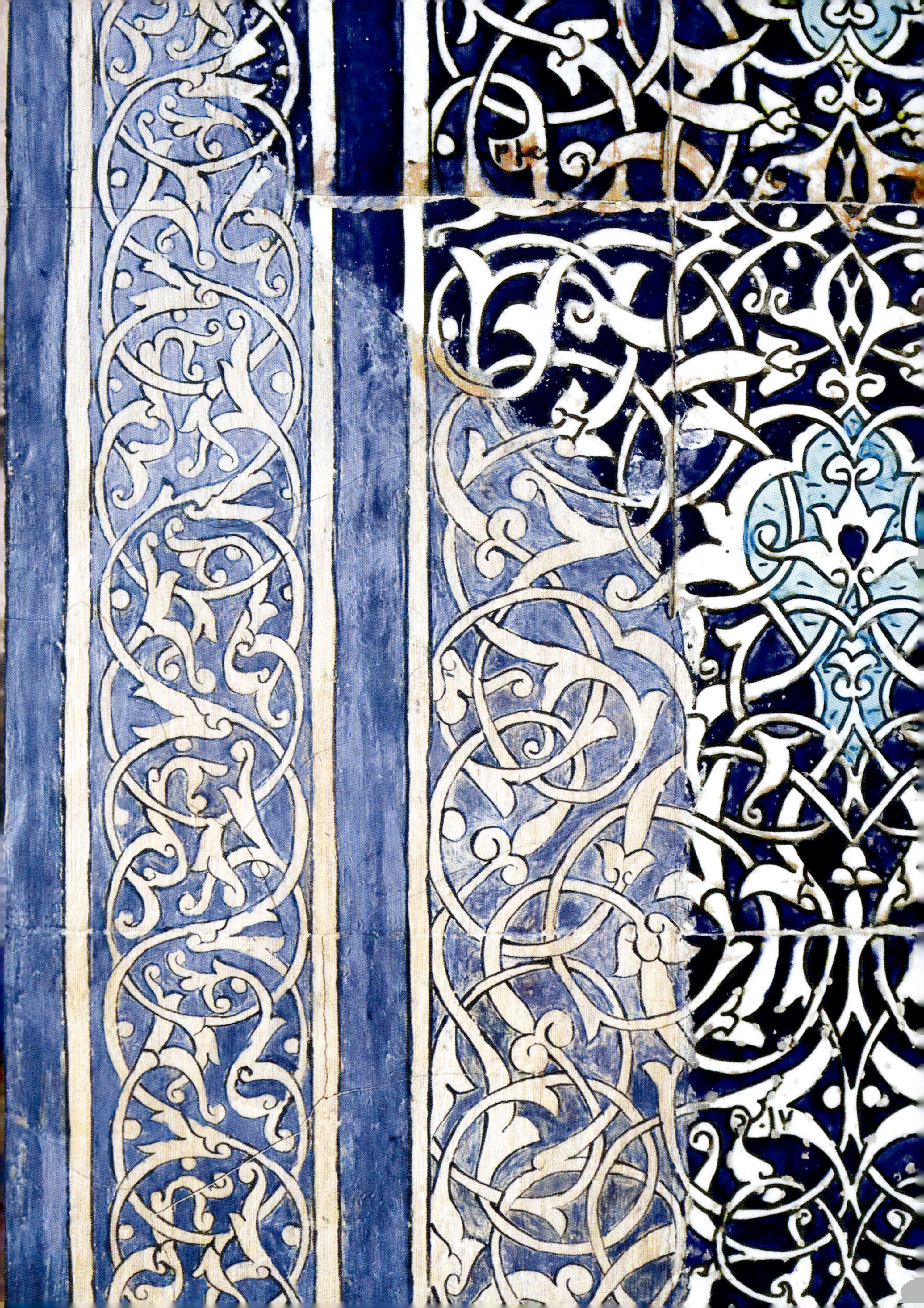

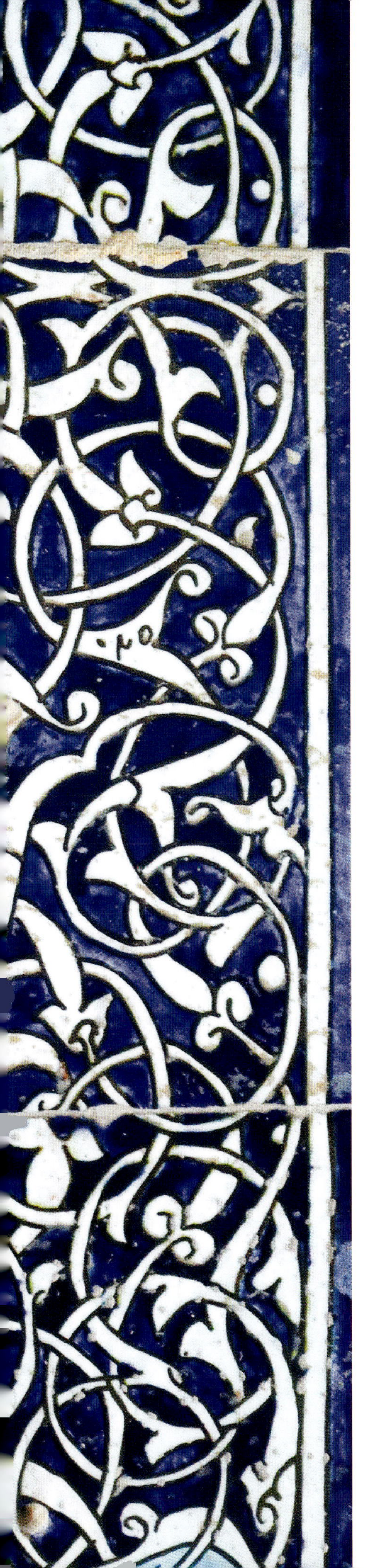

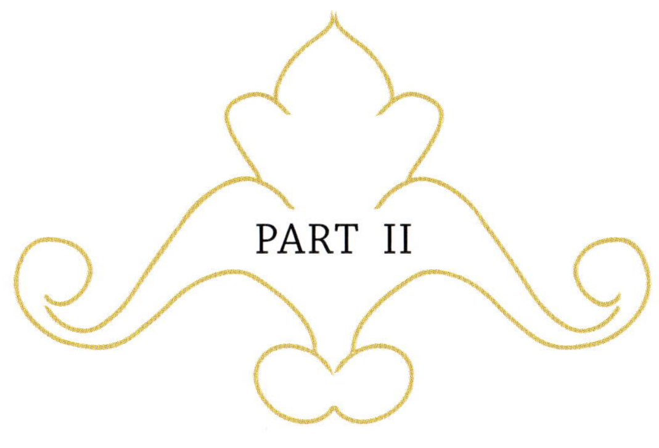

PART II

PATTERN STUDY

I often meet students who are eager to design their own patterns and create their own motifs without relying on any historical references. I was also one of those students when I first started learning this art form. This is an admired type of ambition and curiosity. Our society teaches us to strive for originality and pushes us towards individualism – thus, it is no wonder that creating something new is a common desire.

However, learning old, traditional patterns involves a slightly different process. I mentioned earlier that you must think of the motifs as words of a foreign language – and you cannot speak a language without learning these words. (In fact, you cannot do many things in life if you do not learn the basics!) So, be patient with yourself, start with what you have and learn to really see. If these patterns don't capture your heart, you can return to innovation at a later stage.

In this part of the book, we will be studying 12 patterns, enabling you to be able to reproduce them while understanding their elements. In this way, you will build a visual language of motifs that are commonly used in Islamic biomorphic patterns.

The most important thing to remember is that most biomorphic patterns are based on a geometric grid. There are a number of mathematical possibilities, such as geometric grids based on five stars, six stars, eight stars, ten stars and so on. This book will focus on two essential grid systems – the six-pointed and eight-pointed stars – which will help you to start understanding the patterns. These two grids are mostly used for designing patterns on ceramic tiles and in certain circular designs found in the starting pages of manuscripts, known as a *shamsah*, meaning 'little sun'.

TOOLS AND EQUIPMENT

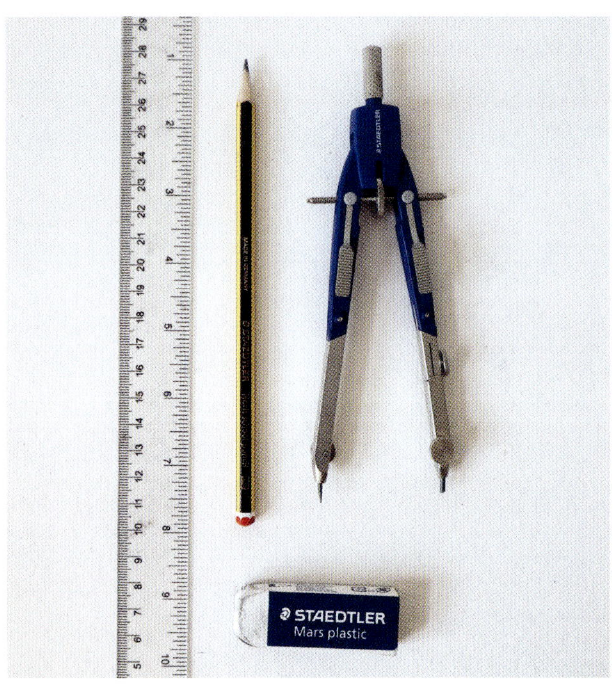

↑ I started with a Staedtler compass and still use it to this day. I find it to be well-built and sturdy; the metal parts are much more reliable than plastic and it comes with an additional expandable arm that gives a larger radius when needed. Opt for a compass with metal parts and a thumbwheel to provide enhanced accuracy and precision.

Before you start with the geometry in the following section, you will need a compass, a straight edge or ruler, a pencil, an eraser and a sharpener. There are many debates over which brand is the best for each, and you will find that even your own preferences change over time. As you develop a love for well-built, good-quality tools, you could start searching the vintage and second-hand market for antique finds.

For the first stage of drawing the geometric grid you will need smooth A4 paper – printer paper is sufficient. The second stage will involve affixing tracing paper on top of this paper with masking tape.

If you intend to paint, make sure the paper is suitable. I do not recommend using the same paper for painting as for drawing, as the excessive use of an eraser could damage the fibre of the paper, meaning that it will no longer absorb paint efficiently.

SIX-POINTED STAR GRID

CONSTRUCTION

The first step in understanding biomorphic patterns is to identify the hidden geometric structure, which might not be obvious at first. This structure is made of circles and lines forming stars and hexagons, all of which act as a guideline for the organisation and placement of the biomorphic motifs. Without this structure, it is difficult to maintain balance and symmetry in the pattern. The composition of the lines gives us a starting point and an organised system to place motifs in a balanced way.

Drawing the underlying six-pointed star grid is the first stage of the next six patterns. The grid construction can be reused by affixing tracing paper to copy the pattern each time. However, taking a moment to draw the geometry is meditative, and even though I have countless grids ready to be used, I love to start my

design practice by drawing the grid with a compass and a straight edge every time. This process is also valuable as it helps me to get deeper in thought and readies my mind for the design to come.

As you construct the lines and circles of the six-pointed star grid, you will notice that it starts with one central circle with six consecutive circles surrounding it. The choice of radius is up to you, depending on how big you want the outcome to be.

Choose a comfortable paper size for you – I suggest either using A4 (21 × 29.7 cm/8¼ × 11¾ in) or A3 (29.7 × 42 cm/11¾ × 16½ in) paper. If you are using A4 paper, use a maximum radius of 5 cm (2 in); for A3 paper, use a maximum radius of 6.5 cm (2½ in) to fill the page.

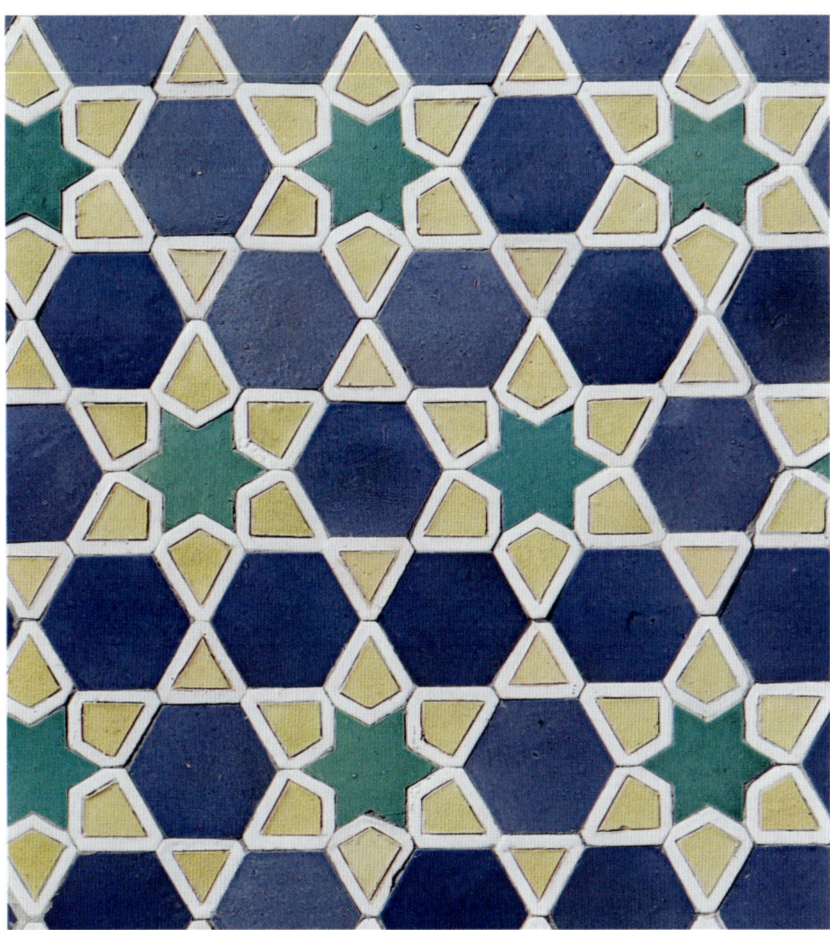

← A six-pointed star pattern, Uzbekistan.

DRAWING THE SIX CIRCLES

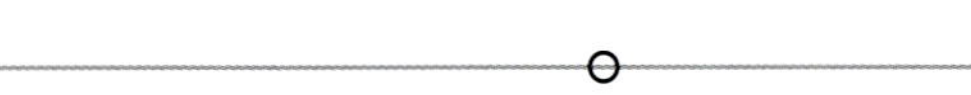

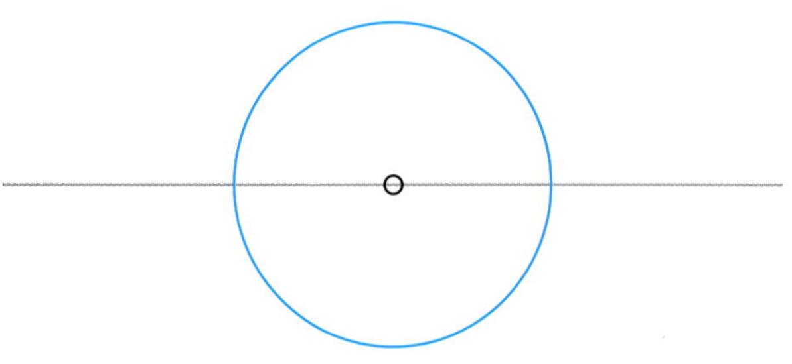

1 Draw a line in the centre of your page and mark the middle point of the line. You can either do this by eye or by measuring the exact distance with a ruler.

2 Draw a circle in the middle of the line using your compass.

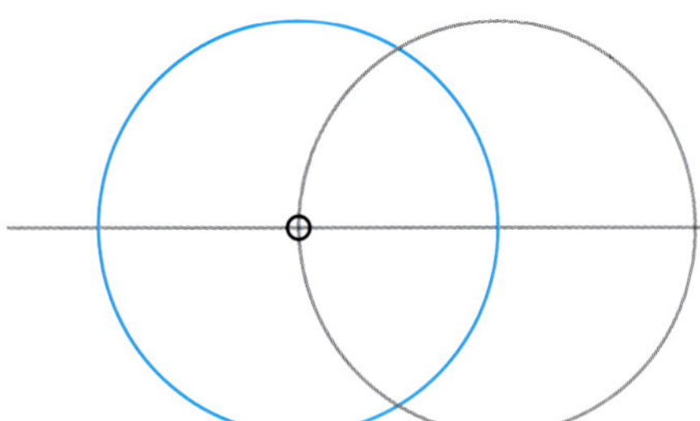

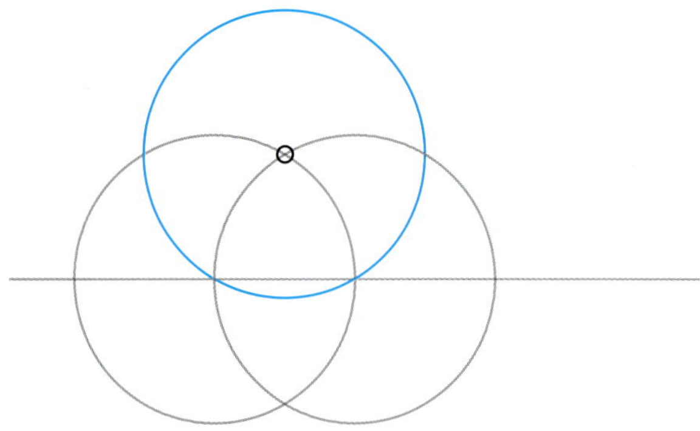

3 Draw another circle on the left, placing the compass needle on the point where the line bisects your first circle.

4 Draw a third circle where the two circles intersect above the line – every time you draw a circle you create a new intersection.

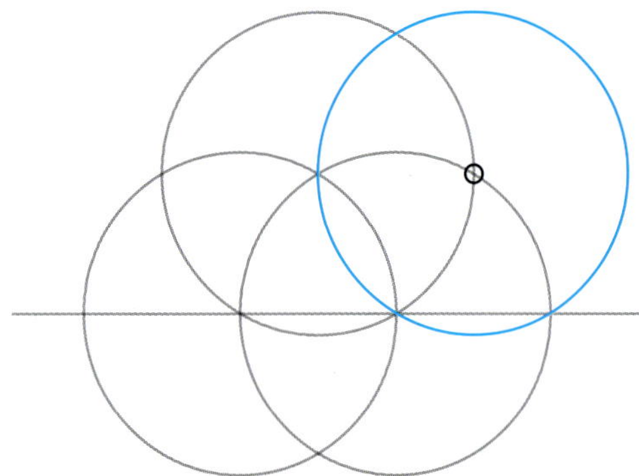

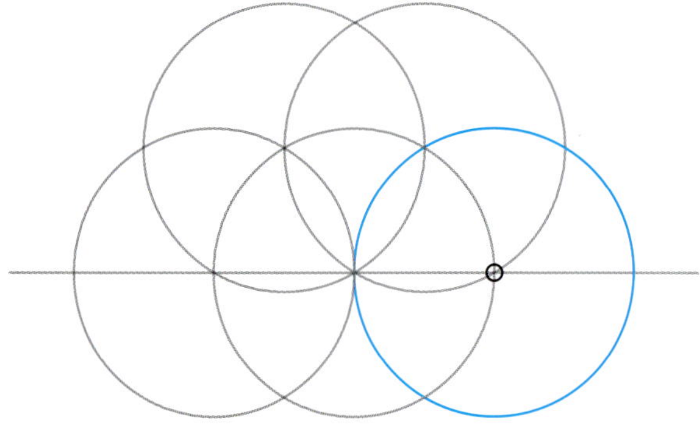

5 Draw another circle clockwise from the new point where the top and right circles intersect.

6 Repeat Step 5 from the next new point of intersection.

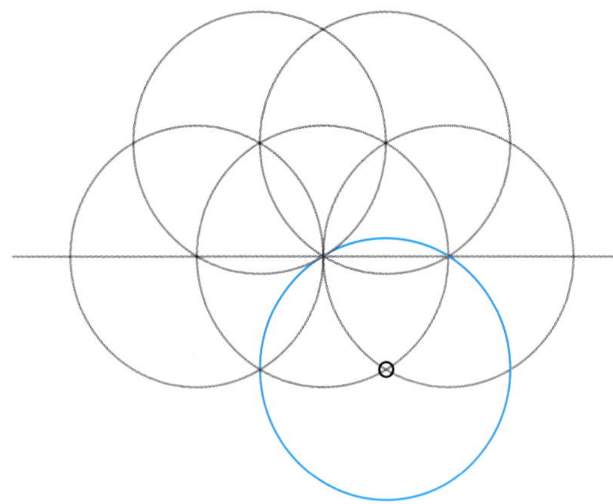

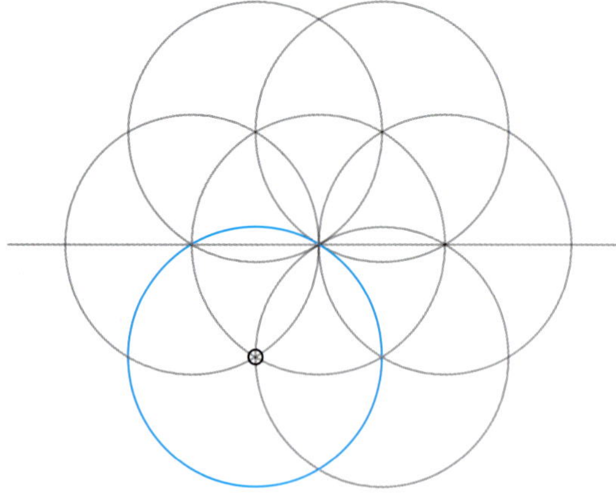

7 Repeat Step 5 from the new point of intersection to add a circle below the line.

8 Draw your final circle. Your drawing is now complete with one central circle and six circles surrounding it.

Once you have completed Step 8, you will have the basic structure on which to build your star. There are two options that determine the orientation of the hexagon:

Grid 1 and Grid 2. You can use one grid for all your drawings and rotate your hexagon as needed, or draw each grid separately as I am doing here.

USING GRID 1 TO DRAW A SIX-POINTED STAR

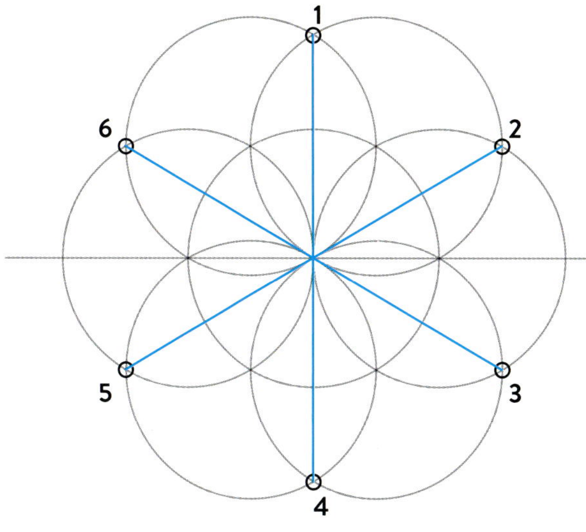

1 Take the completed diagram from Step 8. Number the points from 1 to 6 as shown. Connect points 1 and 4, points 2 and 5, and points 3 and 6 as illustrated, segmenting the diagram into six equal parts.

2 Connect the points consecutively to make a hexagon.

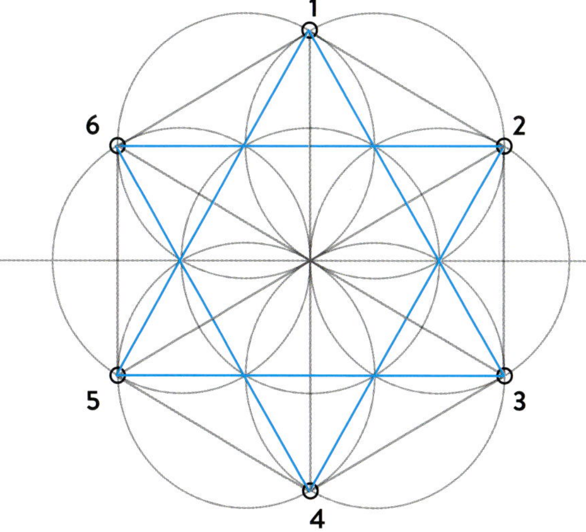

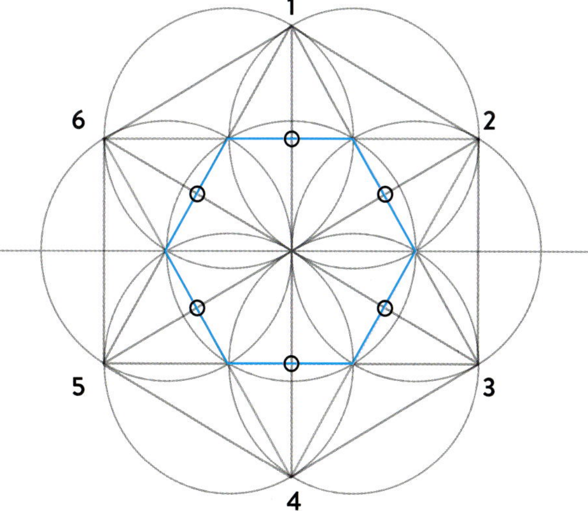

3 Draw two intersecting triangles, one pointing upwards and the other pointing downwards, to form a six-pointed star by connecting intersections 1, 3, 5 and 1 for one triangle, and 2, 4, 6 and 2 for the other.

4 Drawing the six-pointed star creates a new hexagon inside the central circle. Move the marked points to the inner hexagon.

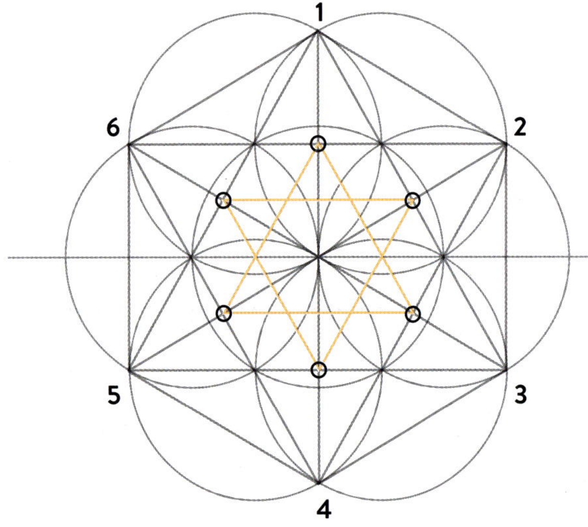

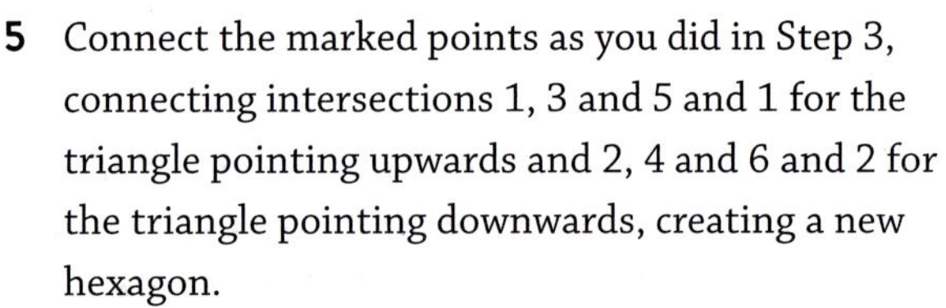

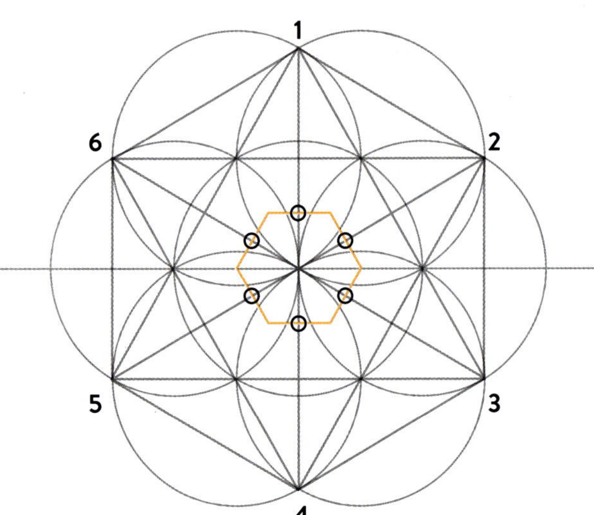

5 Connect the marked points as you did in Step 3, connecting intersections 1, 3 and 5 and 1 for the triangle pointing upwards and 2, 4 and 6 and 2 for the triangle pointing downwards, creating a new hexagon.

6 Repeat Step 4, placing the marked points on the new hexagon.

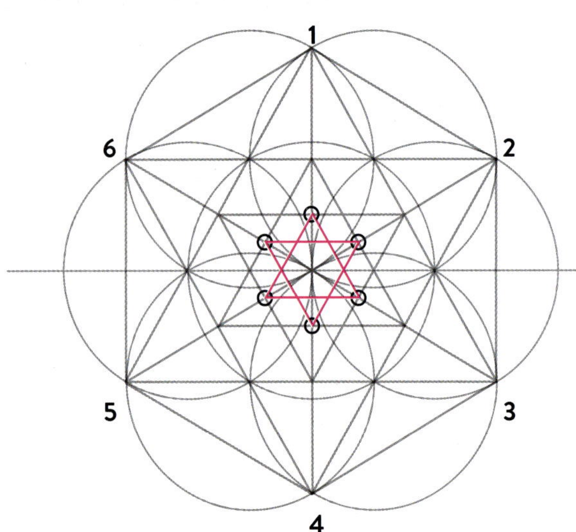

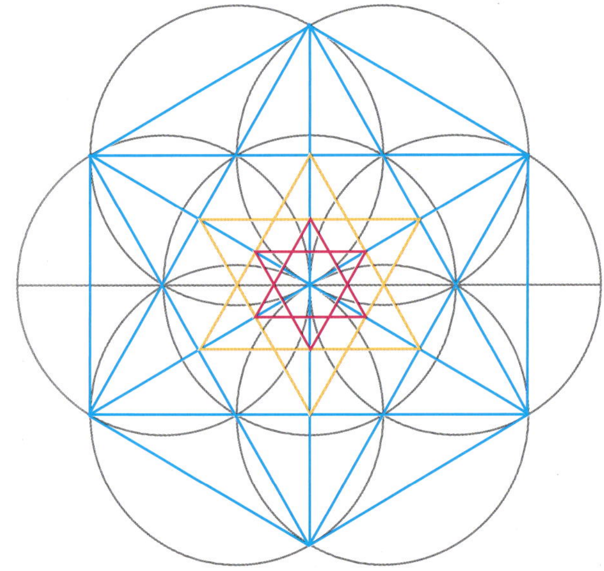

7 Repeat Step 5.

This is the final geometric construction for Grid 1, including a hexagon and three six-pointed stars. The guidelines in this structure will be sufficient to begin analysing many Islamic biomorphic patterns.

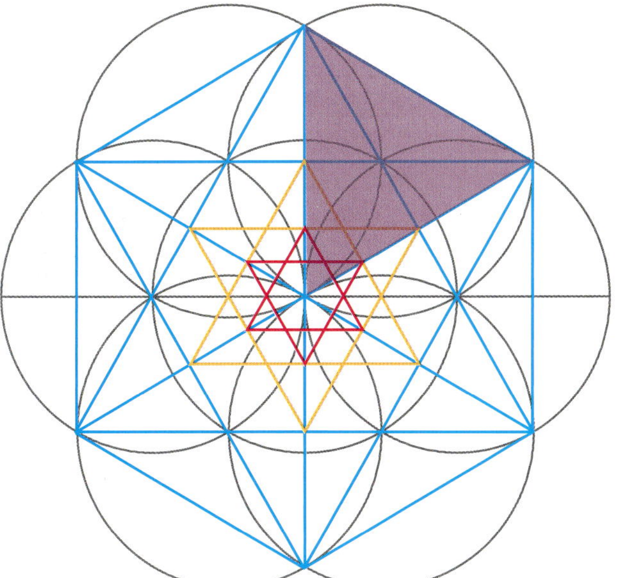

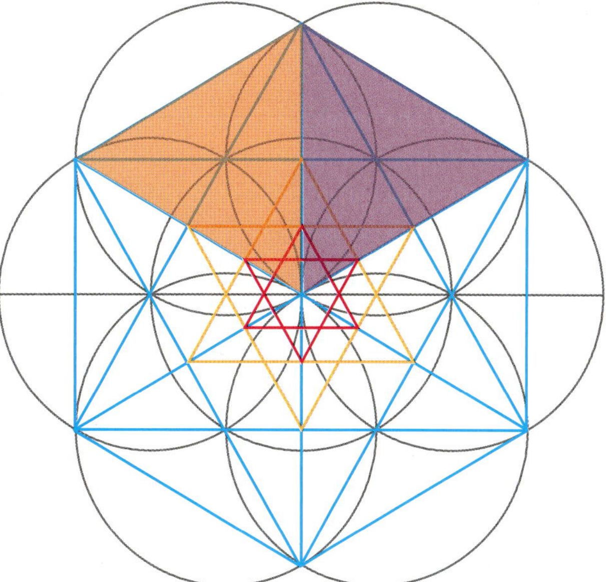

From the full drawing, only one section is needed for our design purposes. This specific section will host all the motif elements that will be needed to complete the pattern. Any design elements must be placed in the section highlighted in purple.

When the design is complete, the triangle section highlighted in purple will be reflected to create seamless symmetry, as shown by the orange triangle, which is called the 'repeat unit'. In some cases, the design section is rotated rather than reflected; however, reflection is the most common style.

USING GRID 2 TO DRAW A SIX-POINTED STAR

The difference between the two grids is the orientation of the hexagon and six-pointed star. In Grid 2, the shapes are rotated 45 degrees.

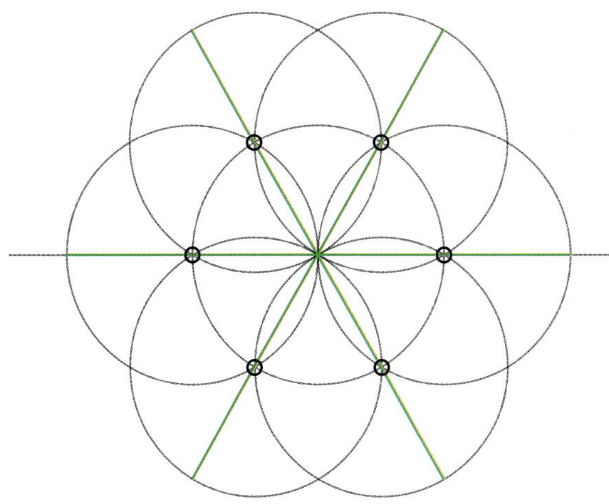

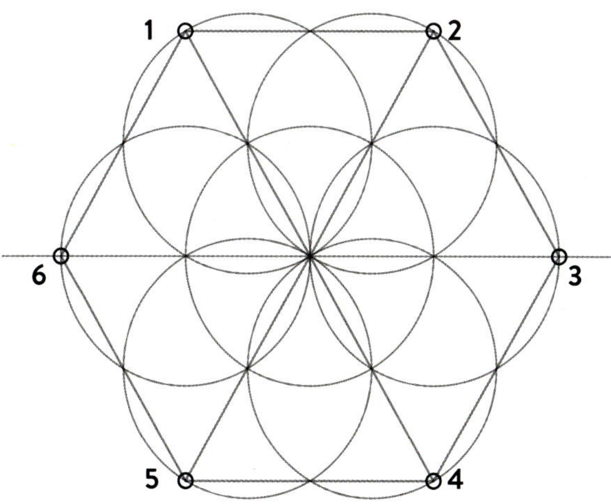

1 Take the completed diagram you created in Step 8 in Drawing the Six Circles, on p.30. Add two diagonal lines to divide the space into six equal sections. These lines go through the inner petals like the central vein on a leaf, and extend to the outer circles.

2 Number the points from 1 to 6 as shown. Connect the points consecutively to make a hexagon.

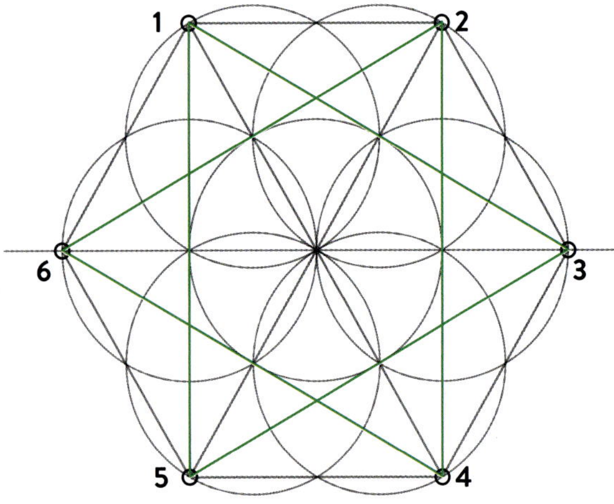

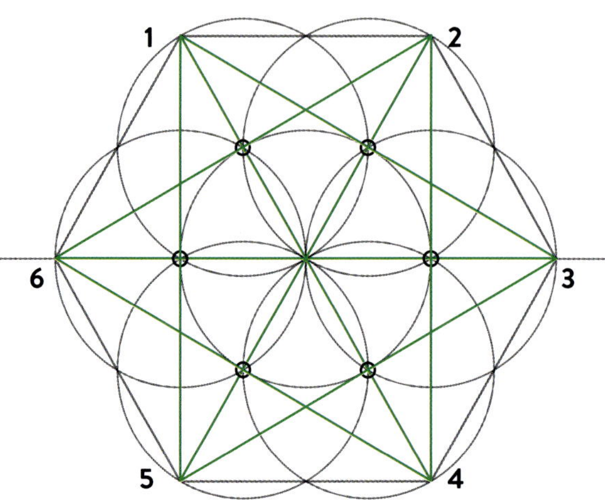

3 Draw two intersecting triangles, one pointing to the left and the other pointing to the right, to form a six-pointed star by connecting intersections 1, 3, 5 and 1 for one triangle, and 2, 4, 6 and 2 for the other.

4 The six-pointed star surrounds the central circle. Move the marked points inwards onto this central circle.

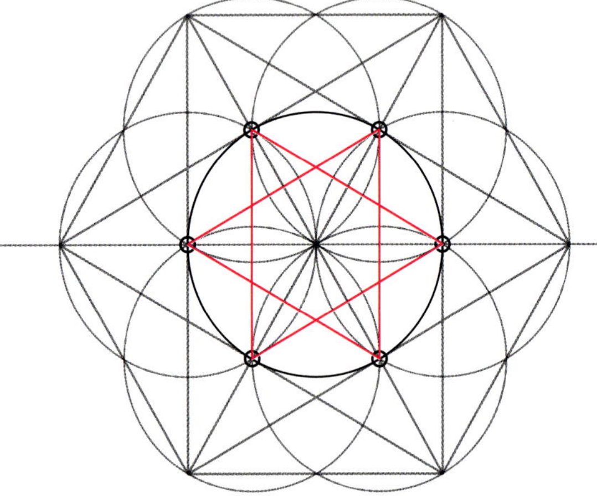

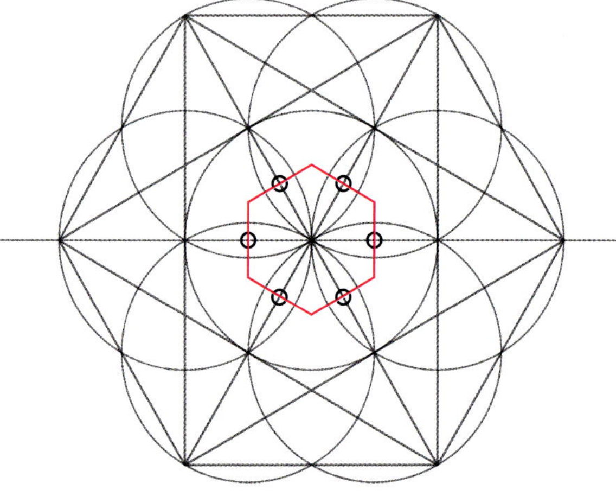

5 Use the points marked in Step 4 to create another six-pointed star by drawing two intersecting triangles. Remember to skip one point each time.

6 The new six-pointed star has created a hexagon within it, so you can use those lines and lower the marked points once more to draw one more six-pointed star.

7 Use the points you marked in Step 6 to create another six-pointed star by drawing two intersecting triangles. Remember to skip one point each time.

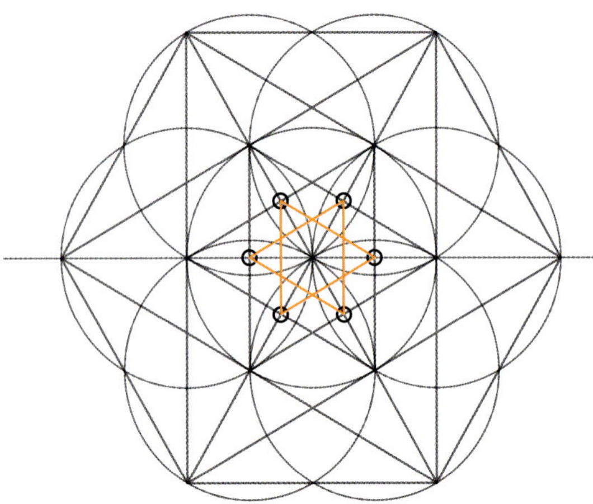

REPEATING AND REFLECTING THE SECTION

As with Grid 1, only one section is needed for our design purposes. This specific section will host all the motif elements that will be needed to complete the pattern. Any design elements must be placed in the section highlighted in purple.

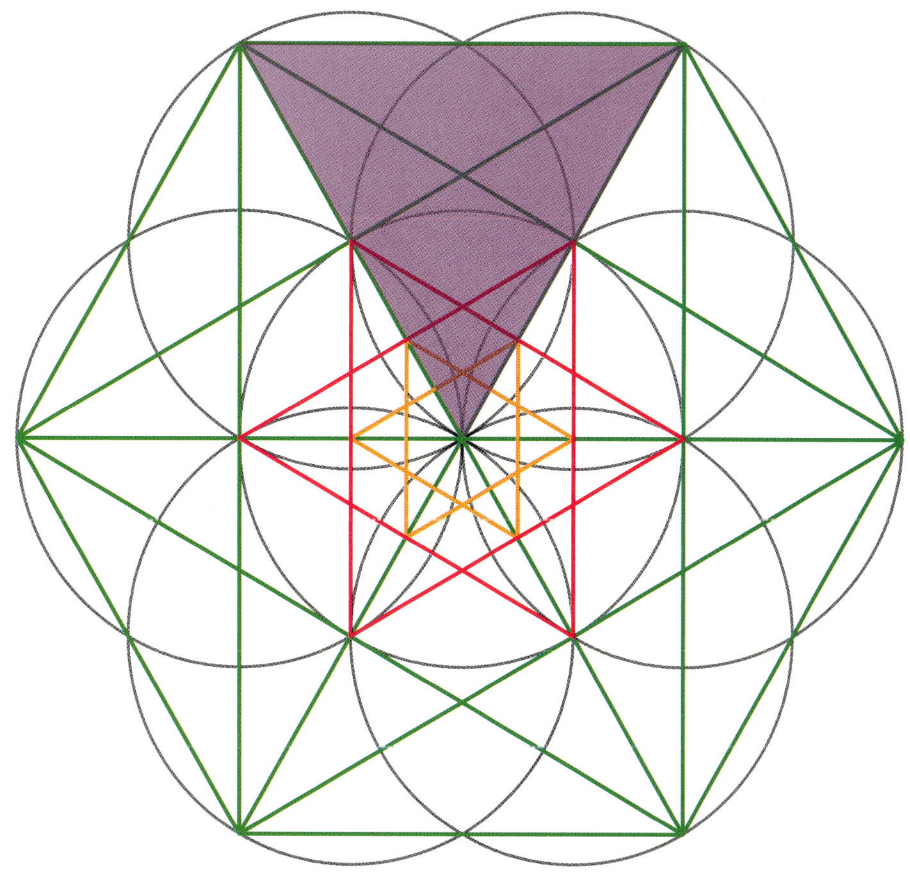

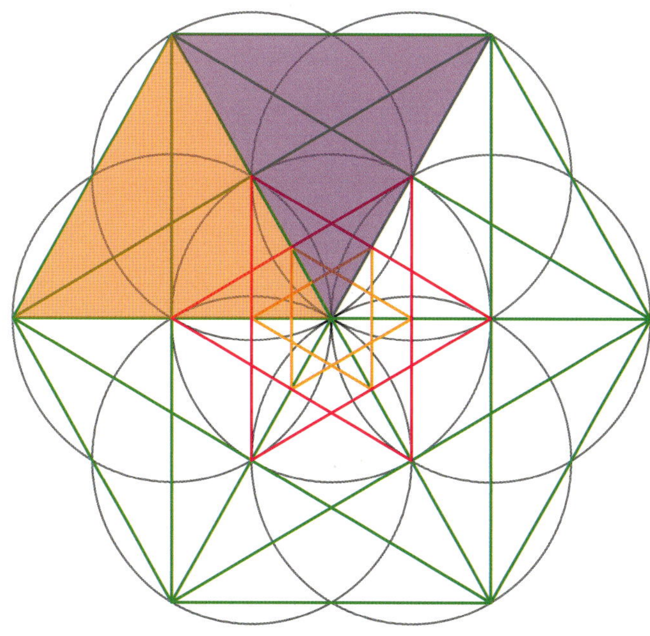

When the design is complete, the section highlighted in purple will be reflected to create seamless symmetry, as shown with the orange triangle. This is called the 'repeat unit'. In some cases, the design section is rotated rather than reflected; however, reflection is the most common style.

THE DIFFERENCES BETWEEN GRIDS 1 AND 2

Having these two grids for the six-pointed star is extremely helpful. The difference between them is that the hexagon is static in Grid 1 and dynamic – rotated 30 degrees – in Grid 2. It amazes me how these two simple but mighty grids are the basis of so many gorgeous patterns in ceramic tiles and manuscripts. The guidelines in these structures will be sufficient to get you started with analysing many biomorphic patterns.

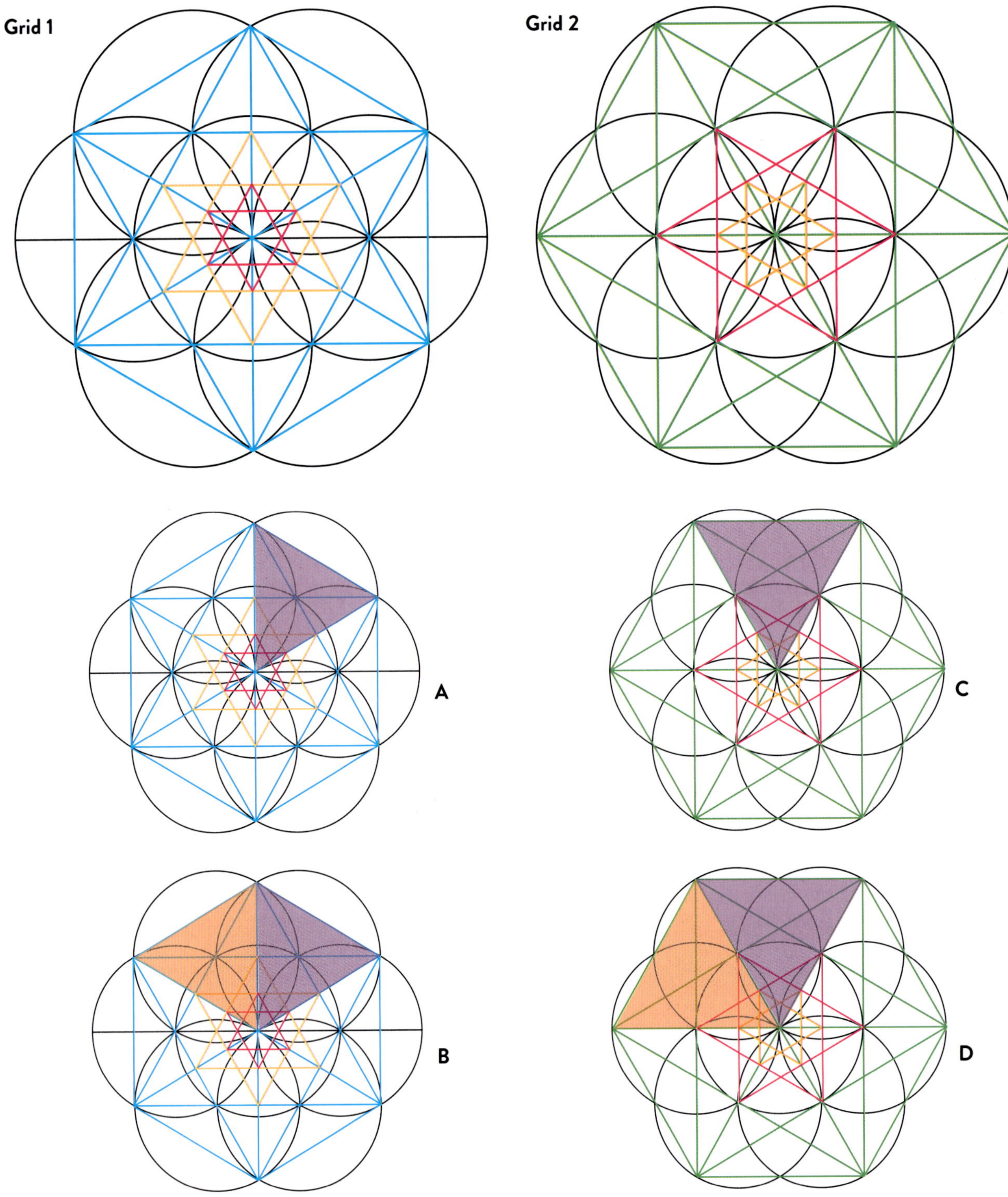

TESSELLATION

A hexagon or six-pointed star is rarely drawn in isolation; it is usually meant to be repeated multiple times, either on a piece of paper or a wall. Therefore, tessellation should be considered to create a series of cohesive and correctly arranged tiles.

Think about tessellation as you would the arrangement of tiles on a floor, a beehive, fish scales or the skin of a pineapple – the organisation of shapes on a flat surface without any gaps. There are three shapes that tessellate seamlessly: hexagons, squares and equilateral triangles.

These can be placed edge to edge to create a repeated geometric pattern.

The three most popular types of tessellation that can be created using a six-pointed star are: regular with hexagonal tiling; semi-regular with hexagonal and triangular tiling; and hexagram and rhombus tiling. They will be applied on Grid 1 and Grid 2. The difference between the two grids will be the orientation – it might not appear very different in diagram form, but it will be more apparent on the pattern itself.

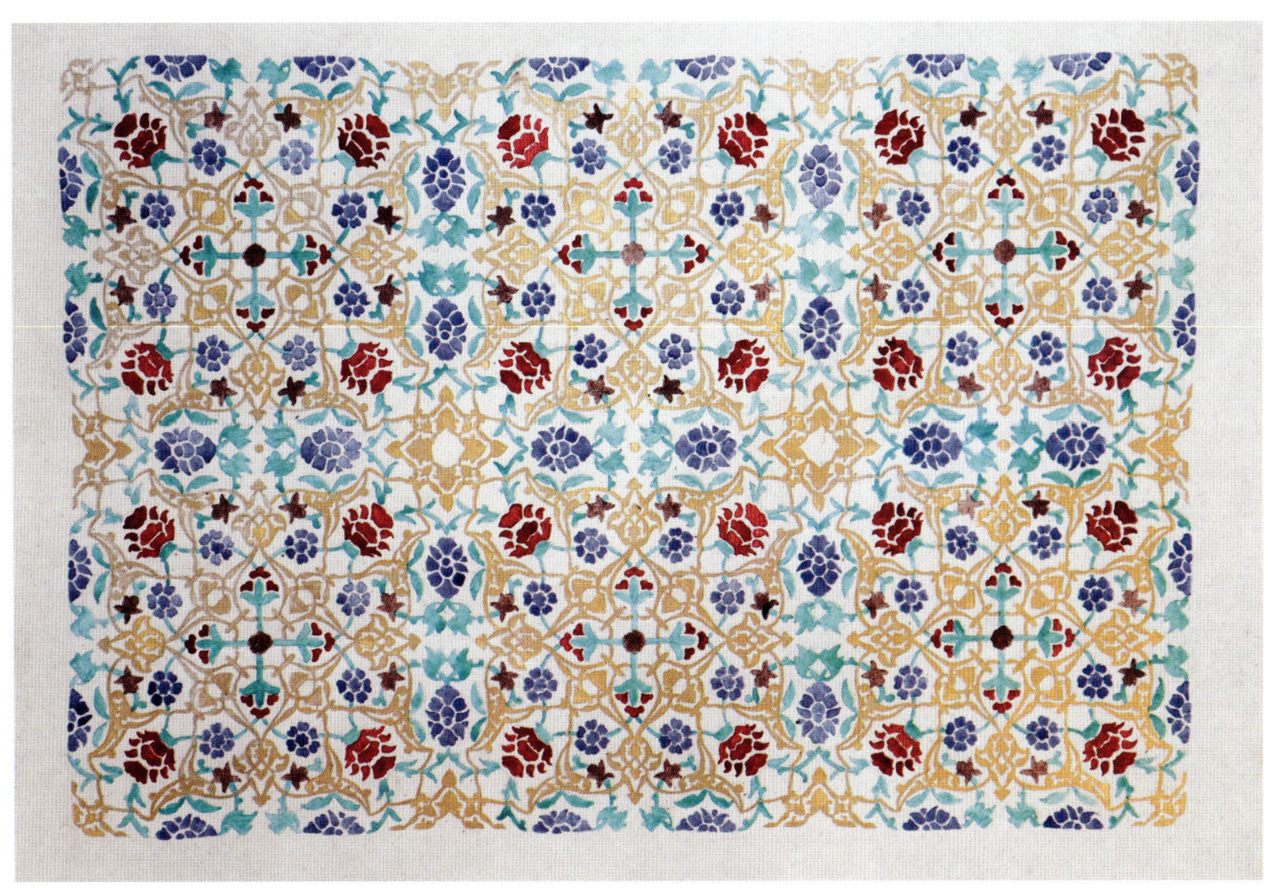

HEXAGONAL TILING

Tessellation A is an example of hexagonal tiling, where all the hexagons are placed next to each other with their sides aligned. This is the most classic tessellation for patterns based on a six-pointed star grid. You can find examples of hexagonal tiling in nature – a popular example is a honeycomb.

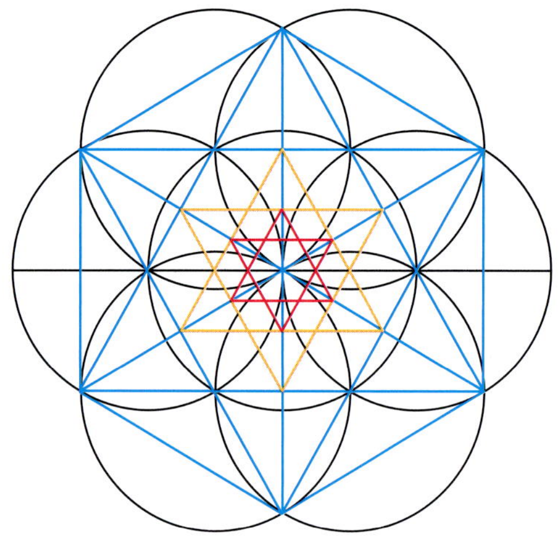 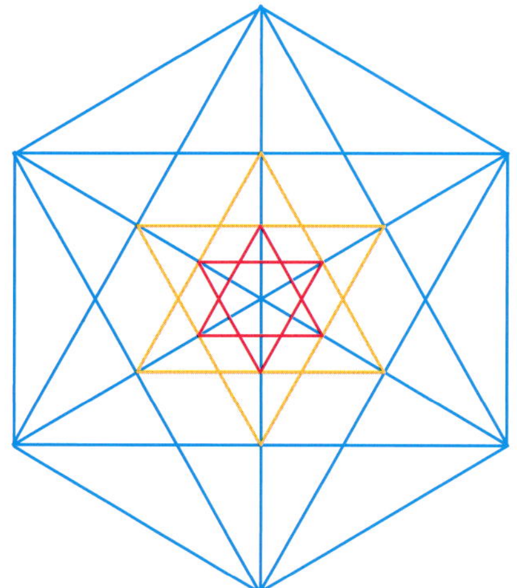

A

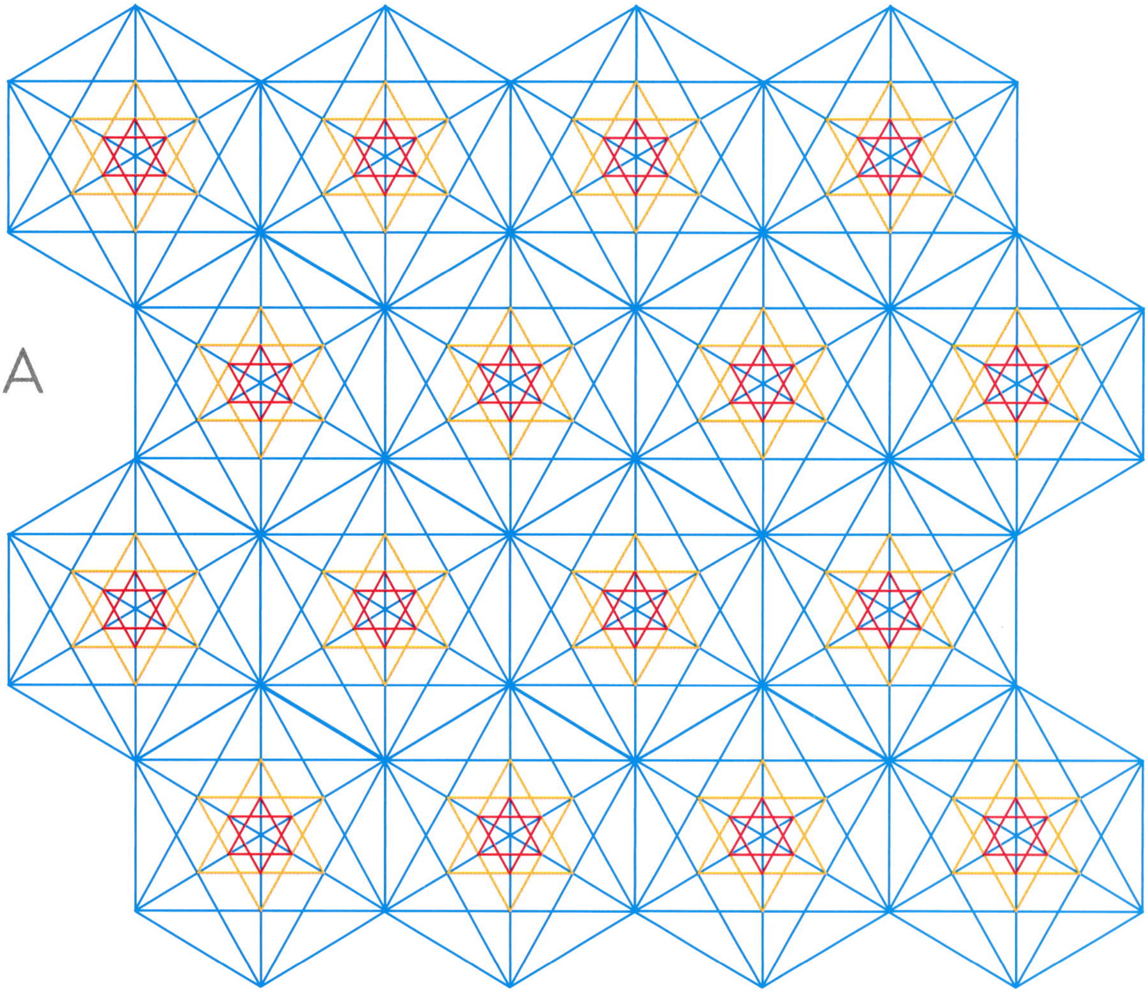

HEXAGONAL AND TRIANGULAR TILING

Tessellations B and C (p.40) show how triangles are created when lining the hexagons vertically or horizontally with their points aligned. The triangles surrounding one hexagon resemble a full six-pointed star. These tessellations will be more obvious with the pattern in place.

In some cases, you will have designed a pattern that only fits in the hexagon, so you will need to draw an additional design for one triangle, which will be repeated in all the triangles.

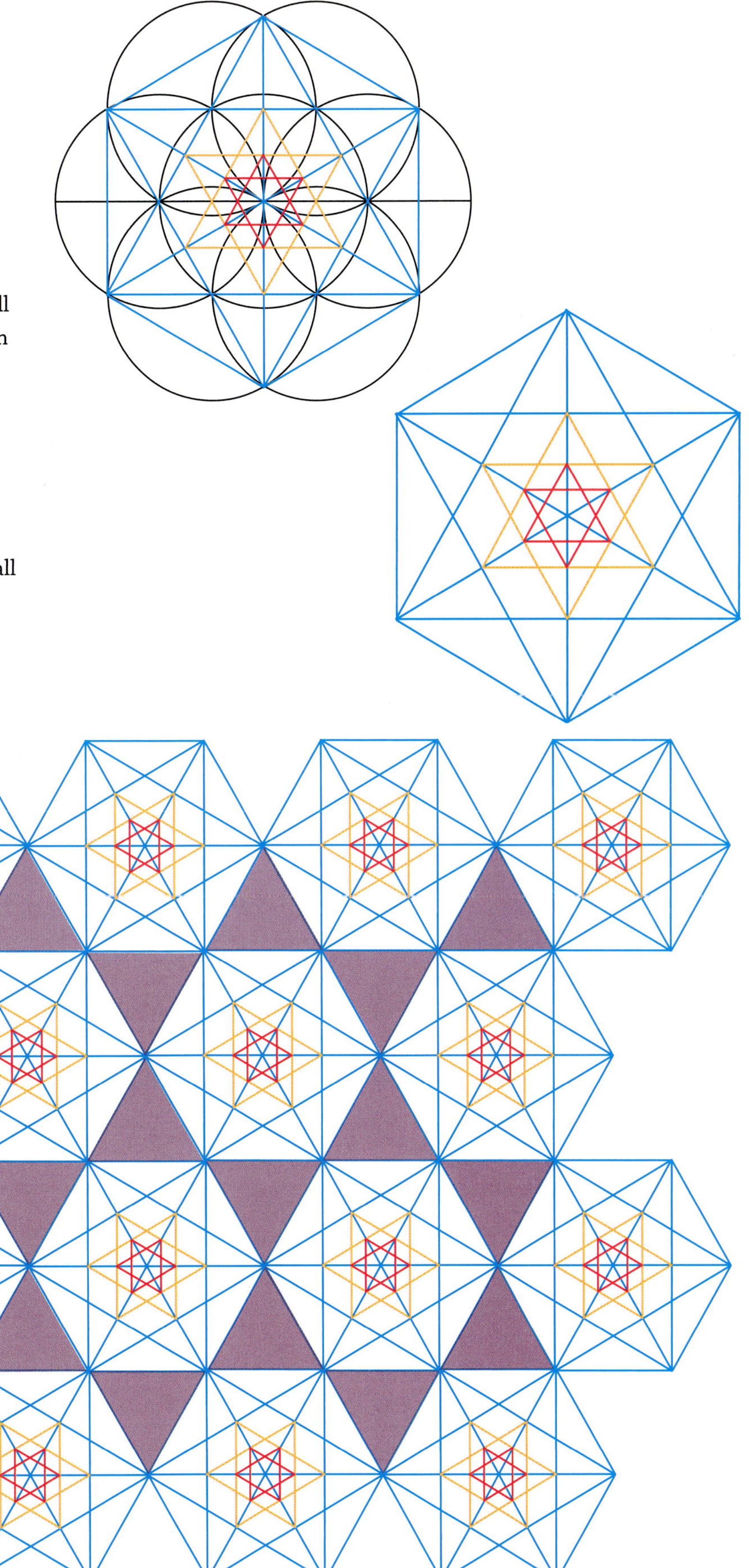

B

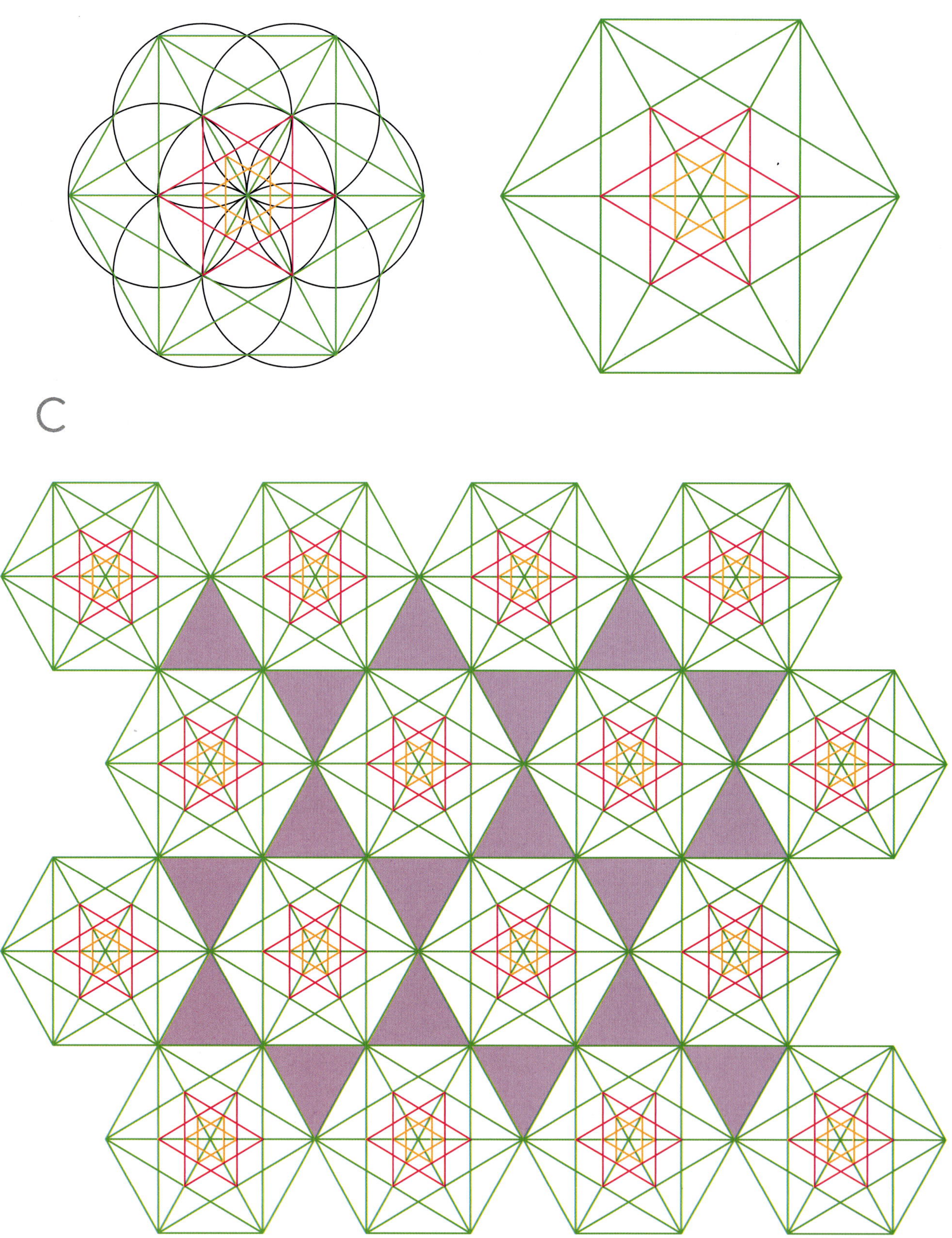

C

SIX-POINTED STAR AND HEXAGON TILING

In tessellations D and E (p.42), the repeat consists of the six-pointed stars
(hexagrams) and hexagons, the latter naturally occur when placing the
stars point to point. It is like a reverse tessellation of B and C, but stars
are dominant rather than hexagons. As with tessellations B and C, D and E
result in the same outcome, but the orientation differs.

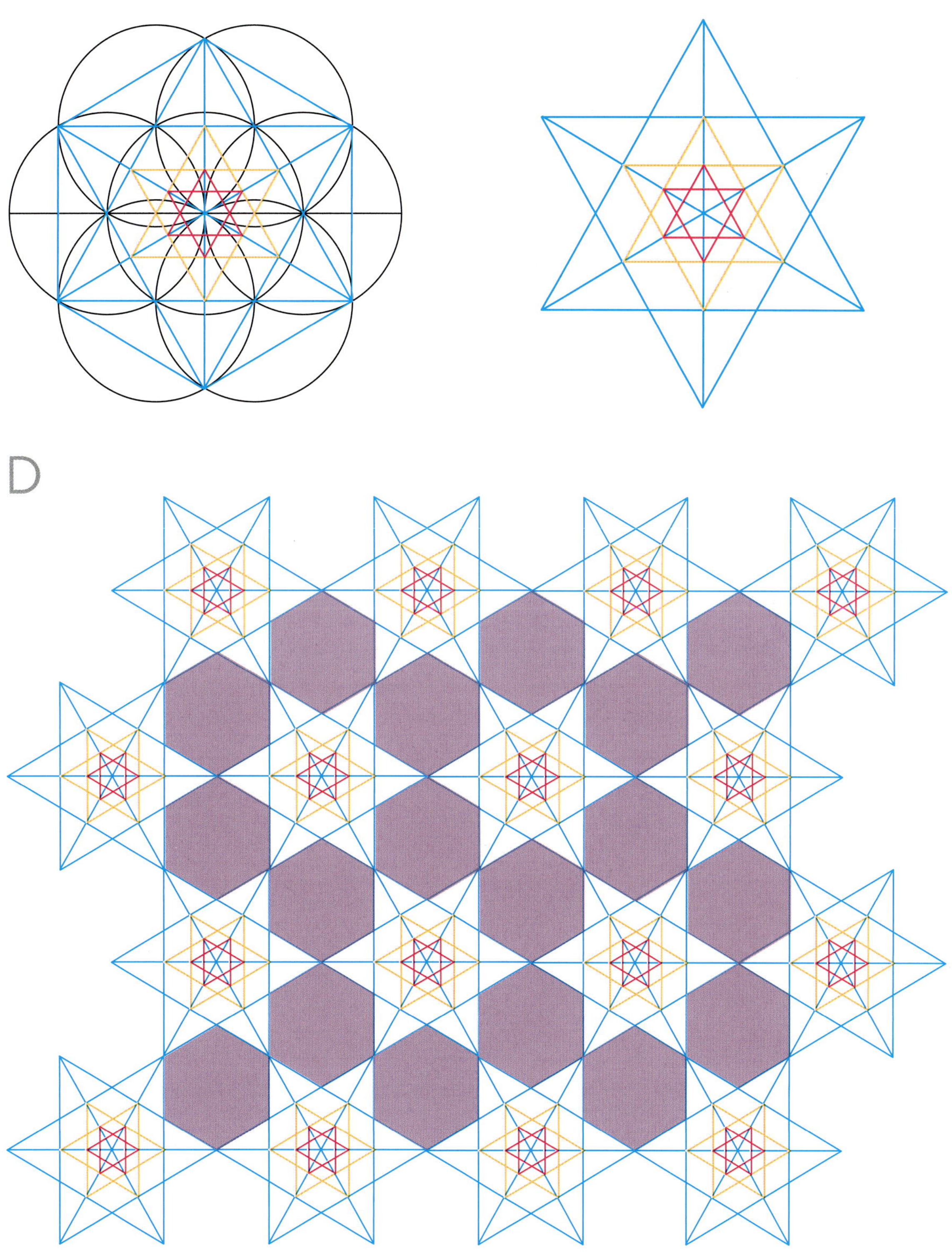

D

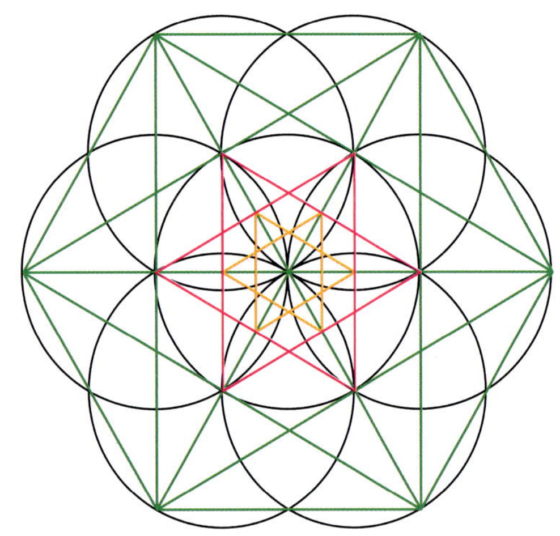 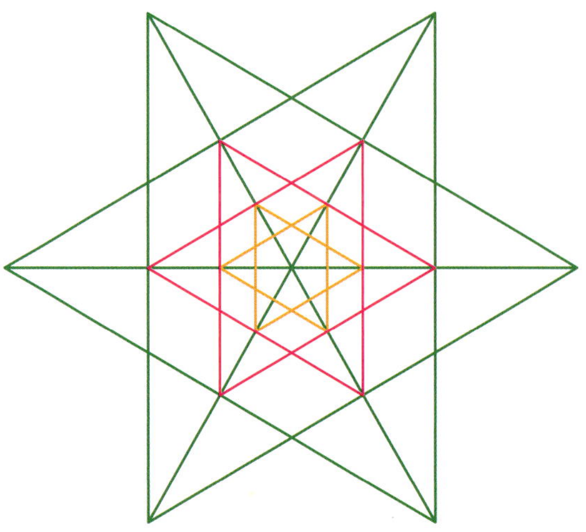

E

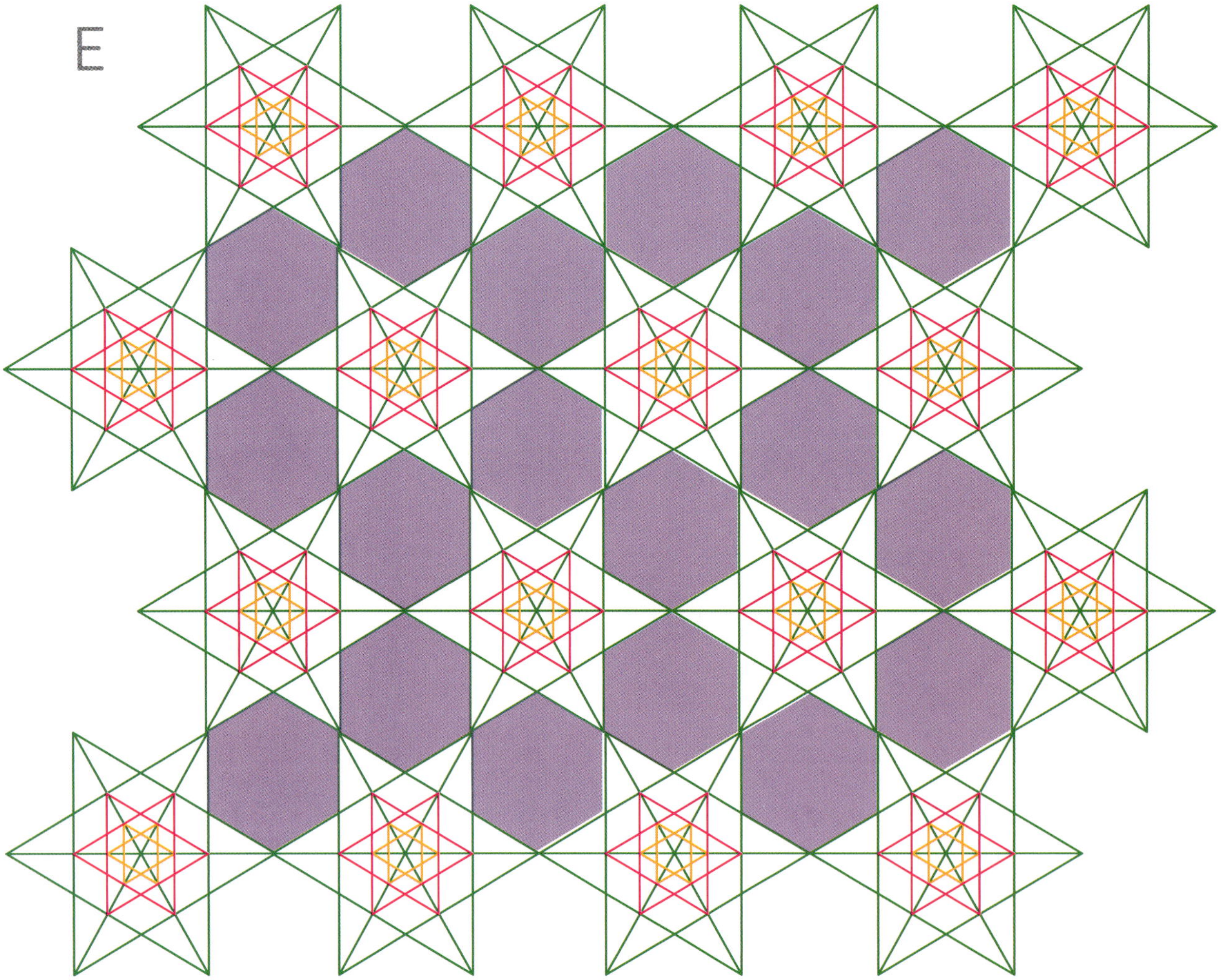

SIX-POINTED STAR AND RHOMBUS TILING

In tessellations F and G (p.44), the repeat consists of hexagrams and
rhombuses. The rhombuses naturally occur when placing hexagrams next to
each other. As with the other tessellations, the two grid systems result in the
same outcome with different orientations, which will impact the look of the
design, especially in Islamic biomorphic patterns – imagine that the branches
and flowers will be directed in a certain way.

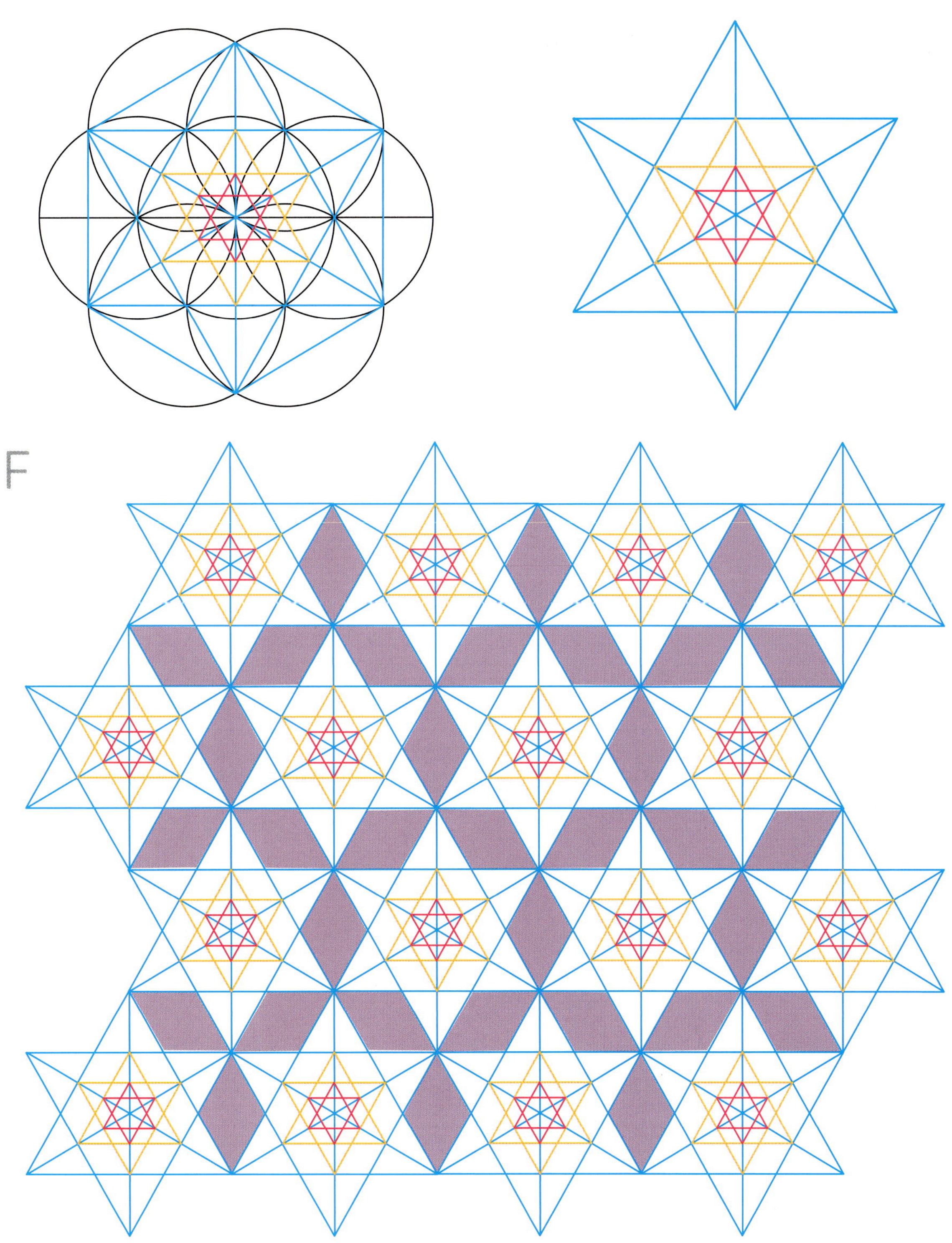

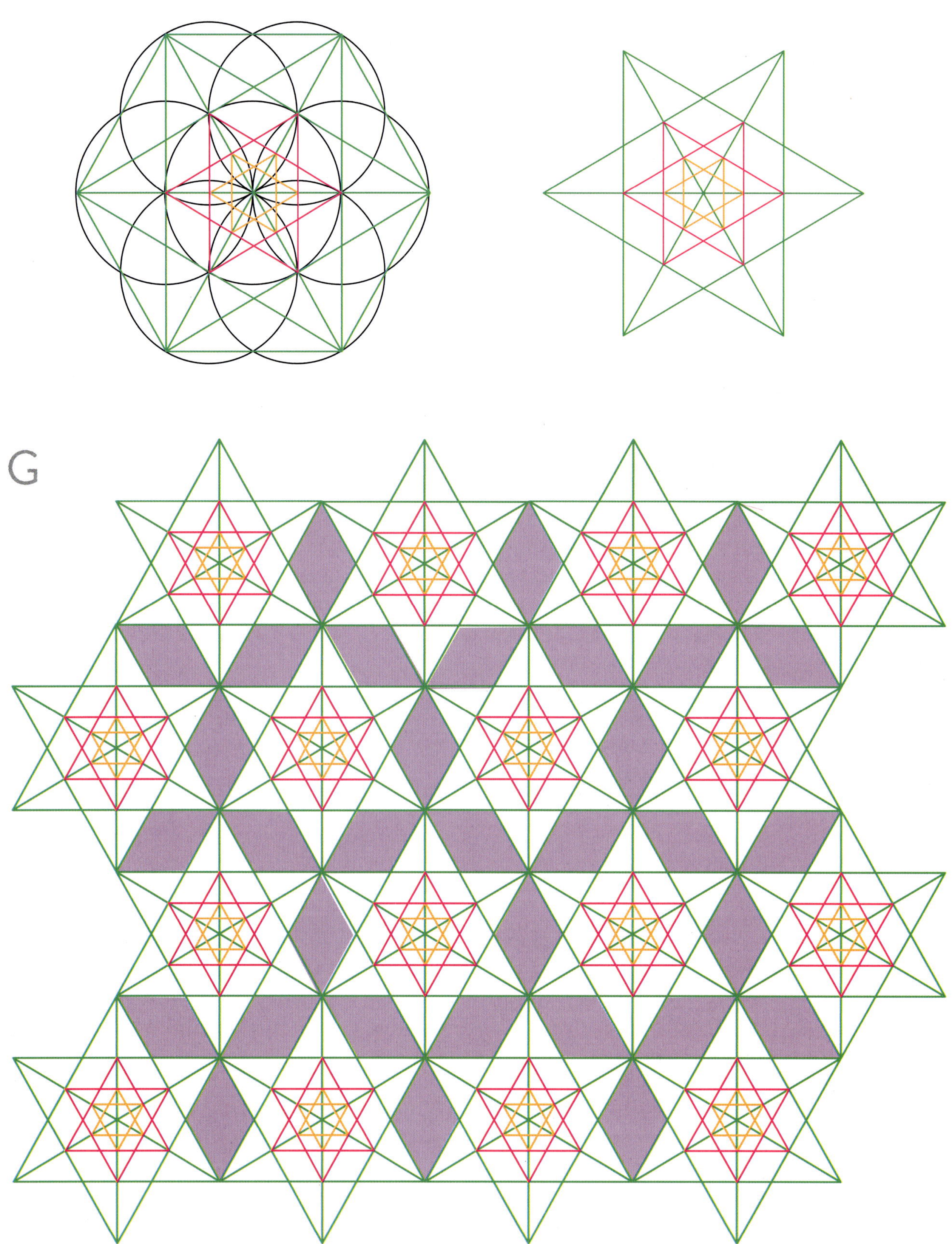

G

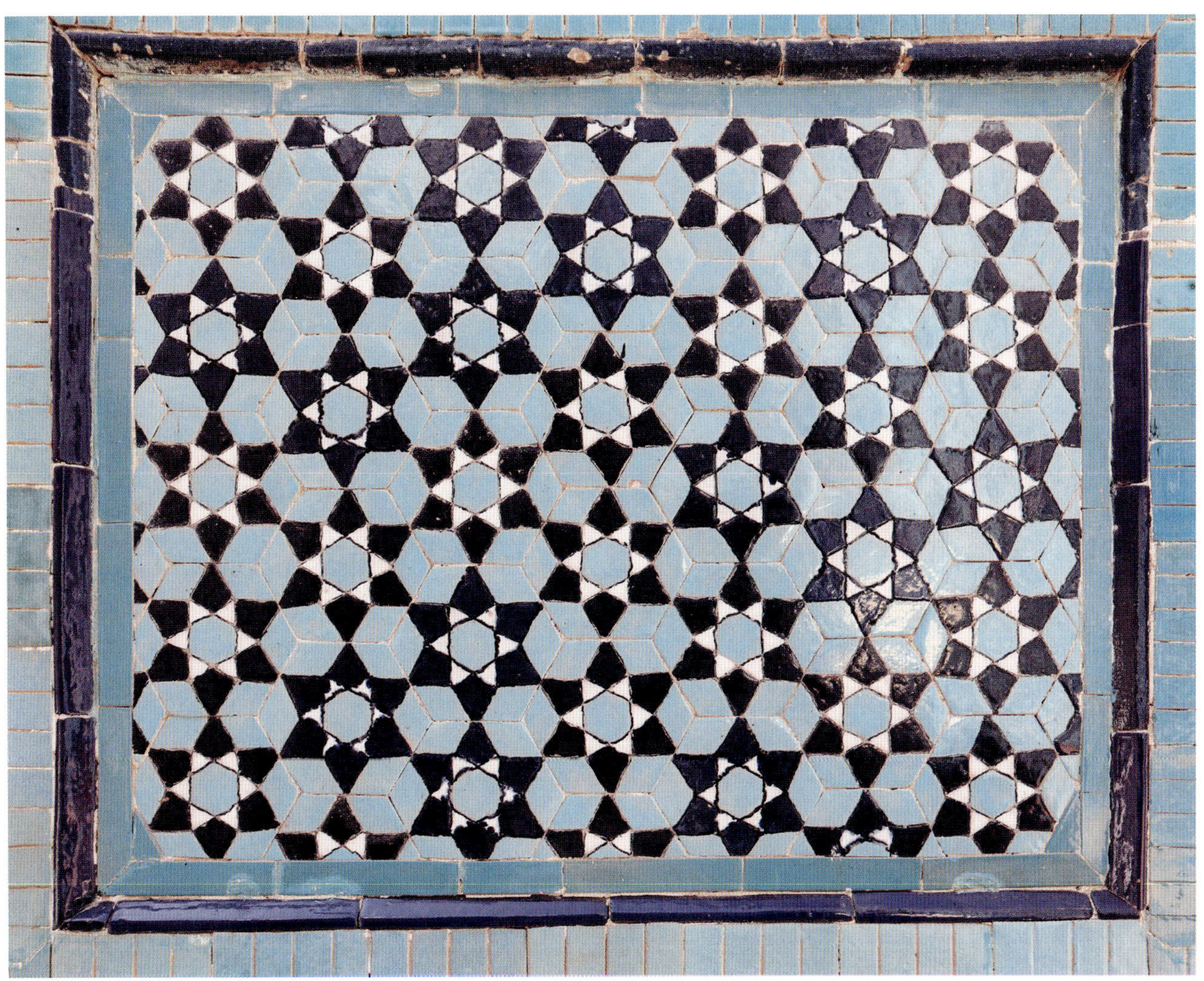

↑ Wall panel in Tashkent, Uzbekistan.

STUDYING BIOMORPHIC PATTERNS

Once you are familiar with the geometric construction
and tessellations, you are ready to start exploring the
patterns using the next section of this book. Without
these structures, freehand drawing will be harder to
achieve and more confusing to learn.

I have noticed that some artists ignore the geometry
and start with folded tracing paper and botanical
patterns; this approach will be harder in the long run
and will result in mistakes with accuracy and balance.
Having some understanding of basic geometry will help
you immensely. You can improve beyond this book by
learning geometric constructions with more complex
star systems.

TYPES OF MOTIFS

Islamic biomorphic patterns include a series of shapes
of two types: motifs based on flora and fauna, and
inorganic shapes. The latter do not have official names,
therefore I usually name them according to objects
found in the home or in nature – a practice that artisans
have followed for years. Local names describing where
some shapes originated can be found in local dialects or
languages in Morocco, Iran and Central Asia, although
due to the language barriers these are generally hard
to find when researching. Some artists have umbrella
names, such as *Rumi* in Turkish books and *Islimi* in
Persian books. In the absence of official naming, I will
use a generic term for these non-botanical shapes
throughout the book: 'ornate inorganic shapes'.

To create the design, the motifs are placed in the design
section on the geometric grid beneath; however, the
arrangement of the motifs is not predetermined by
any specific rules. There is always a motif placement on
the horizontal and vertical lines of symmetry, and in
some cases on the diagonal. The specifications seem to
be flexible and fluid, depending on the creativity of the
pattern designer. It is good practice to study a number
of tiles and designs to have an understanding of popular
arrangements and to be able to compose patterns that
are visually pleasing.

As this may be your first time working with this type of
motif, you can either copy them from the book or you
can draw them free-hand. The latter might not be exact,
but that is OK; your hand will get used to these shapes
and you will be able to draw them better with practice.

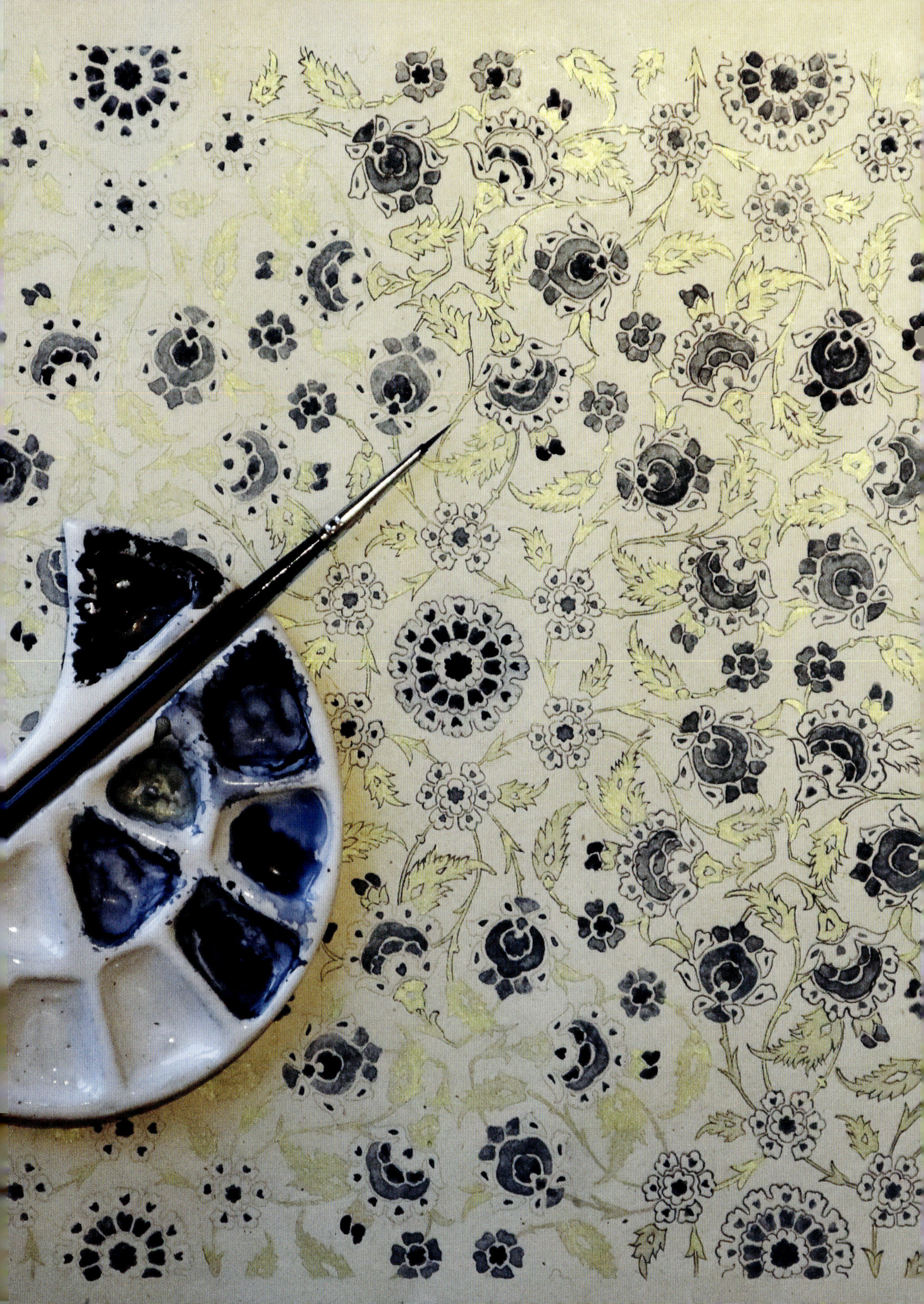

ONE-COLOUR HEXAGONAL TILE

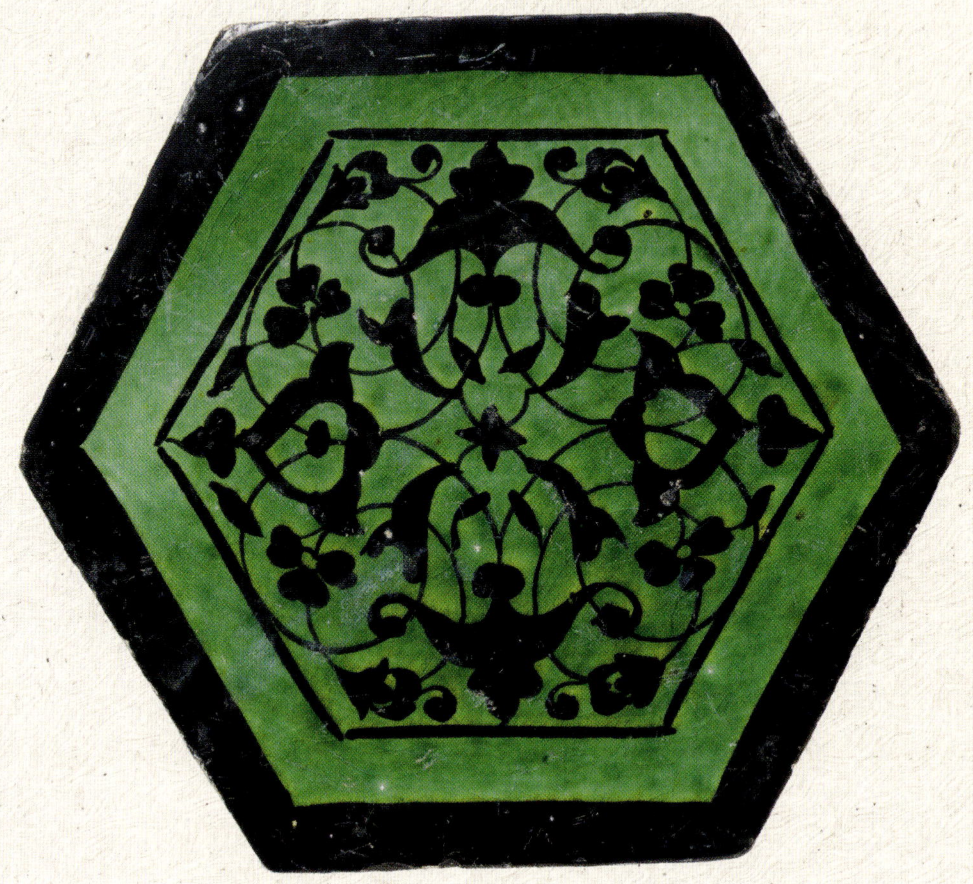

A one-colour hexagonal tile, attributed to Iran and dating back to the end of the fifteenth century.
14 × 15.9 × 2.2 cm. It is important to keep the original dimensions of this tile in mind because we
always tend to draw them smaller than they are.

Looking at the Geometric Structure

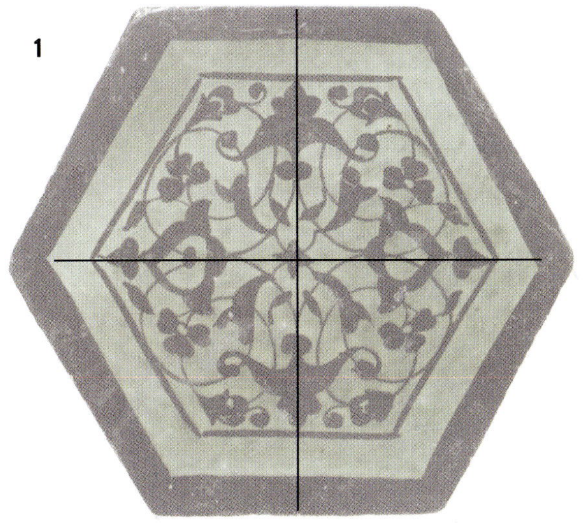

1

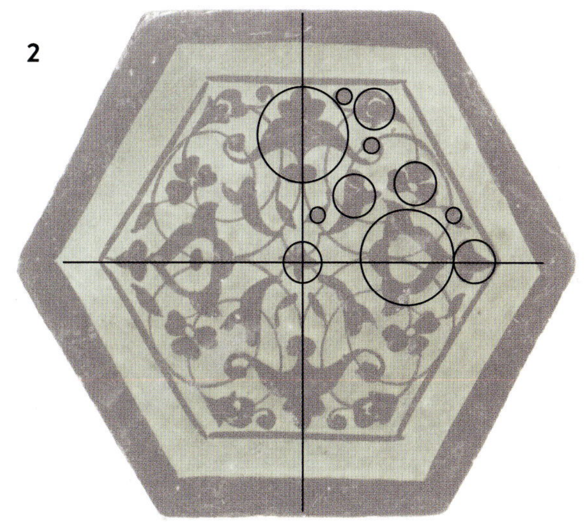

2

The first noticeable aspect is that this is a six-sided (hexagonal) tile that uses Grid 2 (see p.35). However, the inner design is made up of four repeated units, rather than six, which makes it a great starting point (1). The design is usually created in halves to ensure perfect symmetry. Accuracy is easier to achieve when drawing and painting on paper versus tiles, so keep that in mind during your application.

The geometric division also provides us with starting points for the pattern, as seen in the marked circles (2). You will also notice that the tile is not very accurate, which could mean either mean that some of the shapes were painted freehand using only rough measurements, or that the dimensions changed during the tile glazing or firing process.

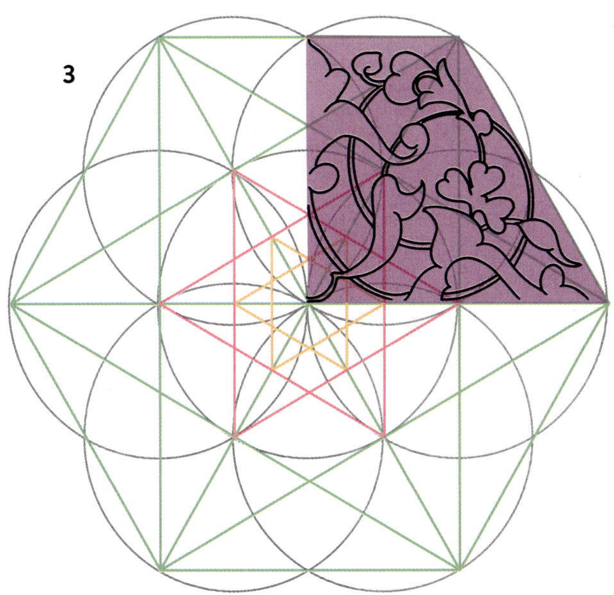

3

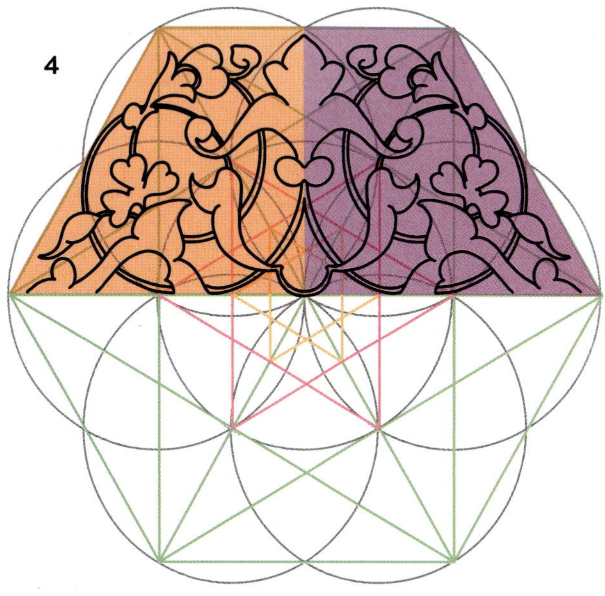

4

The design section is determined by the geometric construction of the hexagon. All the motifs are drawn within that one section, which feels less challenging than drawing the whole pattern without structure (3). The design section is then reflected to create a repeat unit (4), which is repeated once more to complete the design.

Drawing the Pattern

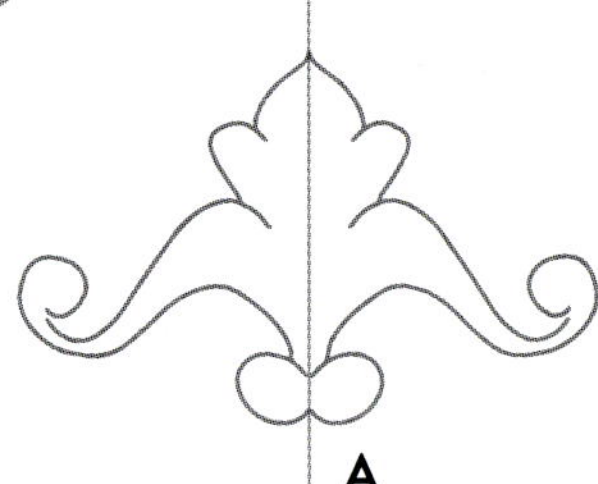

A

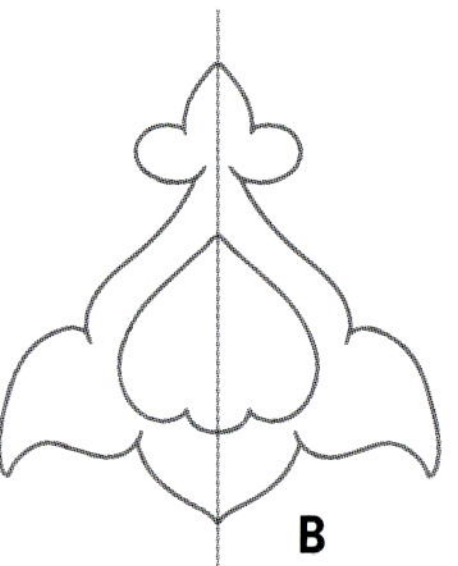

B

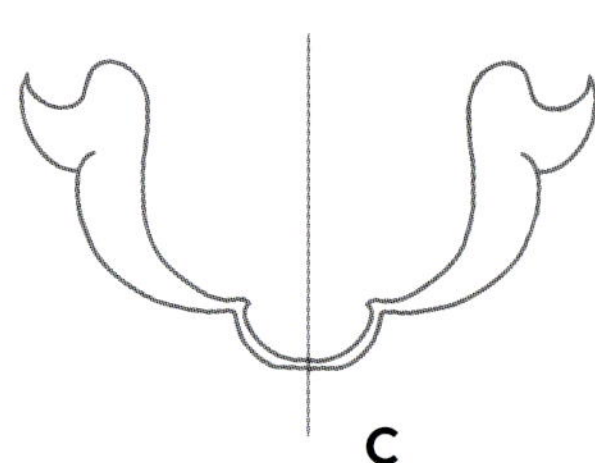

C

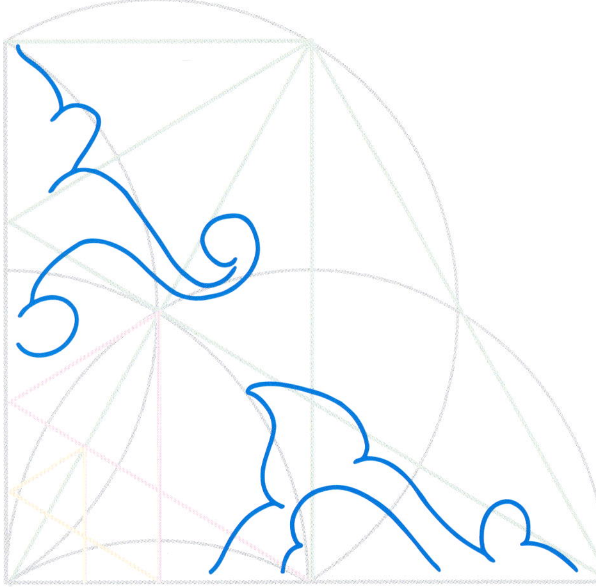

1 This pattern starts with three ornate inorganic shapes (A, B and C). Although they are full shapes, they are placed in the section as halves to ensure the symmetry of the design. It is not very common for a shape to be fully drawn. For example, shapes A and B are shown above as complete shapes, but when you draw them, you will imagine a vertical line cutting them in half.

Place shape A on the vertical line and shape B on the horizontal line. If you are drawing them freehand, start with very light lines drawn with a sharp pencil and keep an eraser with you; keep editing the shape so that it looks as similar as possible to the shape in the illustration.

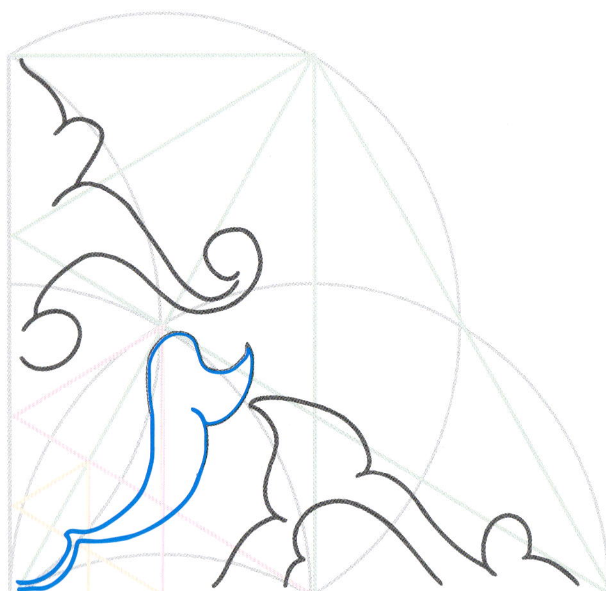

2 Add shape C between shapes A and B.

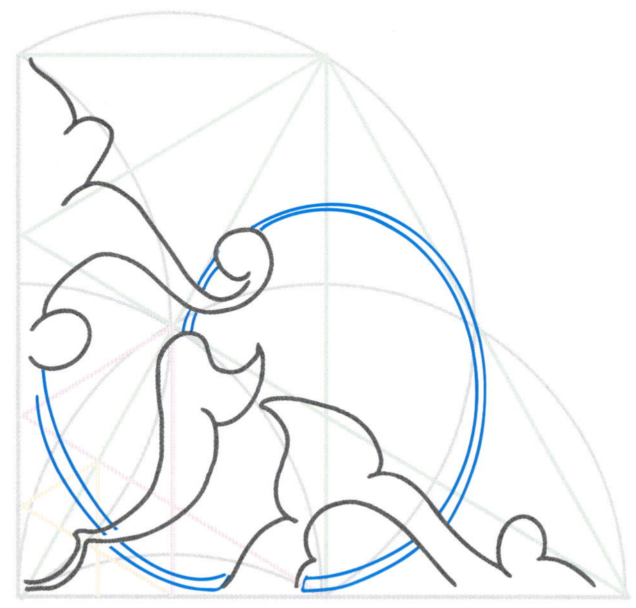

3 It is uncommon for motifs to be floating in space without a connection. One of the preferred ways of connecting shapes is via a spiral. The starting point of the spiral is the motif on the vertical line (A). Loop this into the other two motifs (B and C), leaving spaces for further floral motifs.

4   The floral motifs have a secondary spiral that re-emerges from the spiral created in Step 3. Most floral spirals have a clear starting point from the symmetry lines, however the placement of this one is unusual because it appears from under an inorganic shape. This could be due to the simplicity of the design and the fact that only three additional floral motifs will be added (D, E and F), their placement on the spiral indicated by the circles opposite.

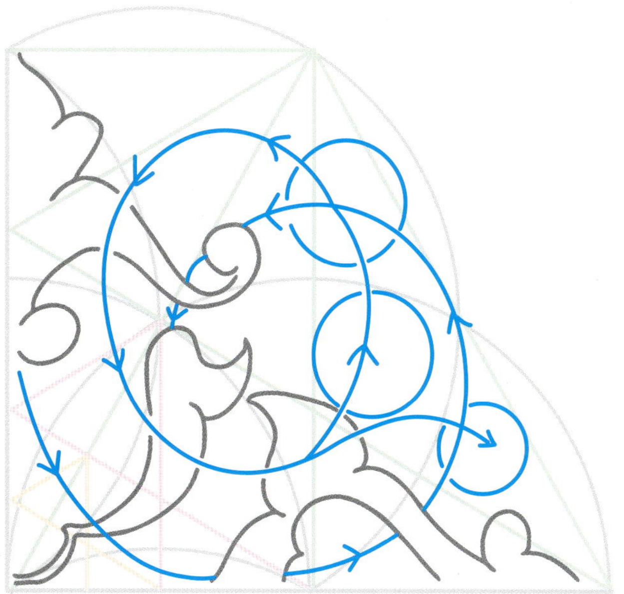

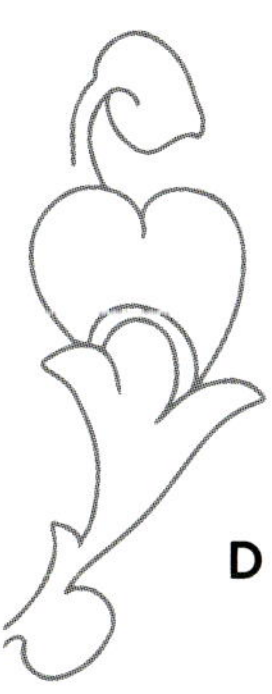

D

E

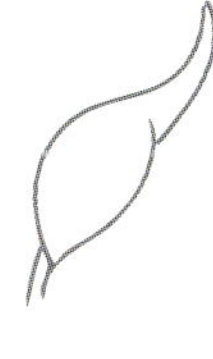

F

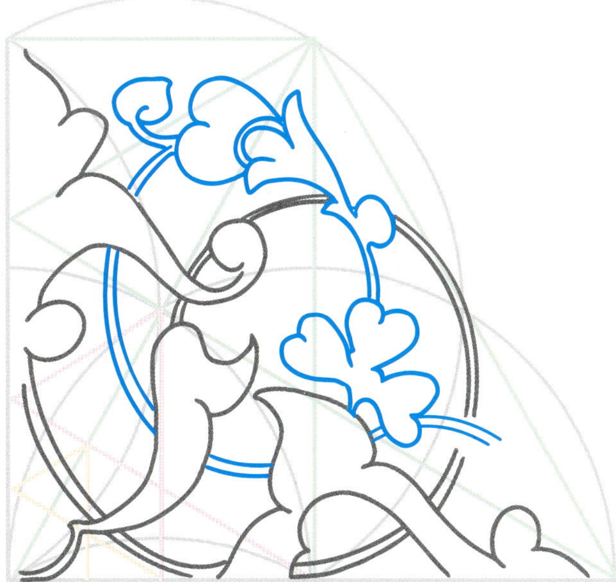

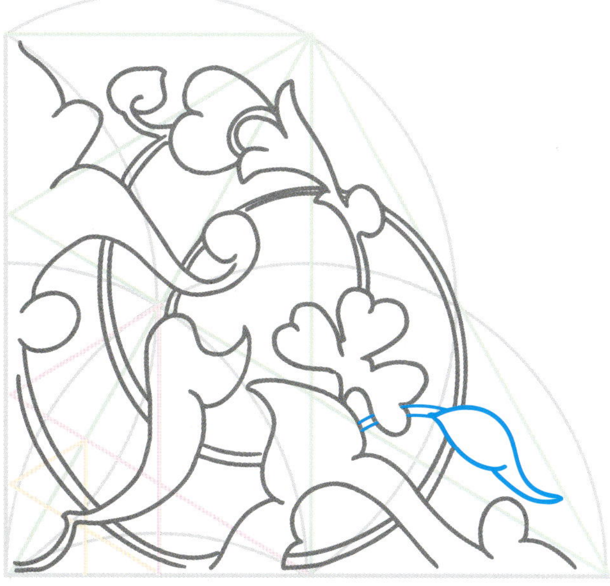

5   Place flower E within the spiral. Add flower D in the slightly bigger diagonal space, since it is a bit more elaborate.

6   The only empty space that remains is above shape B, so add a simple leaf (F) here. Overall, this pattern is relatively simple whilst the repeat looks surprisingly intricate.

7 Reflect the design section to create the full design unit.

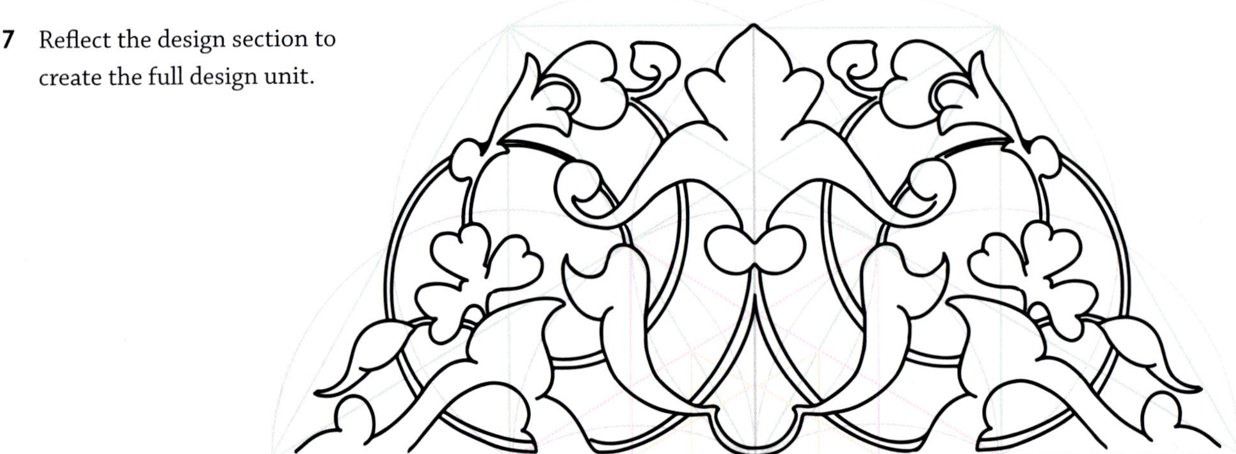

8 Reflect the repeat unit on the horizontal line once more to complete the pattern. This moment of completion always fills me and my students with a great sense of achievement.

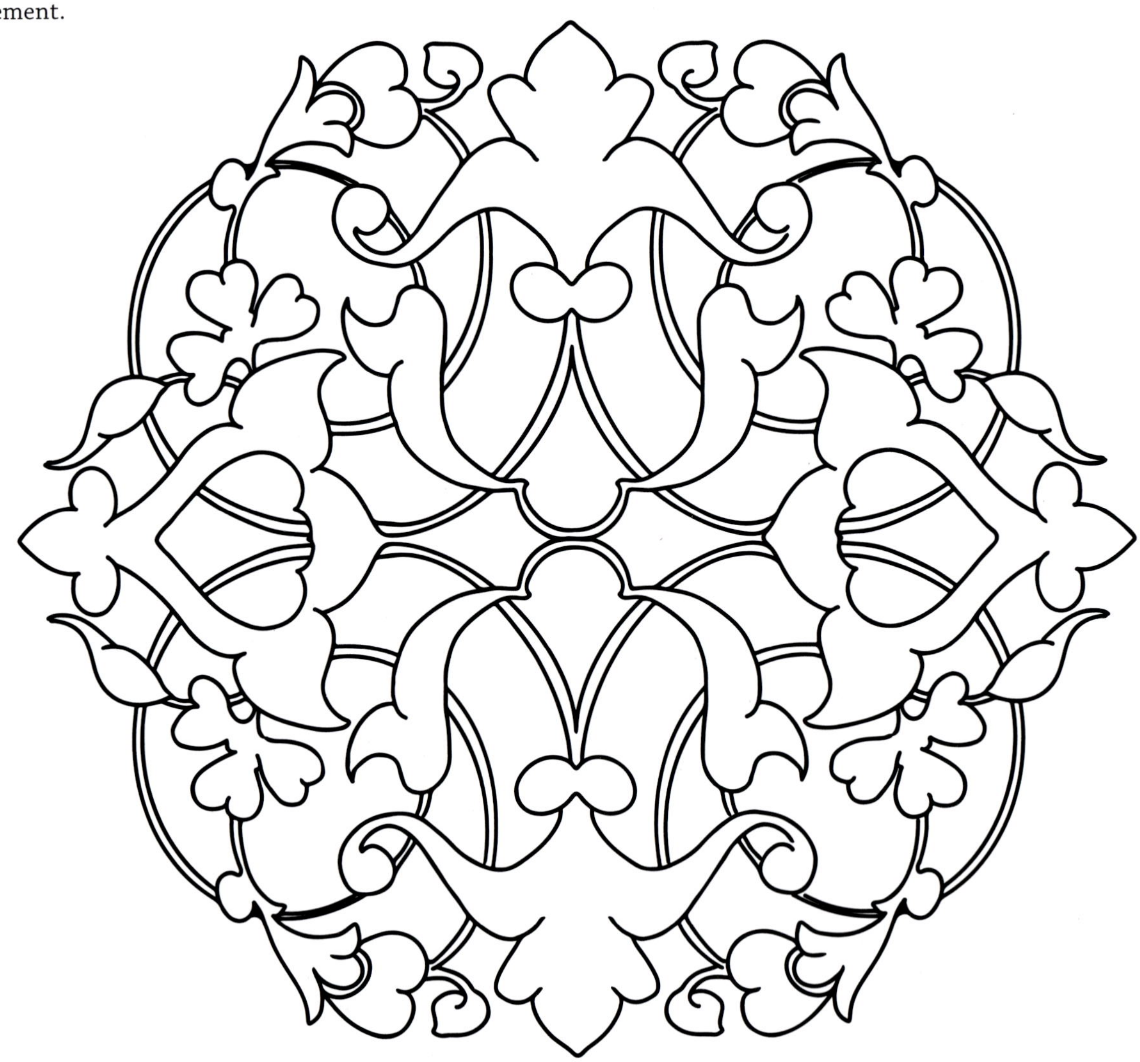

Transferring, Tessellating and Painting the Pattern

When it comes to using this pattern, the easiest way to start is by transferring the design onto paper and then painting it. However, the application is not only limited to paper and can be executed on tiles, glass, embroidery, wood and so on. This is the beauty of simple biomorphic patterns – they are very versatile. Tessellation (see p.37) can also be used to give the whole pattern a different look and feel.

Sometimes painting alone does not satisfy our curiosity. If so, I suggest that you explore different media. If you practise a different art form, incorporate these patterns in your own way. It is amazing to see the different effects that can be achieved.

Part III of this book delves deeper into the painting practice and process (see p.151), but before we move on to the second pattern study, here is a simple way to render this pattern with one colour.

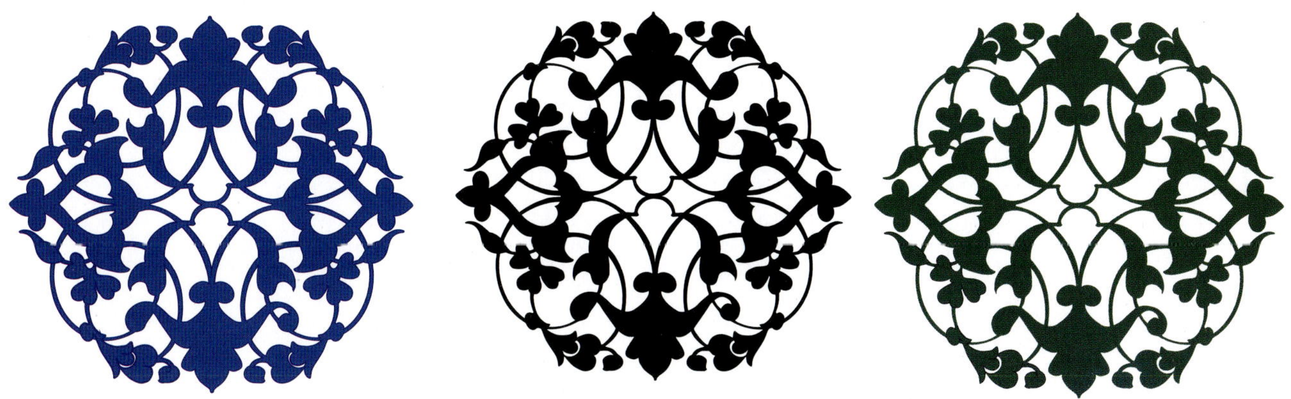

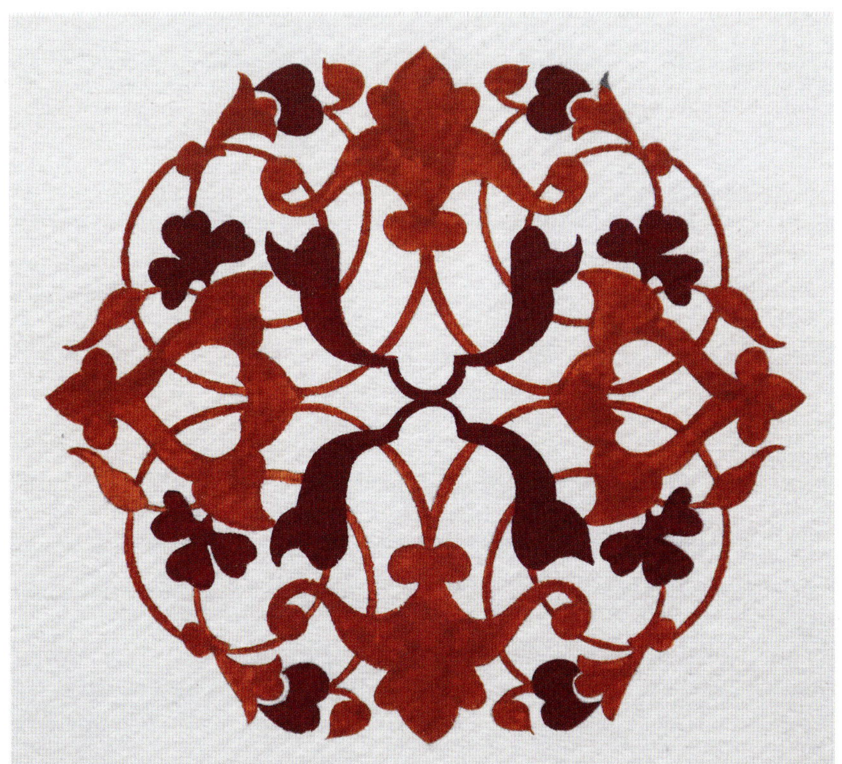

← Here I have painted the pattern in two colours.

IZNIK HEXAGONAL TILE

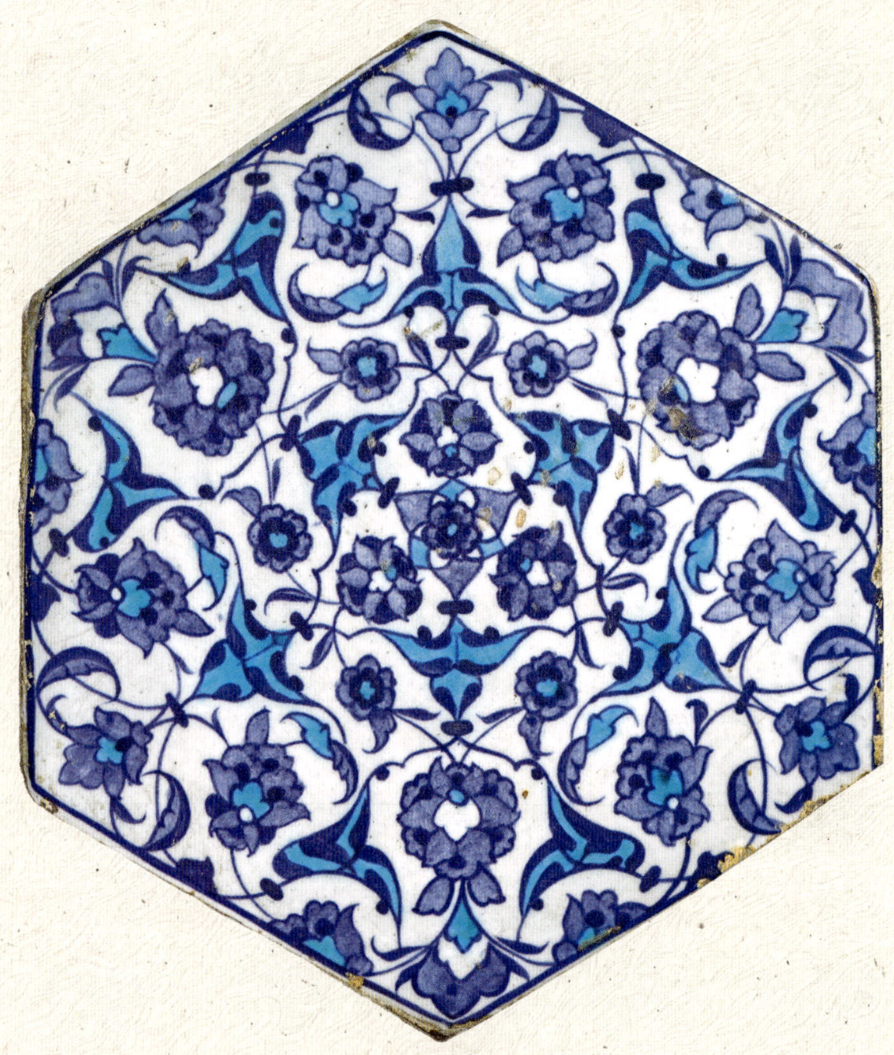

A hexagonal Iznik blue and turquoise pottery tile, c.1525, Turkey.

Looking at the Geometric Structure

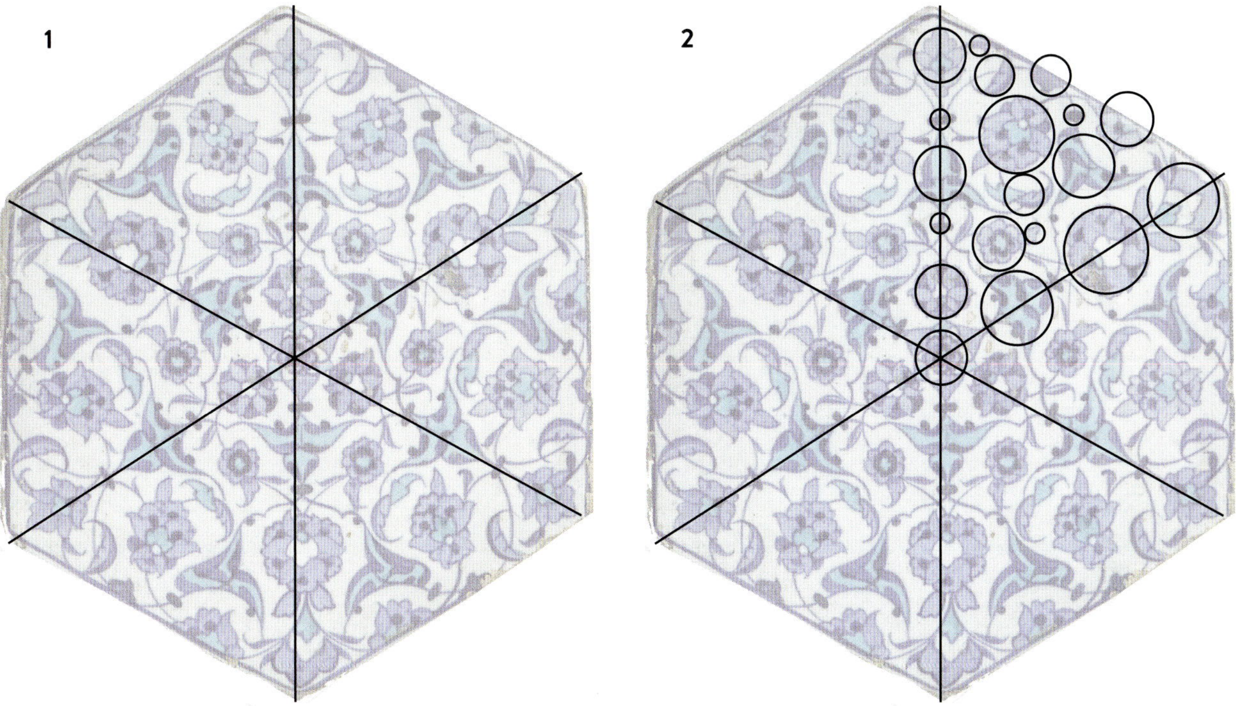

1

2

With its six sides and six lines of symmetry, like our six-pointed star, this tile is a regular hexagon that uses Grid 1 (see p.31). We can place the six lines on the tile (1).

The design section is one triangle of the whole pattern (2).

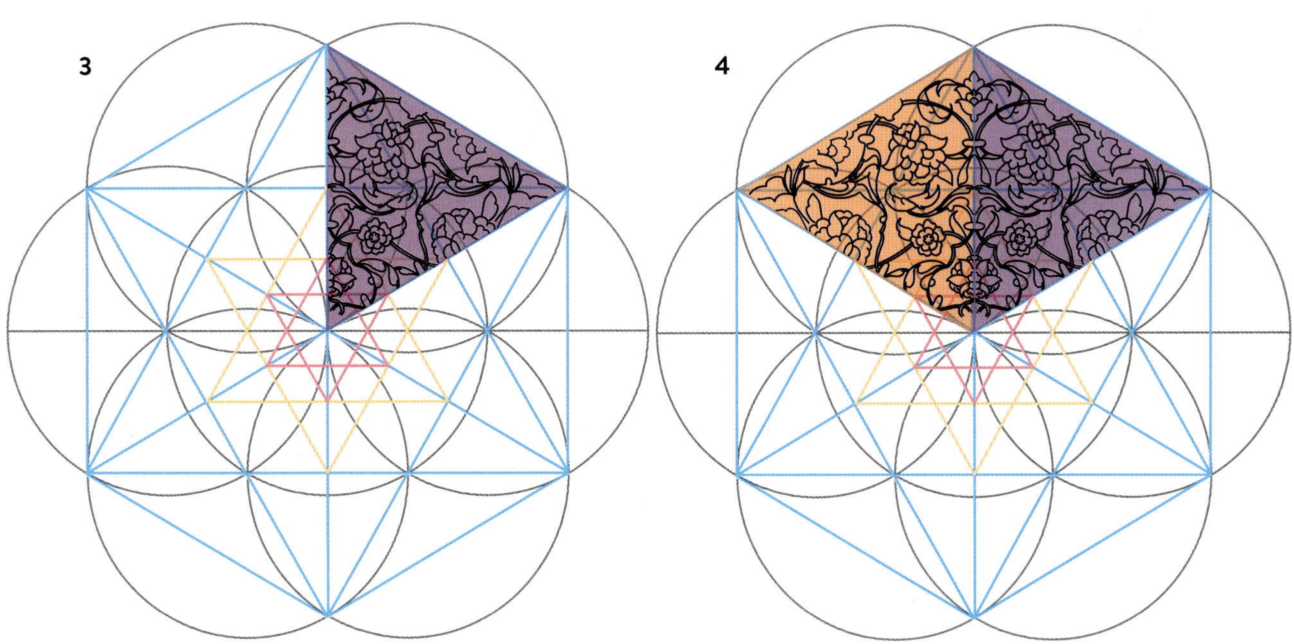

3

4

The design section and its reflection are created by the geometric structure (3 and 4).

Drawing the Pattern

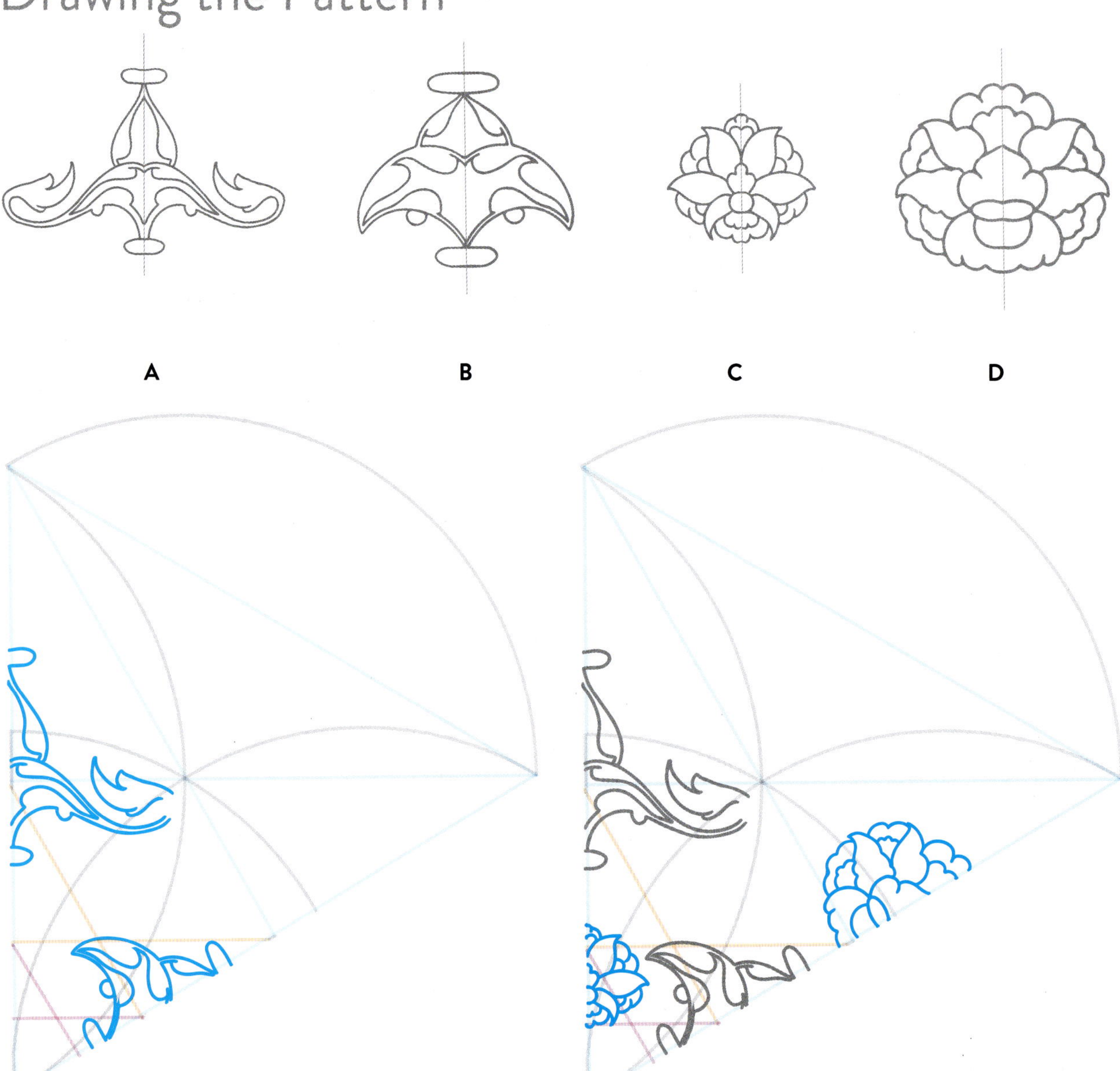

A   B   C   D

1 The start of the design section begins on the vertical and diagonal lines – these are the lines of symmetry in this drawing. Place shape A on the vertical and shape B on the diagonal. Both shapes are placed within the largest six-pointed star. Draw these shapes as halves to ensure the symmetrical quality of the design. You will notice that there is a missing space in there, but this is left for the leaves that will be added later.

2 Place half of flowers C and D on the lines of symmetry. It is interesting to observe that flower C is placed below an inorganic shape, whereas flower D is placed above one. There is a nice balance in this move, and even though it is simple it adds an interesting visual layer to the design.

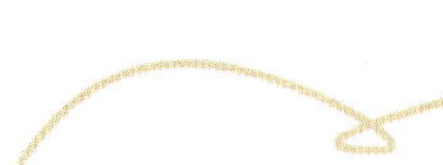

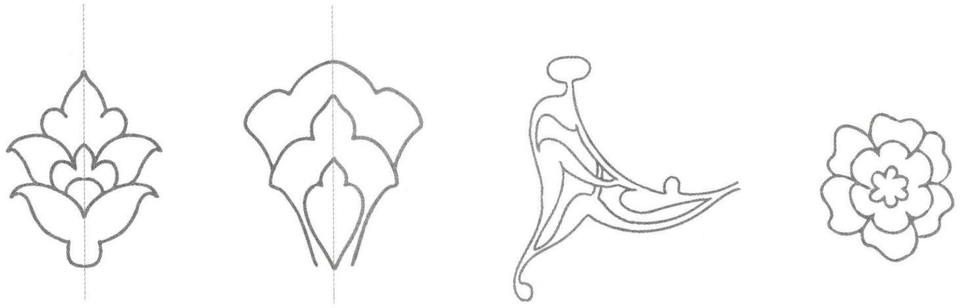

E   F   G   H

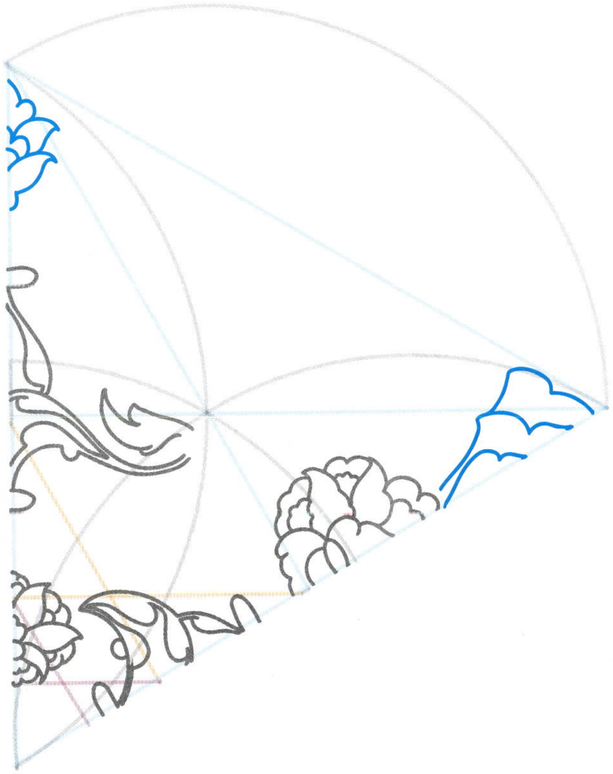

3 Add two more half flowers (E and F) to the lines of symmetry to fill in the gap up to the edge of the geometric lines.

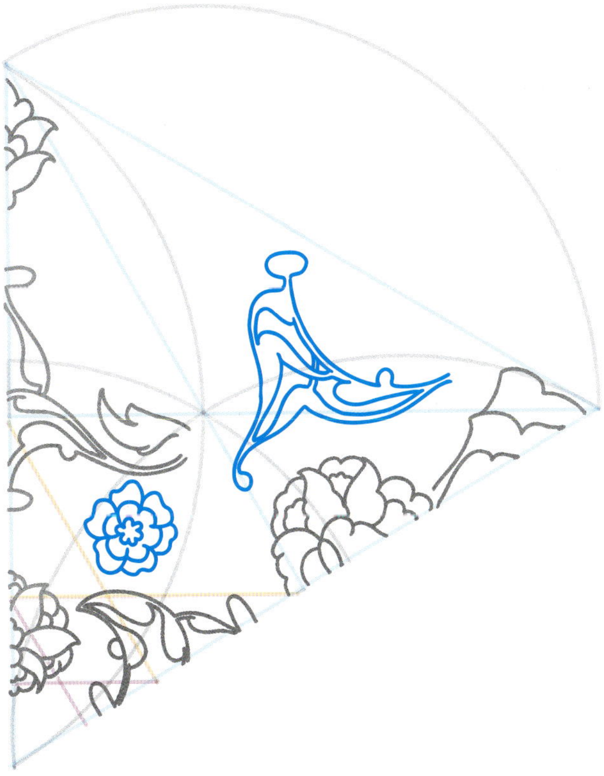

4 Now that the lines of symmetry have been filled with motifs, it is the turn of the central area in between them. These shapes are placed as whole shapes here, rather than halves. Place shape G higher up and flower H nesting within the geometry lines.

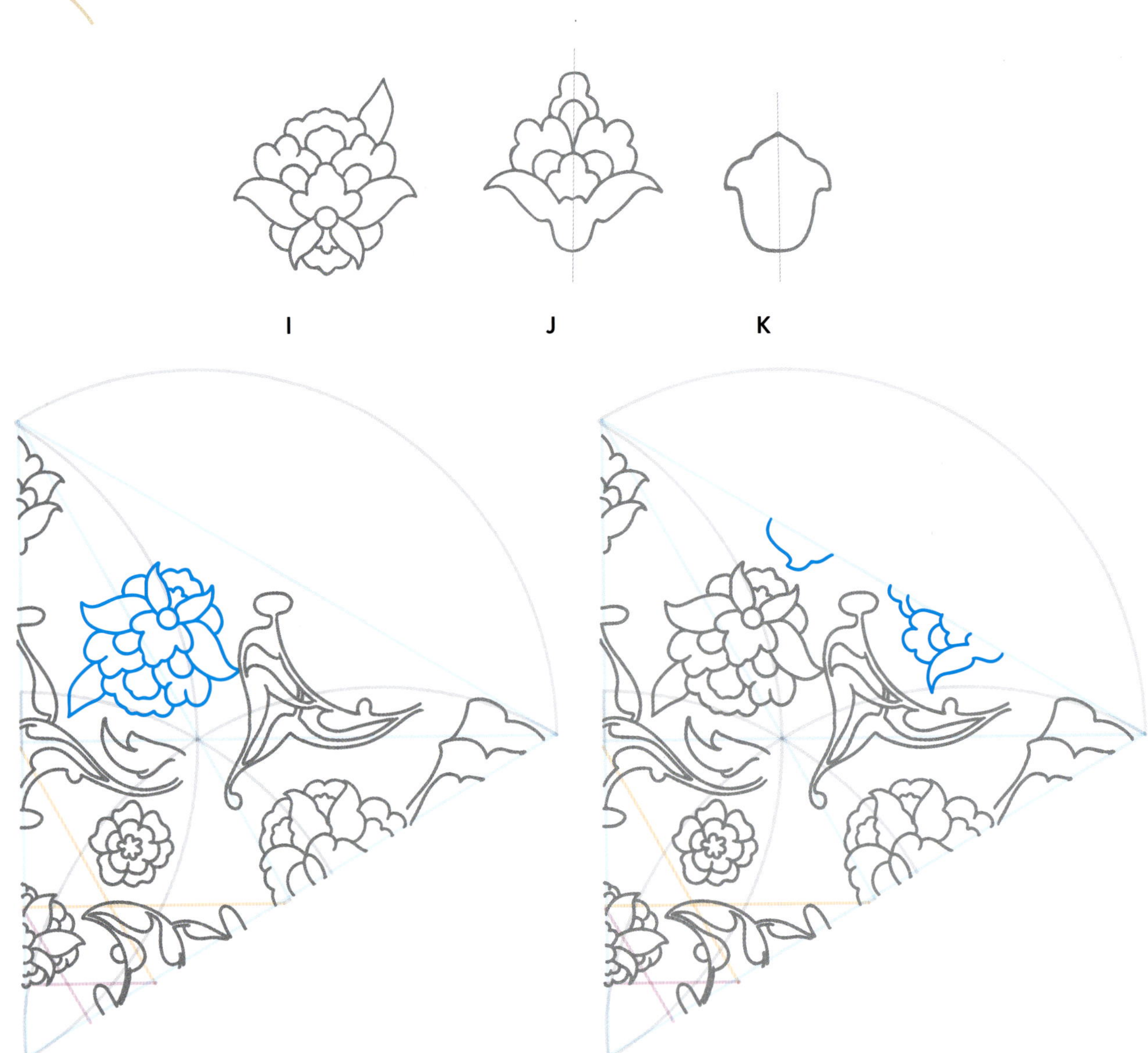

5 Add flower I to fill the empty space. It is a variation of flower C from Step 2, but used as a whole flower rather than a half.

6 One of the hexagon's sides provides an additional line of symmetry. The great thing about this pattern is that this line is also used, so when tessellating a number of tiles together, a new pattern will emerge from those half shapes as well, which you will see at the end of this pattern study. Add half flower J and half shape K to that line. Having one floral motif and one ornate inorganic shape on there complements the types of shape that were added on the vertical and diagonal lines.

Before we continue with the steps, it is good to stop and look at the motifs in the design section and see how they can connect to each other. As previously discussed (see p.50), all motifs must have a connection between them as they cannot be floating in the space. They are also connected as a system. Since there are two sets of motifs, each set is connected to the other: the floral motifs together and all the inorganic shapes together. Each set has its own spiral as well. When observing the pattern, everything looks intertwined as one entity, although they are separate.

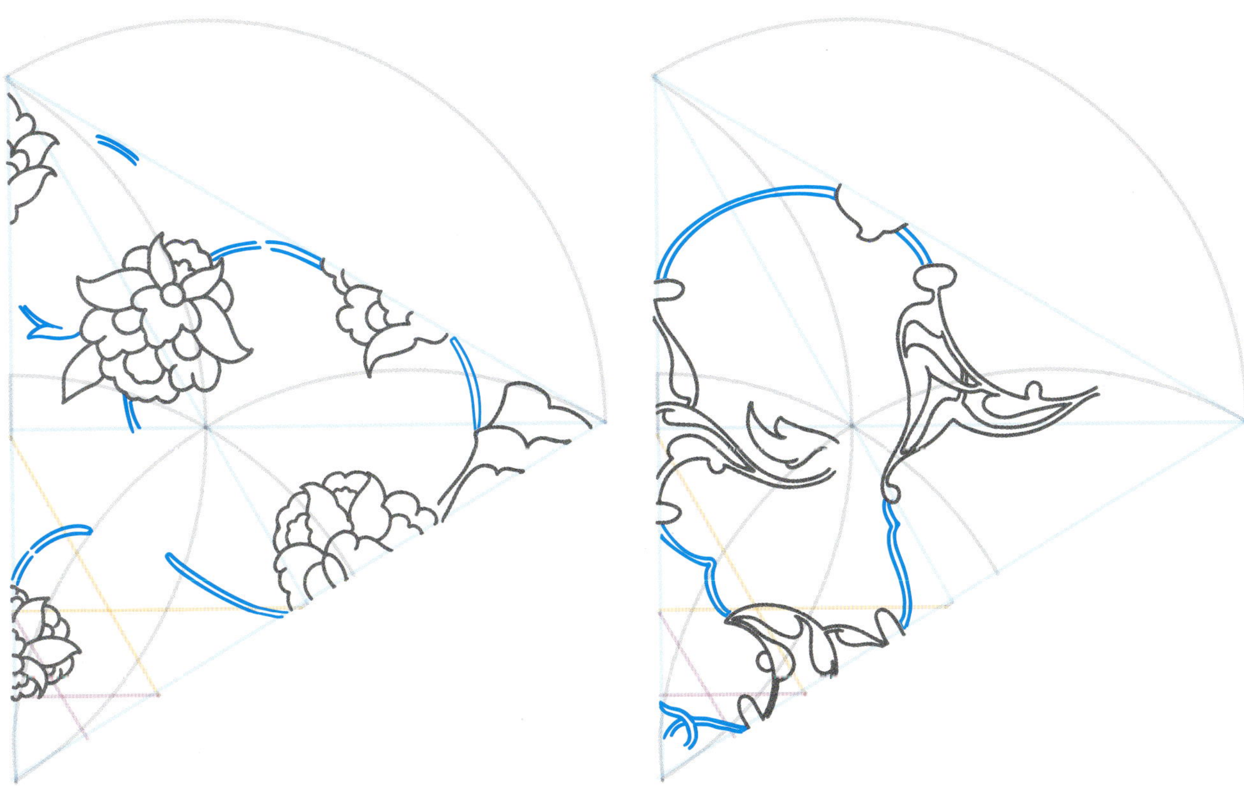

7 Connect the floral motifs with one spiral. Again, you will notice that there are missing spaces for the leaves. In some cases, the spiral is created first and then it is populated with the motifs, so there is more than one way to achieve the same result.

8 Connect the ornate inorganic shapes together as shown. It is helpful to look at each spiral separately to understand how these connections occur.

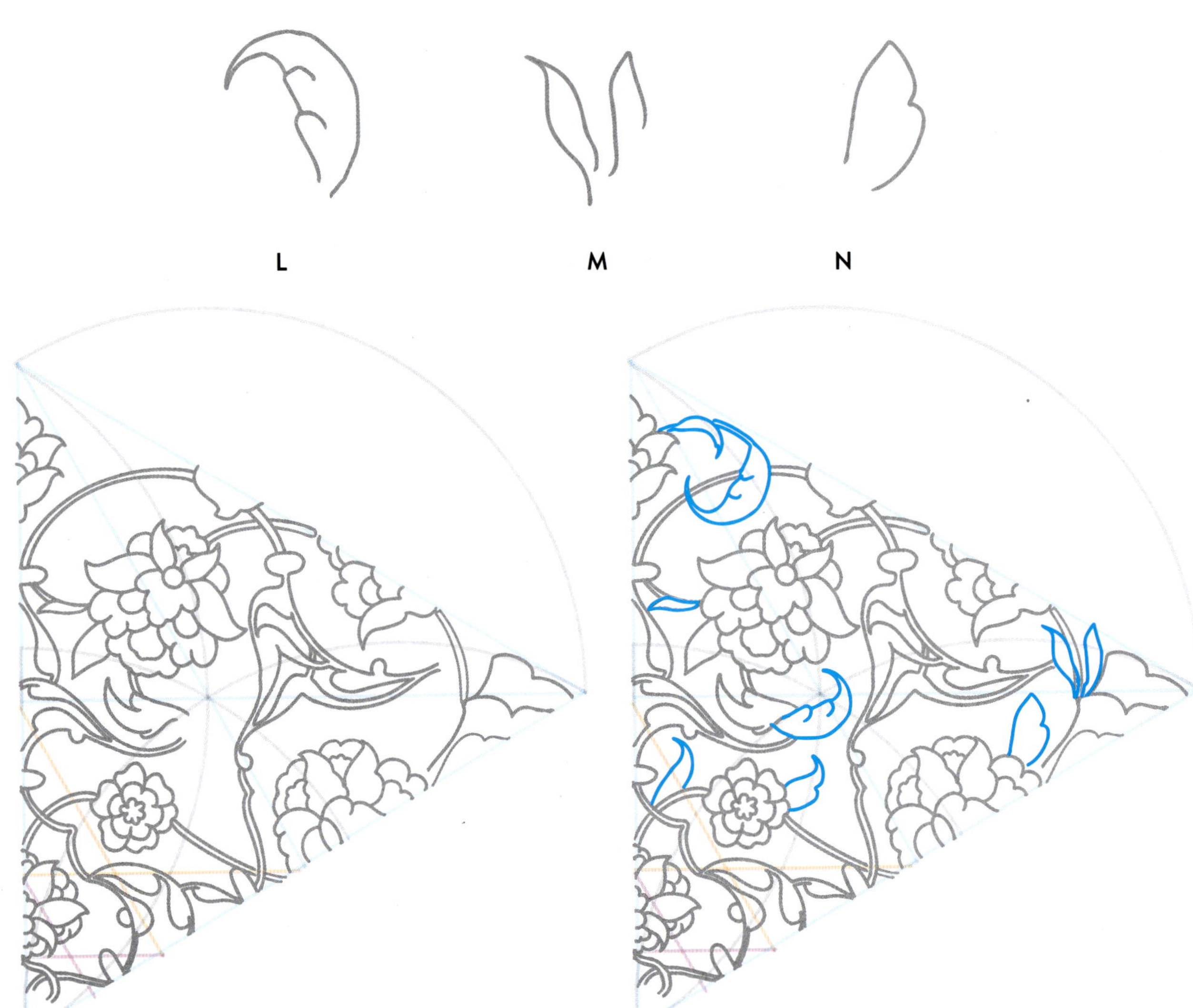

9 There are still empty spaces within the pattern, especially between the floral motifs, and these spaces are usually perfect for adding leaves. Leaves can take many shapes. They can be 'toothed' like leaf L, where one side has two indentations, or follow a simpler design like M and N. Toothed leaves can be more elaborate in bigger designs and can have more indentations on one or both sides.

10 The important consideration when placing the leaves is their direction, which must follow the direction of the flowers on the spiral. In this pattern, the direction is upwards and inwards (anticlockwise). There is no specific science to the placement of leaves; they can be positioned at the discretion of the artist or the designer. All the elements have now been added and the design section is complete.

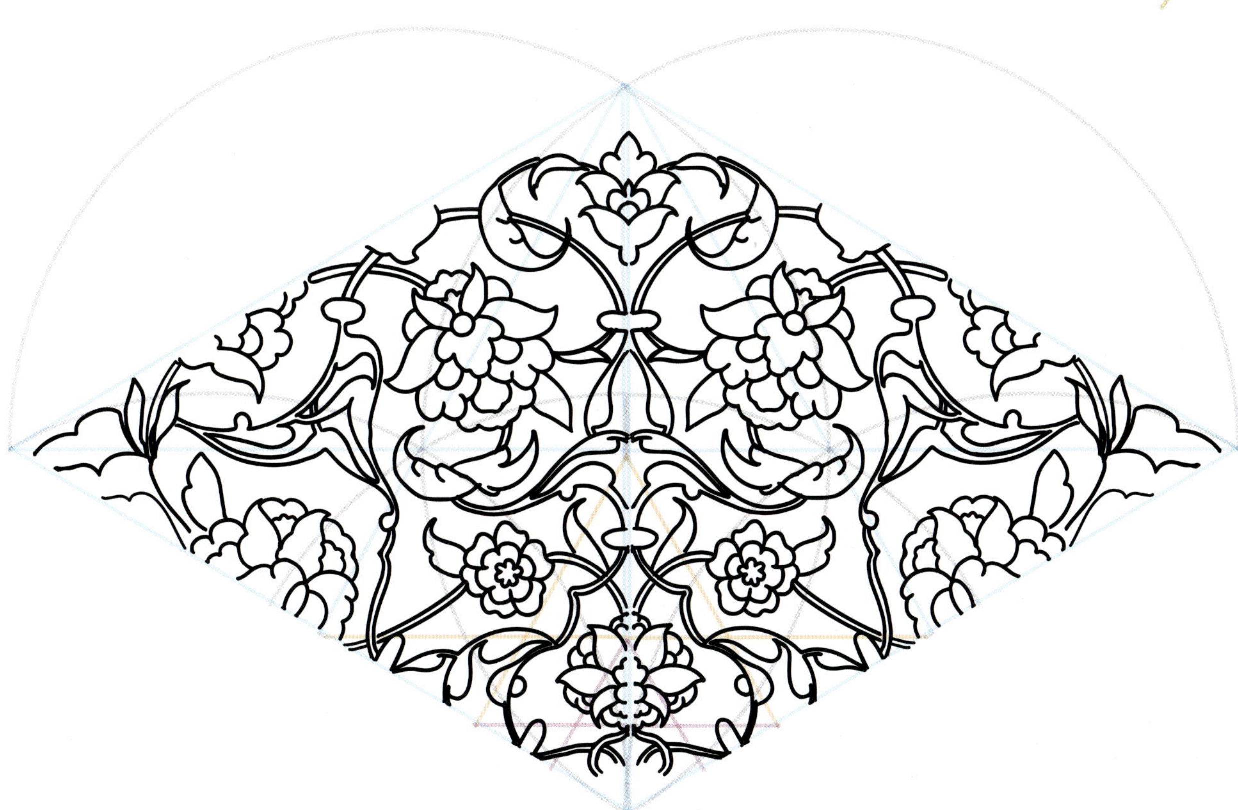

11 Reflect this section. Notice how complicated the design looks as a full repeat unit.

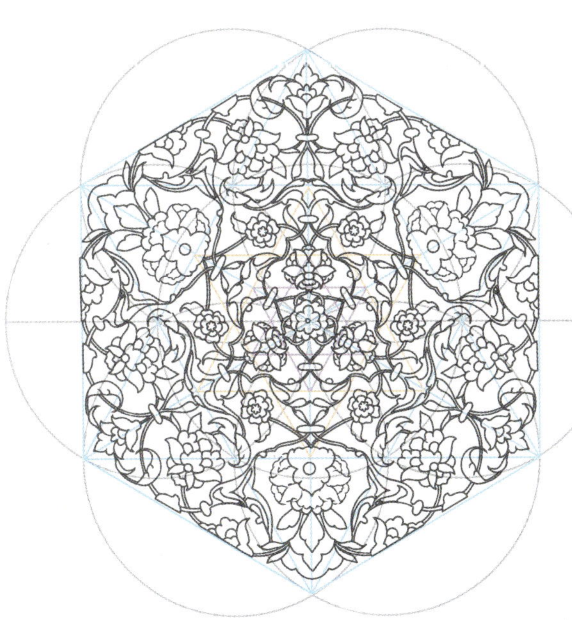

12 Repeat to fill the hexagon to complete the full pattern, which fits perfectly within the shape. The central flower was added at the end, but this can be omitted as the pattern will also look nice without it.

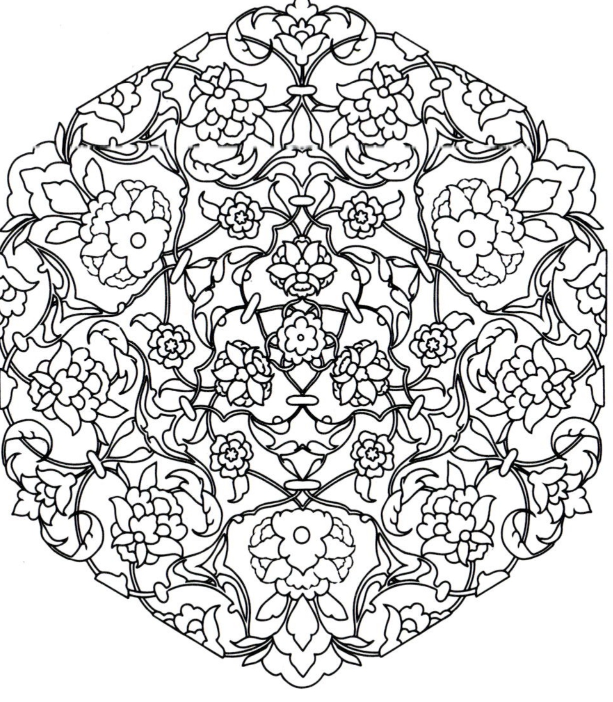

13 The full design is now complete. It is interesting to look at the edge of the hexagon, which includes half shapes as well, suggesting a slightly more complex tessellation.

Tessellating and Varying the Pattern

Tessellate using a hexagonal tiling grid to create a more complex pattern, which you can paint on a large scale.

An example of this pattern painted is given in Part III (see p.166). The possibilities with it are endless. Changing one motif or a few flowers could give you a completely different visual result. The starting point for my students in workshops is always the same but it is amazing how the outcome differs when a curve or a petal are drawn a certain way. So, embrace any 'imperfections' that you might not be happy about at the start because they all look great once the design section is repeated and then tessellated.

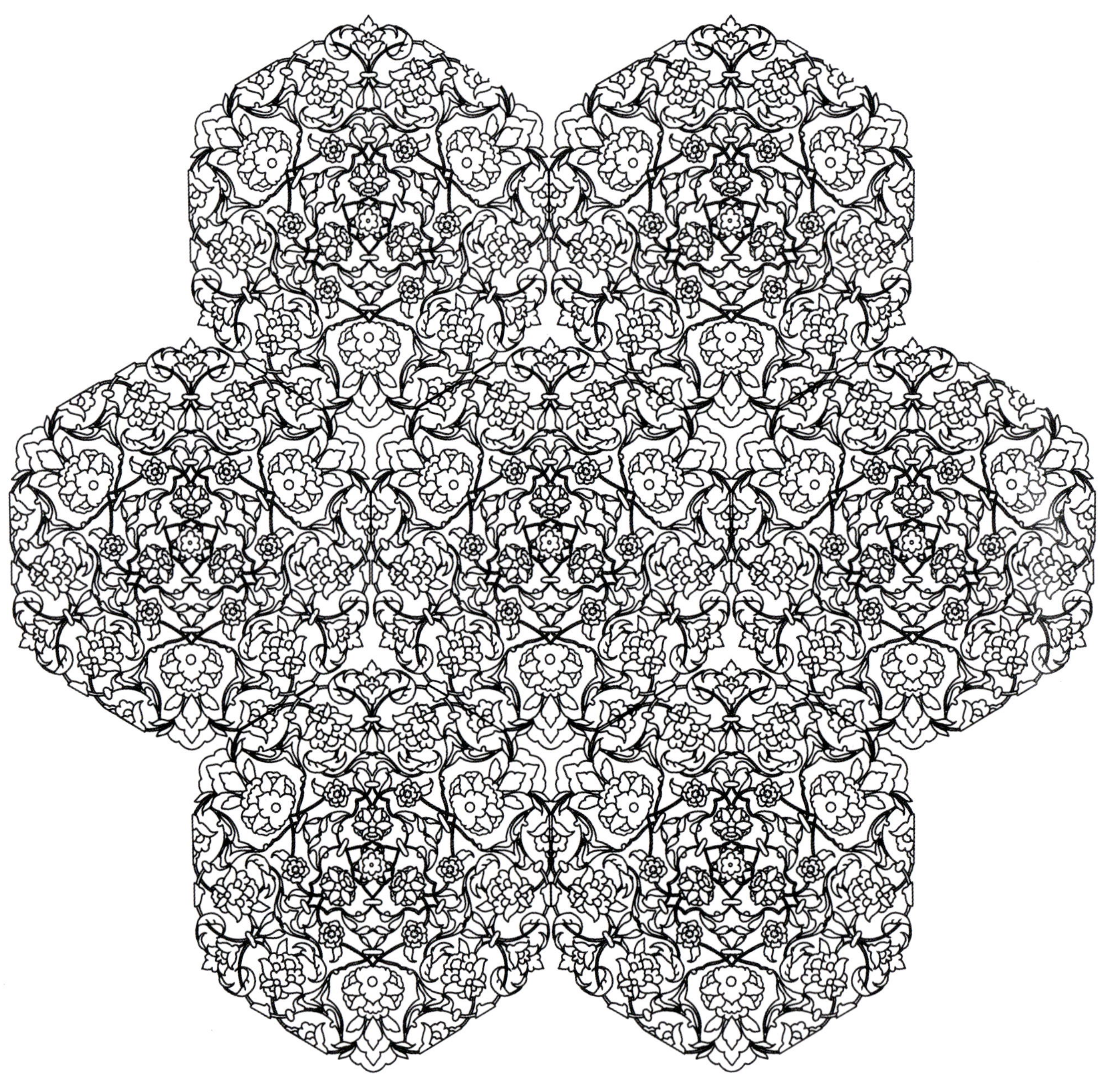

IZNIK FLORAL HEXAGONAL TILE

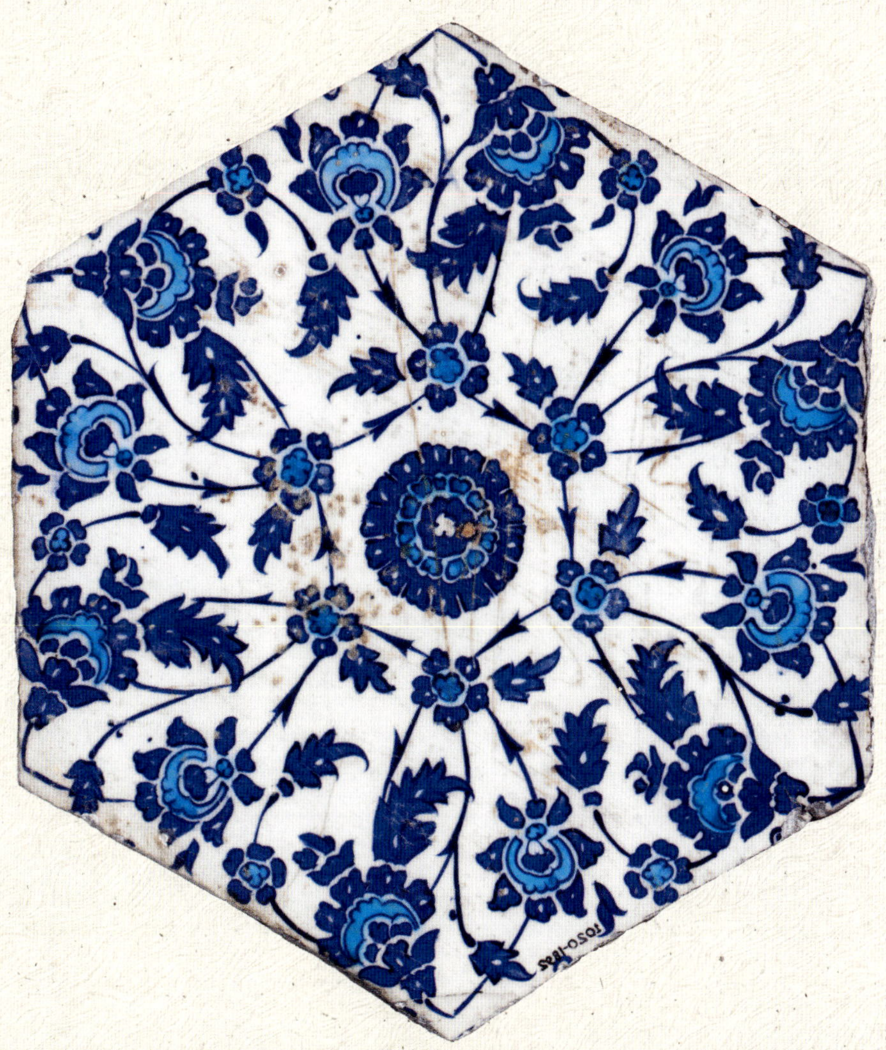

Floral hexagonal tile, 1535, attributed to the city of Iznik in Turkey.
24.6 × 28.3 × 2.1 cm.

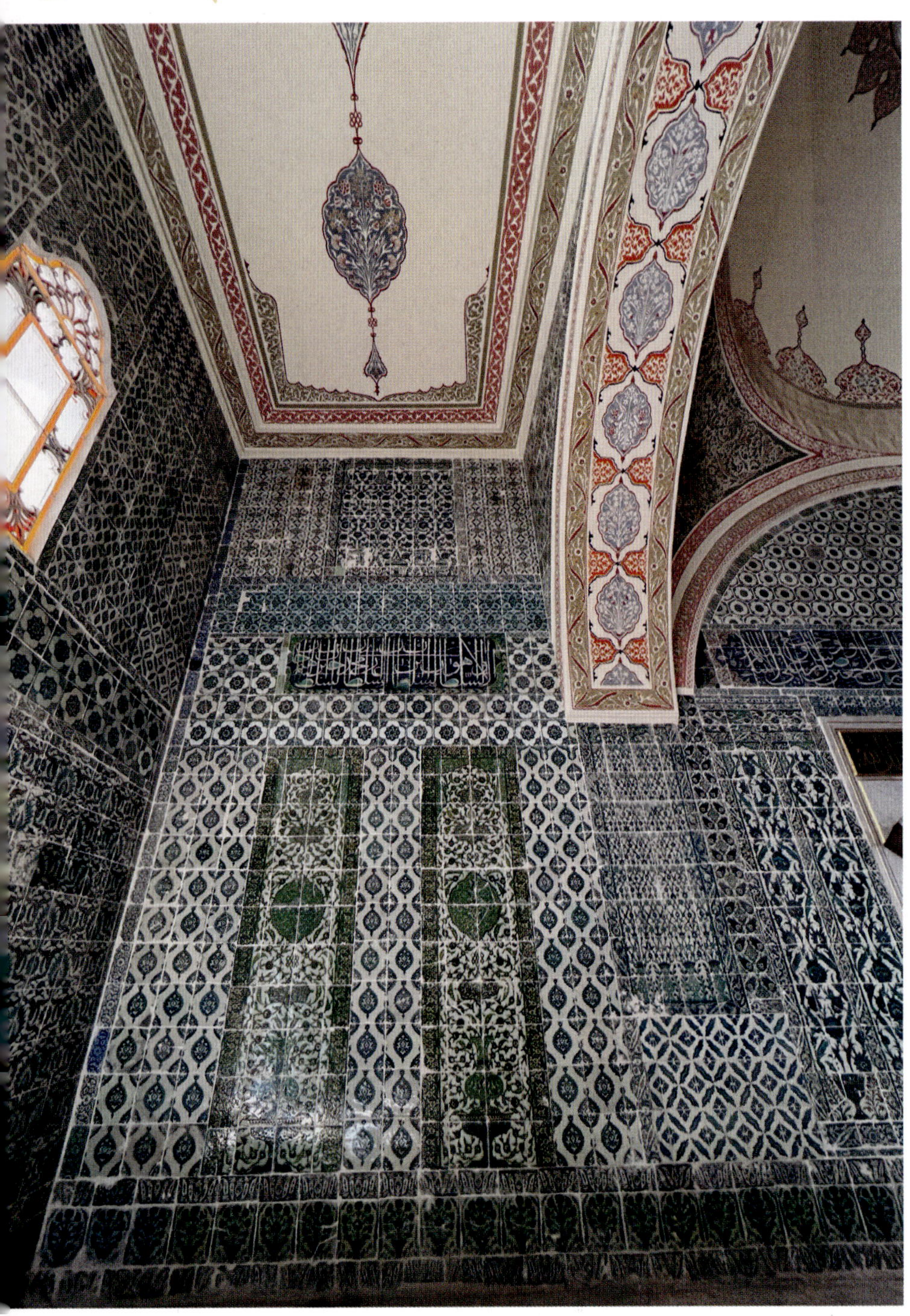

This floral hexagonal tile is dated to the early sixteenth century. It is made of stonepaste and underglaze with polychrome. It is often hard to find the dimensions of a tile because they are not always added as part of the museum or gallery description, but, when available, do come in useful to give us a real comparison when drawing the pattern.

This glazing style has been the signature style of Iznik, north-western Turkey, and many tiles are known as 'Iznik' because of it. The original tile was found in the Sünnet Odasi (Circumcision Room) in the Topkapi Palace, which is located in Istanbul. It was used as the imperial palace during the Ottoman Empire between the fifteenth and nineteenth centuries and is a place filled with history. It is now a museum and is open to visitors from all over the globe to admire. I visited again in 2022; seeing the tiles in person was a privilege and it was worth queuing for over an hour to enter the rooms.

The fascinating thing about this pattern is the number of floral motifs. It consists of four types of flowers; two are repeated in rotational symmetry and two are reflected halves. The flowers can be drawn following a grid, by repeating them using tracing paper or drawing them freehand.

Looking at the Geometric Structure

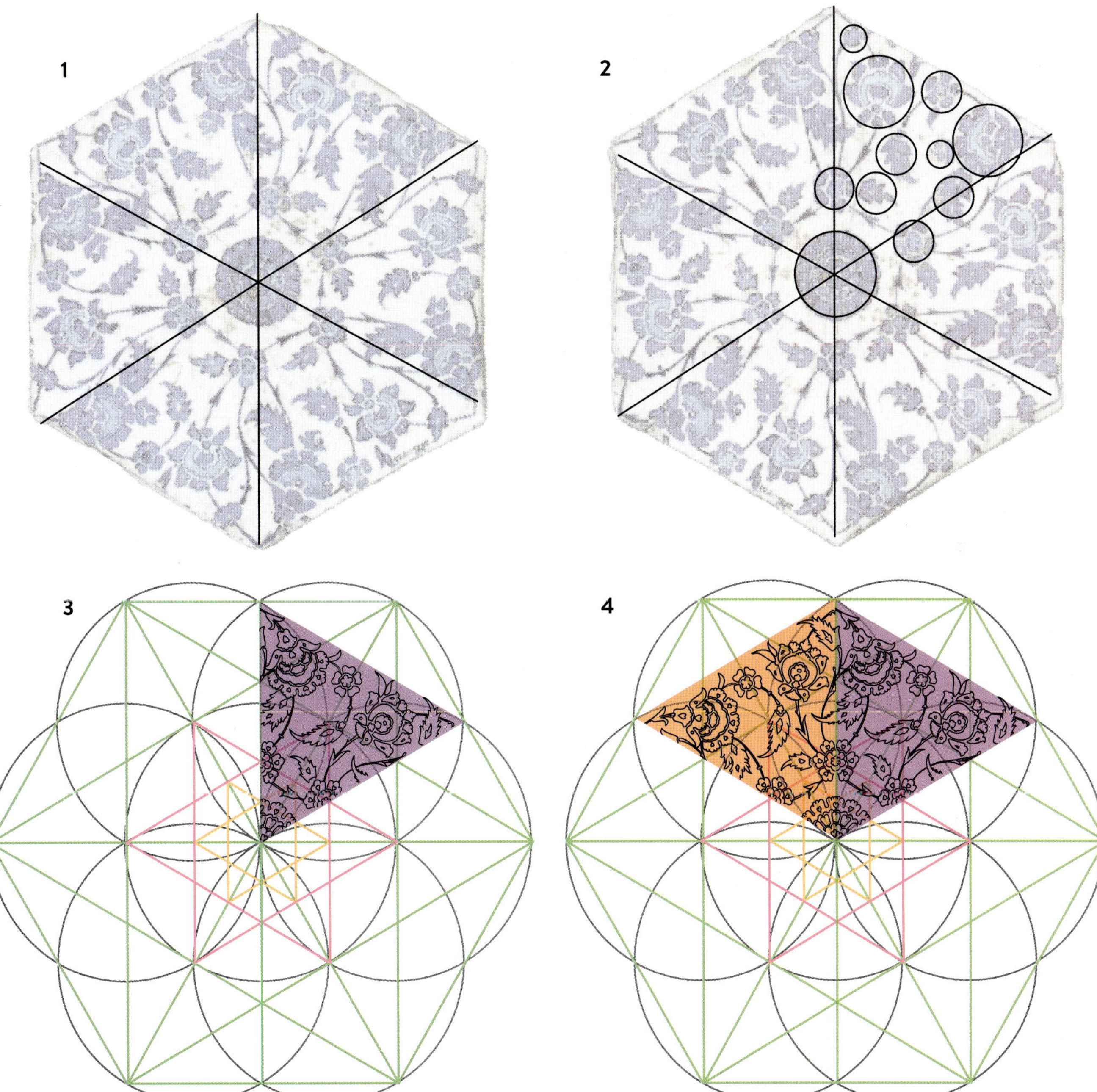

The first stage of the pattern study is to look at the geometric grid and determine the design section (1 and 2). As you now know, the hexagonal shape is an indication that this tile is based on a six-pointed star geometric grid, which determines some of the floral placements within the pattern (3). However, unlike the previous two patterns, the design section is not reflected this time; instead, it is rotated and repeated (4). This style of rotational repeat gives the design a different appearance.

There are many things we do not know from just looking at the original tile, such as the reason the original designers chose these specific flowers and their placement but, since this is a study exercise, we can follow the original placement and predetermined direction of the flowers.

Drawing the Pattern

To draw the elements of this pattern, you will need to follow the steps below. These will help you compose a beautiful, balanced design that is close to the original design of the tile. It is OK if the flowers you draw are not identical to those in the book. Take this as a guide, but you are welcome to add your own touch to the flowers.

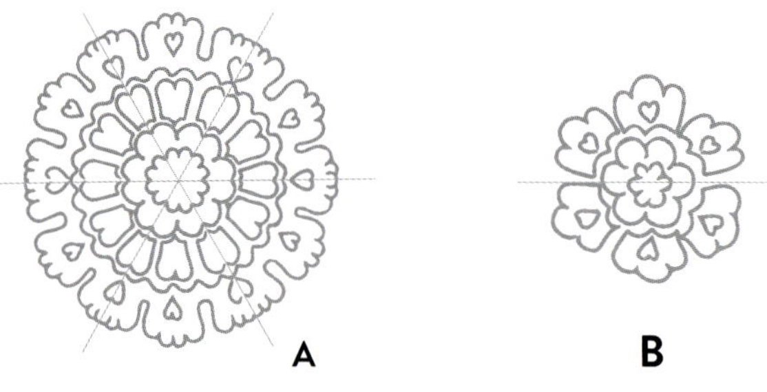

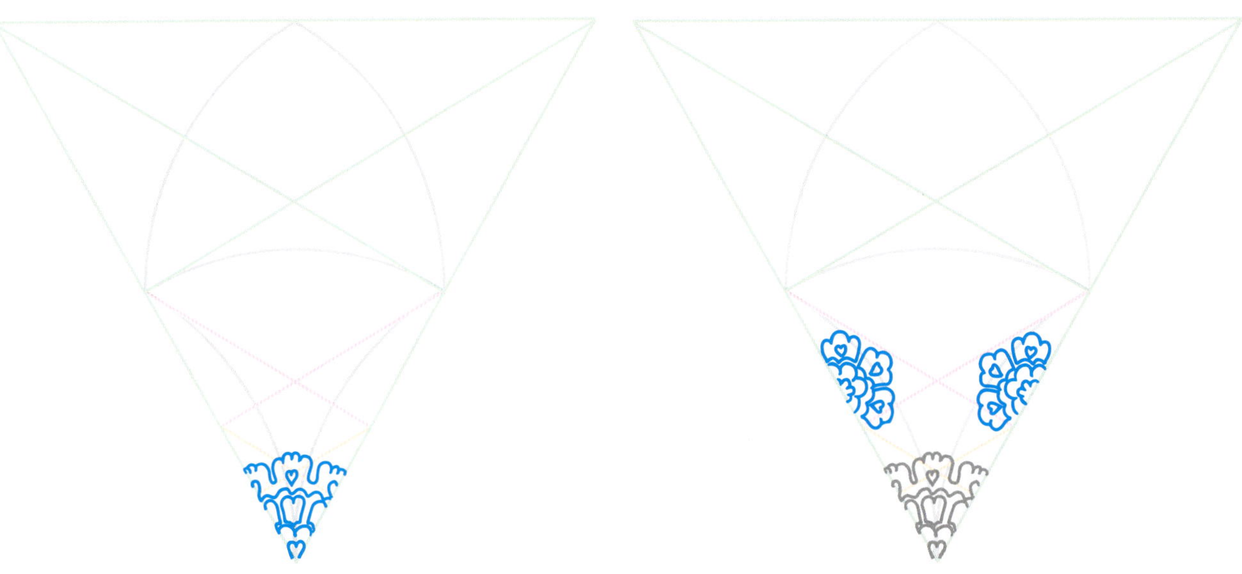

1 The starting point of this design is the central flower, which is placed inside the smallest six-pointed star. Draw part of flower A as shown – it has a total of 12 petals, so only two petals (or one full petal and two halves) will feature in this section.

2 There are two lines of symmetry: the two edges of the triangle. Half of flower B is placed on each line. This flower has six petals, so only three petals of each flower will be used here. Notice how these flowers are placed within the second (pink) six-pointed star.

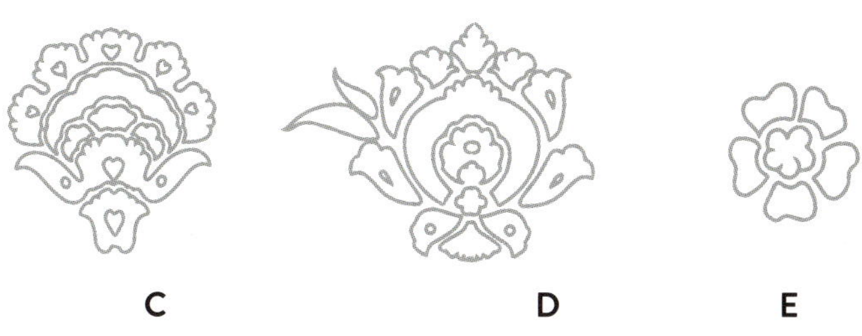

C   D   E

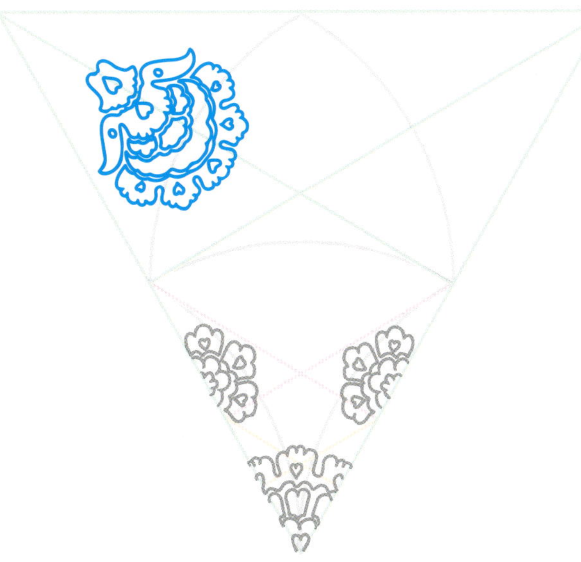

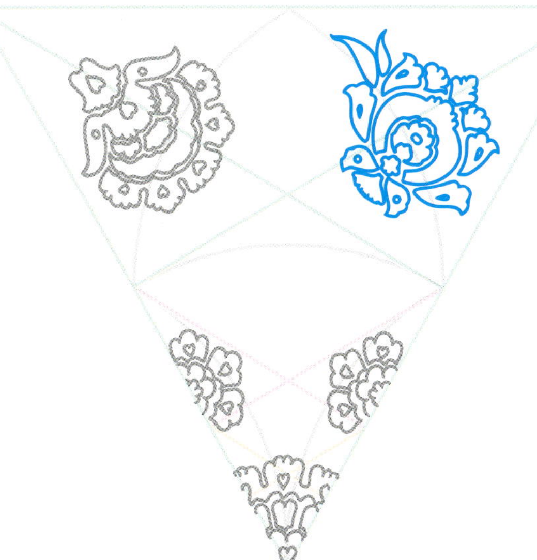

3 Add flower C as a whole on the line of the third (green) six-pointed star, pointing downwards.

4 Add flower D on the other line of the third (green) six-pointed star, also as a whole but this time pointing upwards. Positioning the flowers pointing in different directions creates a new dynamic in the pattern.

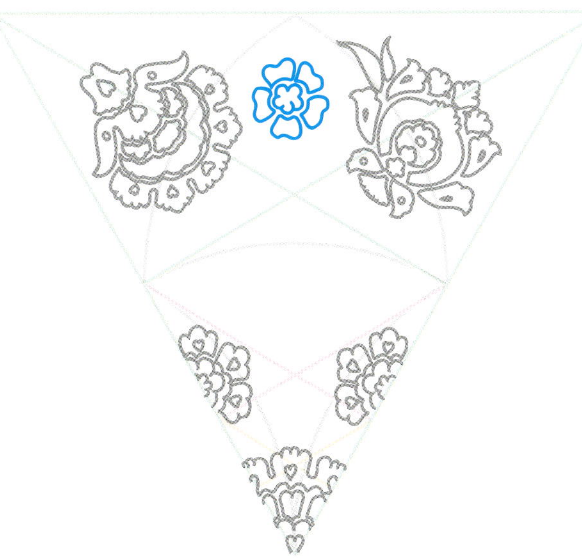

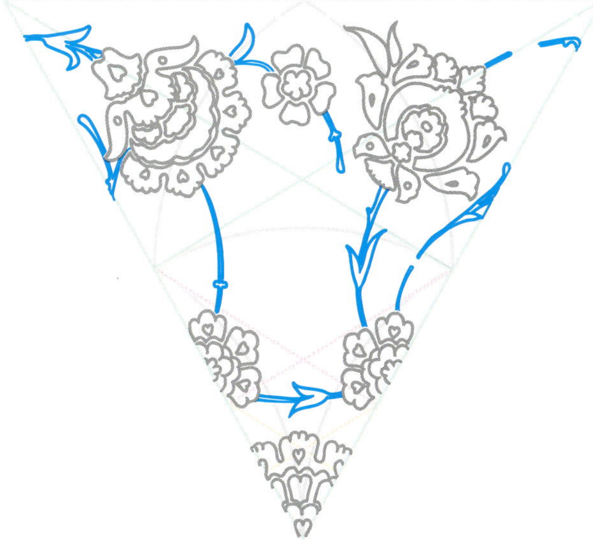

5 Add flower E in the space between the previously placed flowers (C and D). It is much smaller than the others so its effect is more subtle, but it keeps the space nicely populated.

6 When all the flowers have been placed, add branches to connect them together – the rule is not to have any flowers floating in the space without a connection between them. Some artists prefer placing the branches in the design section first and then adding the flowers, while others start with the flowers as I do.

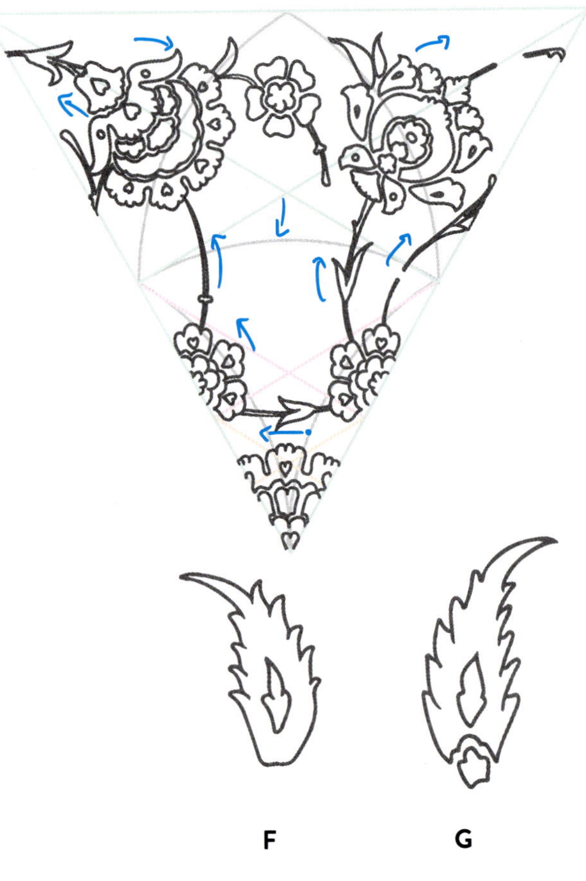

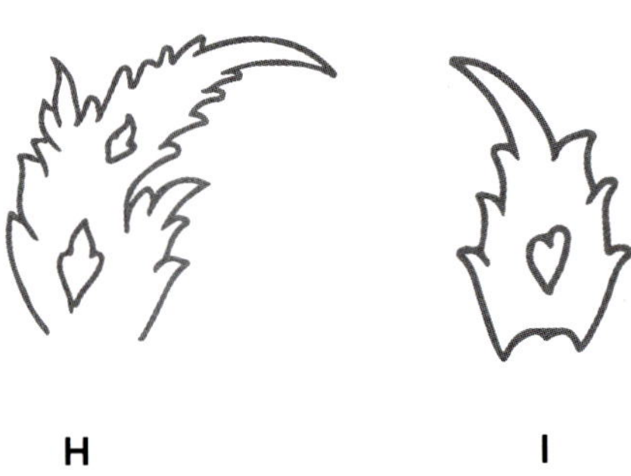

7 The direction of the branches is important for the next step because the leaves need to be placed in a complementary way to the direction of the flowers.

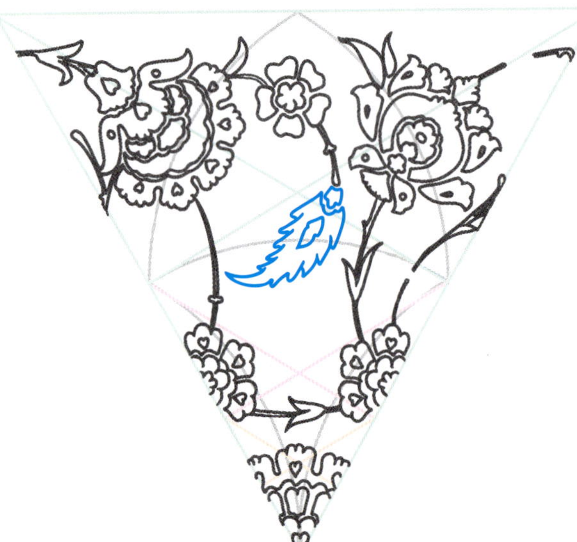

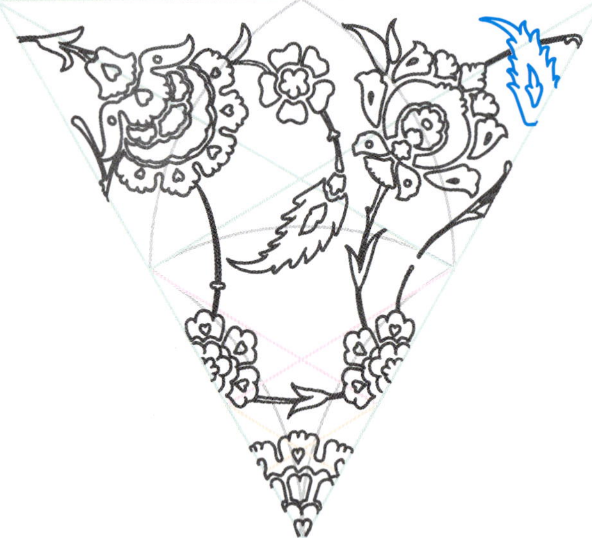

8 The branches are now ready for the addition of the leaves, either whole or as segments. Start by adding leaf G – a toothed leaf with indentations on either side – pointing downwards to complement the direction of the flowers already pointing in the same direction.

9 Add leaf F to the right-side corner. You will notice that it is missing a tiny part. This missing part is actually a part of the branch that will be on the left side of the section, as illustrated in Step 12. As mentioned before, this design repeat is based on rotation so you have to keep that in mind when drawing.

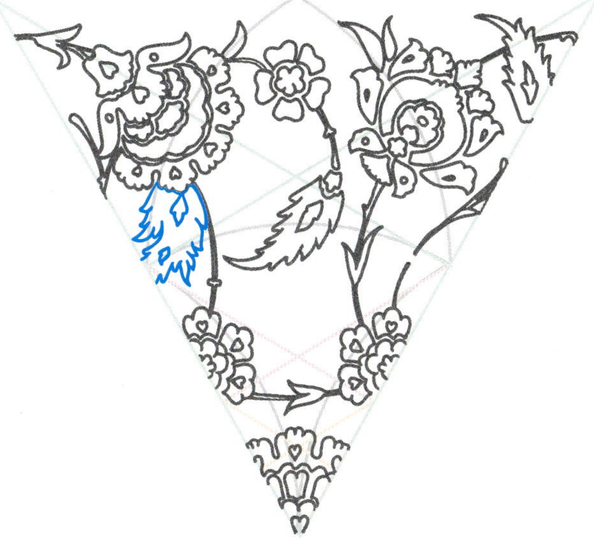

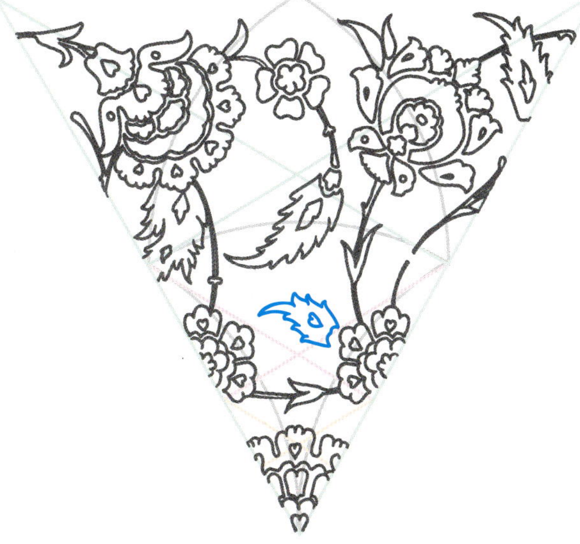

10 Add leaf H as an almost full leaf (as in Step 9, the tip of the leaf will appear on the opposite side in Step 12). If you find this difficult or confusing, you can draw the leaves in full and forgo the small added benefit of this particular style. The rotation will still work with full leaves.

11 Add leaf I in full as an extension of flower B.

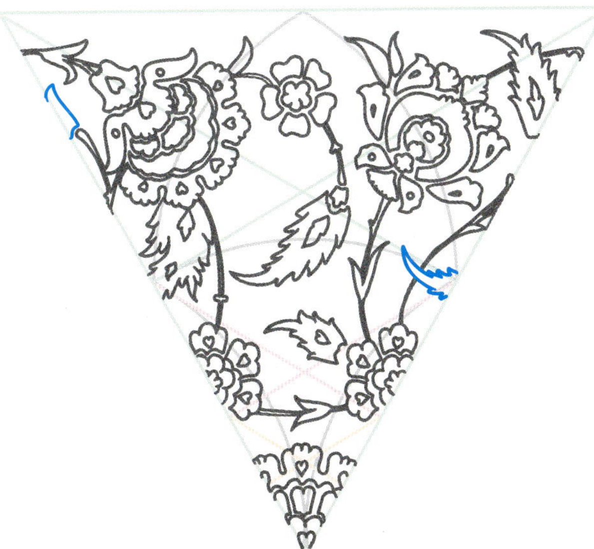

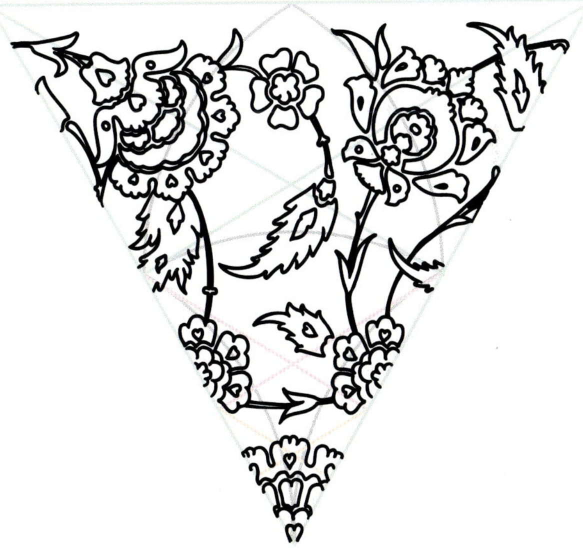

12 Add the missing parts of leaves F and H to the drawing.

13 The design section is now complete.

14 Rotate clockwise and repeat the
section five more times using
tracing paper. Be careful not to
smudge your pencil lines while
using the tracing paper.

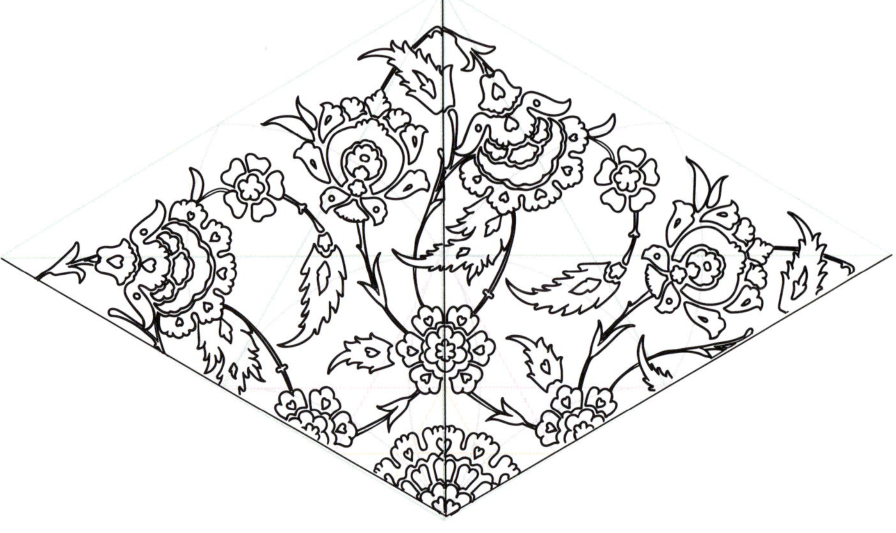

15 Looking at the full design with
the rotation is very pleasing. You
may have some minor edits to
the connections to make as you
rotate the design, but this is to
be expected.

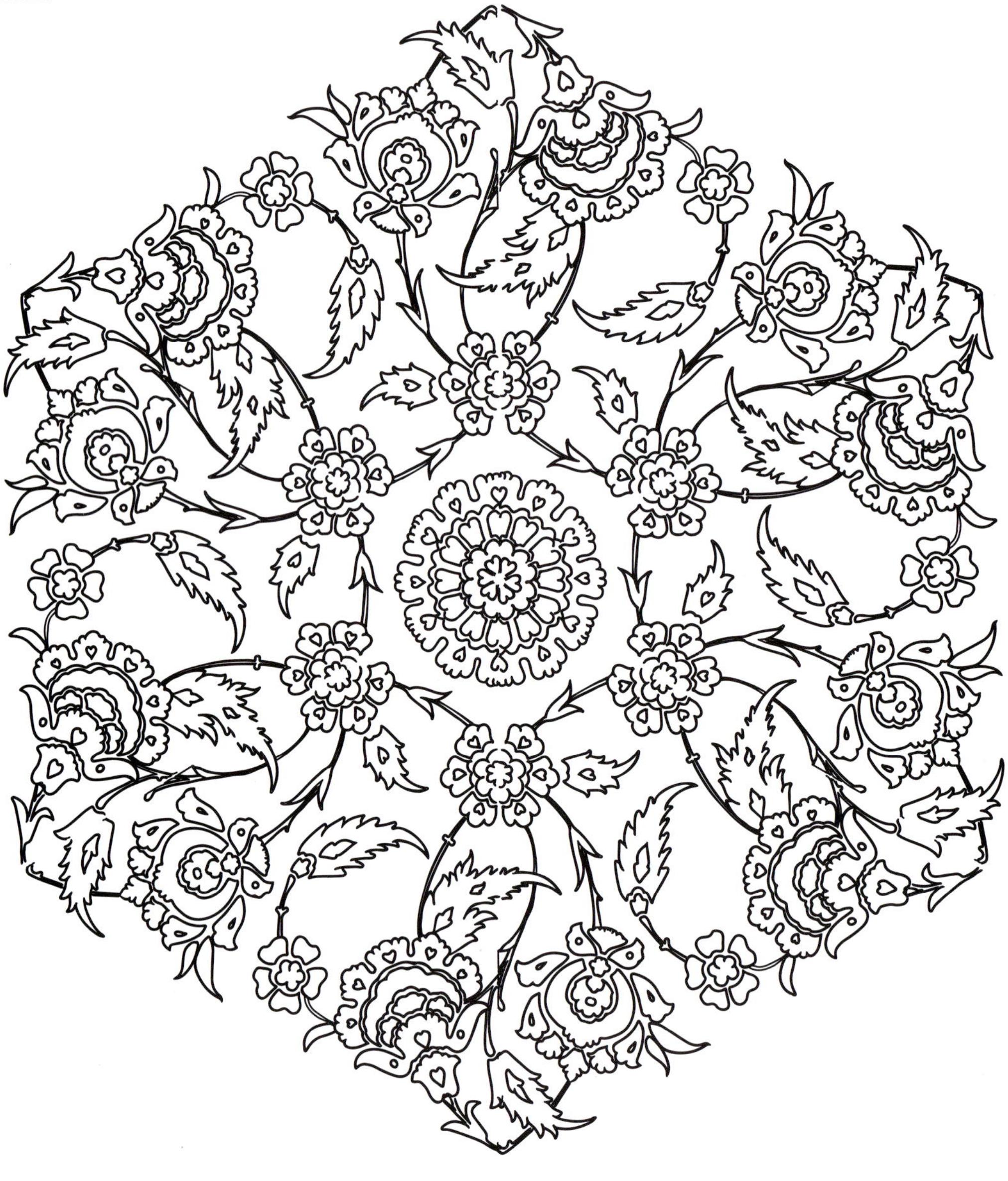

Painting the Pattern

Painting this design is a lot of fun because it can be done in so many ways. You can paint it exactly like the original tile using two colours: cobalt blue and turquoise. Alternatively, painting the whole design in a single colour is very effective, like the one-colour renders below. This shows that one pattern can give you many outcomes depending on how it is painted.

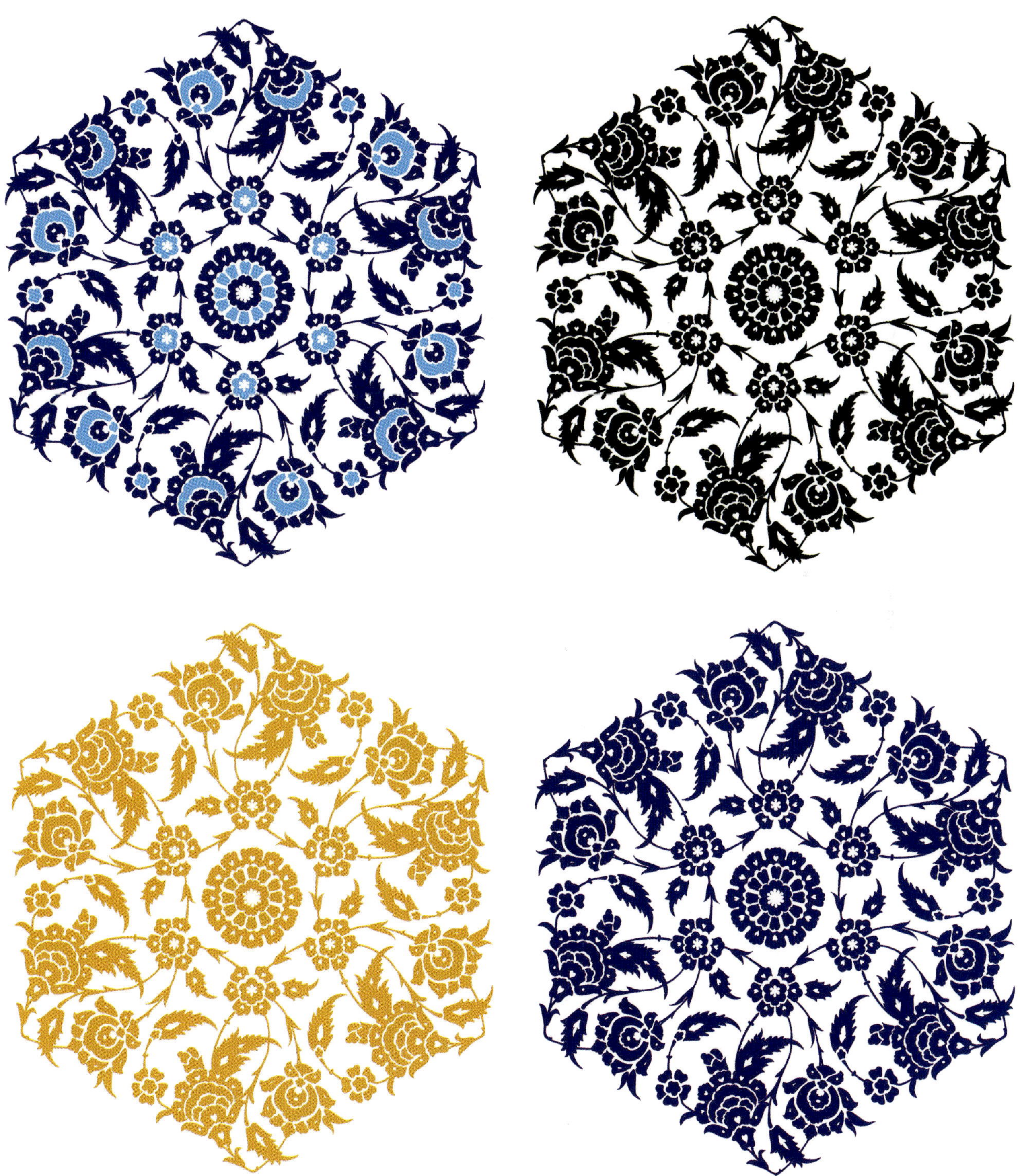

UZBEKISTANI PANEL STAR

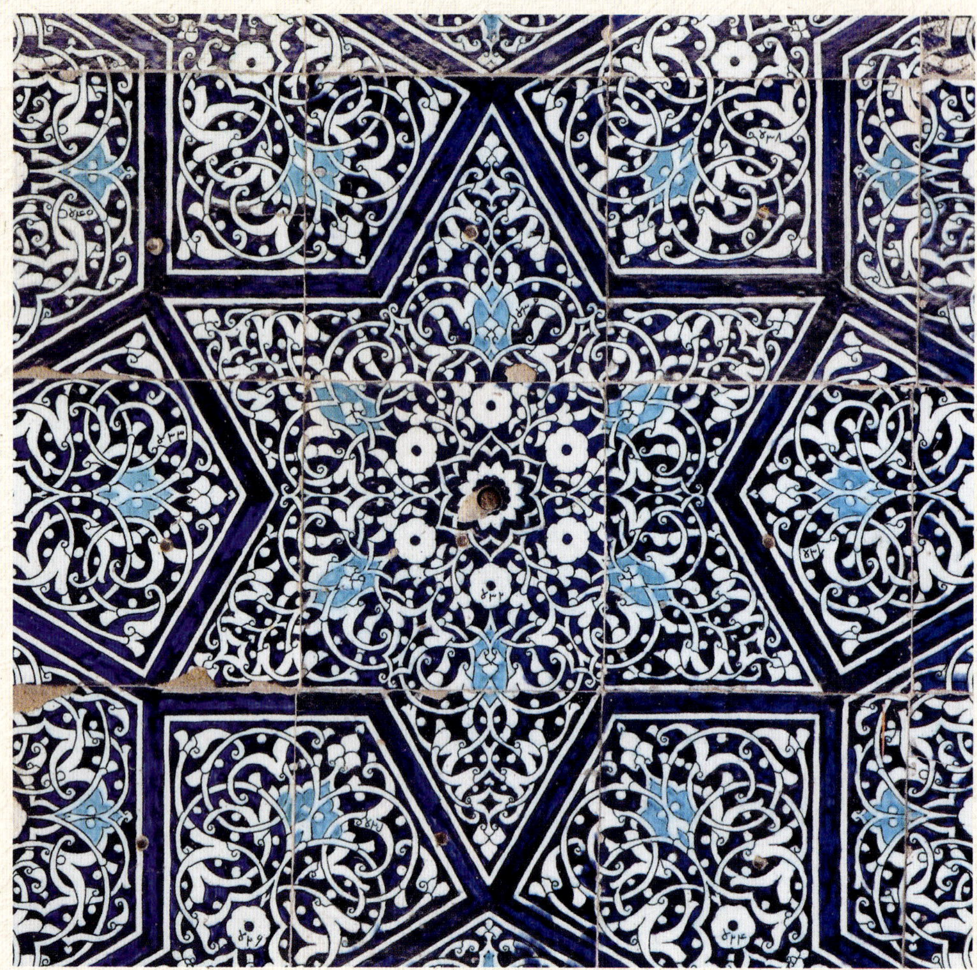

A wall tile from the nineteenth century, Tosh Hovli Palace in Khiva, Uzbekistan.

This pattern is unlike pattern studies 1 to 3, which were found in online museums or private collections to be auctioned; instead, I spotted it on a wall in beautiful Khiva, Uzbekistan when I visited in October 2019. It is truly fascinating seeing huge repeated patterns in person, especially in these calming shades of blue. The repetition draws you in and calms the soul.

Looking at the Geometric Structure

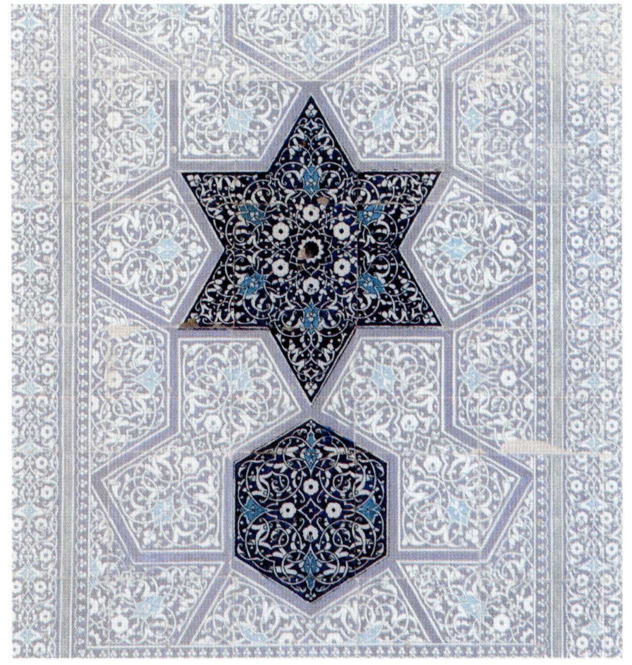
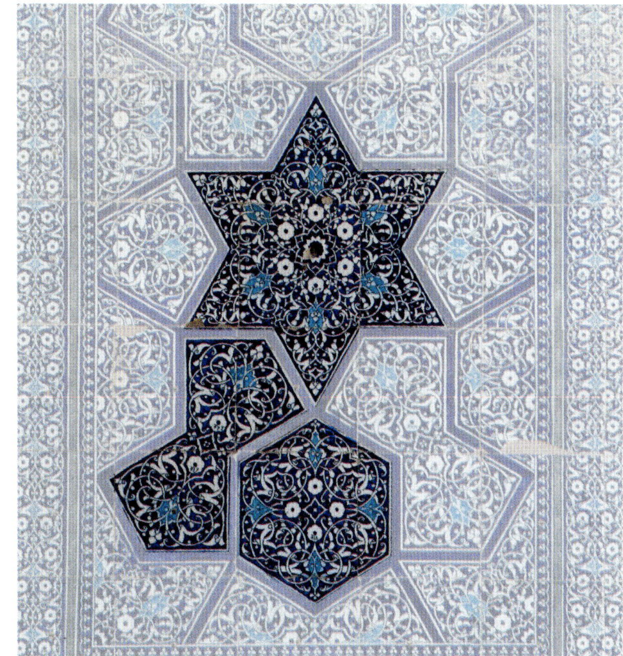

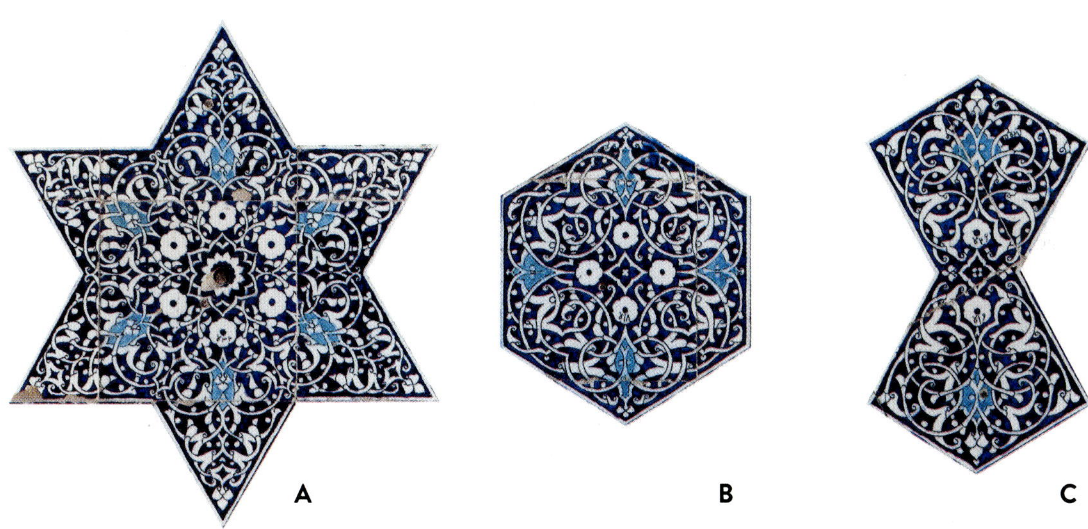

A B C

This pattern is slightly more complicated than the simple construction we previously worked on in the first three patterns because it contains three elements: the star (A), the hexagon (B) and the bowtie (C). The addition of the bowtie changes the proportions and order of shapes and therefore a new geometric construction is required.

1–8 Follow the first eight steps on p.30, 'Drawing the Six Circles'.

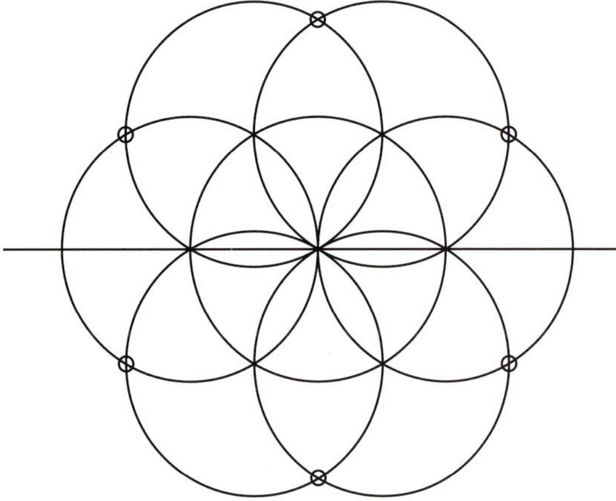

9 Once you have the six circles, mark six points where the circles intersect.

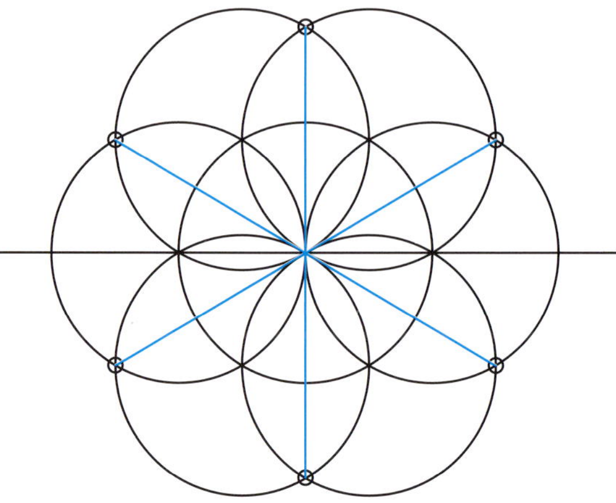

10 From the points, extend lines that go from the point to the centre to the point on the other side.

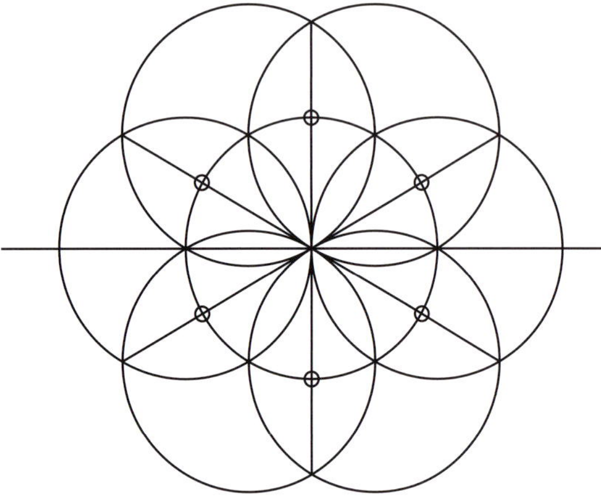

11 Add new points where the lines cross the central circle.

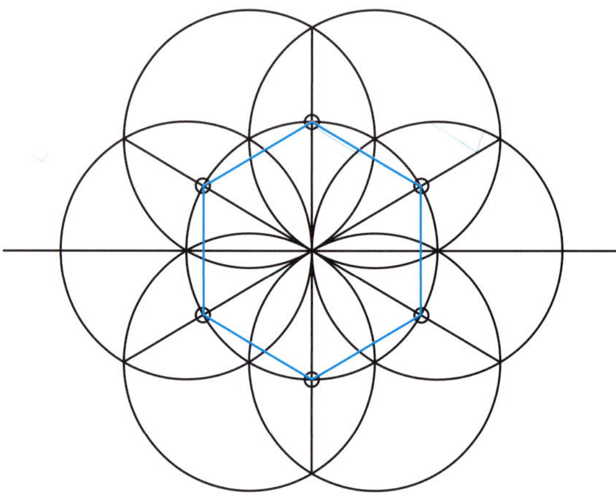

12 Connect the points inside the circle to draw a hexagon.

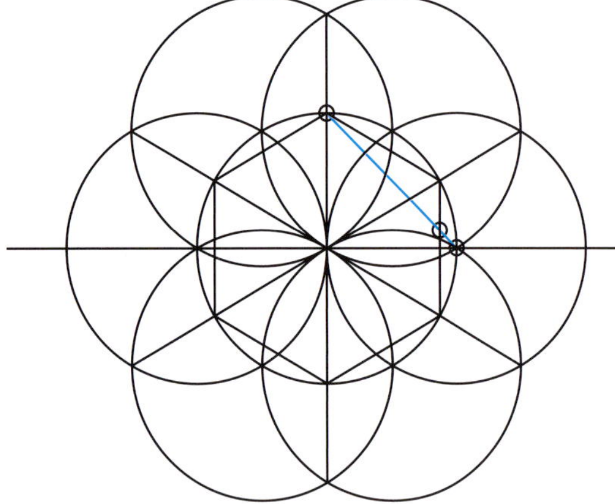

13 A proportional circle is needed, so you need to find its radius. Extend a line from the point on the vertical line to a point on the horizontal line. Circle the point where this line cuts the hexagon.

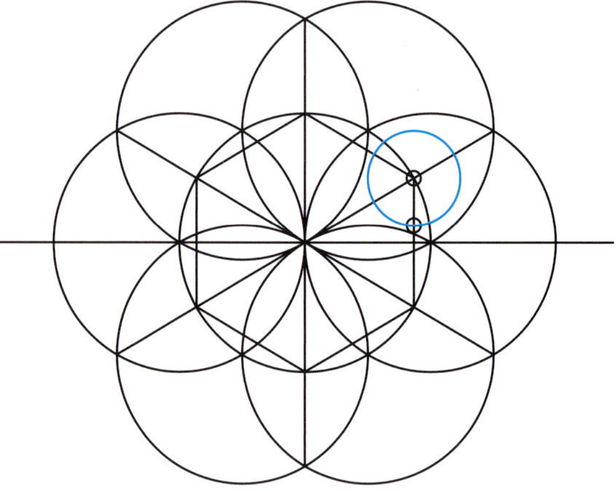

14 The distance from this point and the closest hexagon point to it is the new radius for the proportional circle. You only need to find the new radius once.

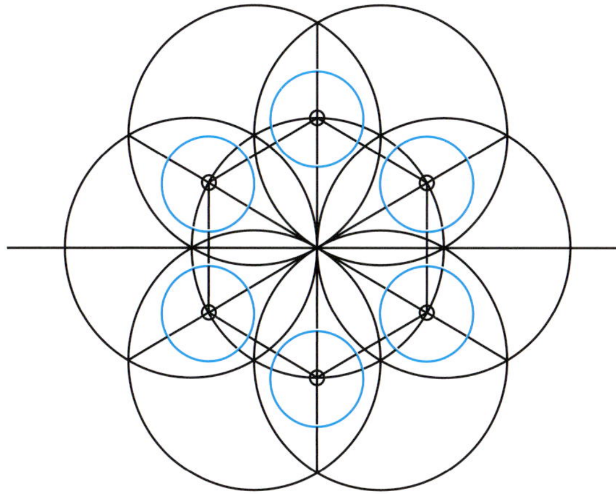

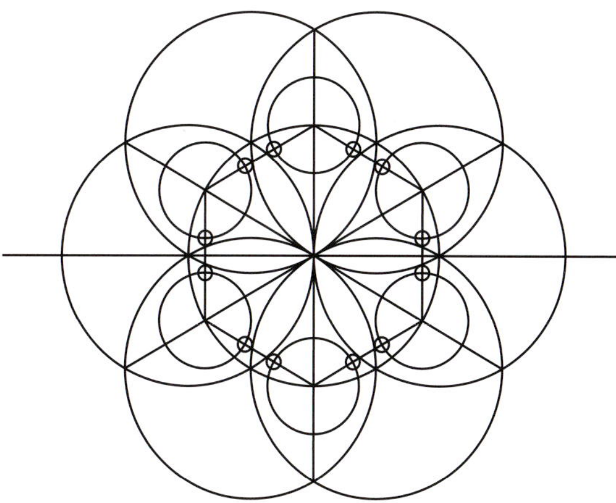

15 Draw the proportional circle following the radius you found in Steps 13 and 14 at all points on the hexagon.

16 Mark two points in each sector where the hexagon and proportional circles touch.

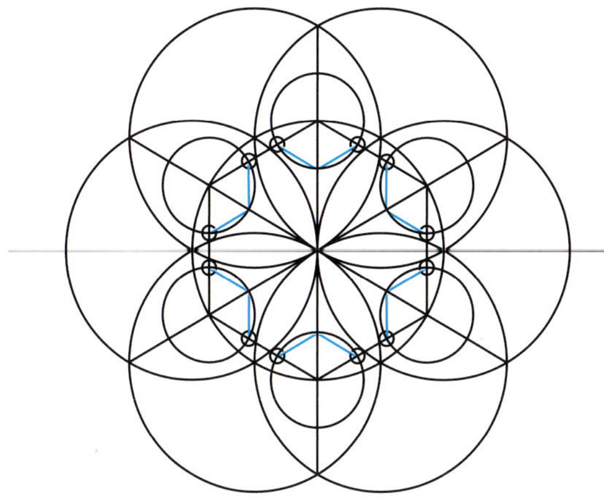

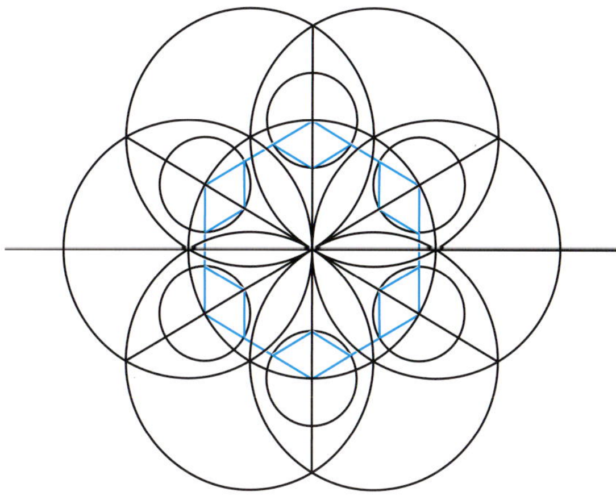

17 Connect each point to the inside edge of the proportional circles.

18 Trace the lines of the hexagon and the lines inside the proportional circles to continue working on a clean copy of the drawing.

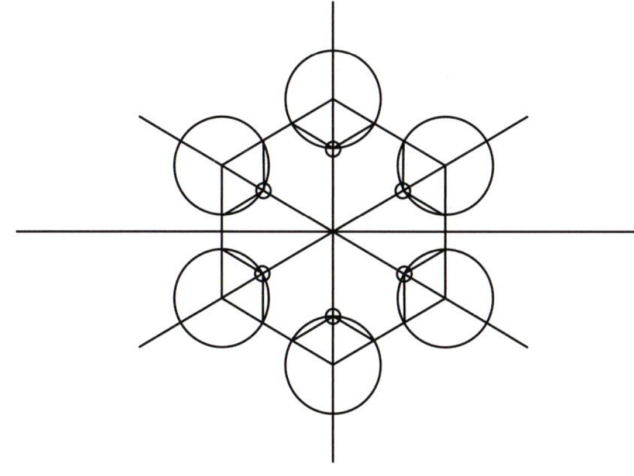

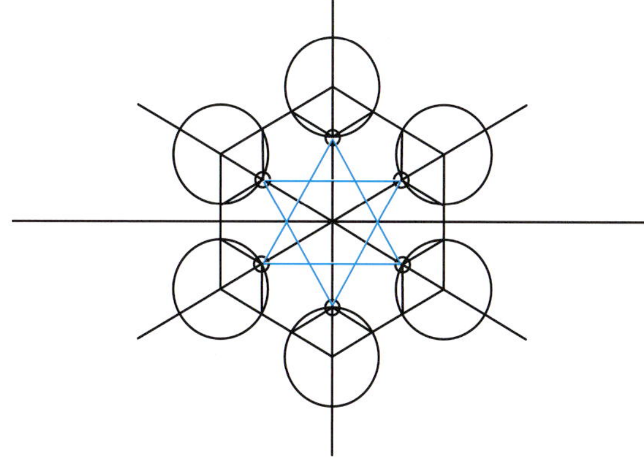

19 On the clean copy, mark where the two lines inside the proportional circles meet.

20 Draw a six-pointed star inside, i.e., two triangles pointing in opposite directions.

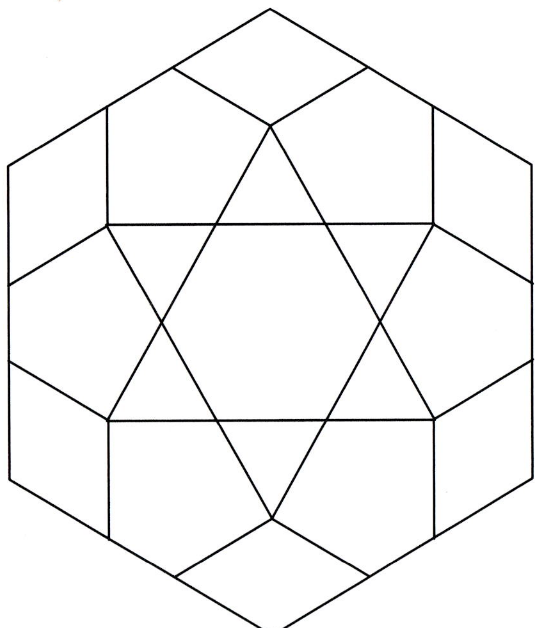

The six-pointed star, the surrounding hexagon and the straight lines within it will form the construction that will be repeated to create the full pattern.

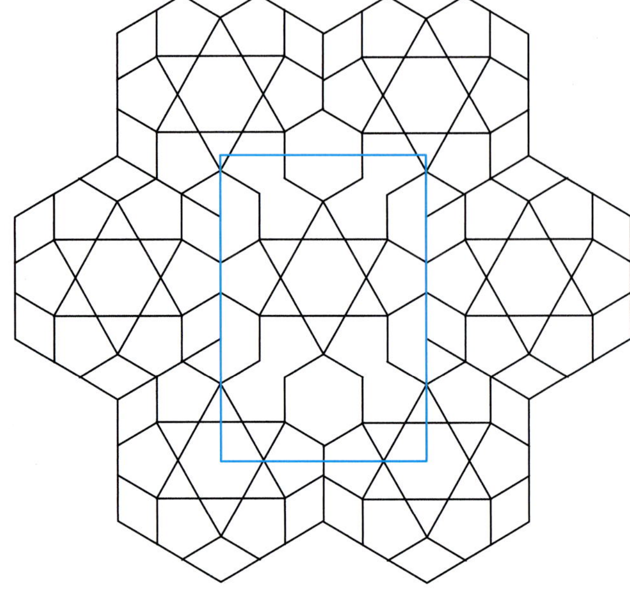

The star is clearly in the centre, but the other two shapes (hexagon and bowtie) will start appearing with the repetition. You will need to erase some of the lines inside the hexagons and bowtie for the shape to appear properly. I have highlighted a rectangle in the middle for the wall panel placement.

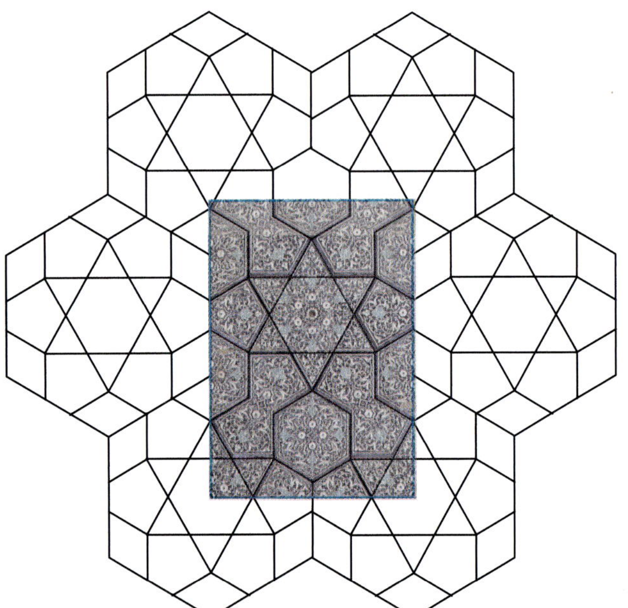

The original pattern is 'woven' which means that you see the border lines doubled to appear thicker. I have skipped this step to keep the pattern simple, but you can experiment with this by following Samira Mian's YouTube video on weaving a geometric pattern: youtu.be/iIvjkR_15h0?si=U4pTIHFAgHdmuucm

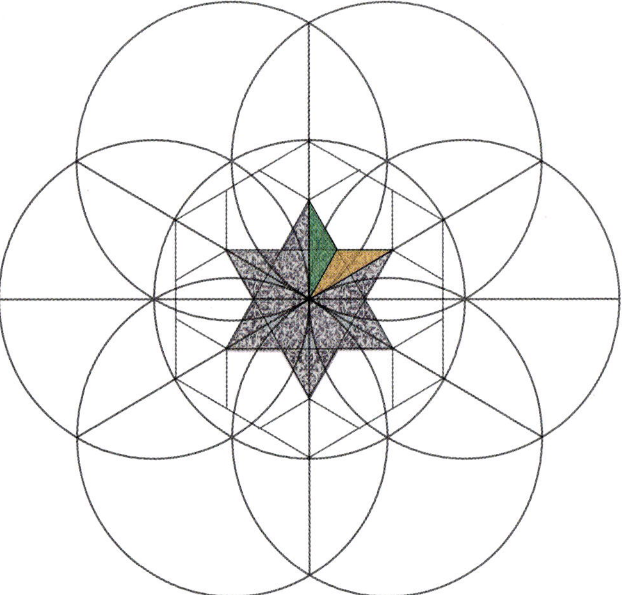

Pattern 4 focuses on the biomorphic construction within the star.

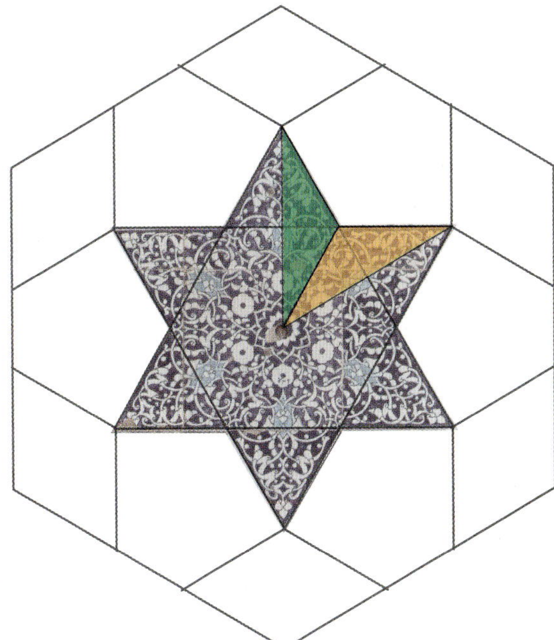 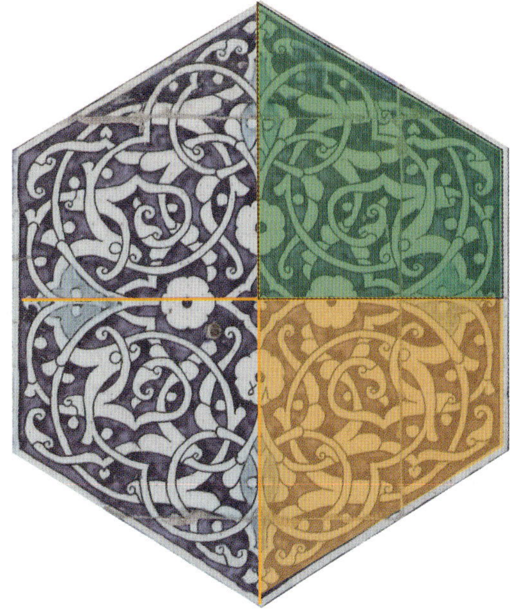

This shows the design section and the mirroring that create the repeat unit.

The hexagon will be studied as Pattern 5. The third shape is the bow tie, which we are not studying, but you can easily read the pattern and its repeat. You can also keep it empty when painting and experimenting with how it looks.

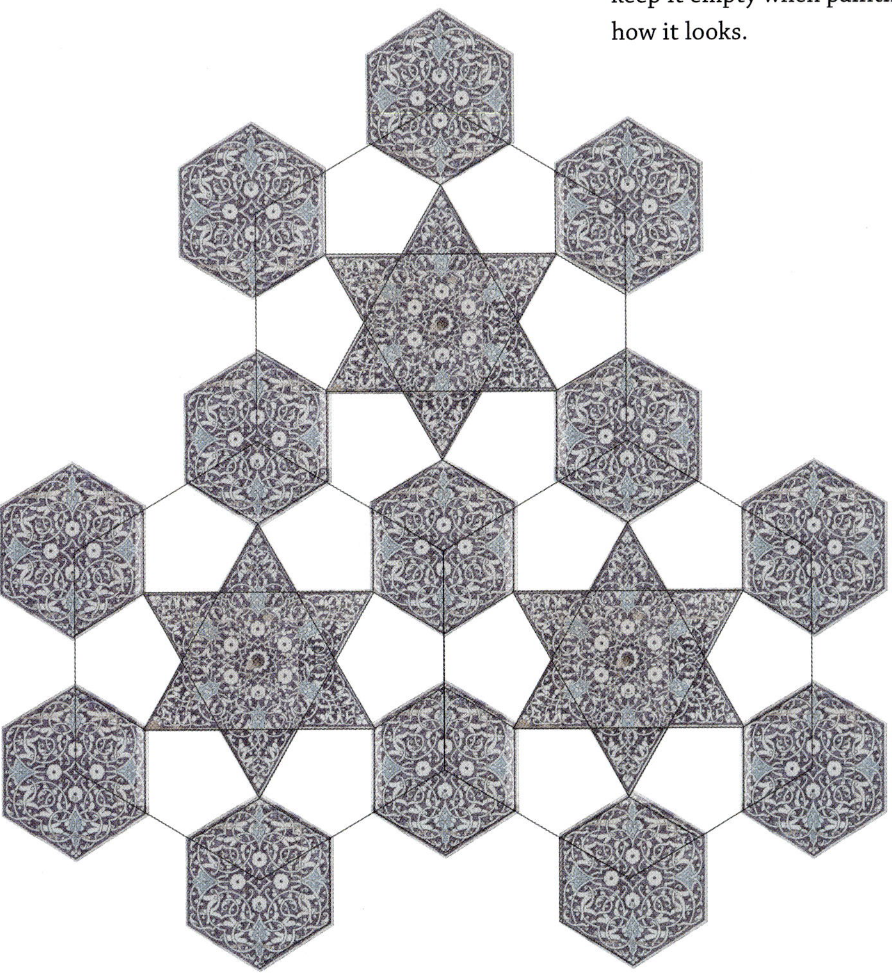

Unlike the three previous patterns where the design section is nestled within the hexagon, this one is only contained within the star shape (1) along with its reflected section. The star section is slim, but it follows the same technique of working with two lines: vertical and the diagonal. Since it is a star, the diagonal line is much shorter than the vertical one.

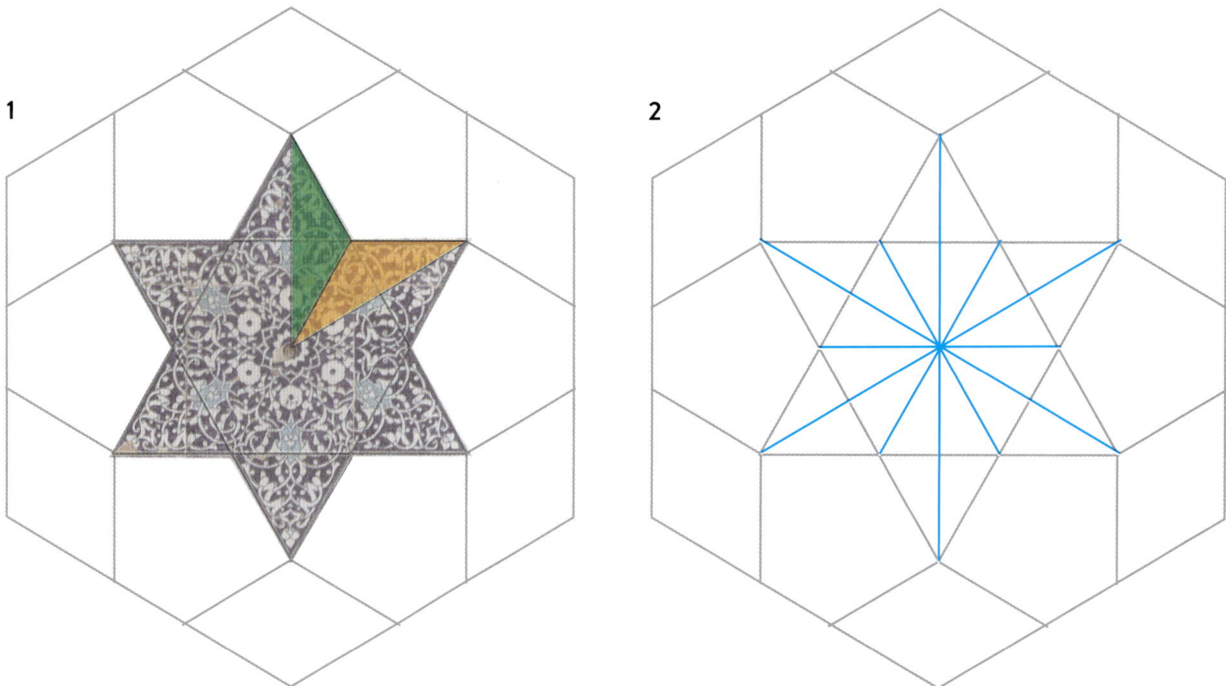

The geometric shape we created in the previous section gives us the star without many construction lines, especially if you traced the design in Step 18 and carried on the work. It is therefore helpful to draw the lines of symmetry inside the star (2). The design section is highlighted and then it is mirrored and repeated (3 and 4).

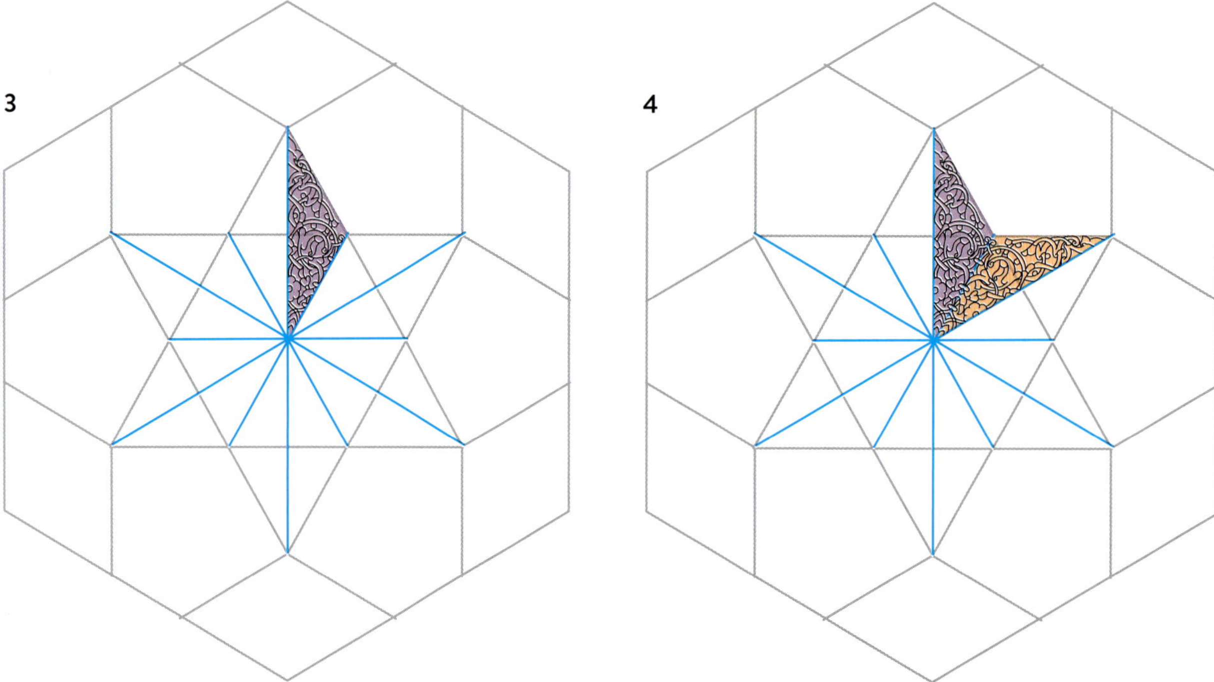

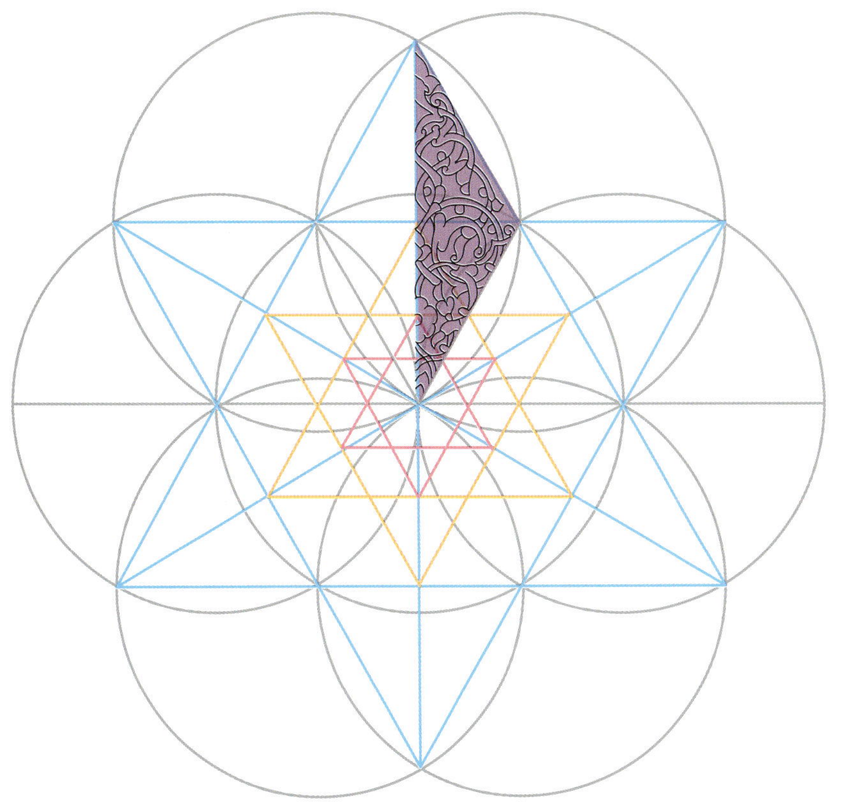

If you feel like you need more construction lines, you can borrow the six-pointed star grid (p.32) to help you place the motifs.

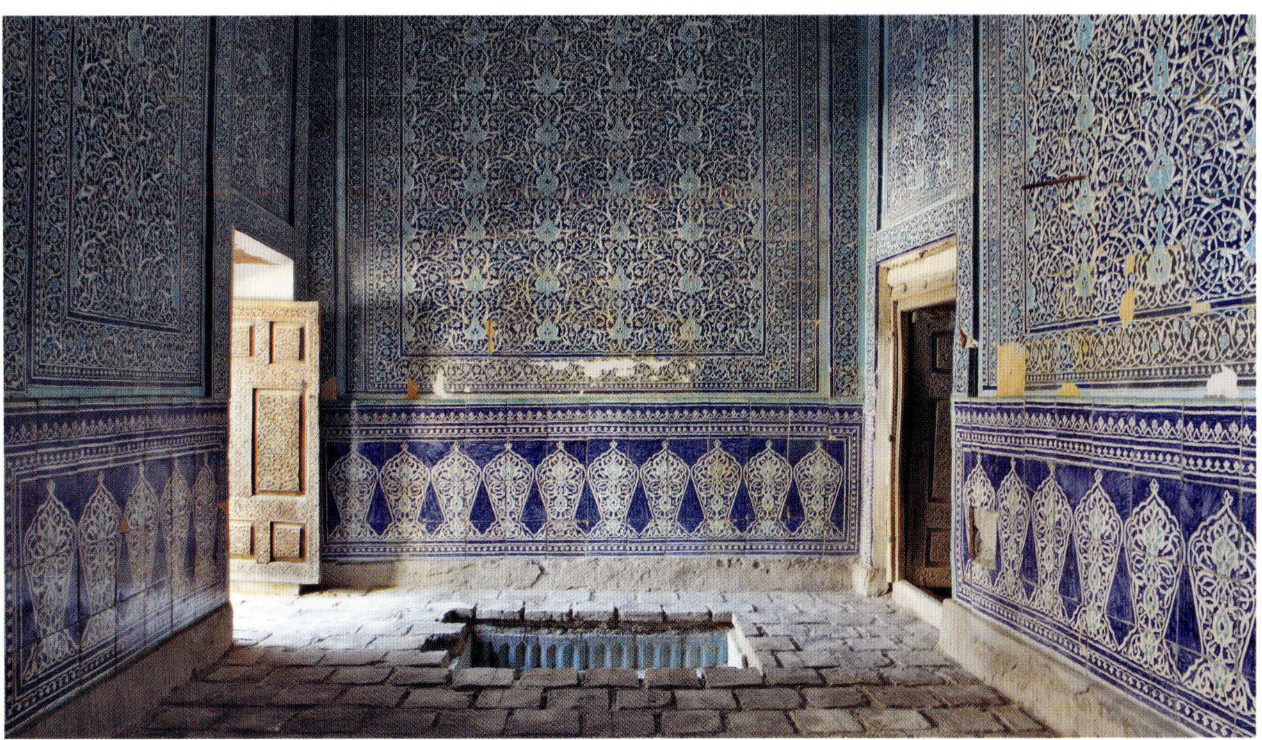

Drawing the Pattern

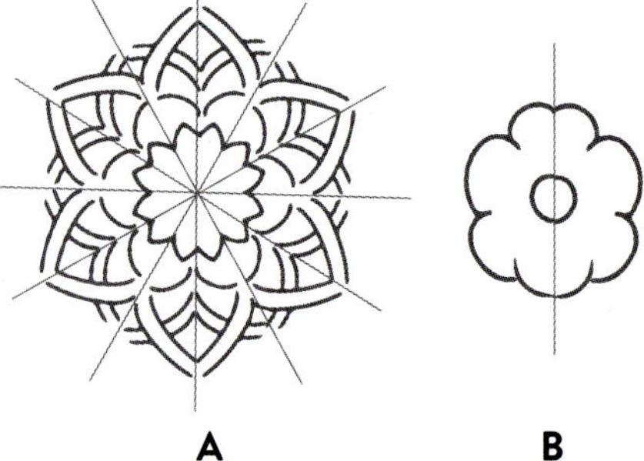 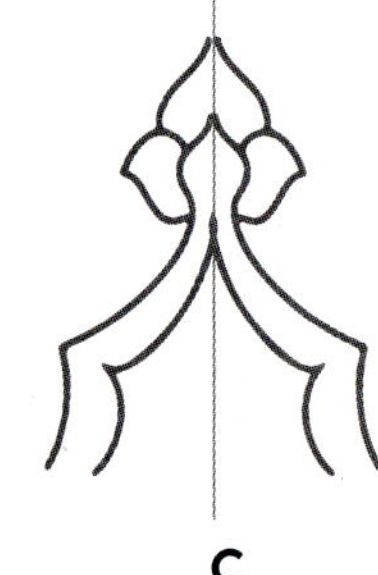 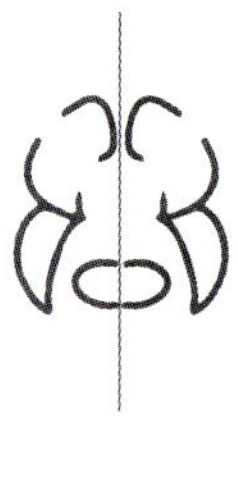 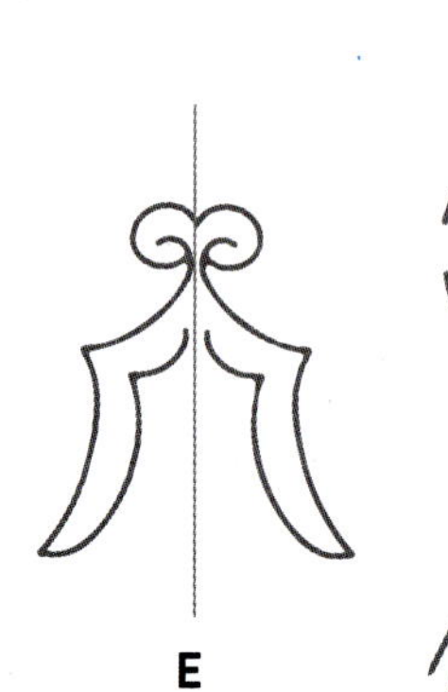 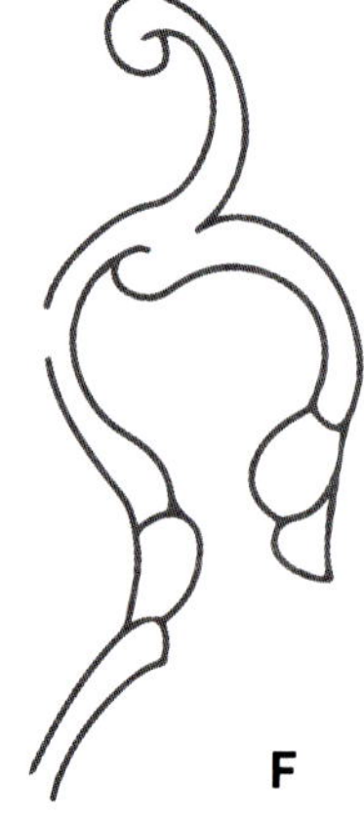

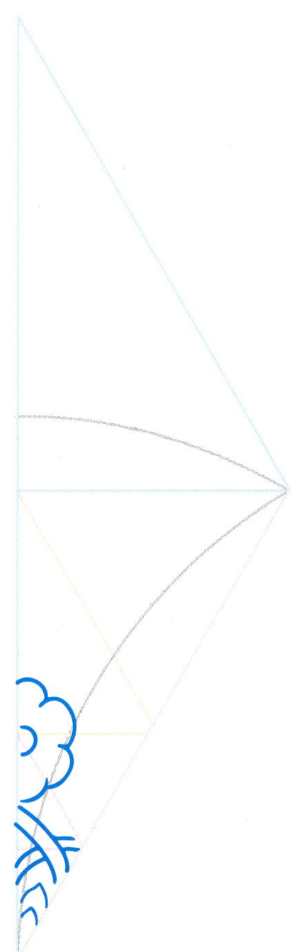 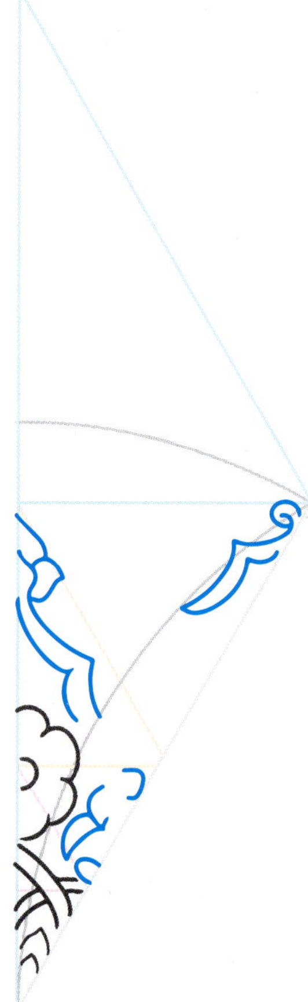 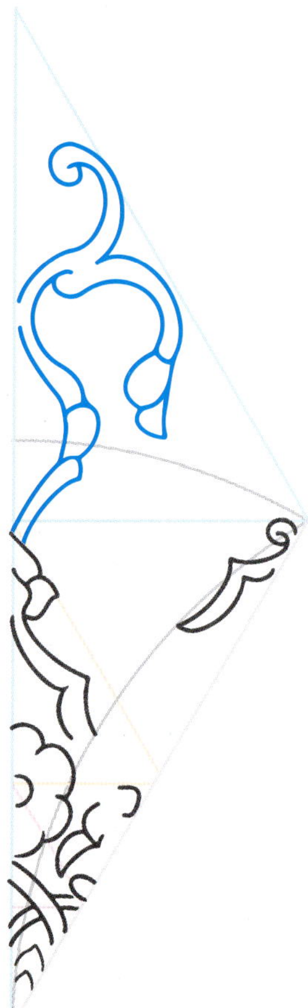

1 The vertical and diagonal lines of symmetry are important as the starting point of the design, where most of the floral and inorganic shapes will be placed as halves. Inside the smallest star created earlier, draw flower A as one petal. On the vertical line, place half of flower B.

2 Add half of inorganic shape C. Then place half shapes D and E along the diagonal line. The placement of the shapes follows the geometric lines of the section. These inorganic shapes might look a little strange, since they are uncommon outside of Central Asia, but they have the same essence as previously drawn ornate shapes.

3 From shape C, a new shape emerges (shape F) that is a combination of curves organised to fill that specific area.

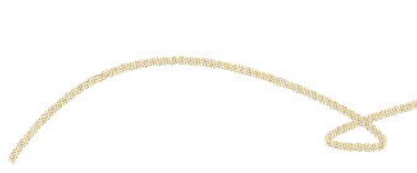

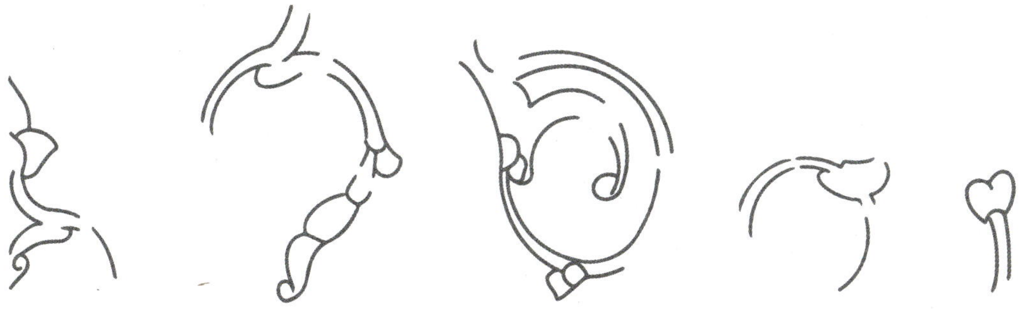

G   **H**   **I**   **J**   **K**

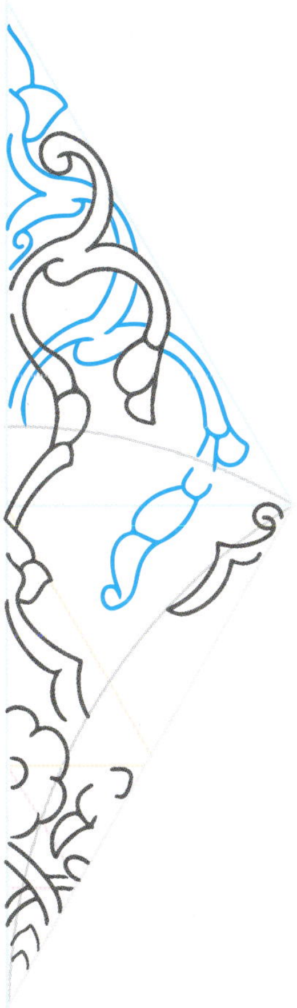

4 To make this pattern more intricate, two new shapes are added (G and H). They are both placed near shape F and are almost intertwined with it.

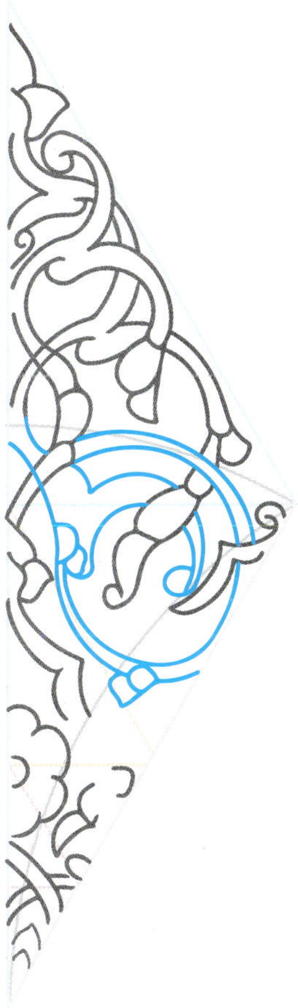

5 The shapes are currently floating without a connection, and the connective curves are what makes this design very special. A new curve (shape I) extends from shape E and connects with shape H. This connection is important as it brings the shapes on the vertical line and diagonal line together.

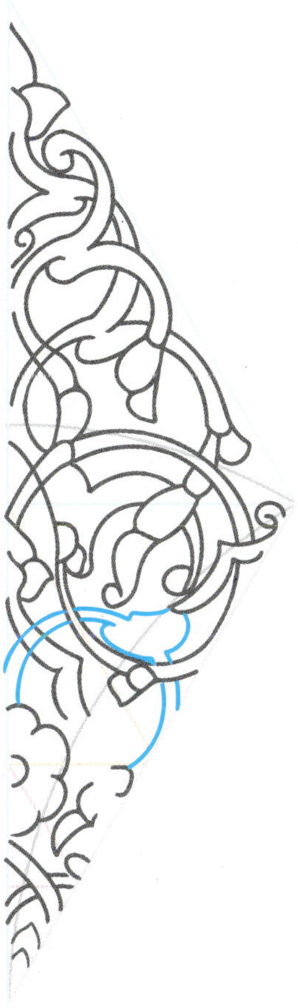

6 A small curve (shape J) extends from flower B to the top of shape D. In the middle of the curve, place a popular inorganic shape, sometimes called a split palmette.

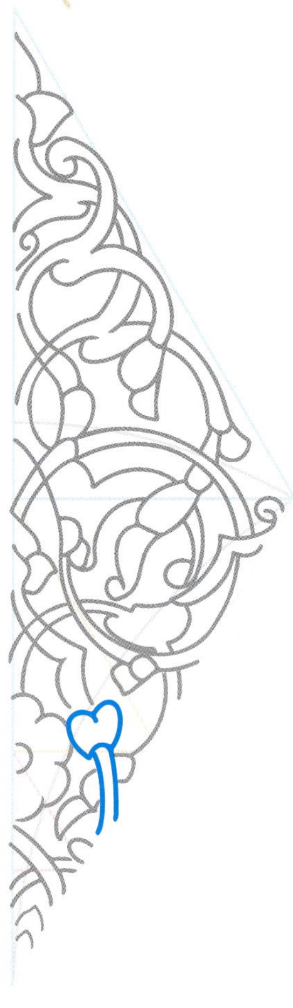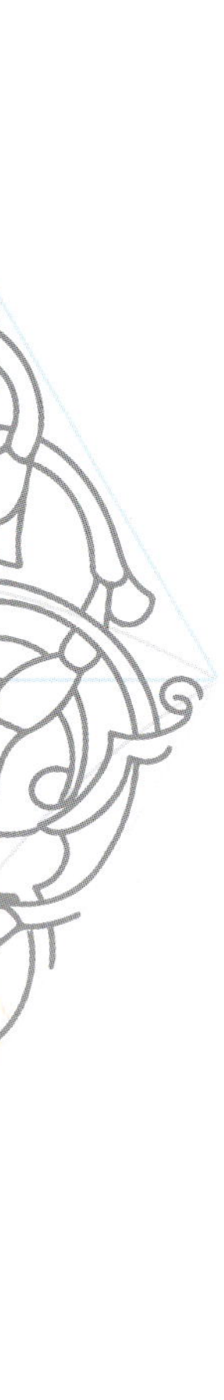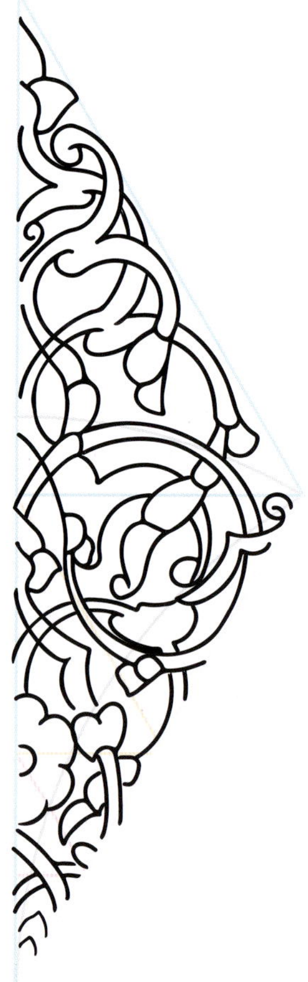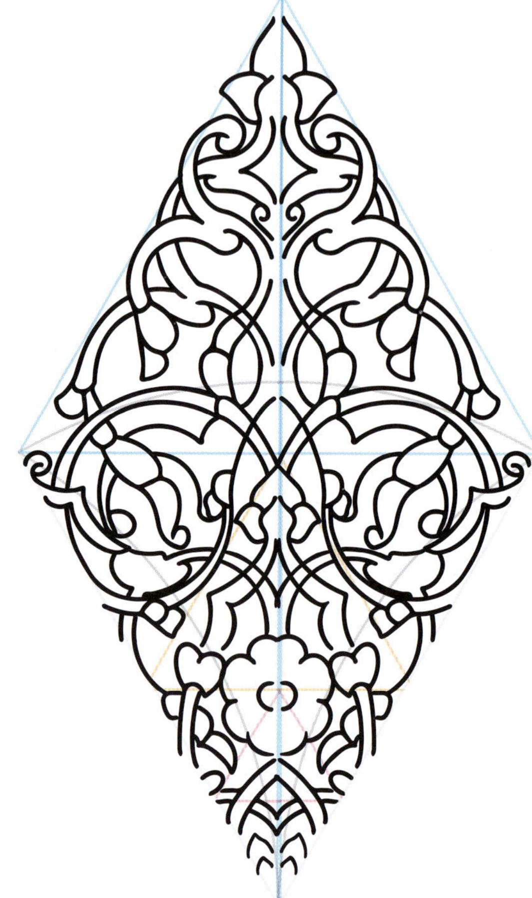

7 Now the only space that remains, is between shapes C and D. Add shape K in there; it looks like a fresh bud that has sprung amongst all the branches.

8 The design section is now complete with all the various elements added. If you want to change anything, do so at this stage.

9 Reflect the completed section to get the full repeat unit that will be completed six times to form the final star.

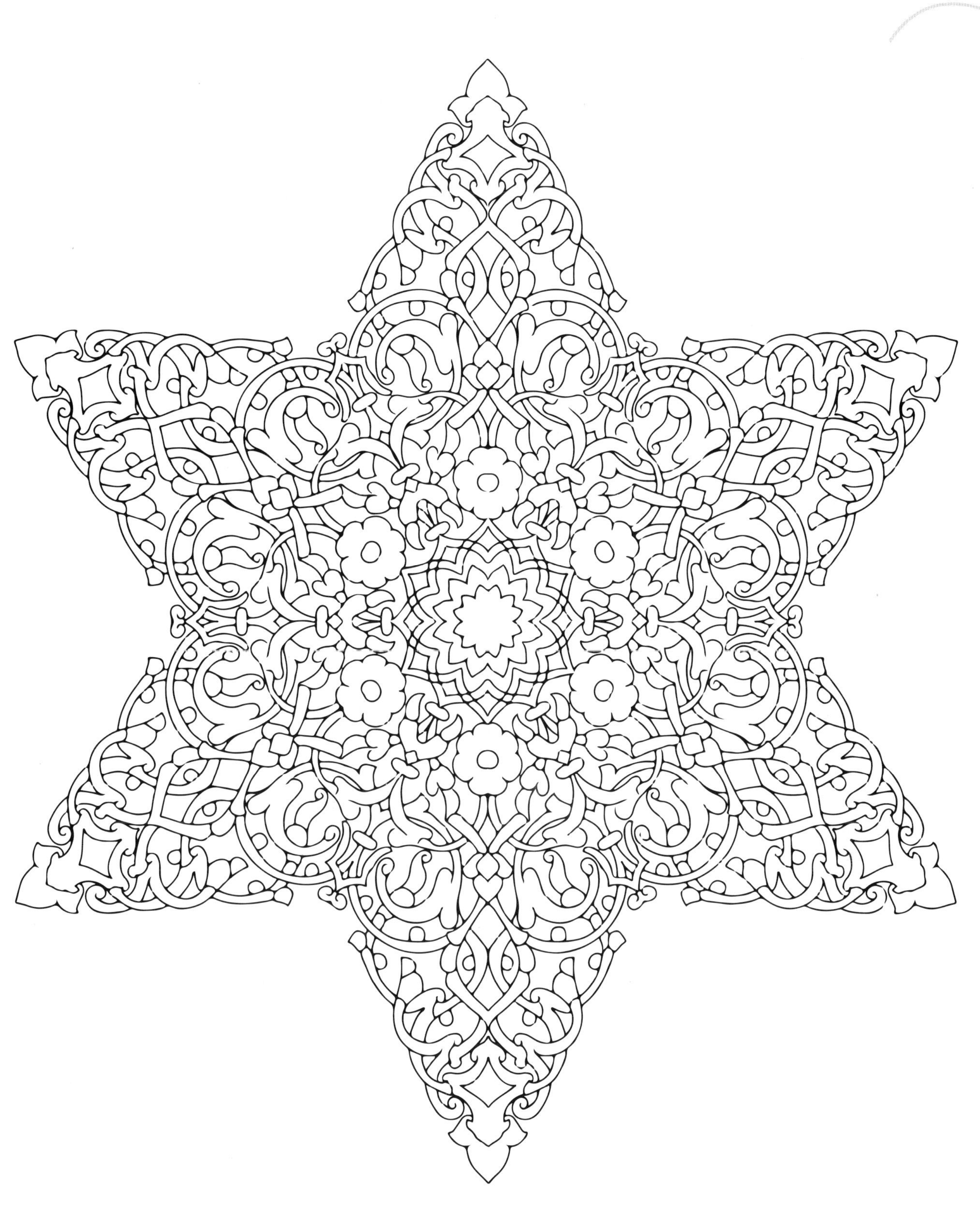

UZBEKISTANI PANEL HEXAGON

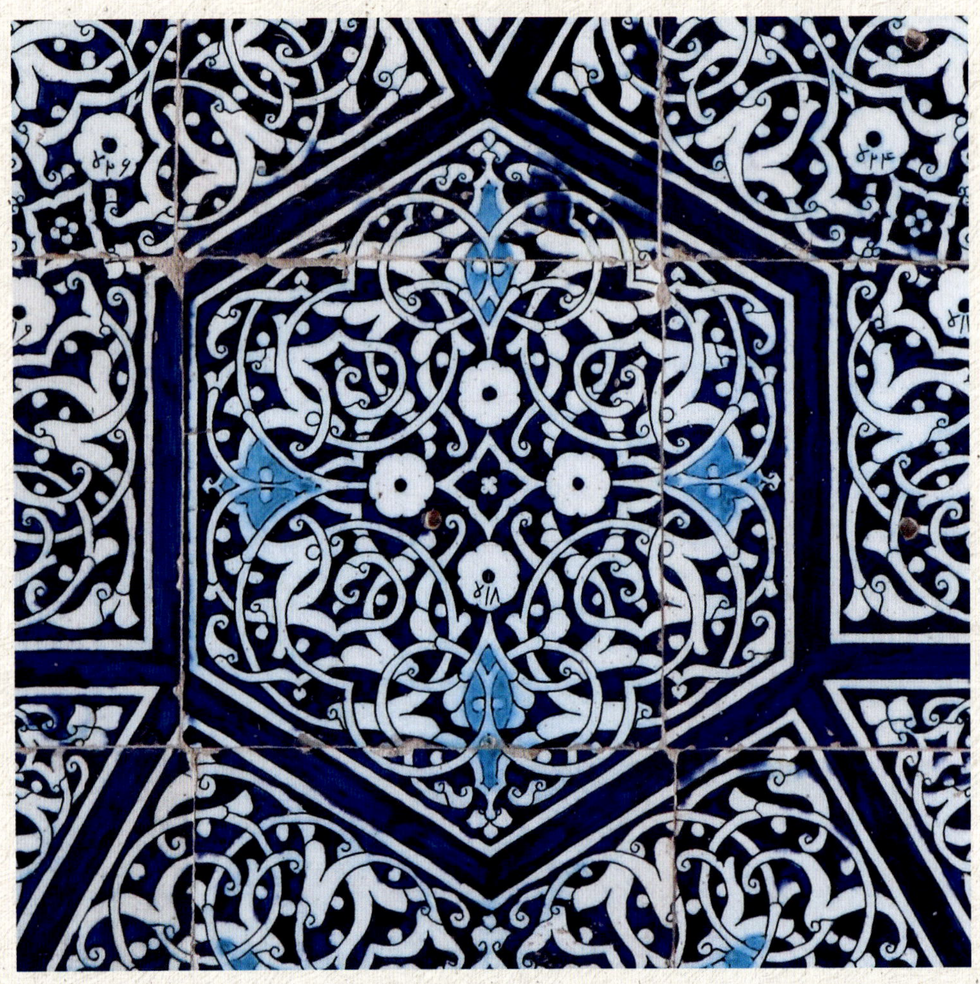

A wall tile from the nineteenth century, Tosh Hovli Palace in Khiva, Uzbekistan.

Looking at the Geometric Structure

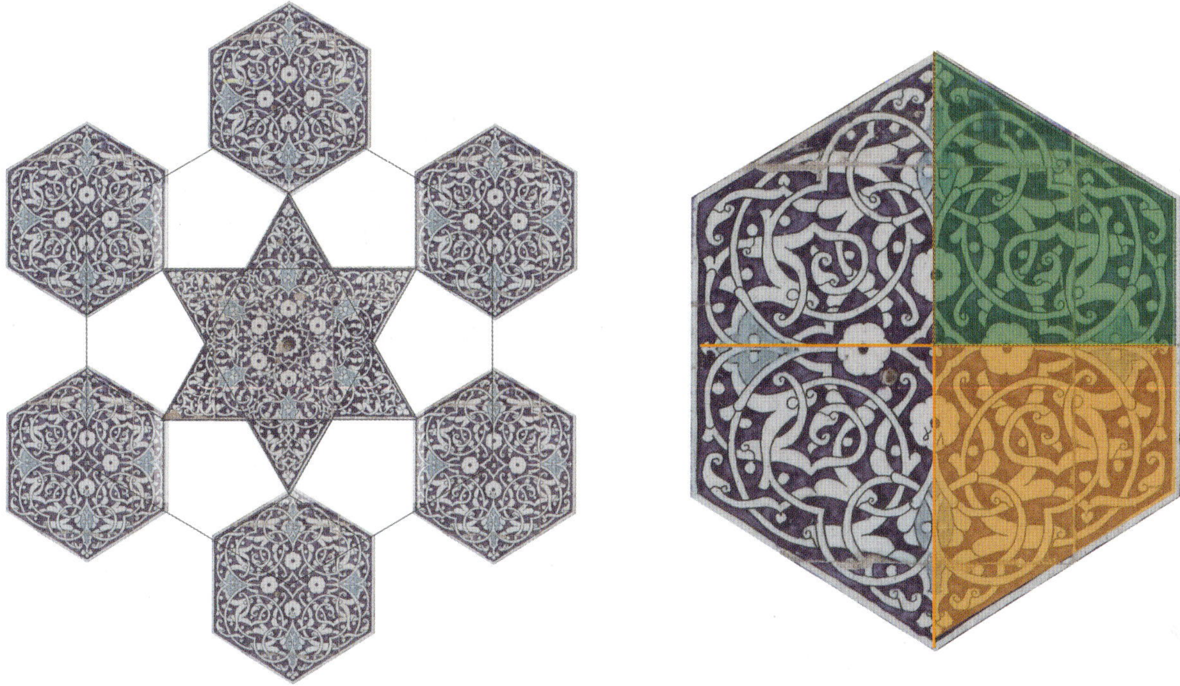

This pattern is the second shape of the same Uzbekistani panel used in Pattern Study 4 (see p.72), which follows the hexagonal tile shape. These hexagons surround the star, and they are created by repeating the pattern constructed here.

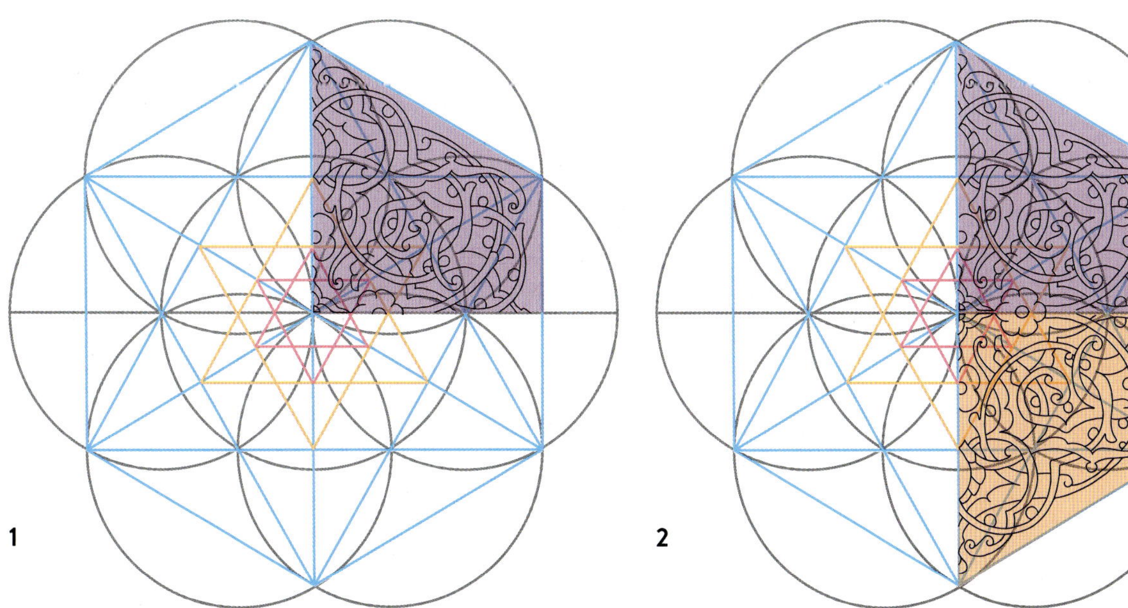

1

If you need more structural lines, you can borrow the hexagon Grid 1 (pp.31–32) to use as additional guidelines to help you with the placement of the motifs.

2

It is interesting to note that the pattern has been designed as quarters of the hexagon, as in Pattern Study 1 (see p.48). The starting point is to identify the two symmetry lines that are apparent in the geometric structure: the vertical and horizontal lines (1). This quarter then is reflected to create the full repeat unit (2).

Drawing the Pattern

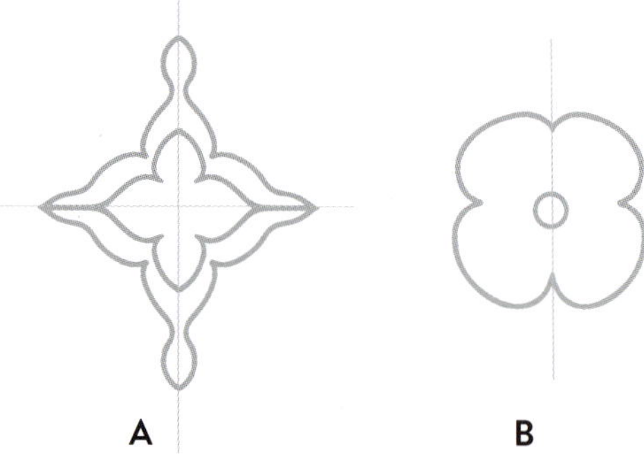

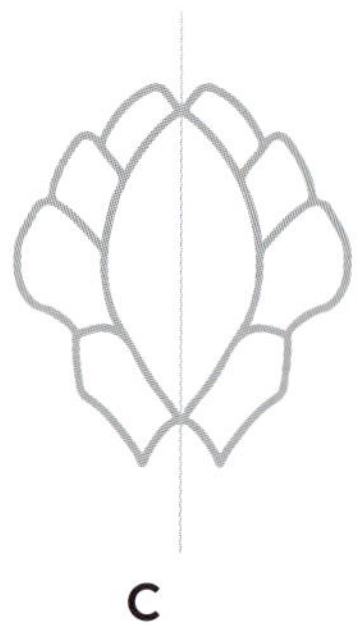

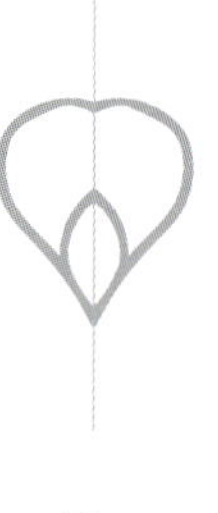

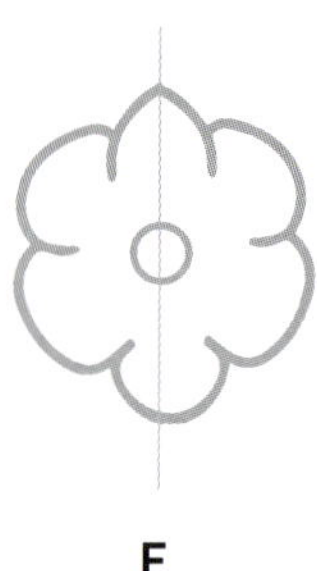

A   B   C   D   E

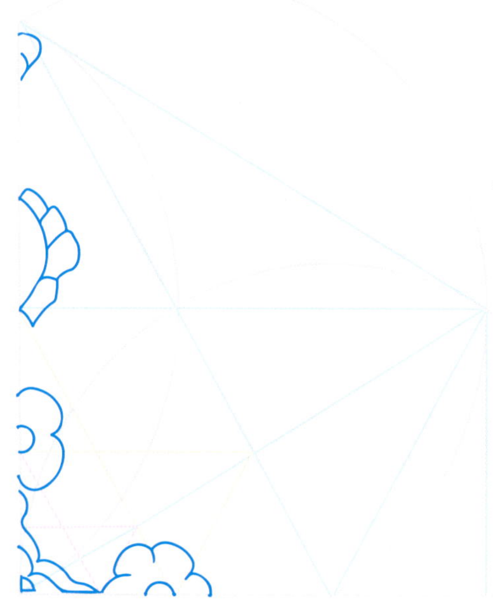

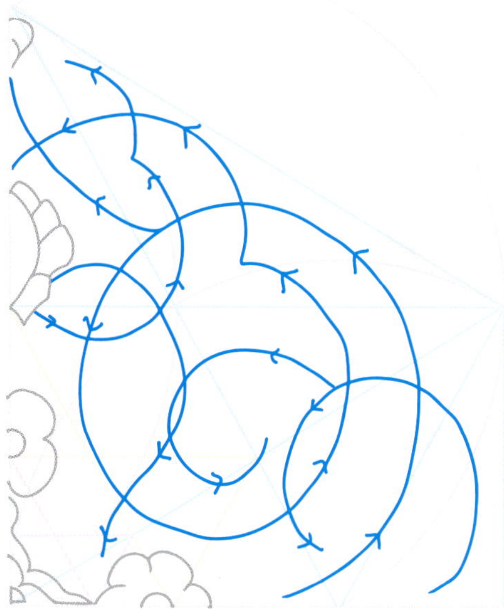

1 The vertical and horizontal symmetry lines are an important starting point for this design, as all the required elements are placed on them. For the sake of a pleasing symmetry, only sections of the inorganic shapes and flowers are placed on the lines. First, place shape A as a quarter in the right-angled corner, then place half of flower B, shape C and flower D on the vertical line, and flower E on the horizontal line. You will notice that the floral elements of this pattern are limited to three. The Timurid period that ruled Uzbekistan much preferred inorganic shapes, as can be observed from their tiles.

2 The connection between all the elements is vital, as in every biomorphic pattern, so it is good to place the spirals along with the determined direction of all the curves. In Pattern Study 2 (p.54), we placed all the flowers before the spiral, but this case is different as most of the additional elements that come with the spiral are part of its composition. The general direction of the spiral is upwards and anticlockwise. It might also be helpful to draw each of the curves and spirals on separate pieces of tracing paper to allow you to see the progression.

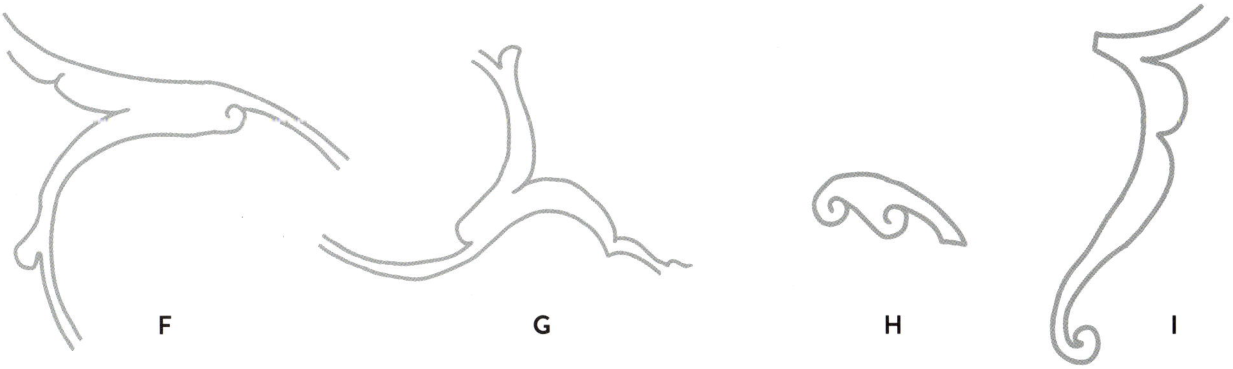

F

G

H

I

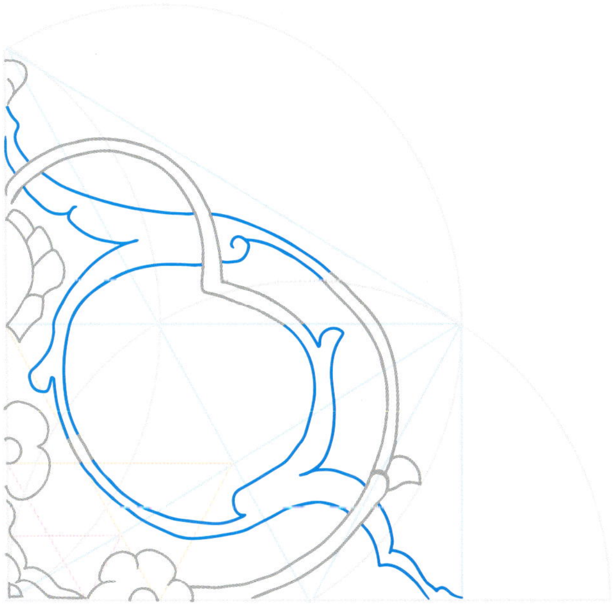

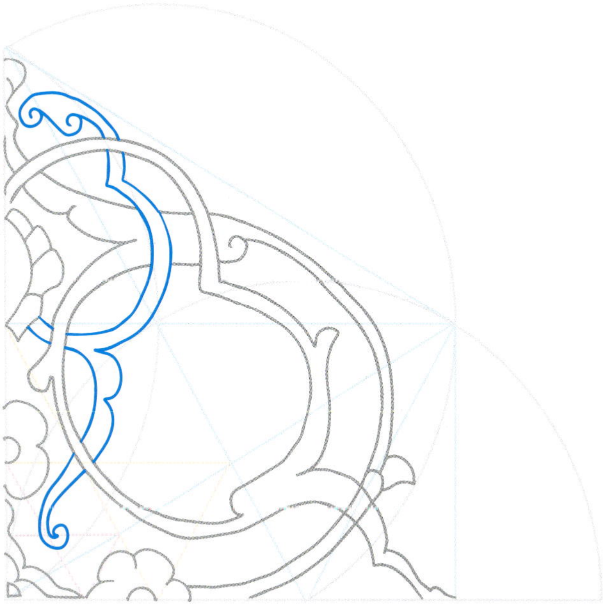

3 Spring the first spiral from flower E on the horizontal line and loop upwards, as shown. The spiral then forms shape F and splits in two. Connect shape G to the lower half of shape F. This shape also splits in two, with one half finishing on the horizontal line and the other curving upwards onto the vertical line. The spiral acts as a frame to the pattern.

4 Spring a double curve from the side of shape C – one curve goes upwards, while the other goes downwards. The upward curve ends with a simple leaf (H), or it could be an inorganic shape – it is hard to make a distinction with these shapes! The downward curve has an ornate inorganic shape (I).

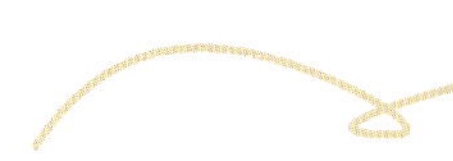

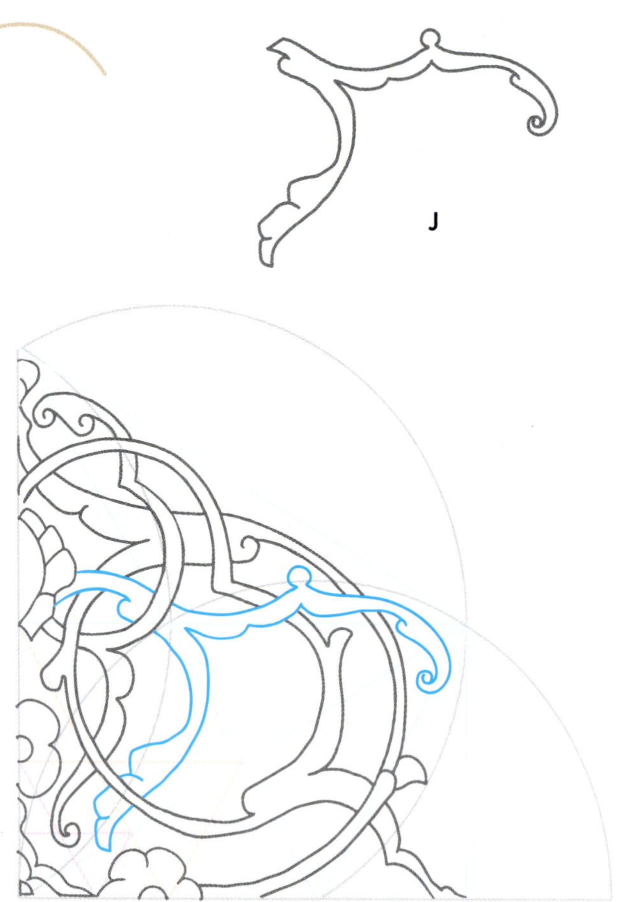
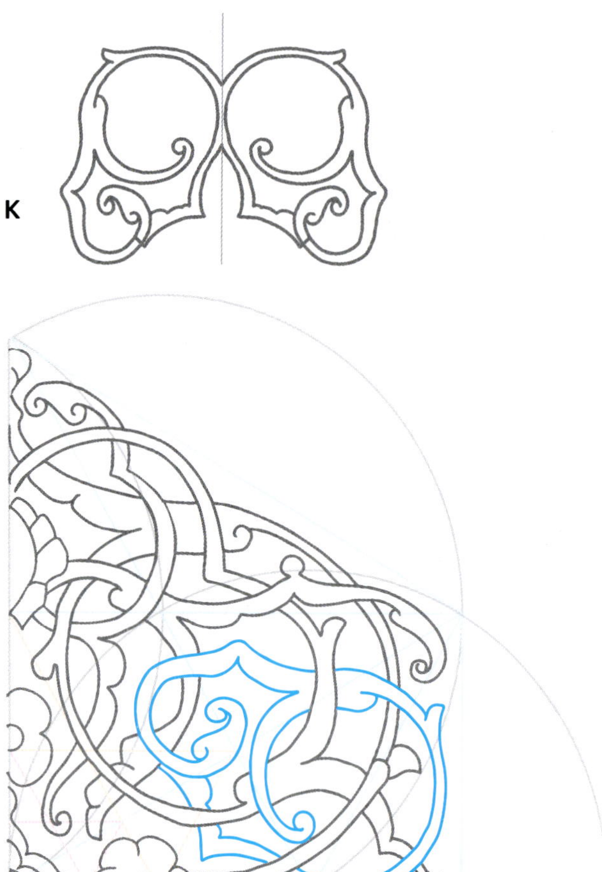

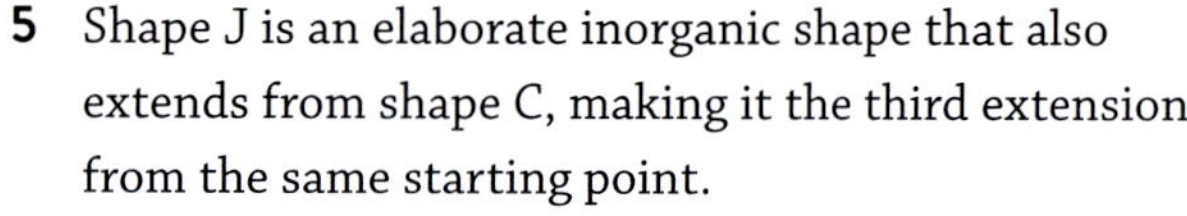

5 Shape J is an elaborate inorganic shape that also extends from shape C, making it the third extension from the same starting point.

6 Rotate shape K 90 degrees and place it as a half on the horizontal line.

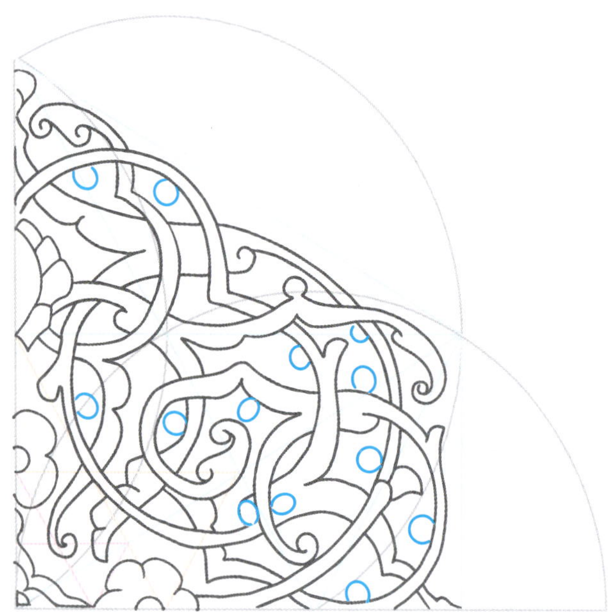
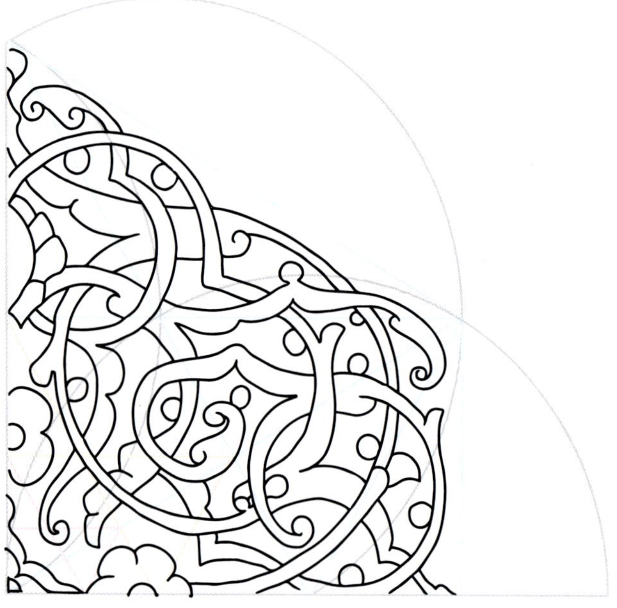

7 The last additions are the circular shapes that fill in the space. They do not seem to have a special order, but they do go under bends and to populate empty areas.

8 When all the additional curves are put together you can see that the design seems very complex and hard to decipher! Thus looking at it one step at a time is the best course of action.

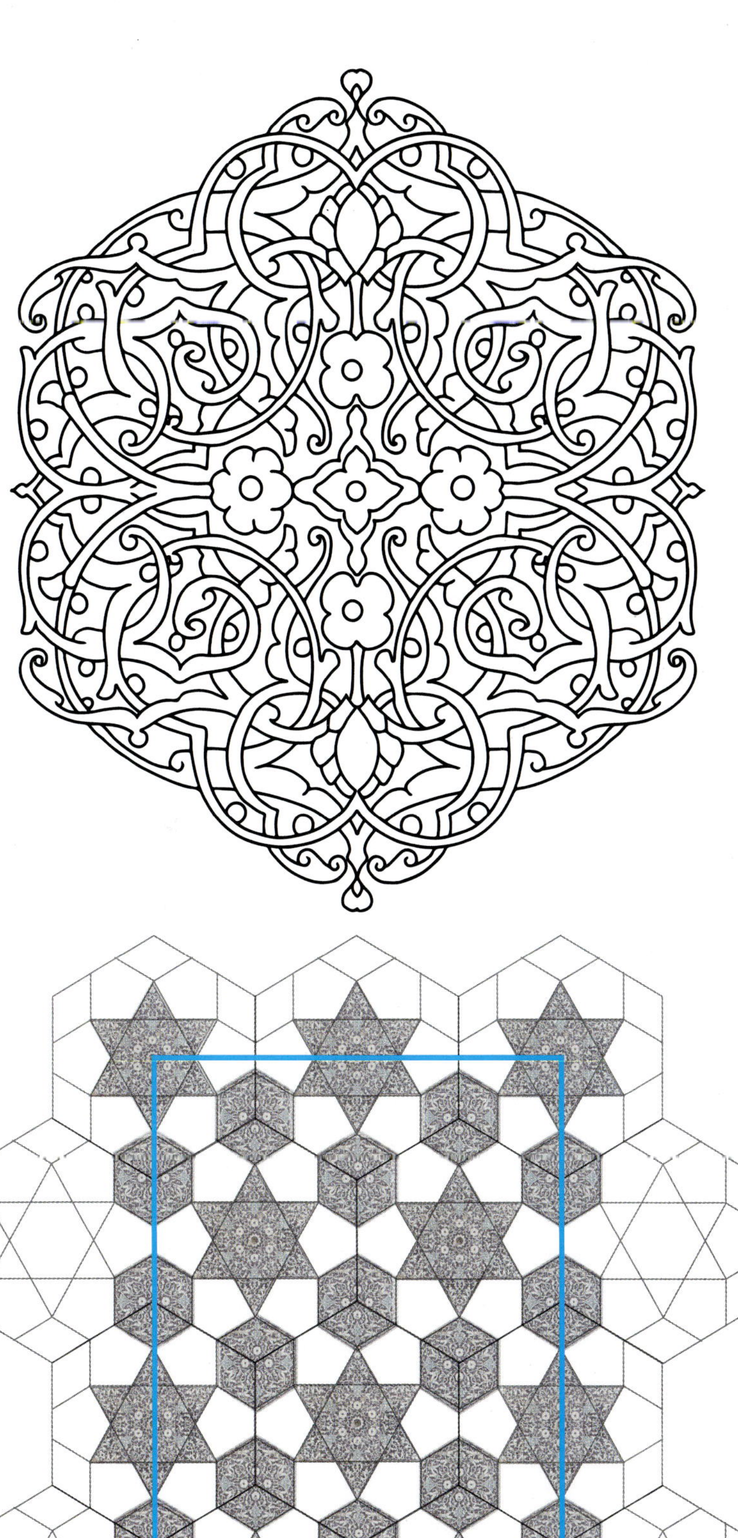

9 The full design is charming. Tessellate it as hexagonal tiling or paint it on its own.

When you have both Pattern 4 (the star) and Pattern 5 (the hexagon), you can create a big composition that fills a whole page, or a smaller one. The number of repetitions will be up to you, but you can get some ideas from the repetition here.

12-POINTED STAR TILE

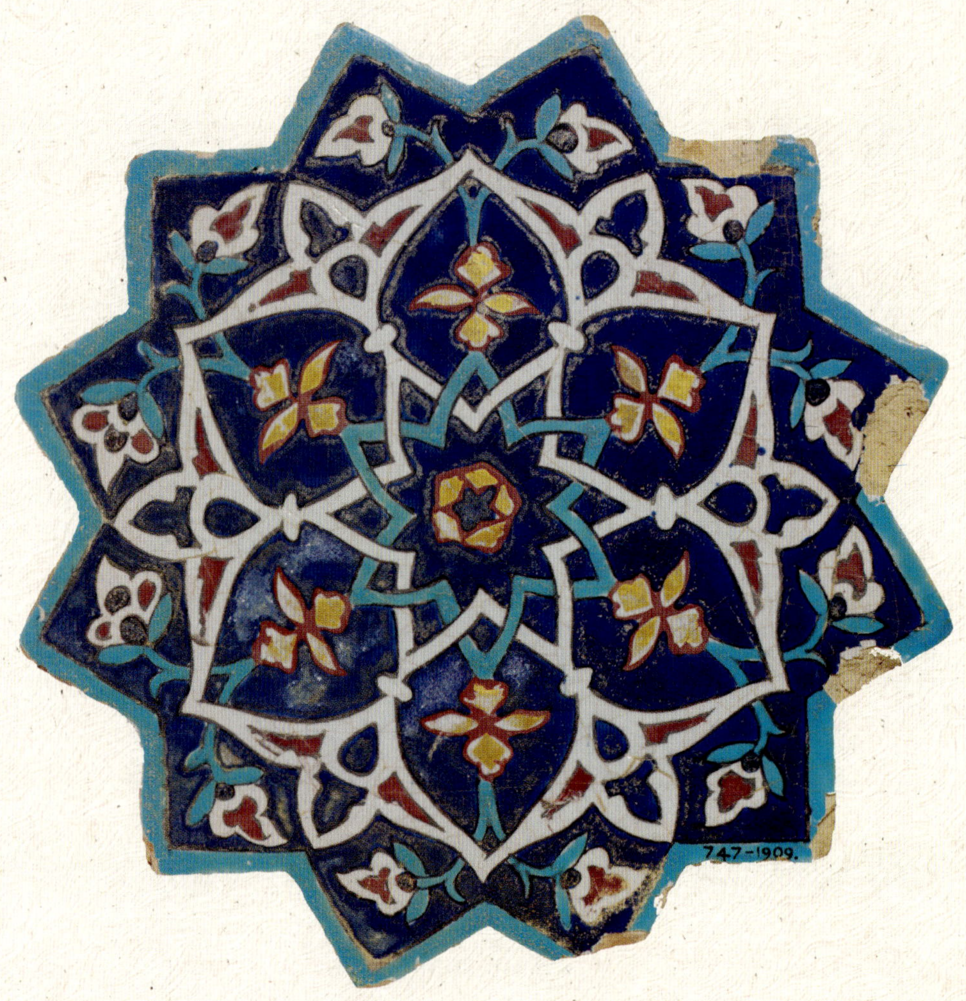

Star-shaped tile. Iran, 1444. Fritware.

This tile is thought to have come from the west iwan of the Ghiyathiyyah Madrasah at Khargird in Khurasan, Iran, founded by the vizier of the Timurid ruler Shahrukh. The simple motifs within it are considered a signature style for the Timurid period and can be seen in a few architectural examples from the same period in parts of Iran and Uzbekistan (see p.21).

Looking at the Geometric Structure

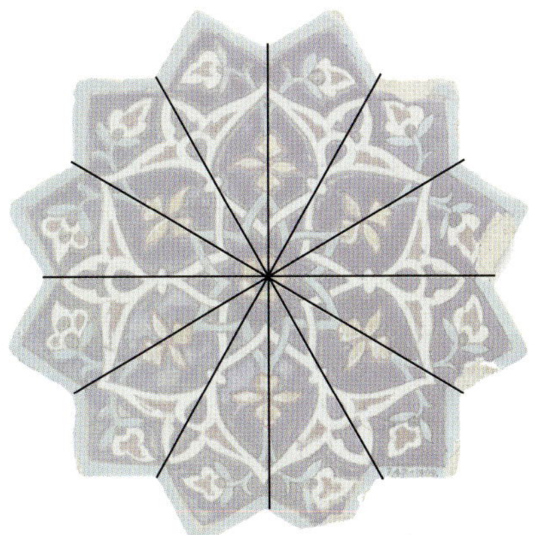 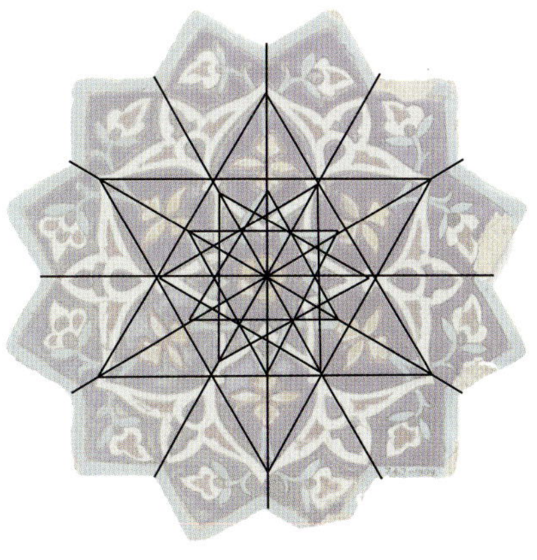 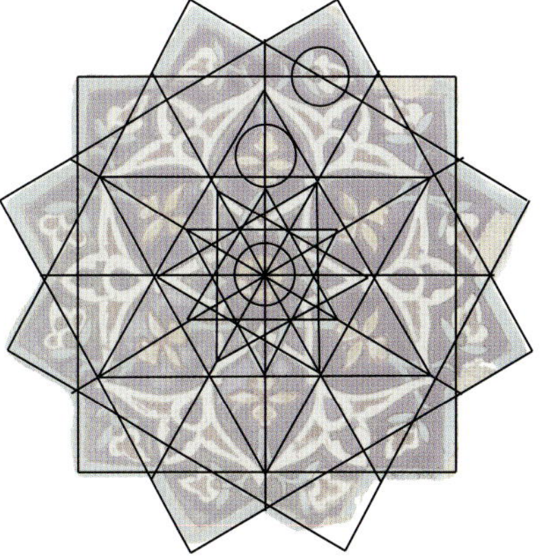

This pattern is based on a 12-pointed star, which has the same starting point as the six-pointed star and shares Steps 1–8 with it (see p.30). However, there are a number of additional steps to construct the outer shape of the tile.

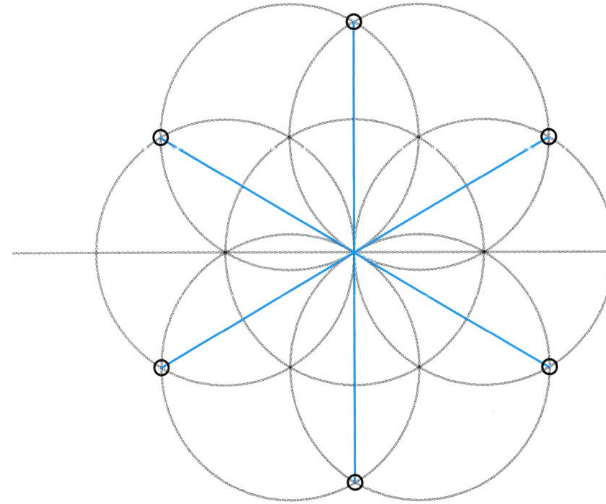

9 Mark the points between the intersecting circles and extend lines from one point to the centre and to the point opposite.

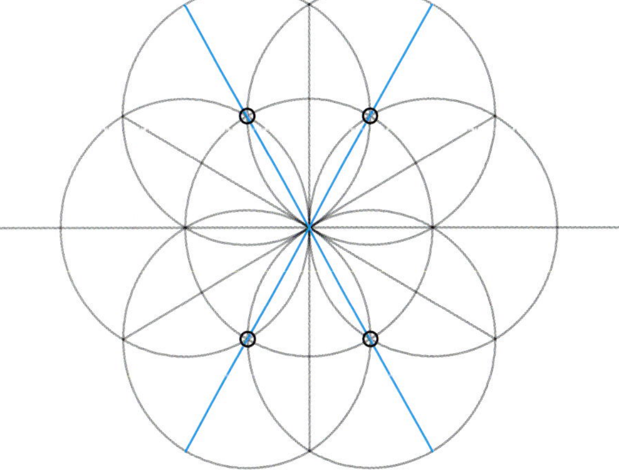

10 Bisect the two diagonal floral shapes inside the circles with lines extending to the outer edges of the circles.

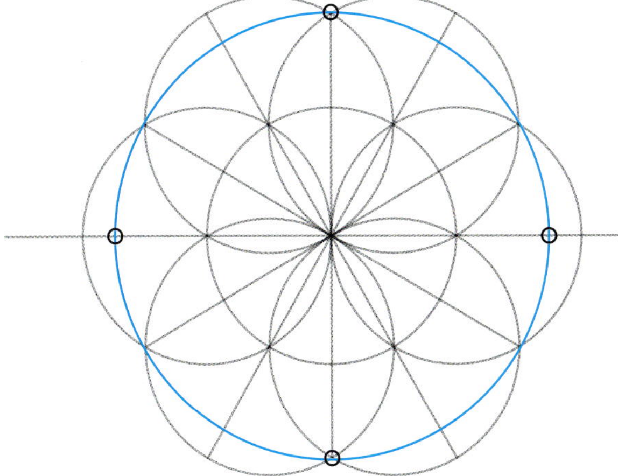

11 Draw a circle containing the whole inner construction, and mark where it meets the horizontal and vertical lines.

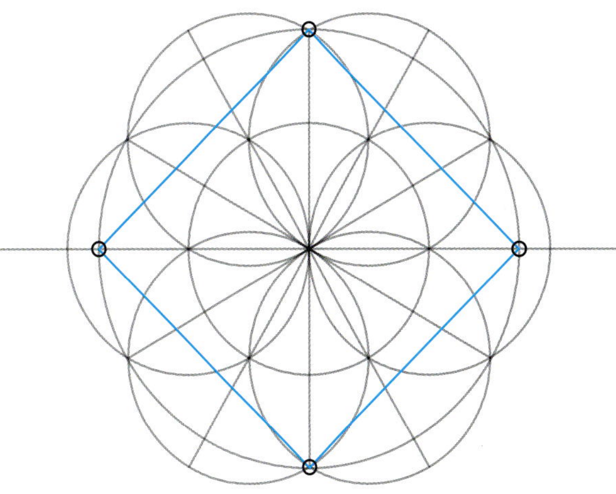

12 From the vertical and horizontal points on the circle, draw a dynamic square, which is a square turned 45 degrees.

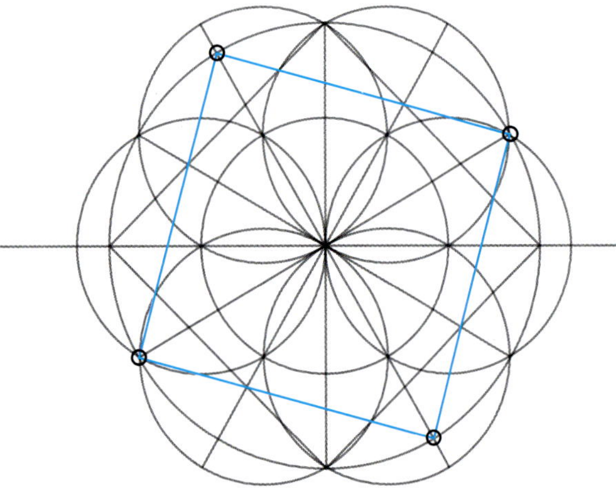

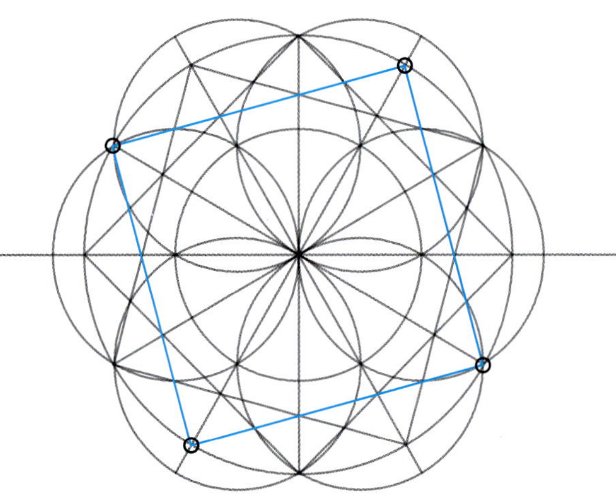

13 Draw another dynamic square, moving its corners anticlockwise to the next intersection.

14 Use the remaining four points to draw the third square inside the circle. You now have three squares making the 12-pointed star.

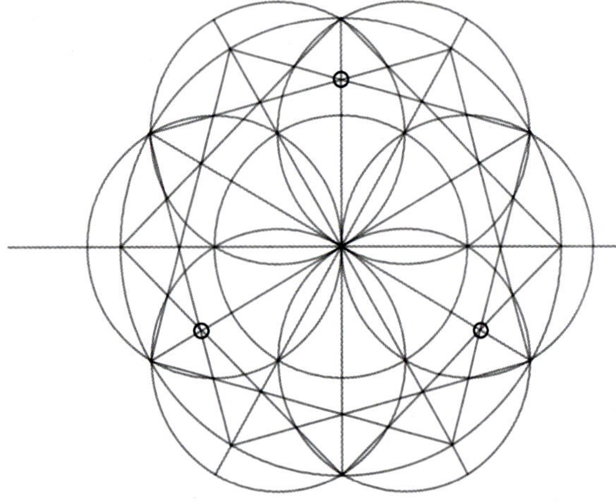

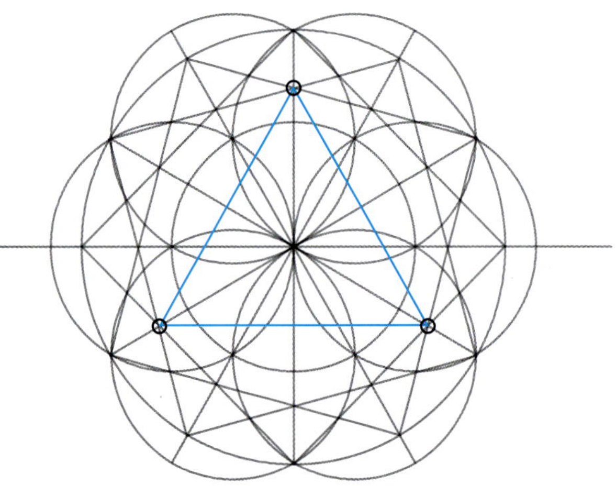

15 You will be drawing a six-pointed star, so start with marking three points where the dynamic squares cross for the triangle placement.

16 Draw a triangle from the chosen points.

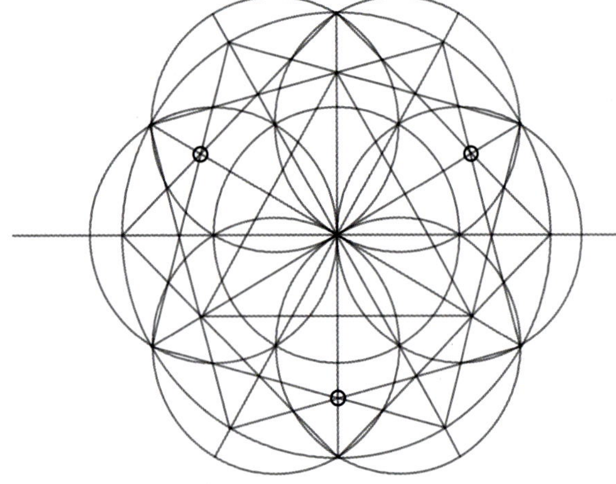

17 Mark three points for the upside-down triangle.

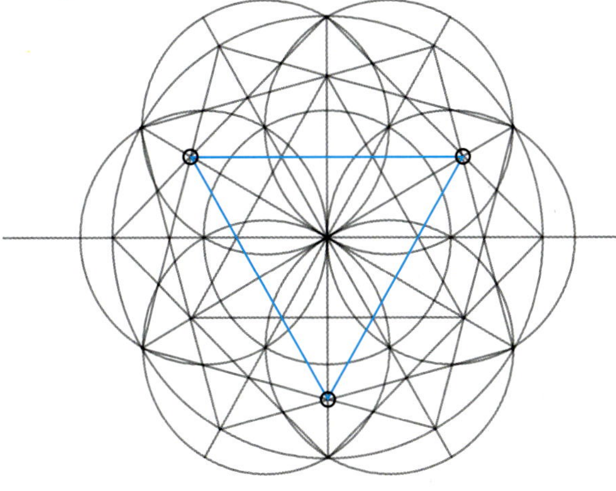

18 Draw the upside-down triangle from the chosen points.

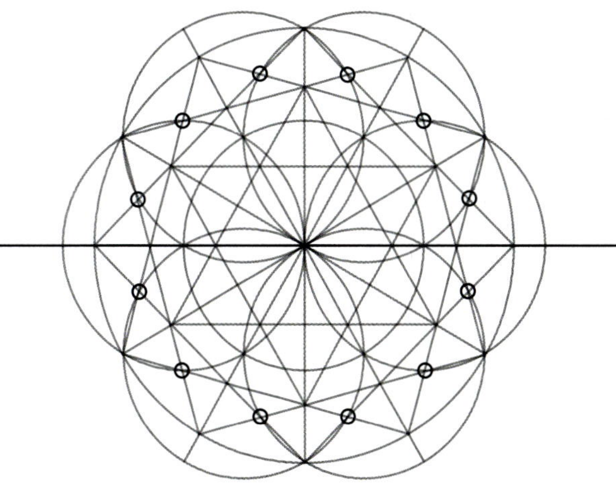

19 Mark 12 points where the squares intersect with the circles.

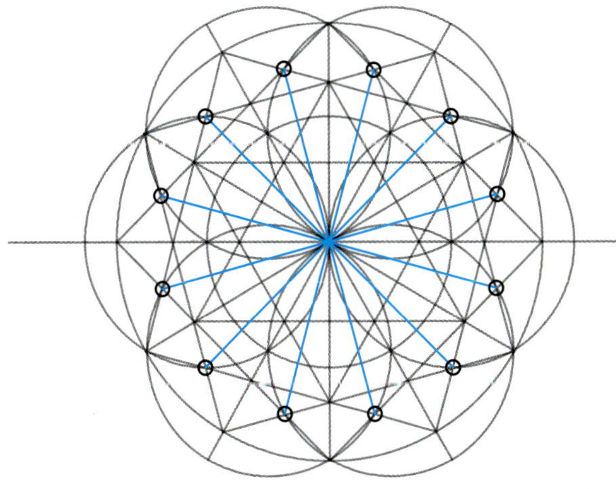

20 Extend lines from the points to the centre and to the point opposite.

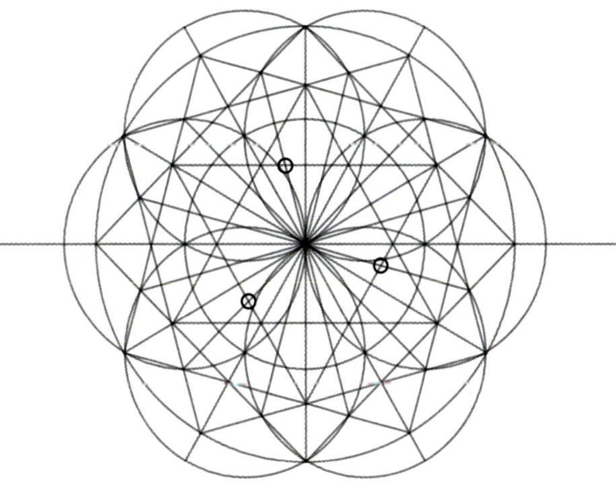

21 Mark three points on the six-pointed star (drawn in Steps 16–18) in order to draw a small triangle. There are three points between each selected point.

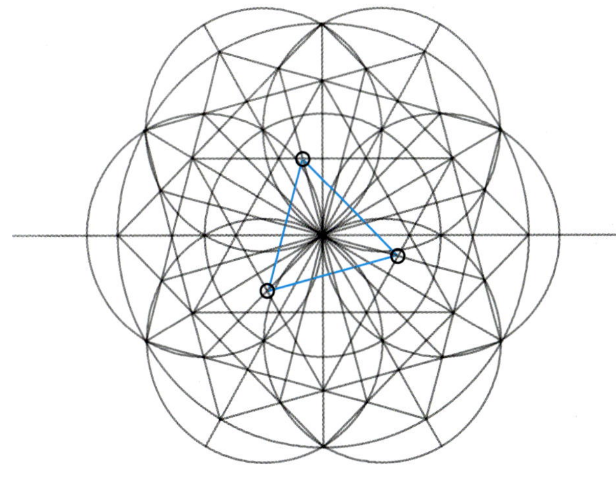

22 Draw the first triangle.

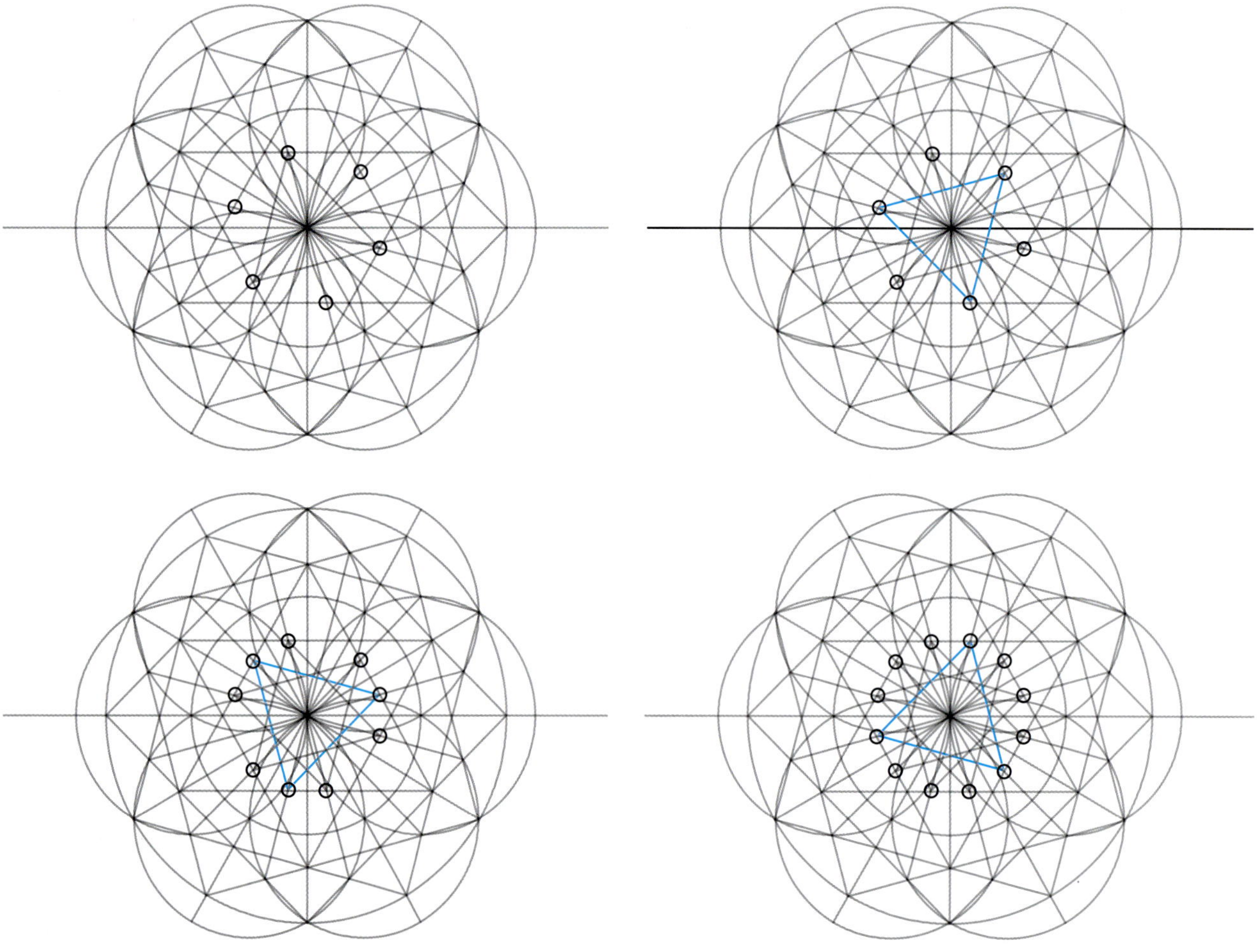

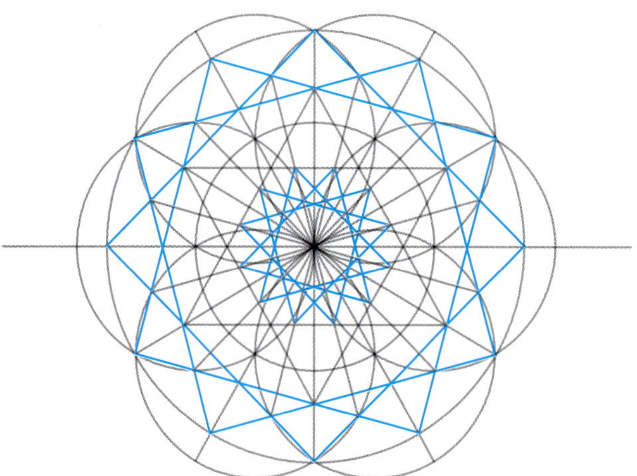

23–26 Repeat the process until you have four triangles and a new 12-pointed star.

27 Note that there are two 12-pointed stars in this design. The first one is made up of squares and is defining the tile borders, whilst the second is made up of triangles inside the design to make it even more detailed.

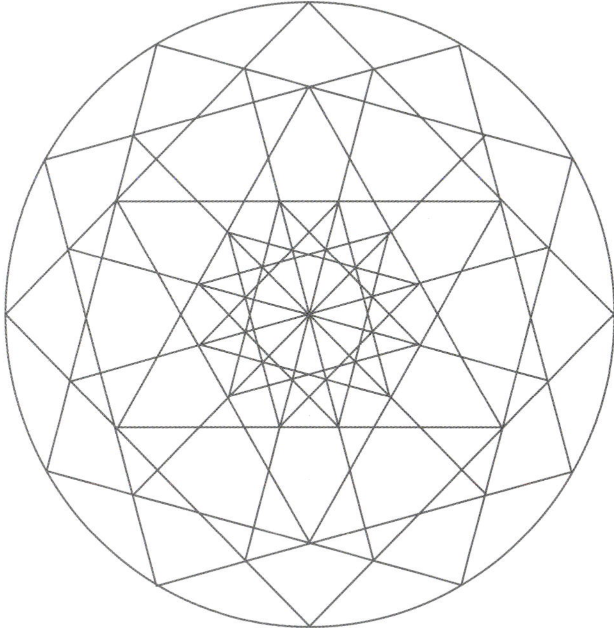

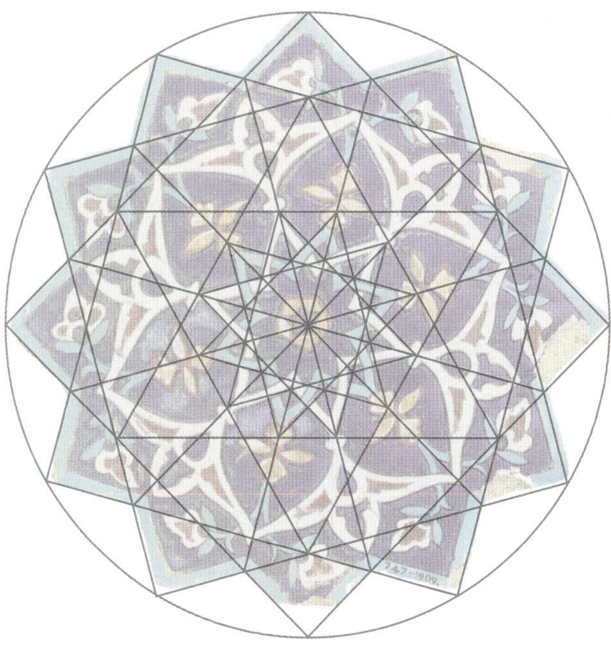

28 You can trace the design without any of the intersecting circles to have the complete layout of the tile. You can keep the biggest circle encompassing the design if you want the outcome to be contained, or you can forgo this if you want the sharp tile borders.

29 Overlaying the tile image shows us how geometry is essential to help us make decisions about where to place the motifs.

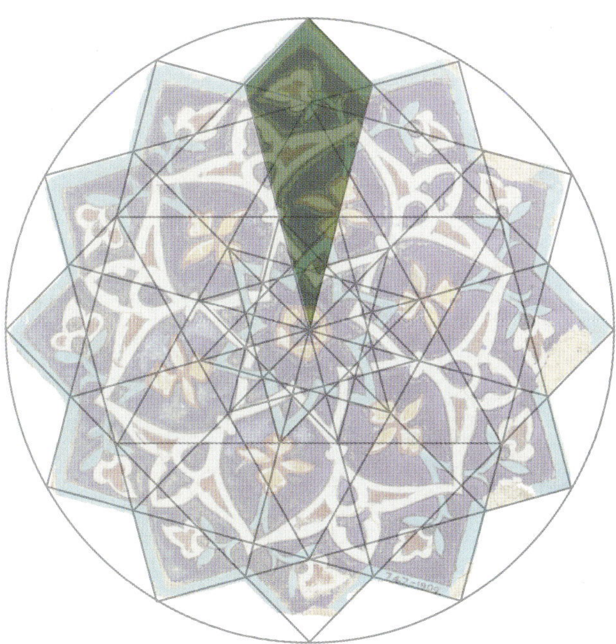

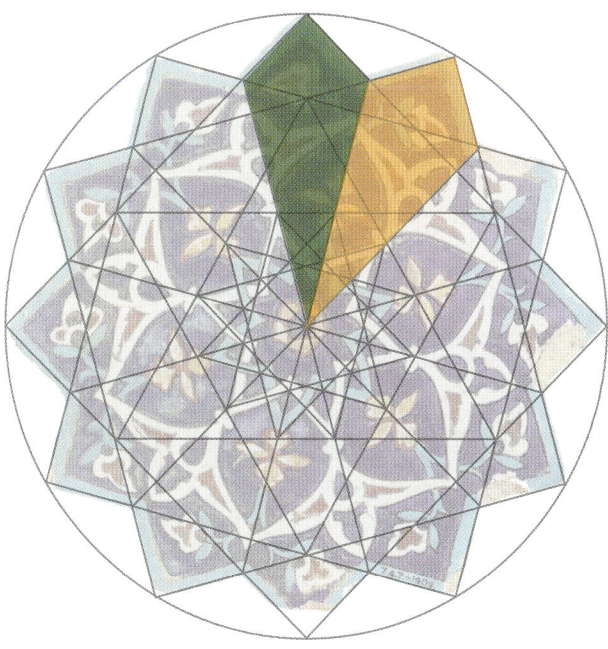

30 As always, a design section is selected where the pattern is created.

31 Finally, it is mirrored and repeated to create a complete design unit.

Drawing the Pattern

This pattern is very simple and made of only five elements: three flowers, an inorganic shape and the central star. Its simplicity is very attractive and can look very striking once painted.

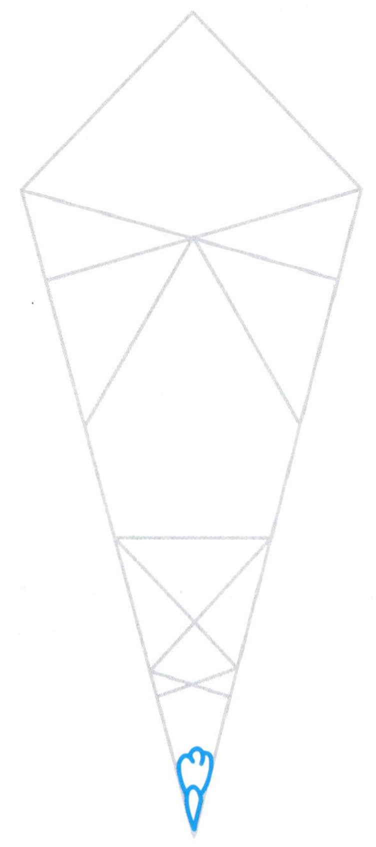

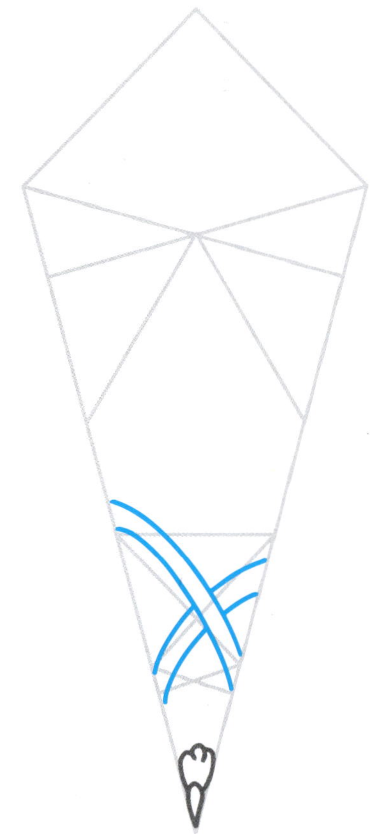

1 Start at the centre of the design and draw one small petal – toothed and with a round detail in the middle.

2 Follow the straight lines of the inner 12-pointed star and curve them slightly. You can draw the whole star in this step, or you can do it in single design sections as I have done. You can keep the lines straight like the star, if you prefer, but make sure to double the lines to give yourself a wider area to paint.

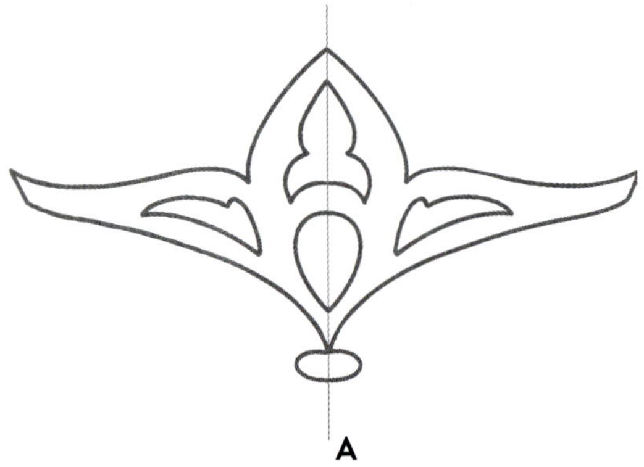

A

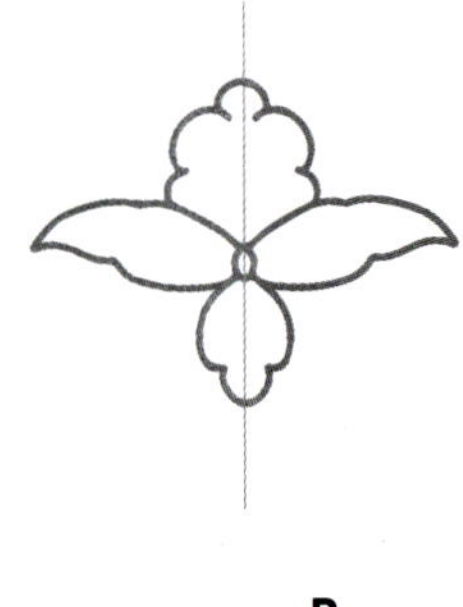

B

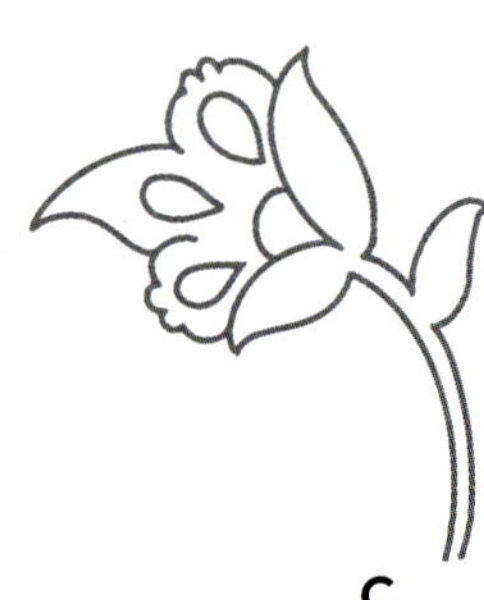

C

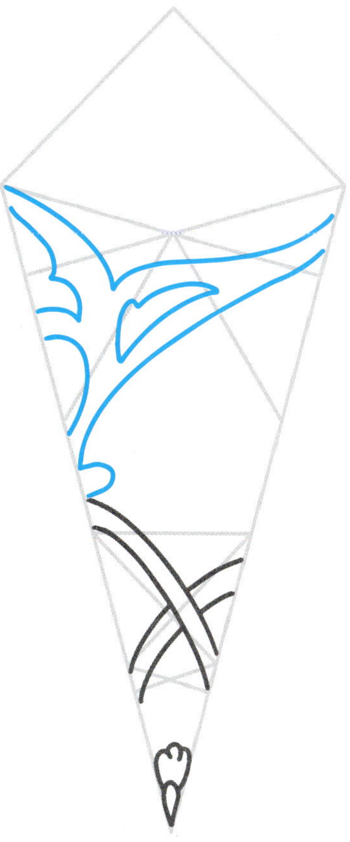

3 There are two diagonal lines of symmetry, which are important in creating the motifs. Place half of inorganic shape A above the curved lines of the star from Step 2 and fill the space until you reach the other line of symmetry.

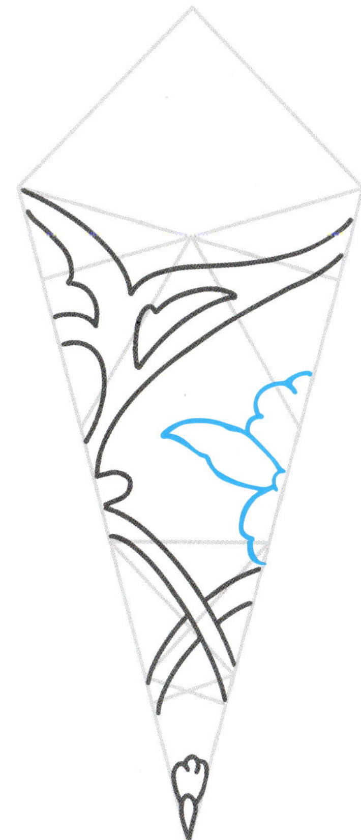

4 On the second line of symmetry (the other diagonal) draw half of flower B and place it above the curved star's line from Step 2, but leave some space between it and shape A.

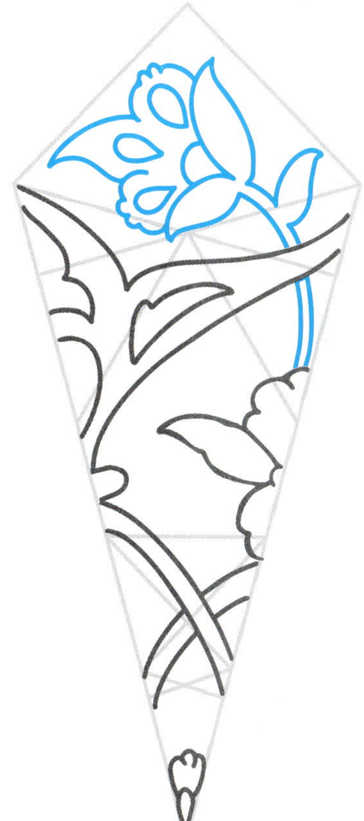

5 Draw flower C springing from flower B to fill the top space.

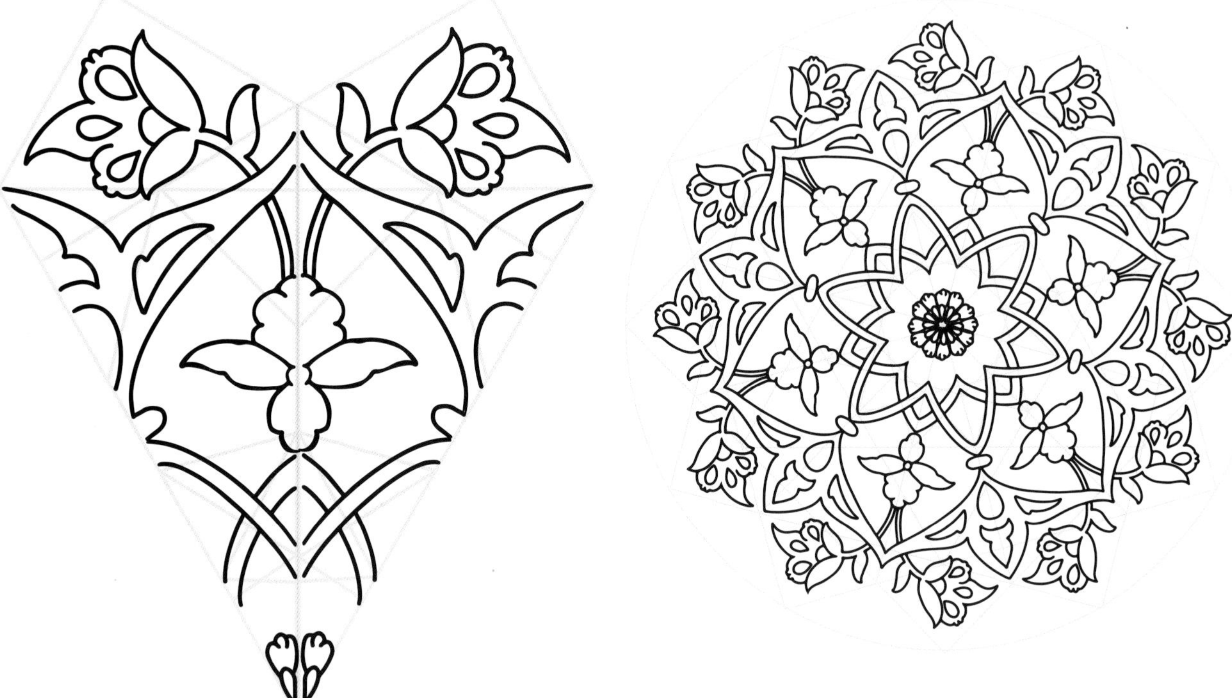

6 The design section is now complete and it will need to be mirrored and then repeated.

7 Once all the sections are repeated inside the tile, you will have the complete pattern.

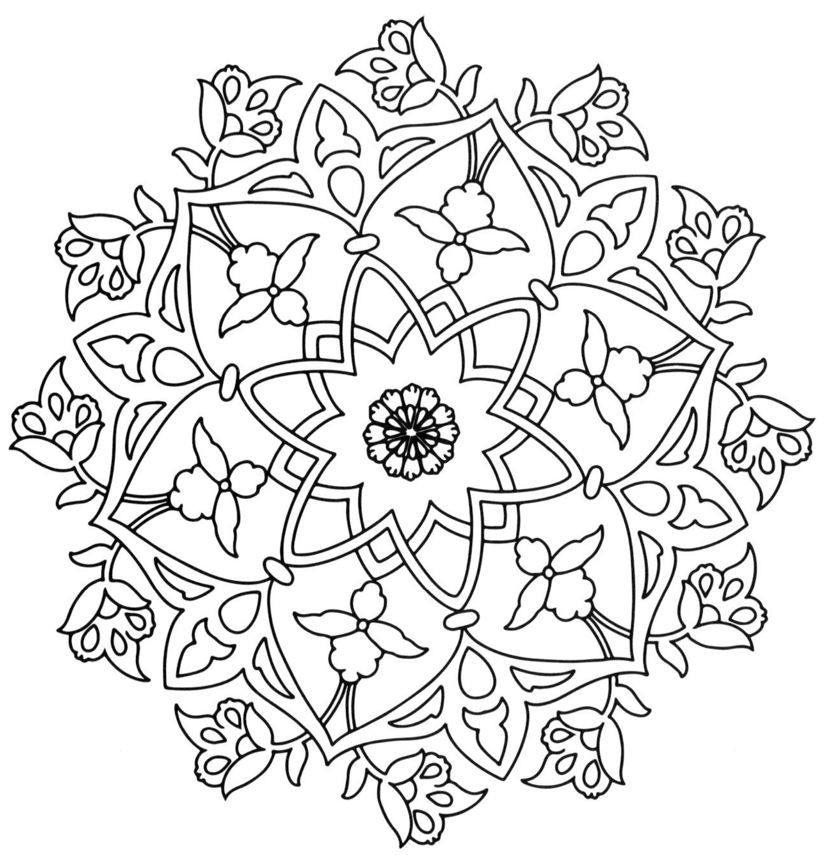

8 If you prefer a flowing design, you can remove the tile edges – the design is beautiful with and without them. The painted image on the cover of the book follows this design!

EIGHT-POINTED STAR GRID

As you have seen from the previous pattern studies, a grid system is very important in order to organise the pattern visually. It is the backbone of any Islamic biomorphic design – the building block that the motifs rely on to be structured, symmetrical and harmonious.

In this section, you will learn the eight-pointed star grid system before we progress on to the pattern studies.

It is considered an easy and essential grid. As with the six-pointed star grid (see p.29), you have the option to draw only one grid and use it for all of the pattern studies or you can draw a new one each time you start a pattern design. I would advise the latter because it is a relaxing practice that helps you think, and your skills will improve each time you draw the grid.

CONSTRUCTION

The grid can be used on its own or tessellated to create an even bigger pattern. The patterns in this section are designed using a single grid. The guides for tessellating will be helpful when you are ready to take the patterns further and create larger-scale artworks.

DRAWING YOUR FIRST EIGHT-POINTED STAR

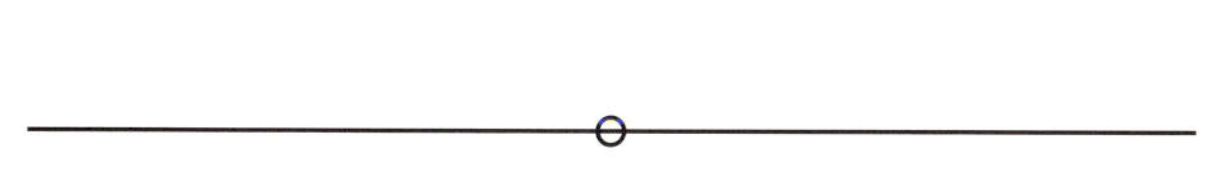

1   Draw a line in the centre of your page and mark the middle point of the line.

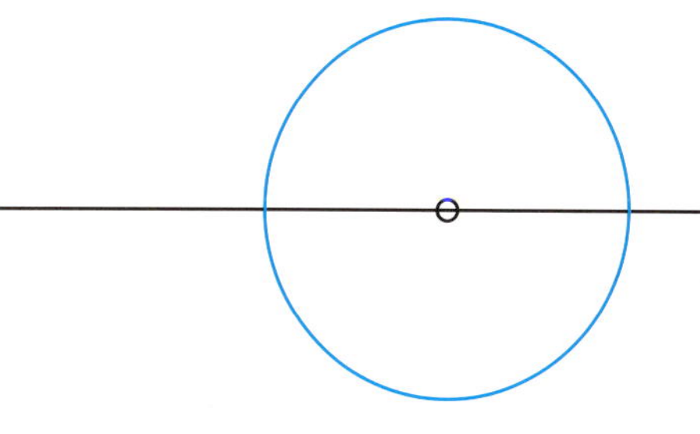

2   Draw a circle in the middle of the line using your compass.

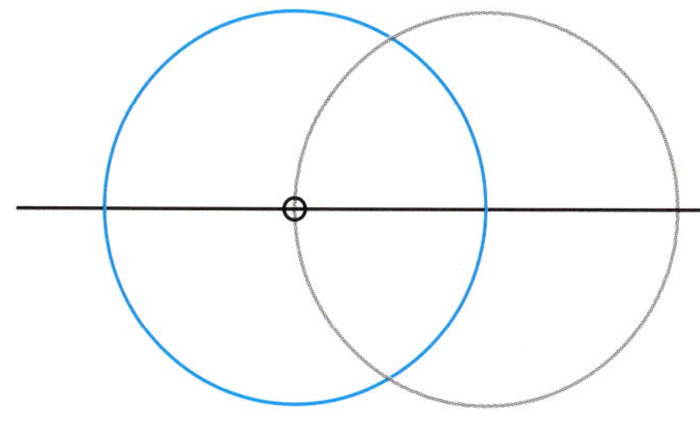

3   Draw another circle on the left, placing the compass needle on the point where the line bisects your first circle.

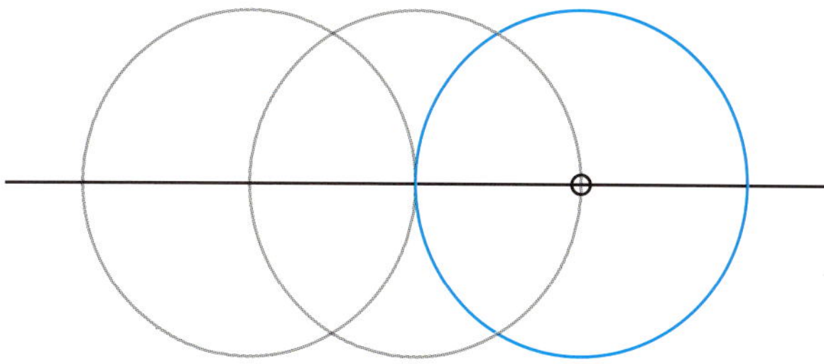

4   Repeat Step 3 to the right of the central circle.

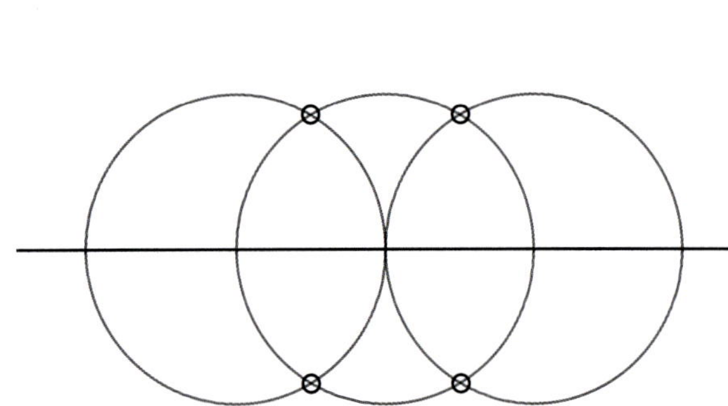

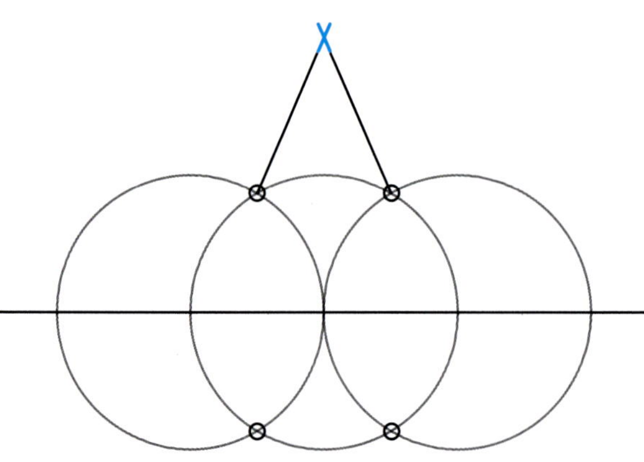

5 You need to find the vertical line using geometry rather than guessing its placement. Mark four points on your central circle where it intersects the side circles.

6 Place your compass needle on each of the top points to draw a small curve to make an X shape.

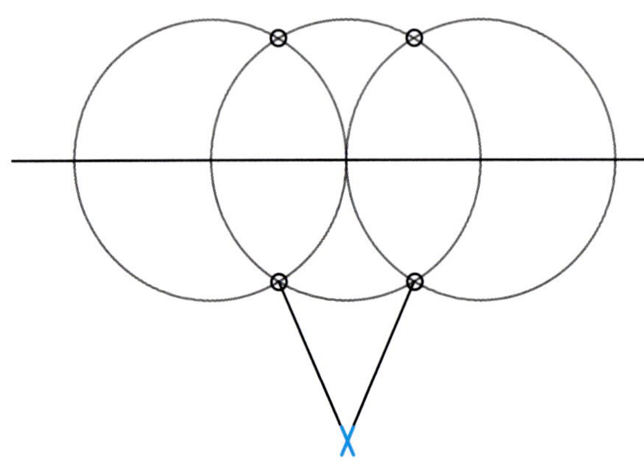

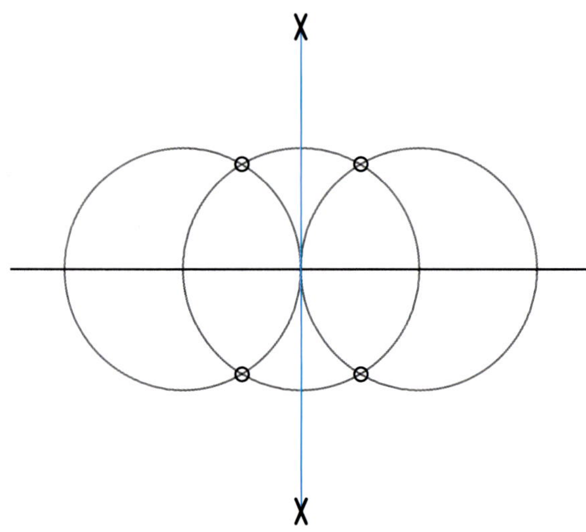

7 Place the compass needle on each of the bottom points to draw a small curve to make an X shape.

8 From the points created in Steps 6 and 7, draw a straight vertical line that will pass through the top, centre and bottom points.

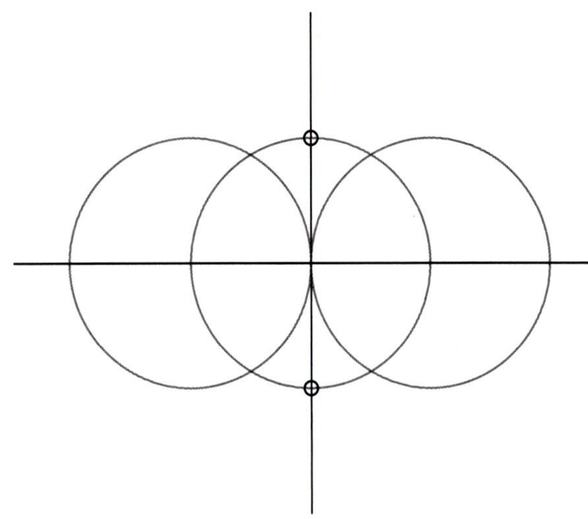

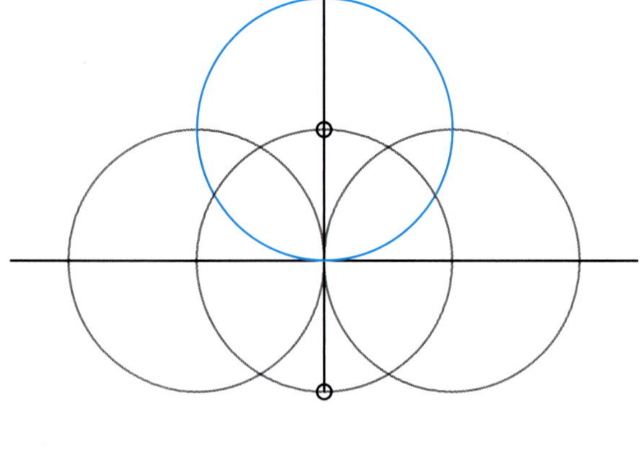

9 The vertical line has created two intersections on the central circle. Mark these points.

10 At the top point on the central circle, where the vertical line bisects it, place your compass needle and draw another circle.

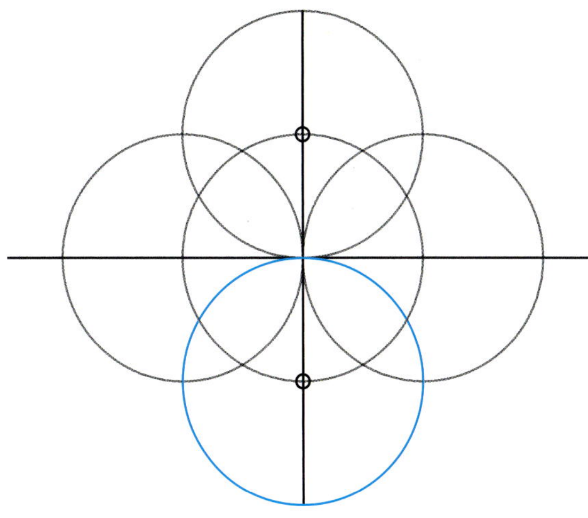

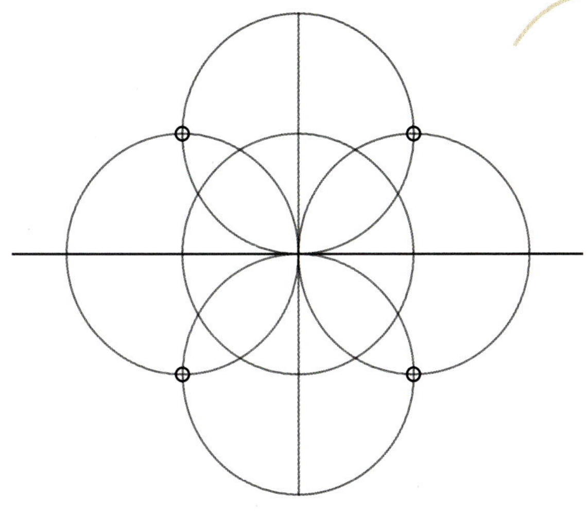

11 At the bottom point on the central circle, where the vertical line cuts in, place your compass needle and draw another circle.

12 You will notice that the four additional circles that you have drawn have formed four petals in the central circle. Mark the points at the end of these petals.

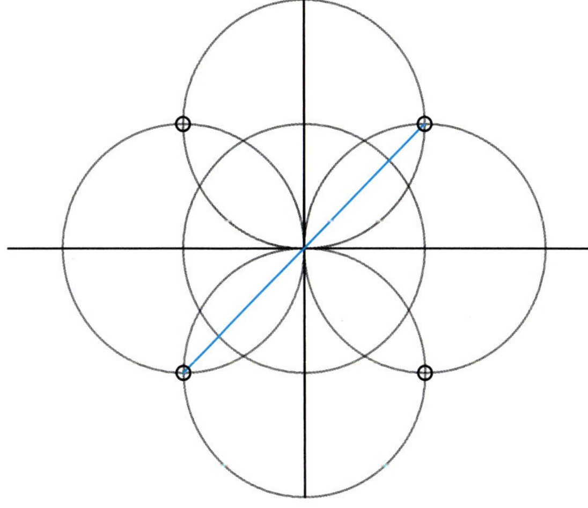

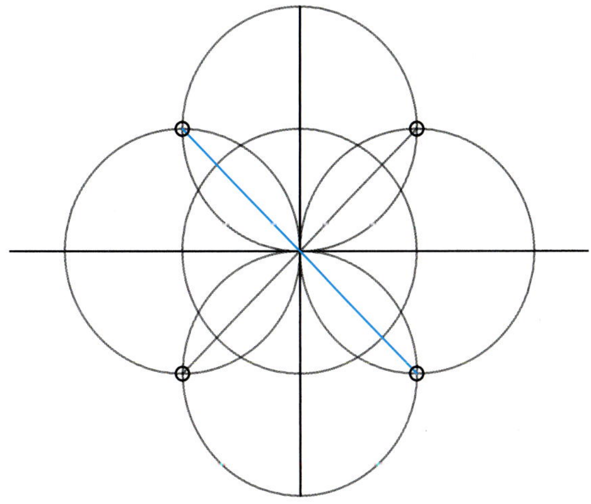

13 Extend a diagonal line from the top right point to the bottom left point.

14 Extend a diagonal line from the top left point to the bottom right point. Your two lines will create an X.

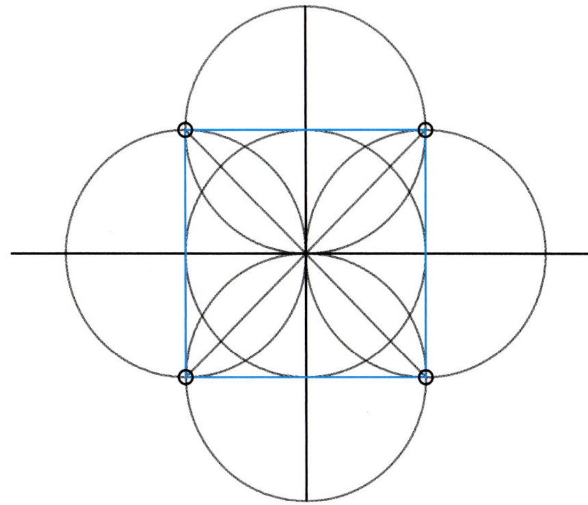

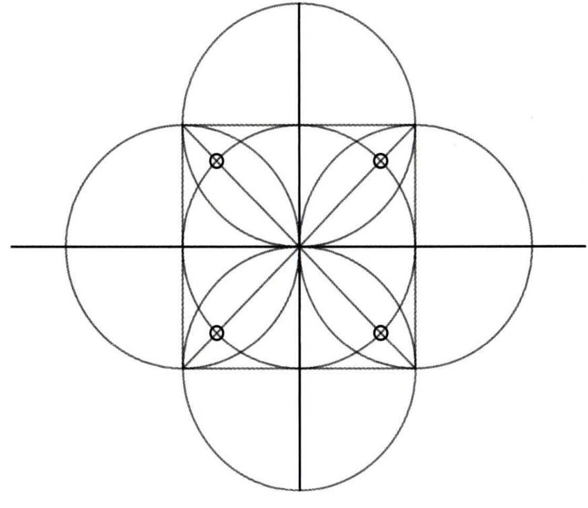

15 Use the same points to draw your first square, which will frame the central circle. This is also indicative of the tile size we will be working with in the design.

16 Mark four points on the central circle where the diagonal lines intersect with it.

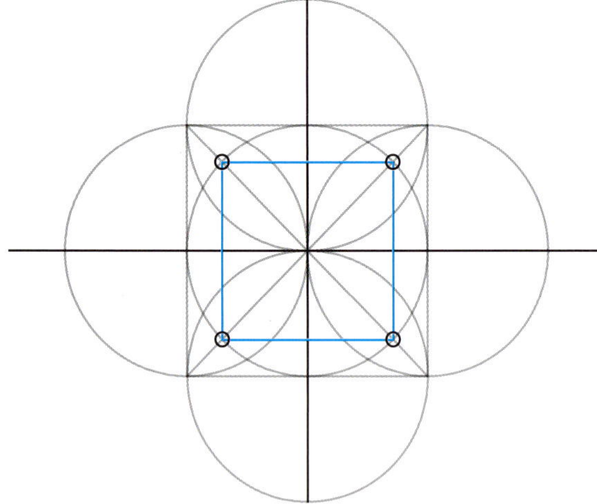

17 Draw a second square from these points.

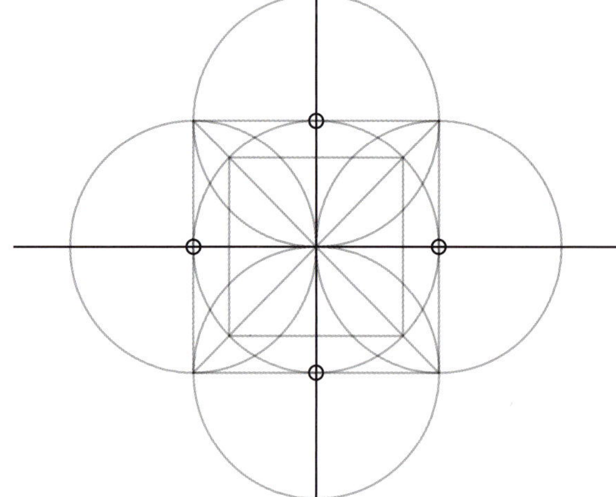

18 On the central circle, mark four points where it meets the vertical and horizontal lines.

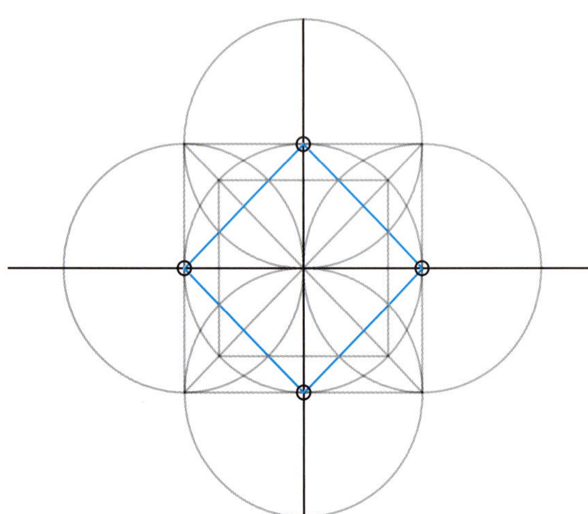

19 Draw a dynamic square from the points you marked in Step 18.

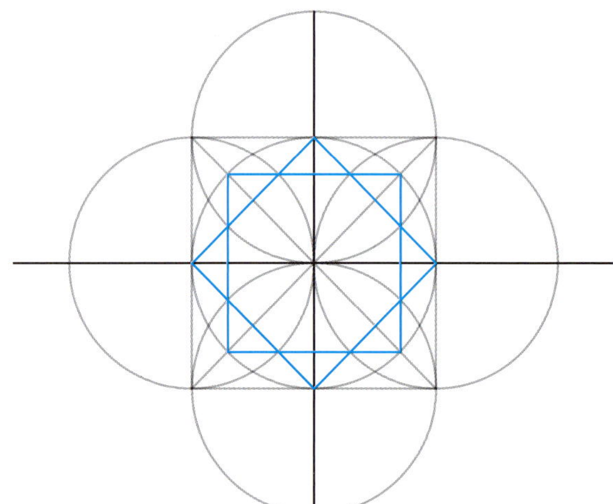

20 You will now have your first eight-pointed star inside the central circle.

DRAWING YOUR SECOND EIGHT-POINTED STAR

One eight-pointed star is not sufficient to give us the guidelines to work with for biomorphic patterns – we need more lines to guide us, hence you will need to draw three more eight-pointed stars.

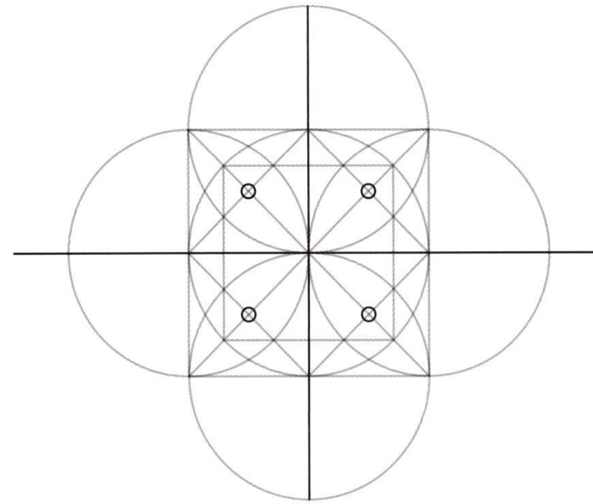

21 Mark four points on the diagonal lines where they intersect with the inside of the eight-pointed star.

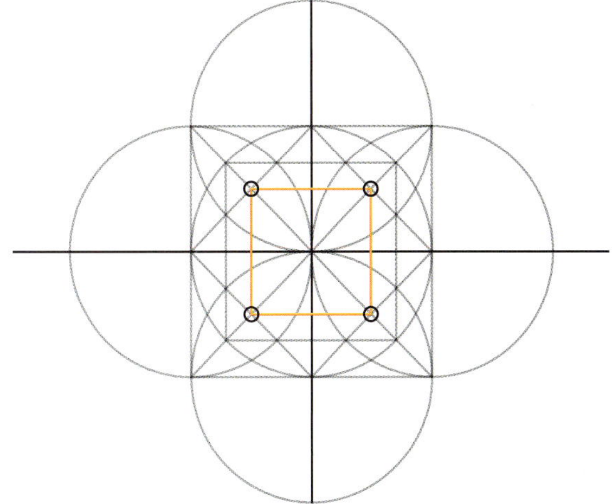

22 Draw a regular square from these points. You will notice that it is enclosed within the previous (blue) eight-pointed star.

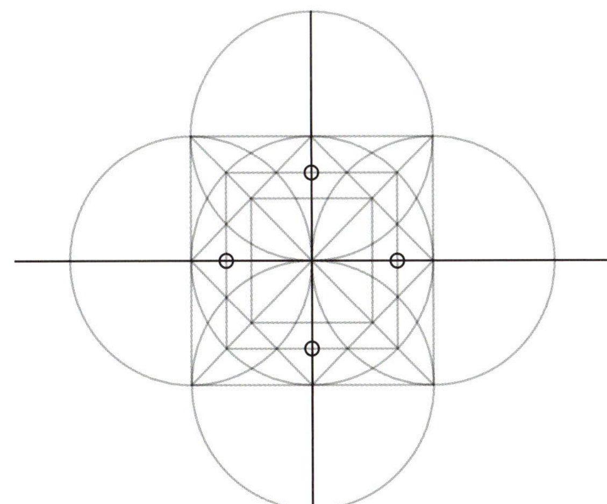

23 On the horizontal and vertical lines inside the previous eight-pointed star, mark four points.

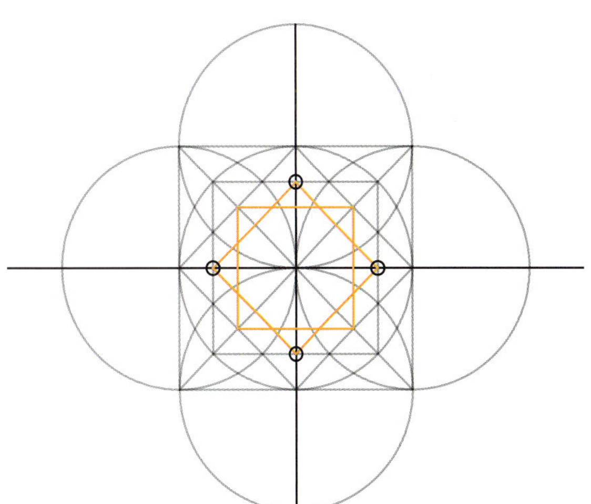

24 Draw a dynamic square from these points to make your second eight-pointed star.

DRAWING YOUR THIRD EIGHT-POINTED STAR

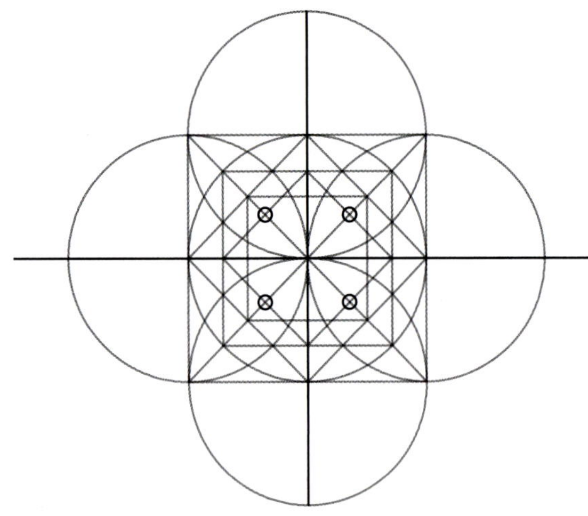

25 Mark four points on the diagonal lines where they intersect with the inside of the second (orange) eight-pointed star.

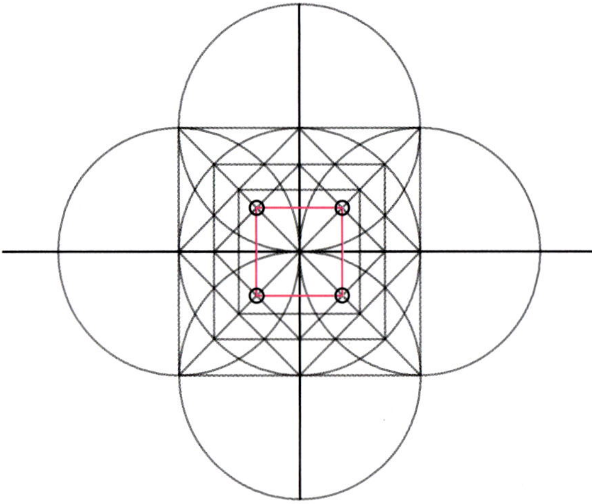

26 Draw a regular square from these points. You will notice that it is enclosed within the previous (orange) eight-pointed star.

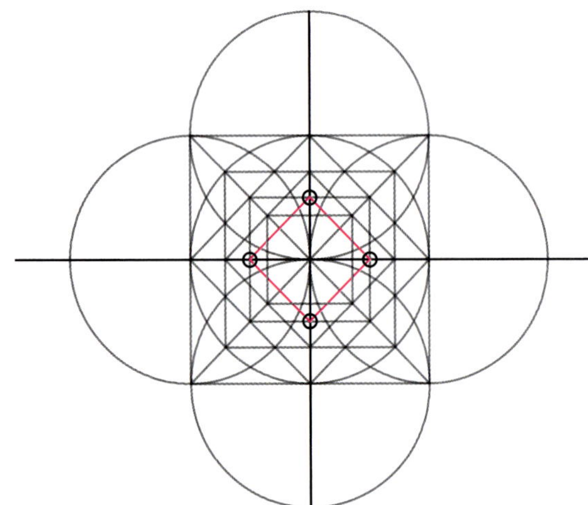

27 On the horizontal and vertical lines inside the second (orange) eight-pointed star, mark four points.

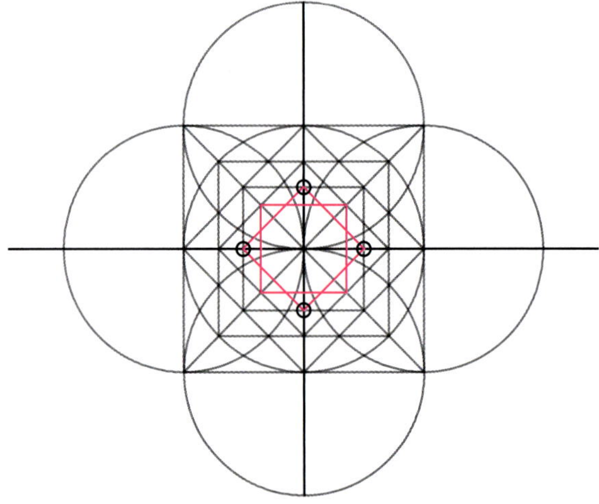

28 Draw a dynamic square from these points to make your third (pink) eight-pointed star.

DRAWING YOUR FOURTH EIGHT-POINTED STAR

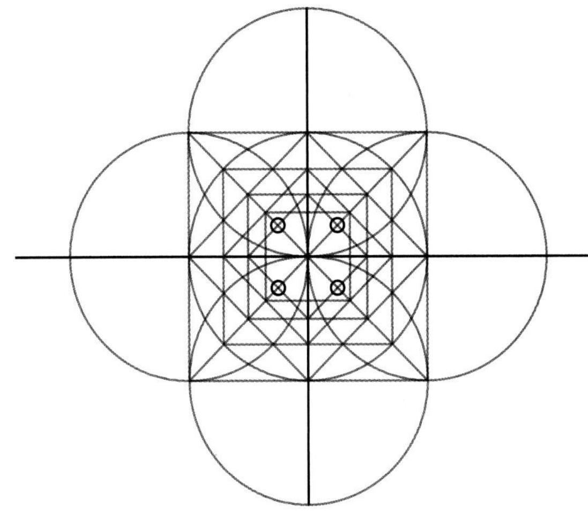

29 Where the diagonal lines on the inside of the third (pink) eight-pointed star intersect, mark four points.

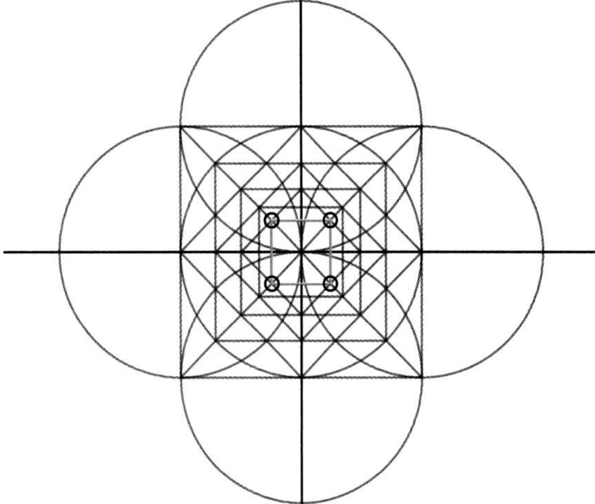

30 Draw a regular square from these points. You will notice that it is enclosed within the previous (pink) eight-pointed star.

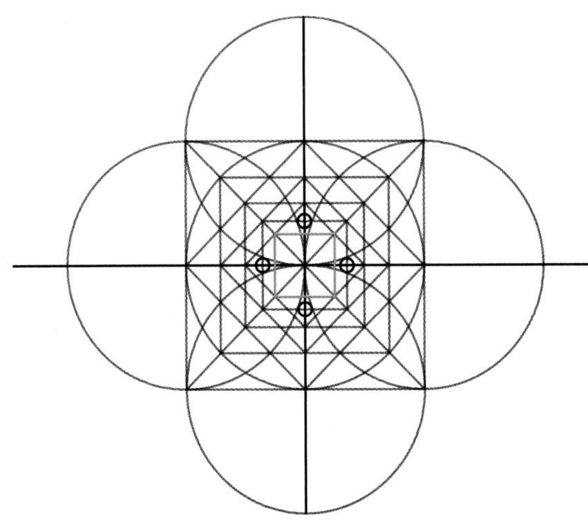

31 On the horizontal and vertical lines inside the third (pink) eight-pointed star, mark four points.

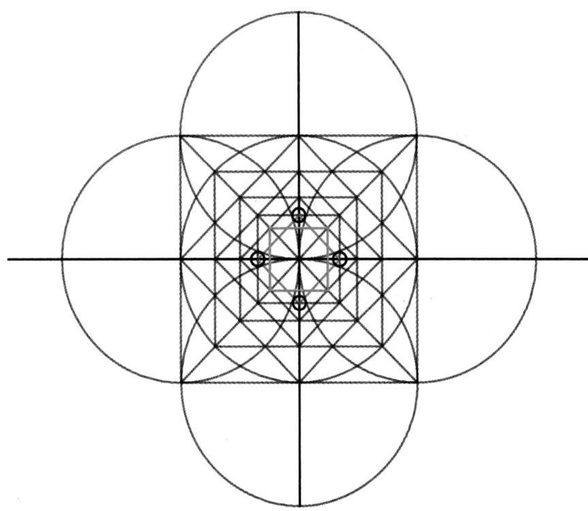

32 Draw a dynamic square from these points to make your fourth (green) eight-pointed star.

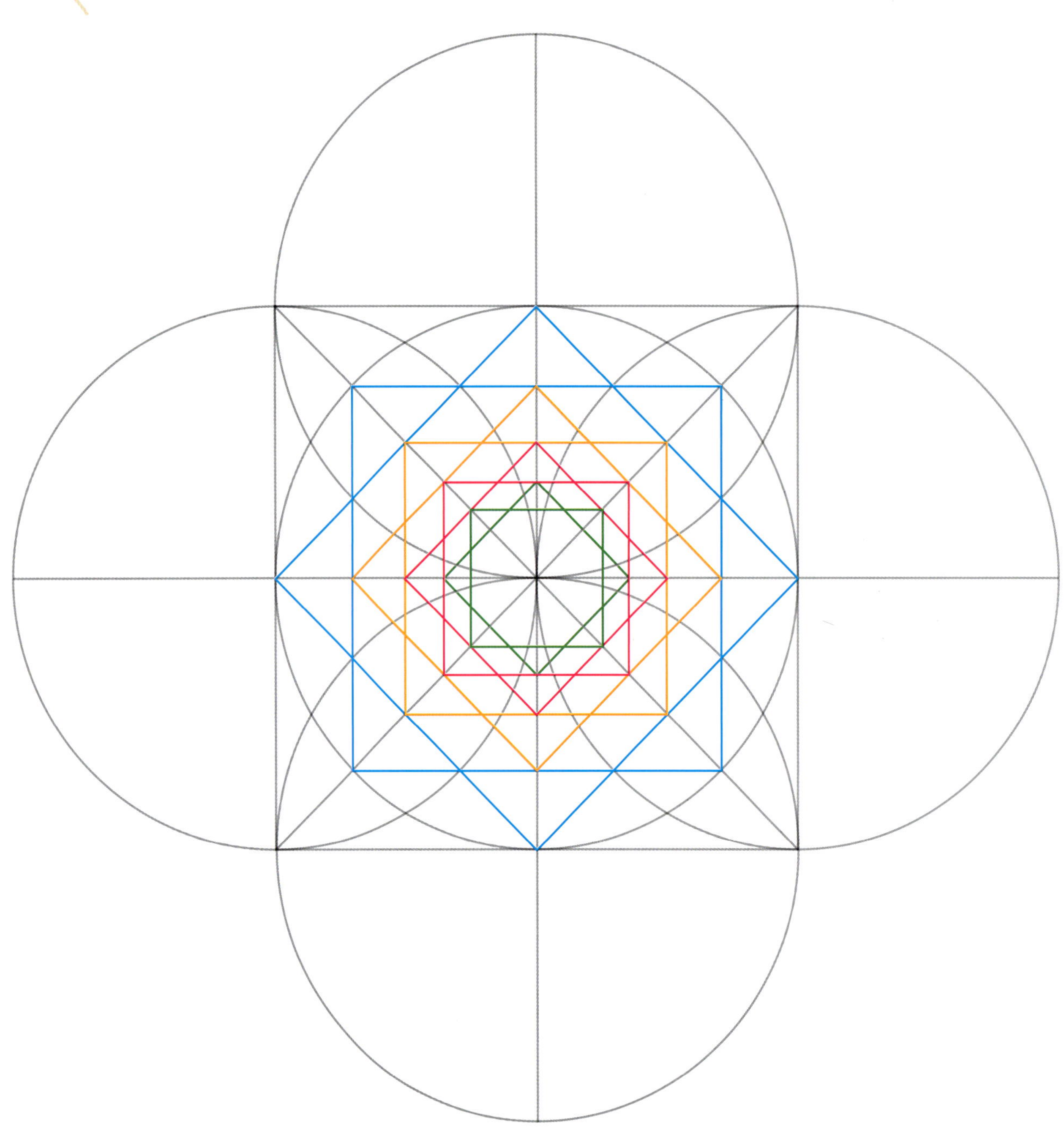

33 This is the final construction of the simple eight-pointed star that includes four eight-pointed stars. As you can see, there are plenty of guidelines for us to work with to create beautifully balanced biomorphic patterns. In the following pattern studies, you will see how we design them in sections in a similar way to the six-pointed star grid we studied previously (see p.29).

TESSELLATING THE PATTERN

Tessellation is an important part of the pattern-making process because it allows us to expand our patterns from a small unit to a large decorative panel, as seen in mosques and palaces across the Islamic world.

The classic tessellation for an eight-pointed star grid is the star and cross tessellation (A). According to Keith Critchlow (1933–2020) – artist, geometer, author and pioneer in Islamic patterns – this pattern is called the 'Breath of The Compassionate', referring to the movement of breath that is reflected visually in this tessellation.

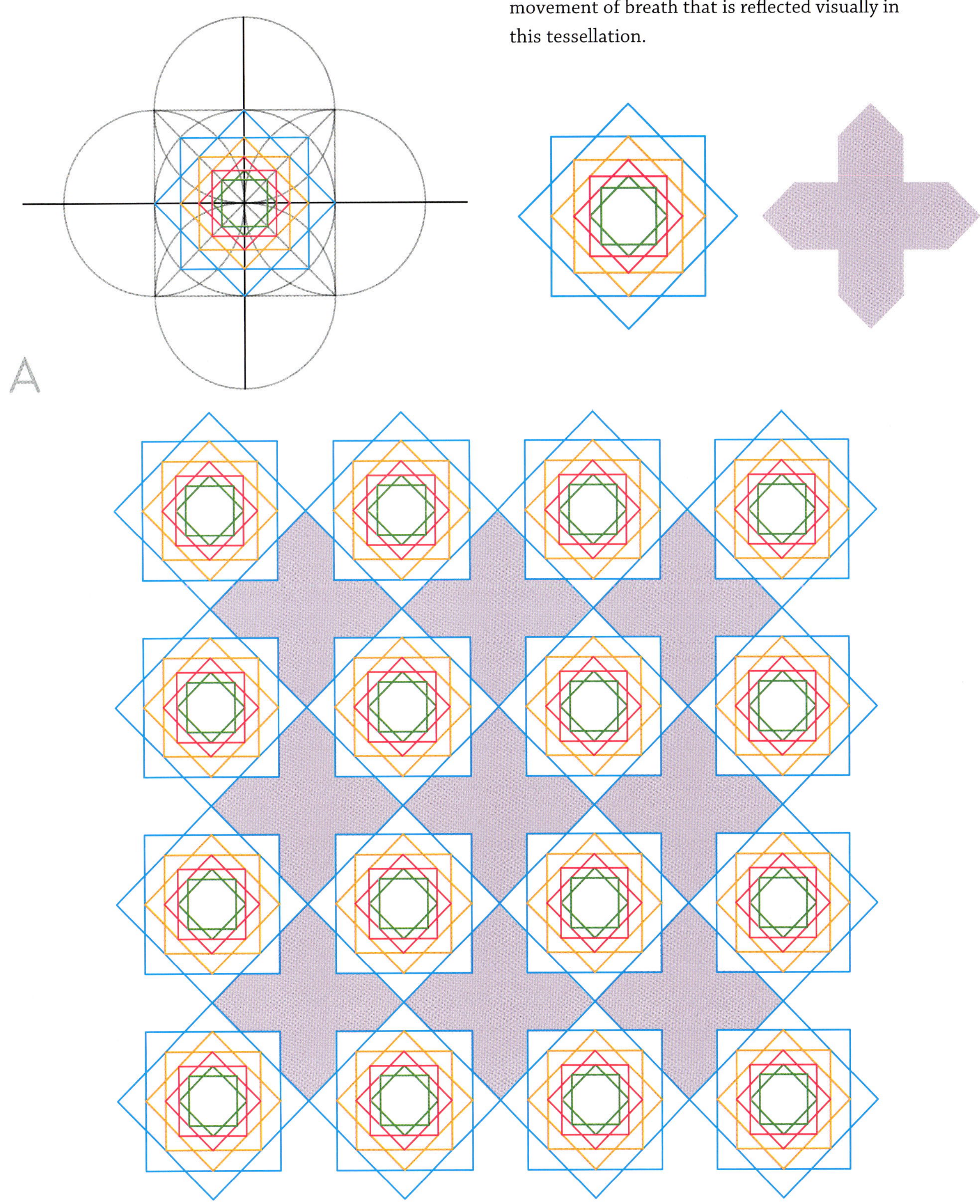

A

There are more forms of tessellation that can be conjured from an eight-pointed star grid, such as B, C and D. These are irregular and not commonly used in Islamic patterns. I have included them here to show you some possibilities, but you can leave them for a future point when you advance your practice and want to create more pattern styles.

Now that you are familiar with the grid and its possibilities for tessellation, you are ready to explore a new set of six patterns from tiles and manuscripts that are based on the eight-pointed star structure. This coming section will give you a new way to see patterns when you are visiting beautifully patterned locations.

B

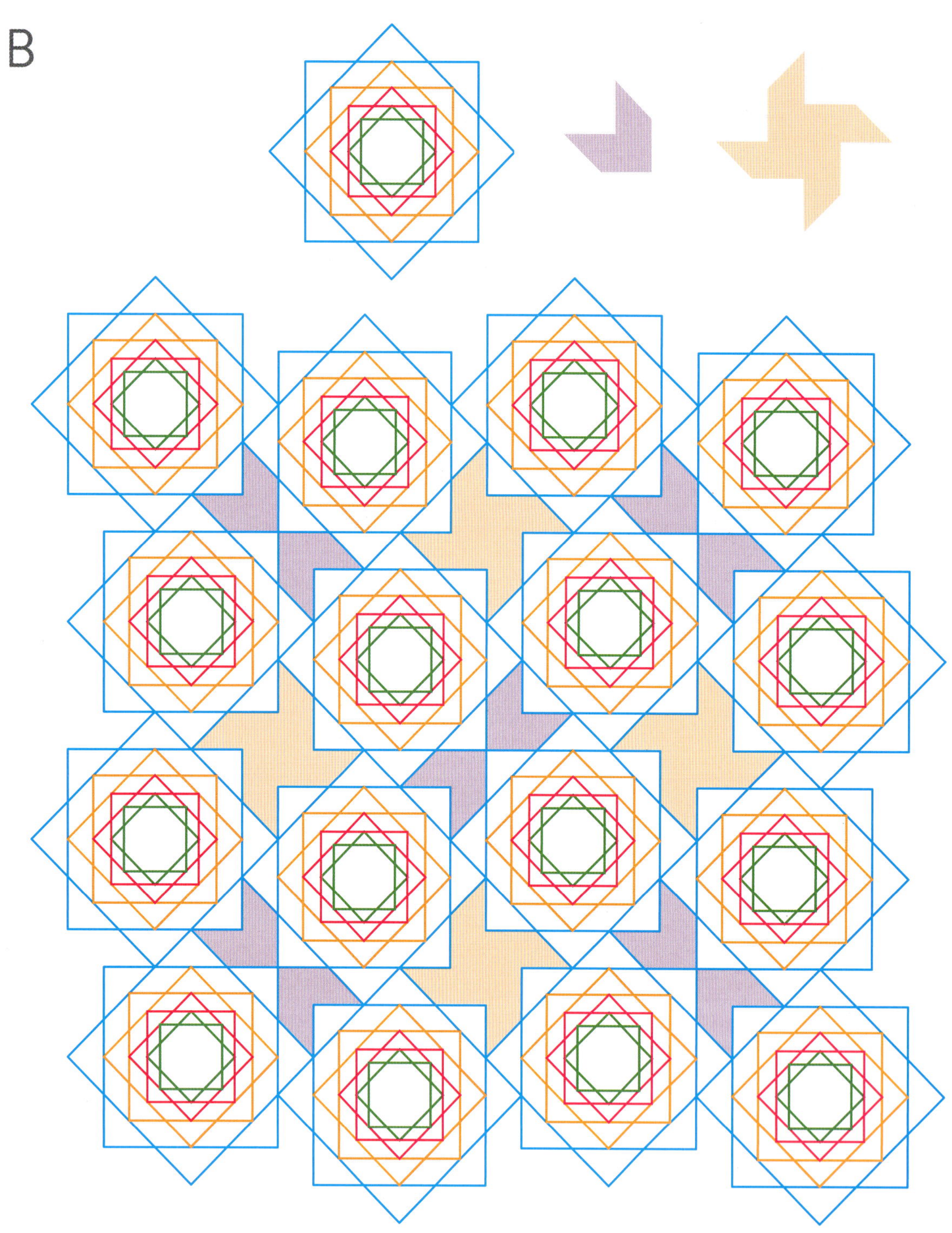

C

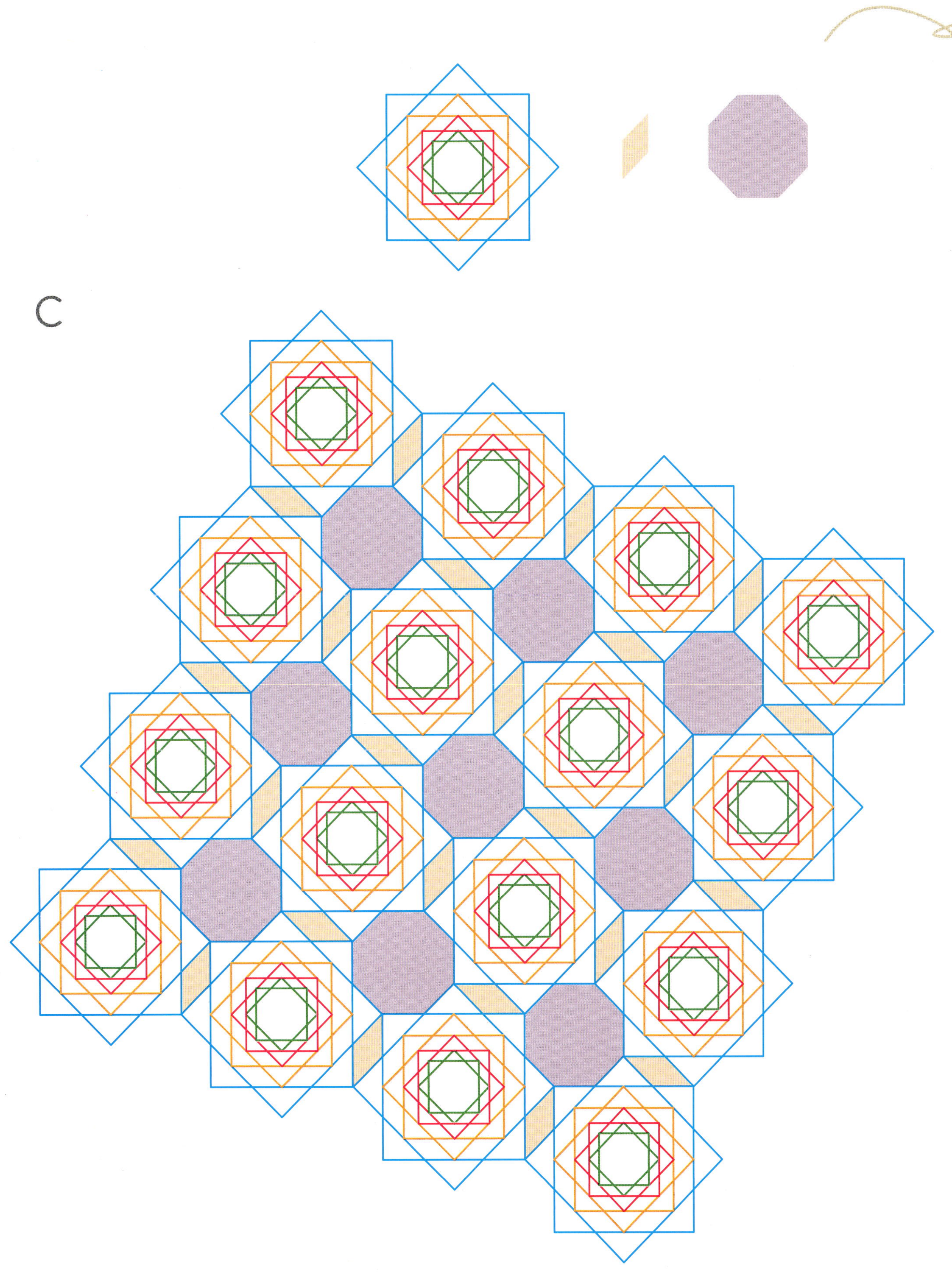

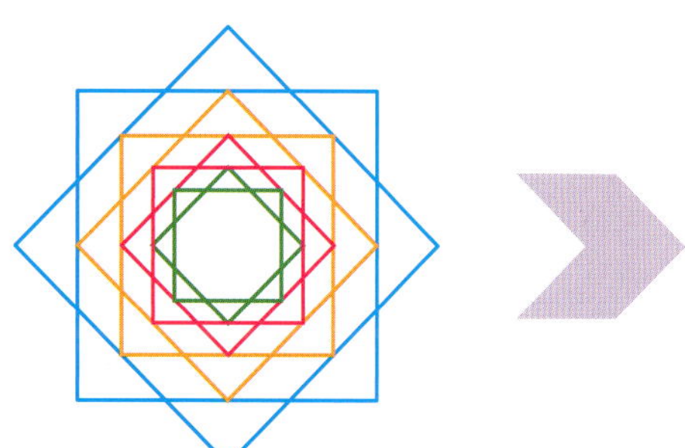

D

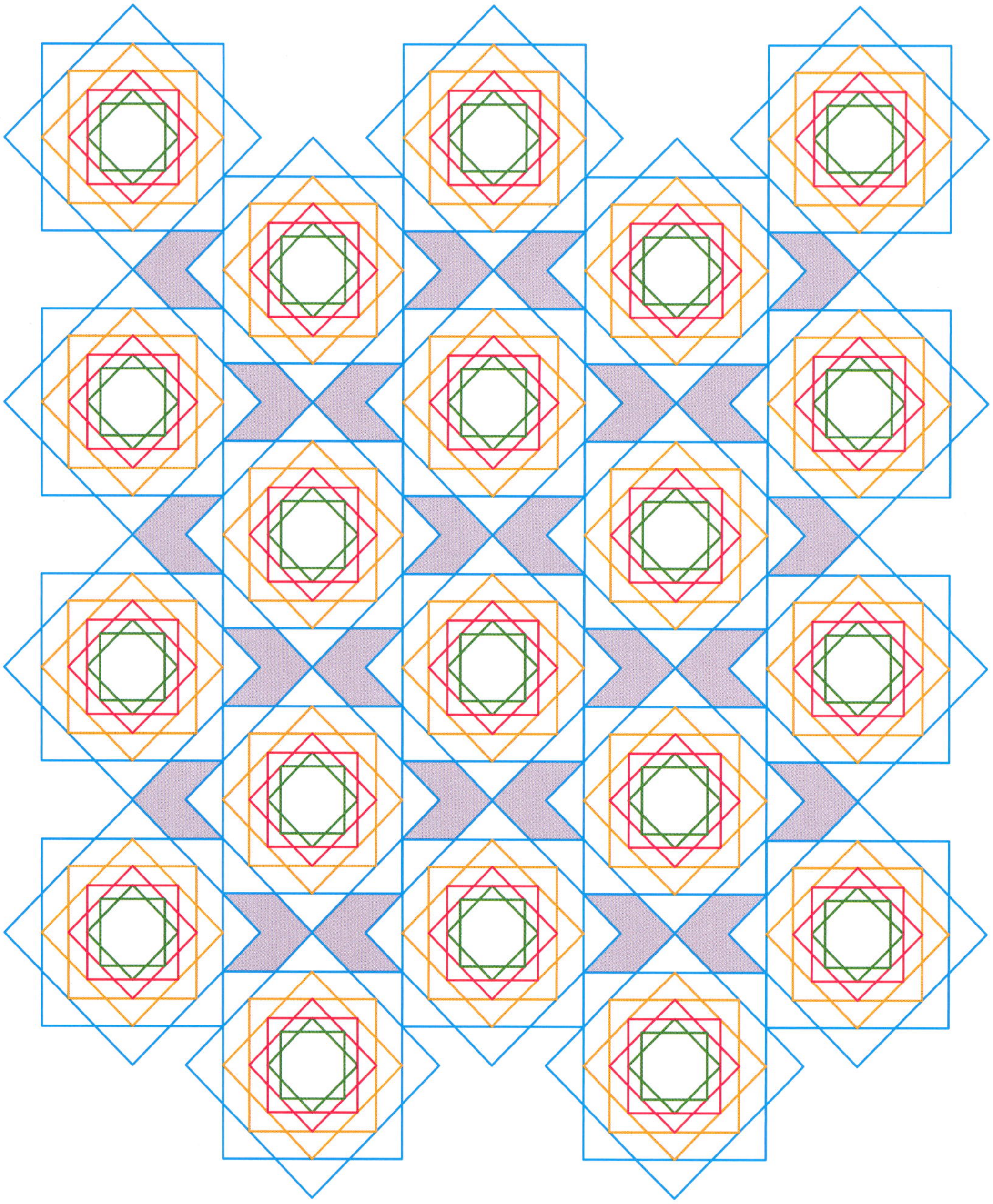

IZNIK POLYCHROME TILE

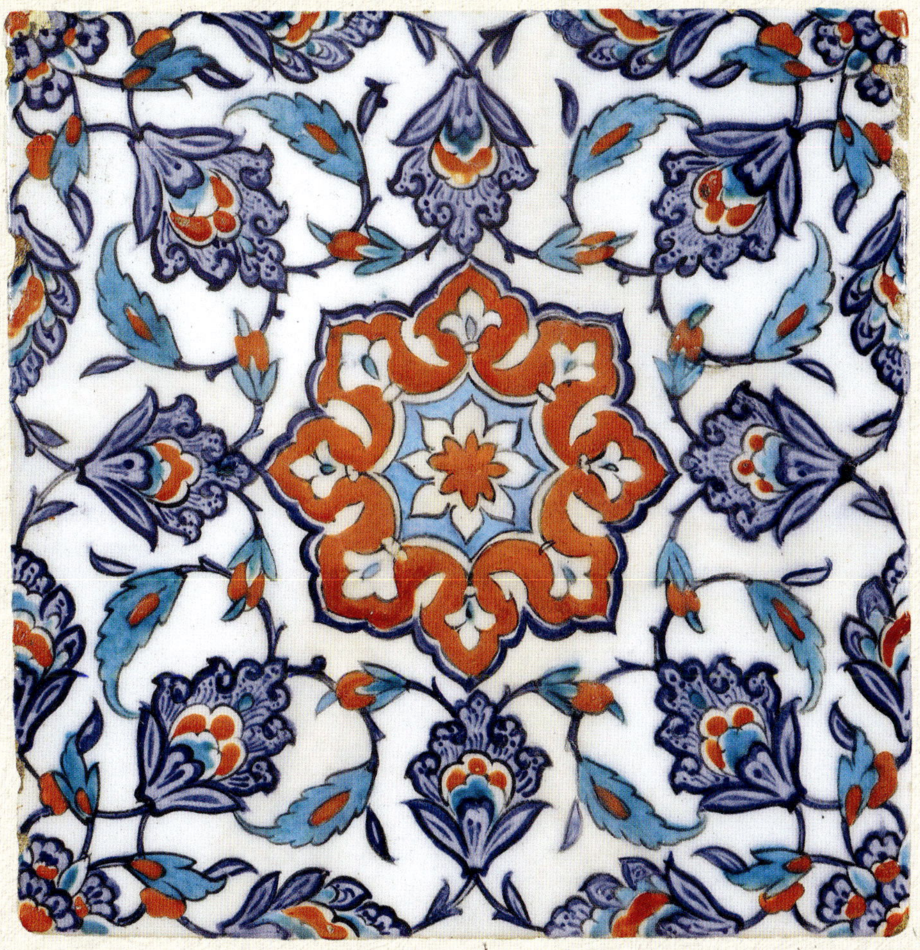

An Iznik polychrome tile, Turkey, c.1580.

Looking at the Geometric Structure

This beautiful Iznik tile from Turkey is the first pattern of the eight-pointed
star grid series. The section that will be designed is only an eighth of the
total pattern. It will be reflected to form a complete unit and then repeated.
You can see this in the tile images below and on diagrams 1 and 2.

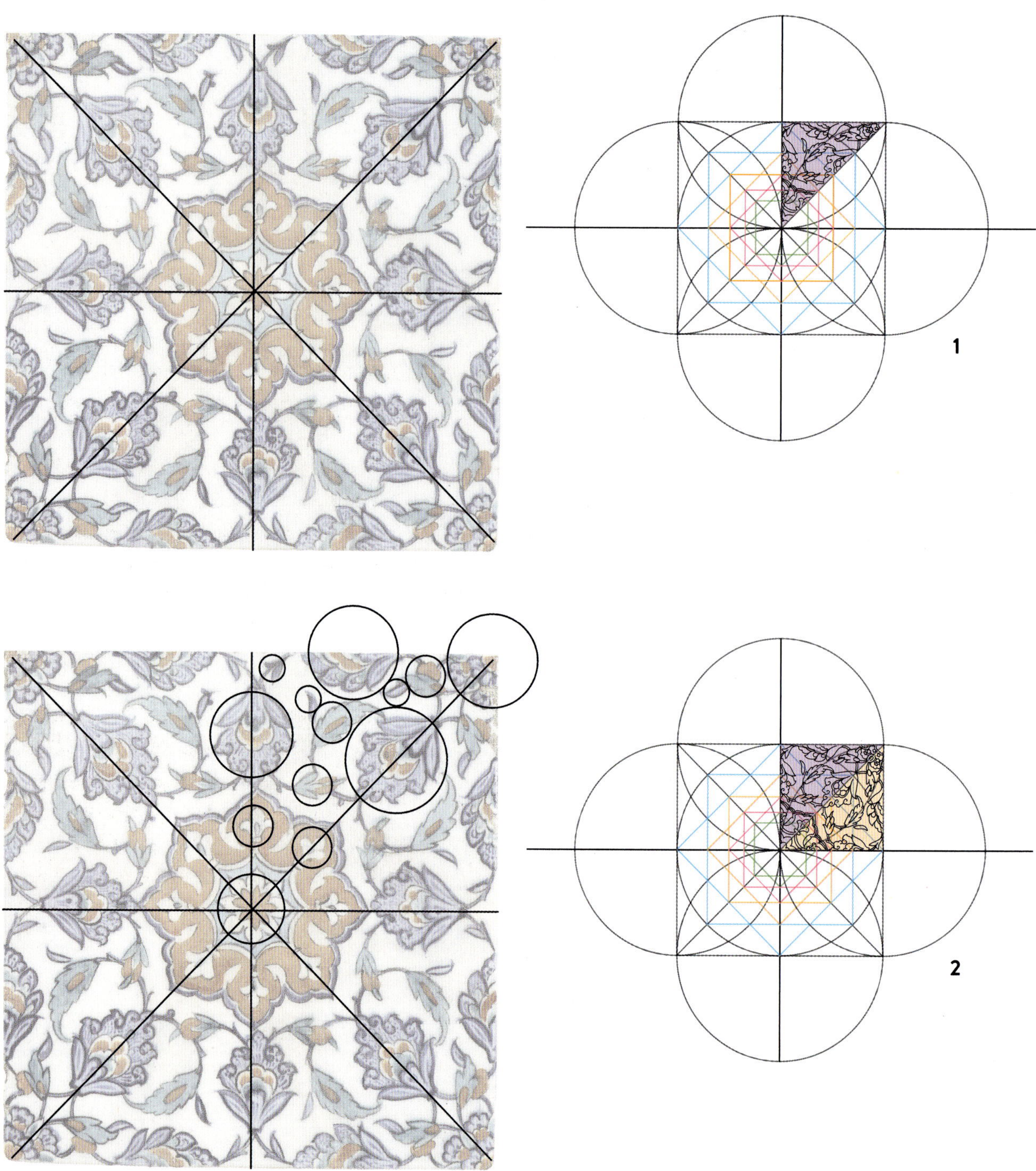

Drawing the Pattern

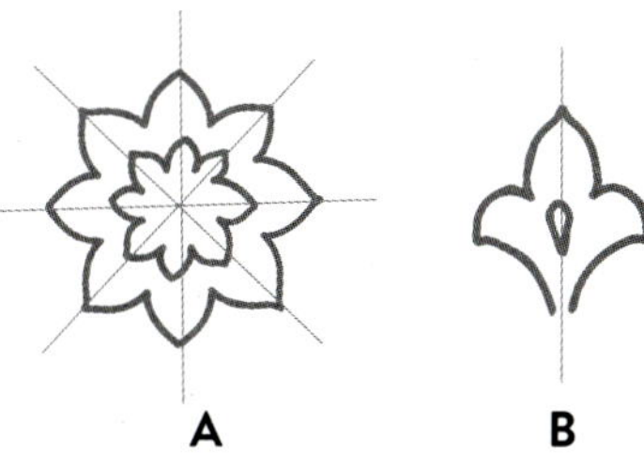

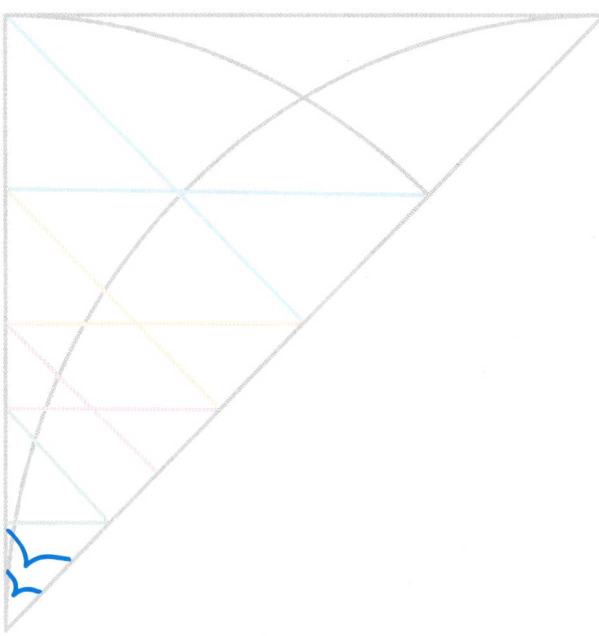

1 The starting point of this design is the centre, which, like the rest of the elements, is designed in sections. Start by drawing just two half petals of flower A.

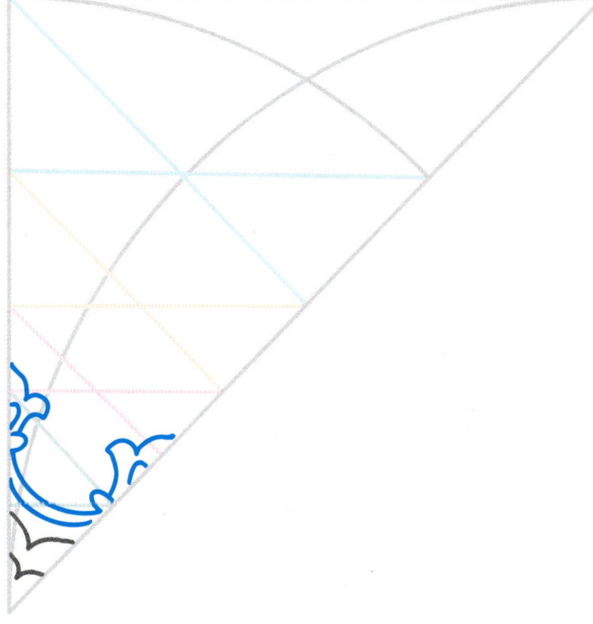

2 Near flower A, inside the pink star section, draw two halves of shape B. One half will be placed on the vertical line; the other will be placed on the diagonal. Extend a small curve connecting both halves from the bottom.

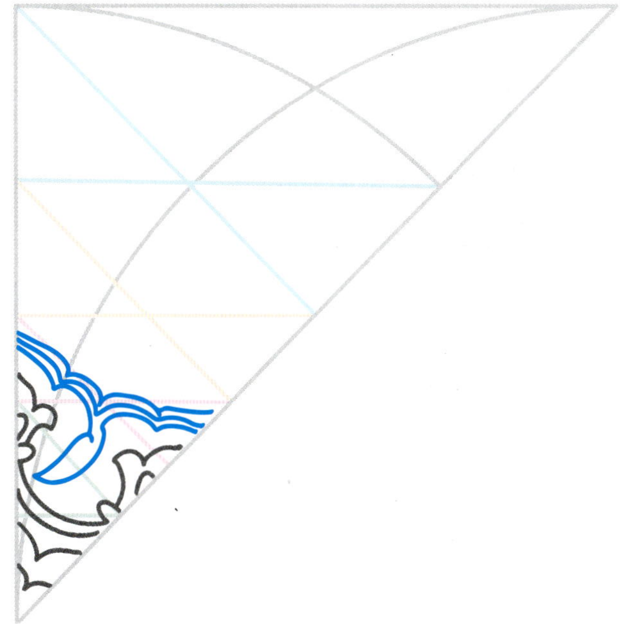

3 The guidelines of the pink star creates a great guideline for us and we will use that to draw two sets of four small curves to act like a frame. Between the two sets, draw a leaf pointing diagonally. You can draw this shape as shown in the diagram or you can use your own style of drawing a curved frame, making sure you are following the guidelines of the star.

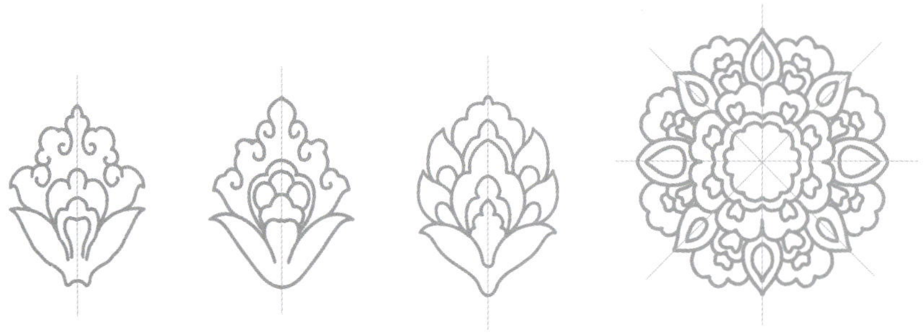

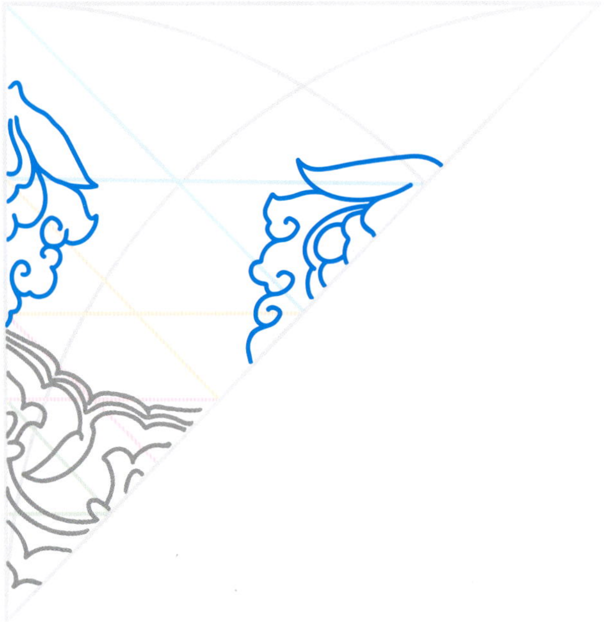

4 Turn flower C upside down and carefully place half of it on the vertical line, inside the guidelines we have in the section. Place half of flower D, also upside down, on the diagonal line, mostly within the guidelines.

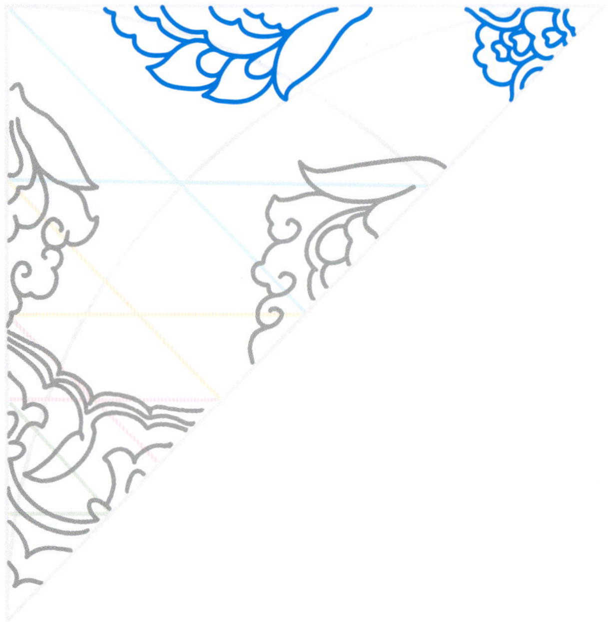

5 Place half of flower E onto the horizontal line at the top of the triangular section. Add a section of circular flower F in the far right corner. Having elements on that line helps to create a beautiful repeat when the tile is tessellated and placed many times.

6 Connections between the flowers are a must; they cannot be left floating in the space without branches attaching them to each other. The easiest way to look at this is to extend a small branch from the top and bottom of each flower.

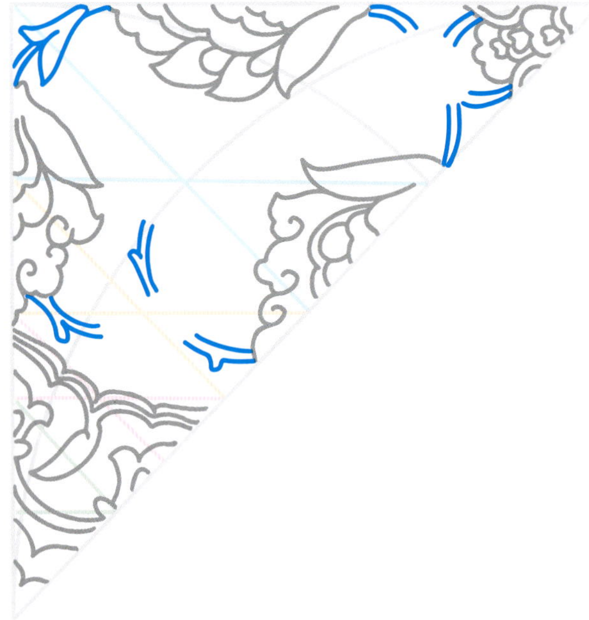

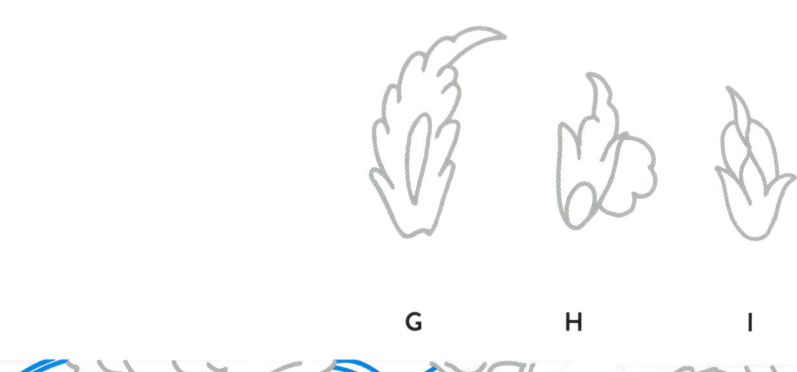

G   H   I

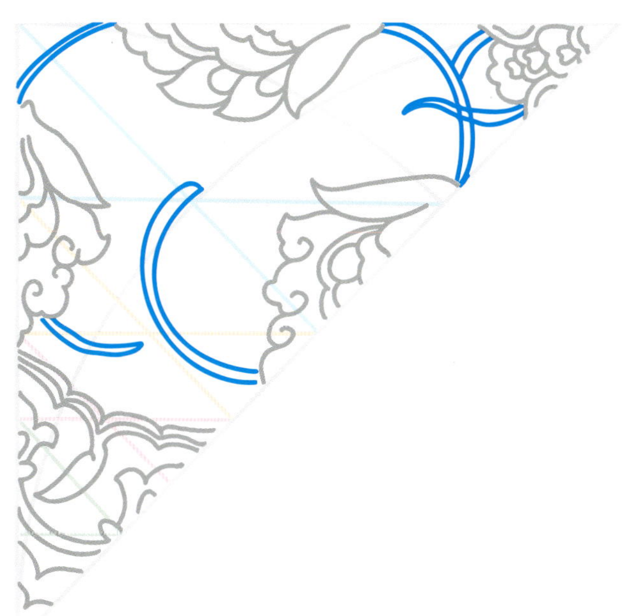

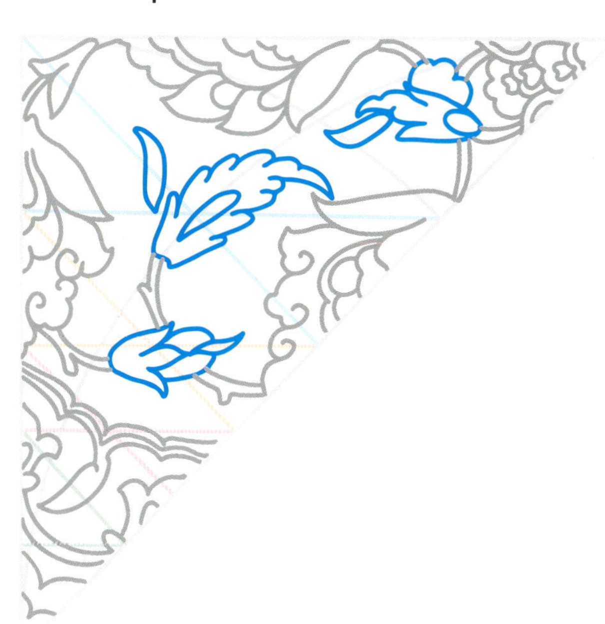

7 When the branches are fully extended, they curve.

8 There is plenty of space remaining between the flowers and this is where leaves come in. Add leaves G and H to the branches, along with flower I.

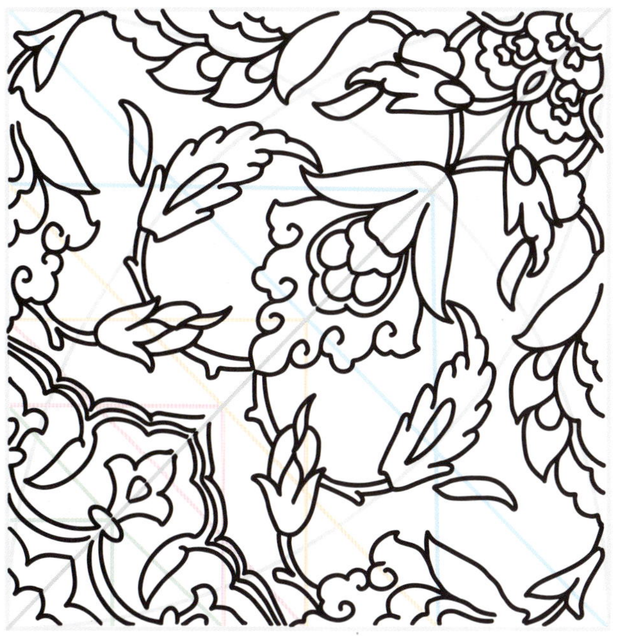

9 When that eighth is completed, reflect it to complete the full quarter, then reflect again and repeat to complete the design. It is important for all the half motifs to connect in the repeats to create a full pattern for you to enjoy. You can also change certain components in the flowers if you are keen to create your own pattern.

Tessellating the Pattern

In Step 5, I mentioned that the half flowers placed on top of the triangular section will create a different appearance when the pattern is tessellated. If you look at the tessellation, you can see how this small addition has given us another pattern with a different floral centre which is also very charming.

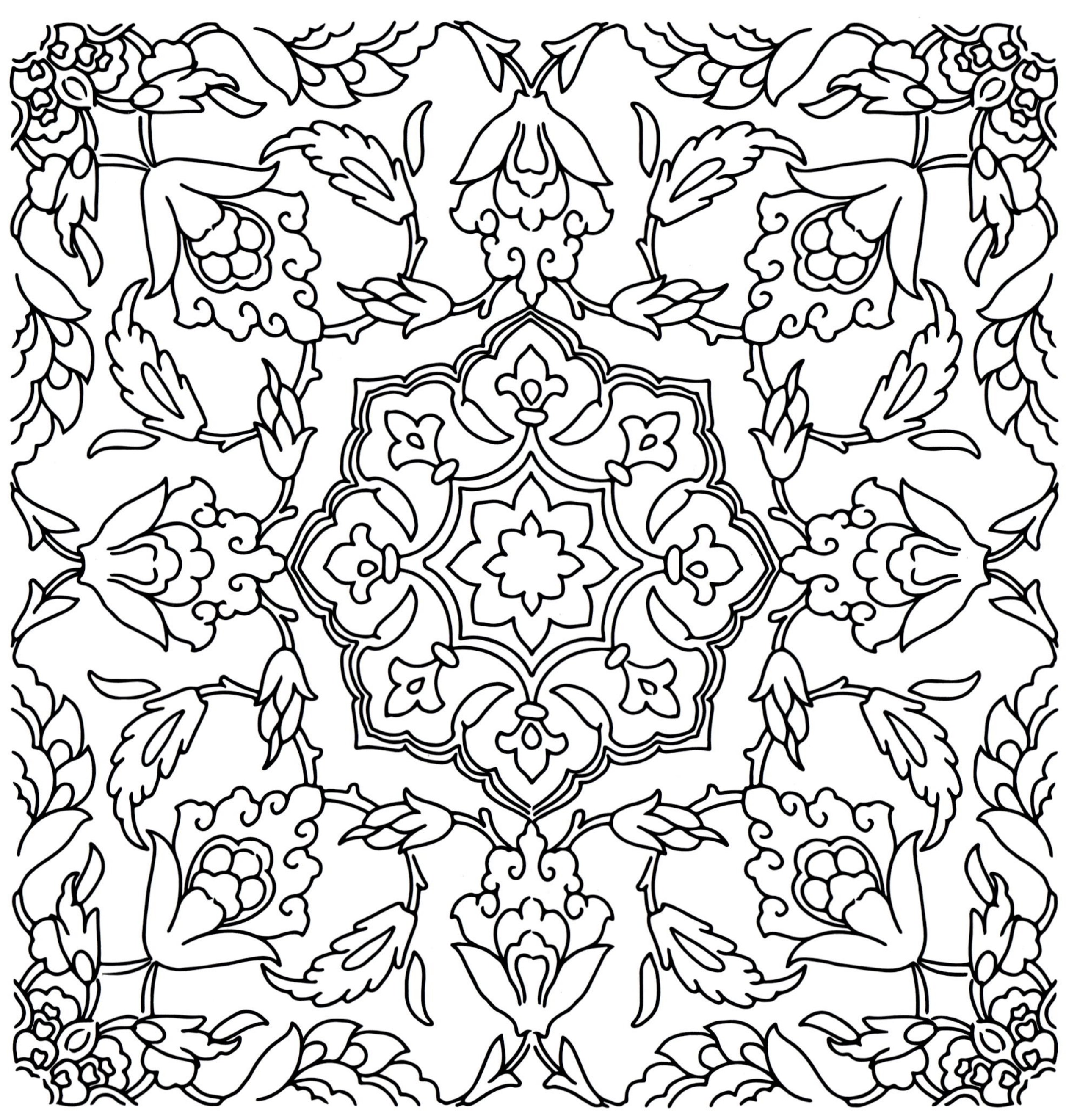

TURKISH QURAN CARPET PAGE

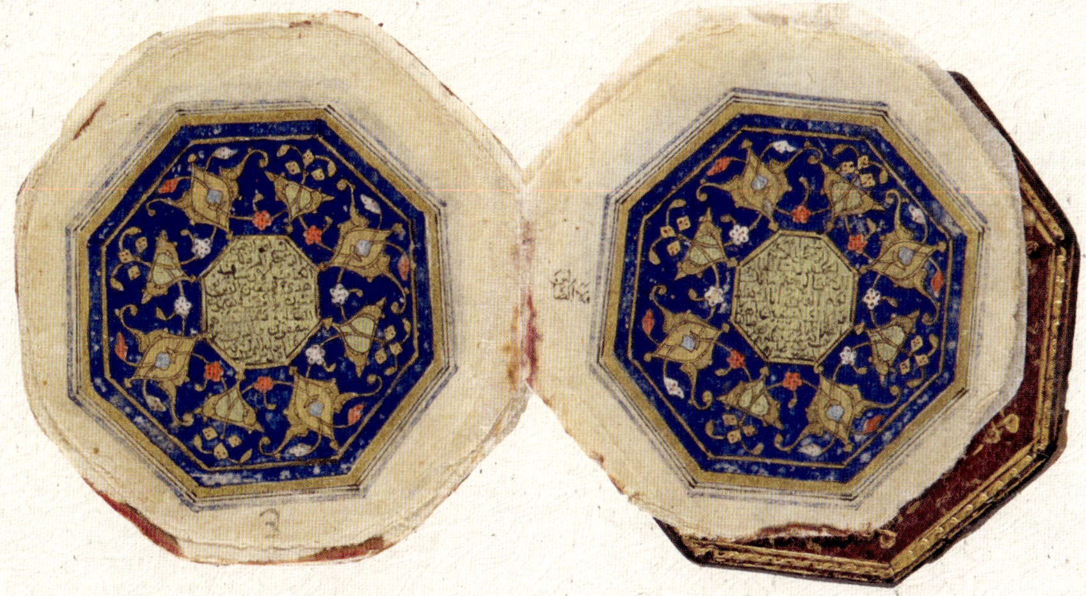

An illuminated miniature Quran, Turkey, Ottoman, sixteenth century.

For our eighth pattern, we will study a stunning carpet page from a very small Turkish Quran produced in the sixteenth century. This Quran is made of 338 pages and the script used is Ghubari, copied by Husayn ibn Hasan al-Hasani during the Ottoman period. These pages are part of the opening section of this Quran, hence their extra detail and ornamental nature.

Patterns in manuscripts are often either too advanced or have a different geometric consideration from the star grids that I have provided for you to study. It is also generally a challenge to find patterns which are available and copyright-free. They are always a treasure when found, though.

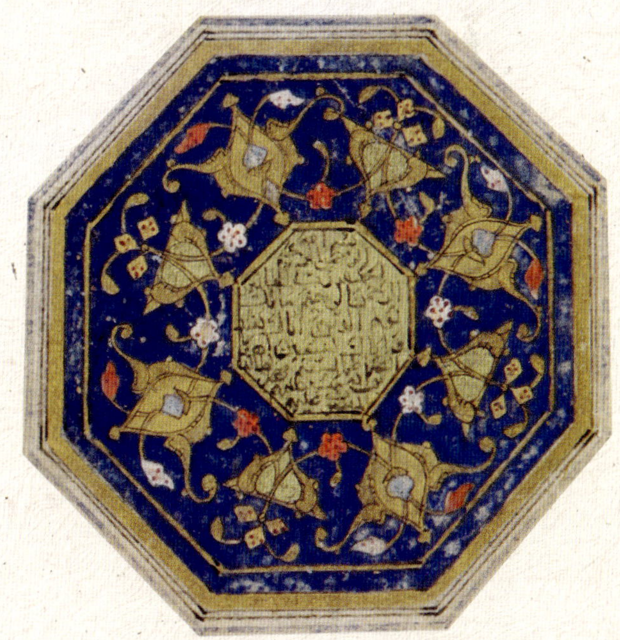

Looking at the Geometric Structure

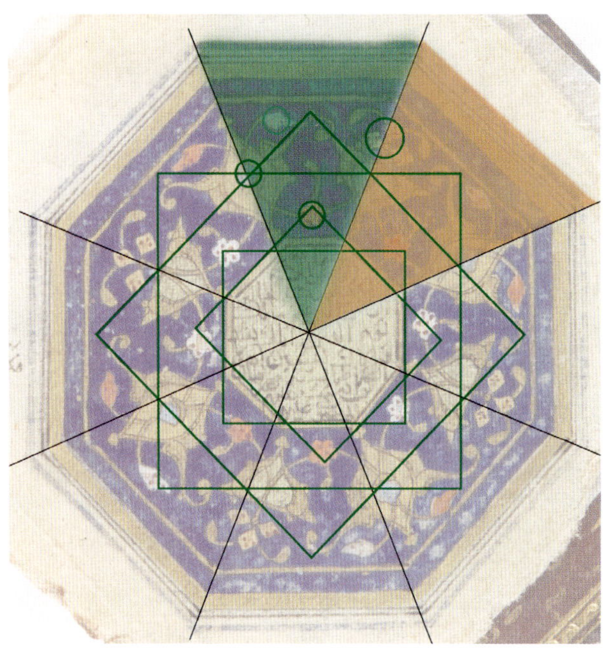

There are some inaccuracies in the pattern and the octagonal shape, but it is a great starting point for beginners, since the inner shapes are considered very simple and are also popular in many other examples. The method of designing in one section and reflecting it is the same as in previous pattern studies.

Adjusting the Geometry to an Octagonal Design

Since you will be working with the octagonal shape rather than the eight-pointed star, there are some additional considerations to be taken into account. You will need to follow the next ten steps to adjust the geometry before starting.

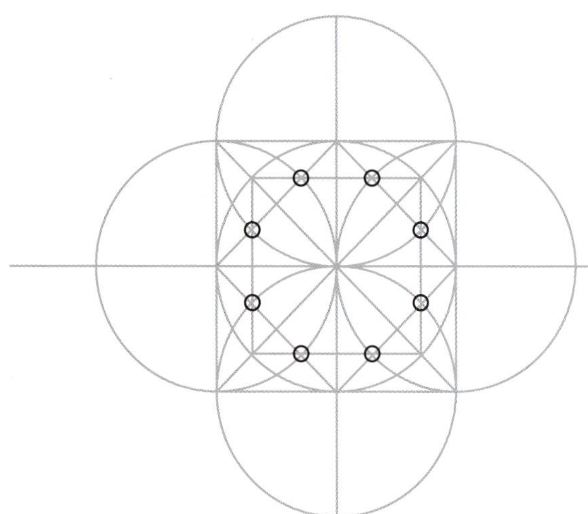

1 Use the pattern from Step 20 of the eight-pointed star grid (p.102). Mark eight points where the regular and dynamic squares intersect.

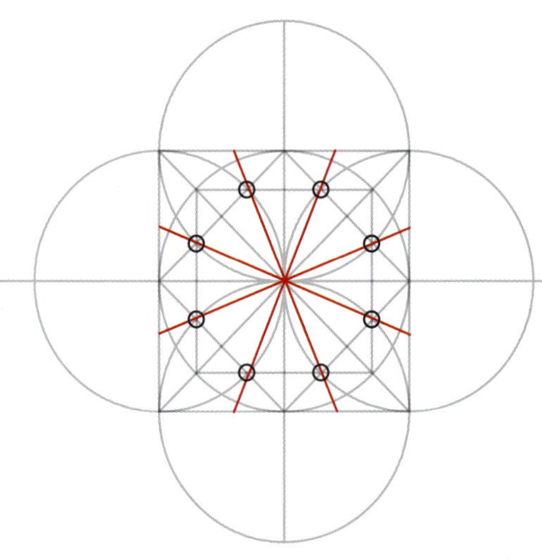

2 Extend diagonal lines from these marked points to pass through the centre to the corresponding opposite point. Make sure the lines extend to the largest square.

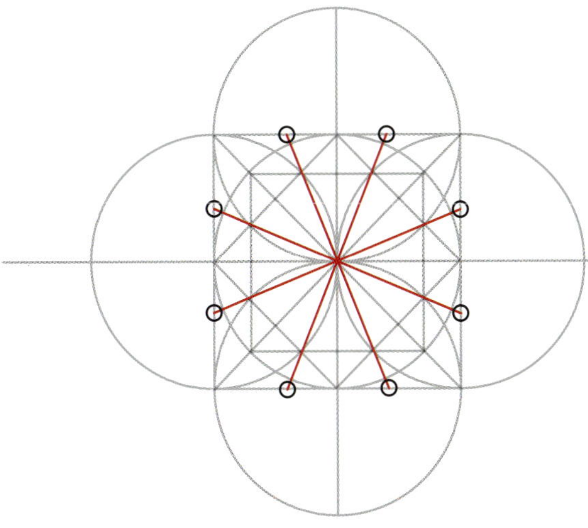

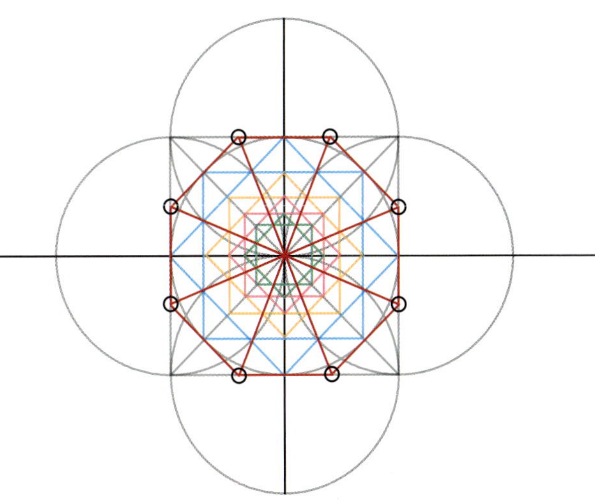

3 Mark the ends of these lines on the largest square.

4 From these marks, connect the lines from the top to create an octagon that will frame the central circle.

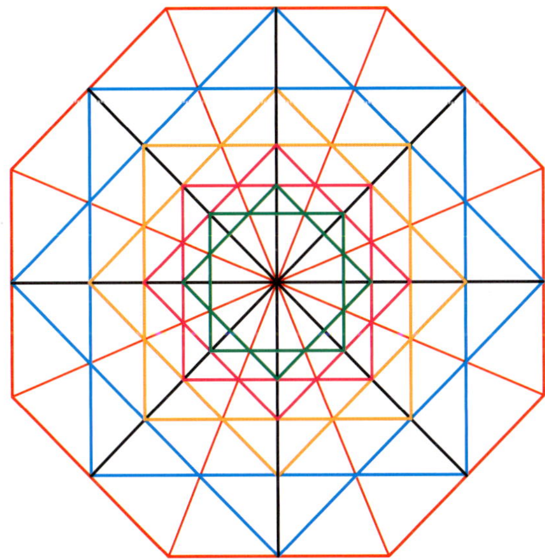

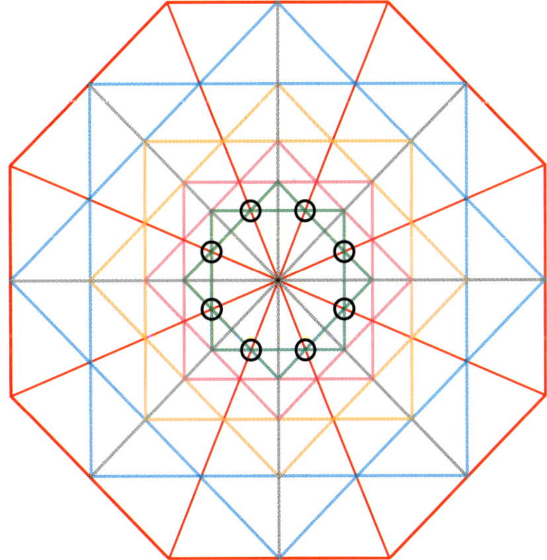

5 You can trace the design using tracing paper to pick up the octagon and the four eight-pointed stars, so you do not get confused by the circles or the additional marks you previously made.

6 Going inwards to the smallest (green) eight-pointed star, mark the points where they meet the lines you made in Step 2 (the red lines).

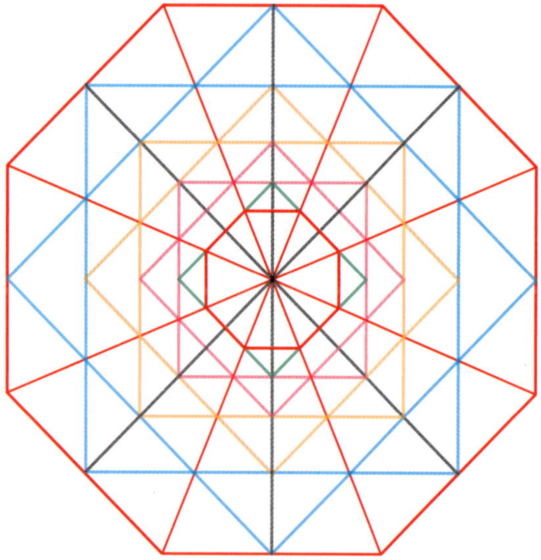

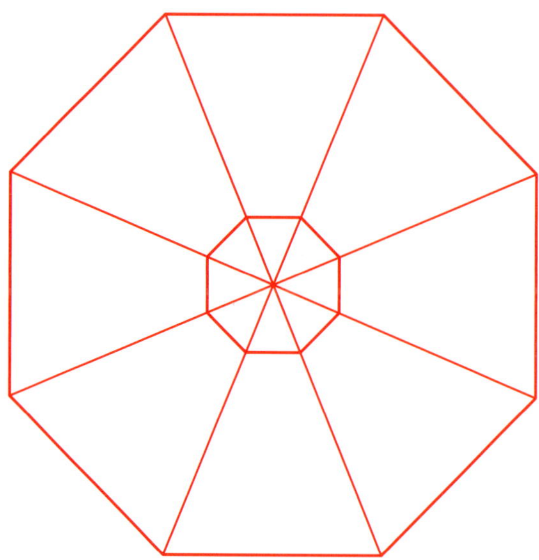

7 Draw a small octagon inside the smallest (green) eight-pointed star, which would frame any text that appears on the page.

8 You can trace the diagram once more, this time only including the two octagons. This is useful to see the main shapes you will be working with, without all the lines. However, you will need the lines for the actual design, so do not discard any of your process papers.

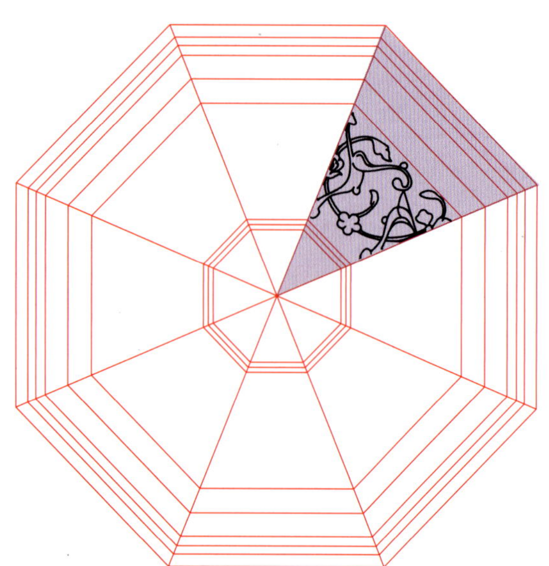

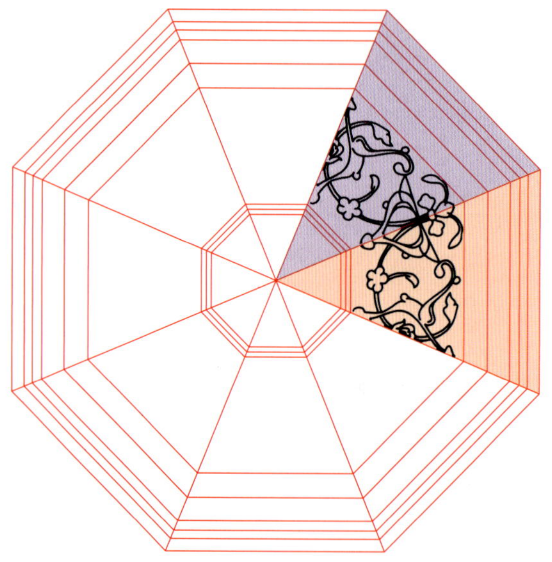

9 The design has a lot of framing and a number of additional octagons that progress inwards. There are inaccuracies in the original, I think the placement of the octagons was guessed, but you can calculate where you want to place them and draw them as shown.

10 Reflect the design section to make the repeat unit. Repeat across the octagon to create the whole pattern.

Thinking About Tessellation

Before the pattern is drawn, it is interesting to think about a tessellation made up of the octagonal shape and the dynamic square. It is another way of looking at how the design can be expanded upon.

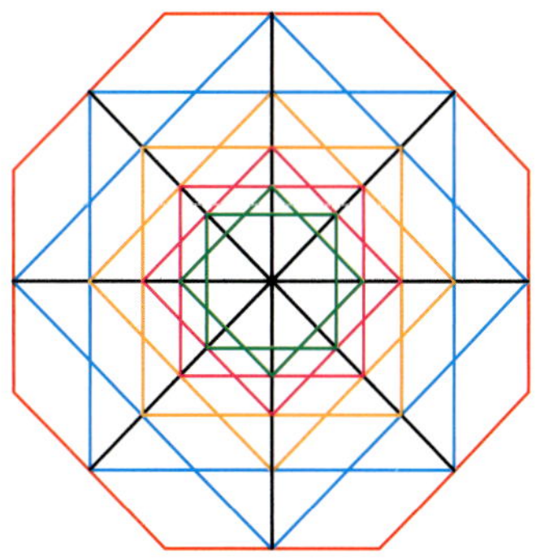

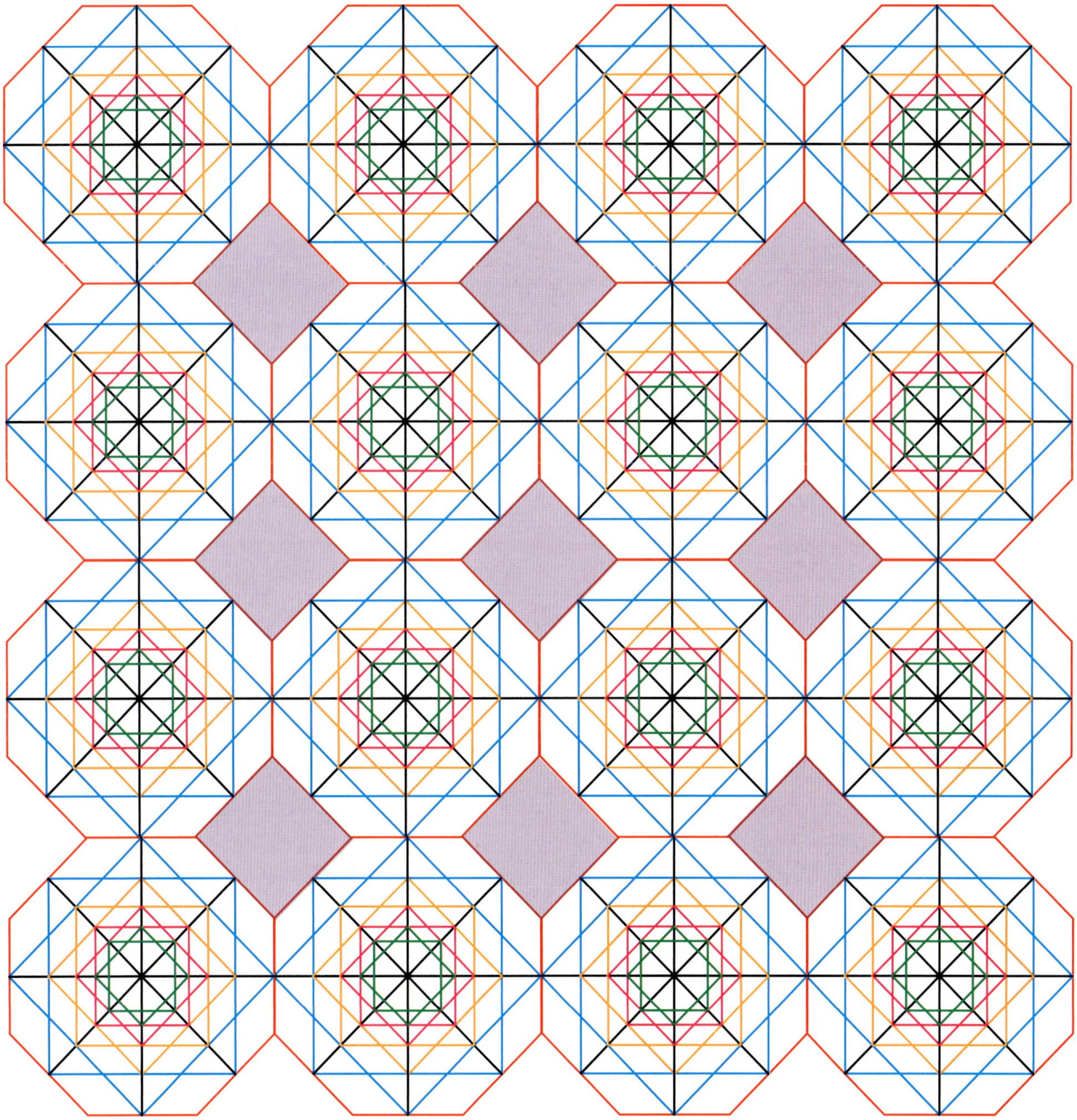

Drawing the Pattern

You will notice that this design is simple, once you figure out the geometry and the design section.

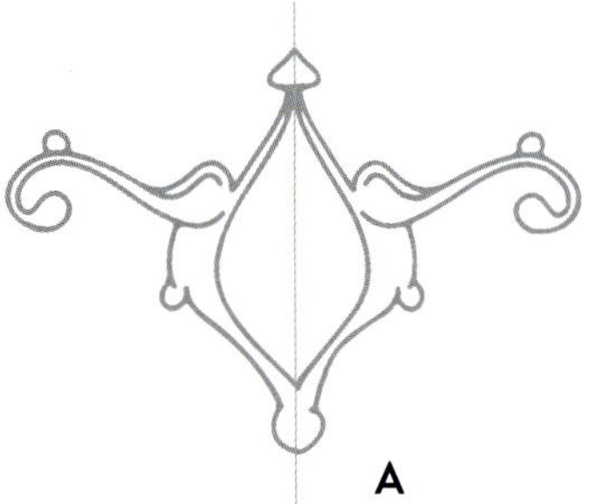

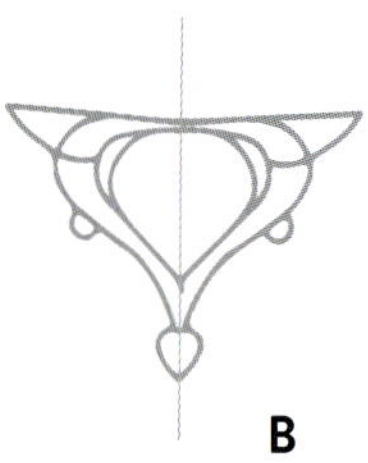

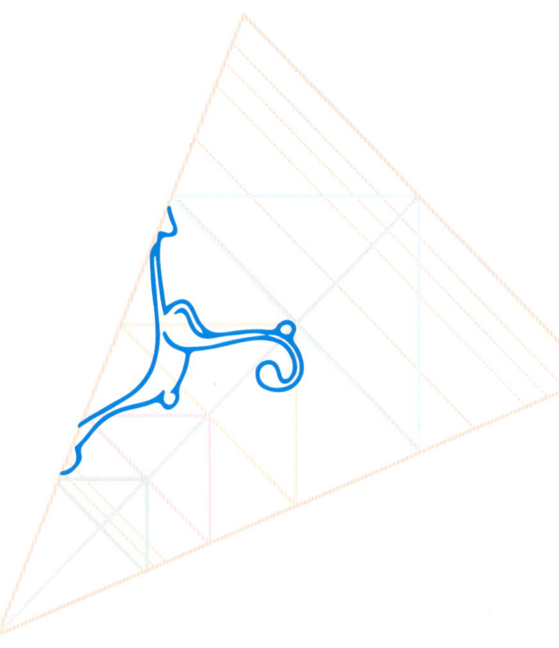

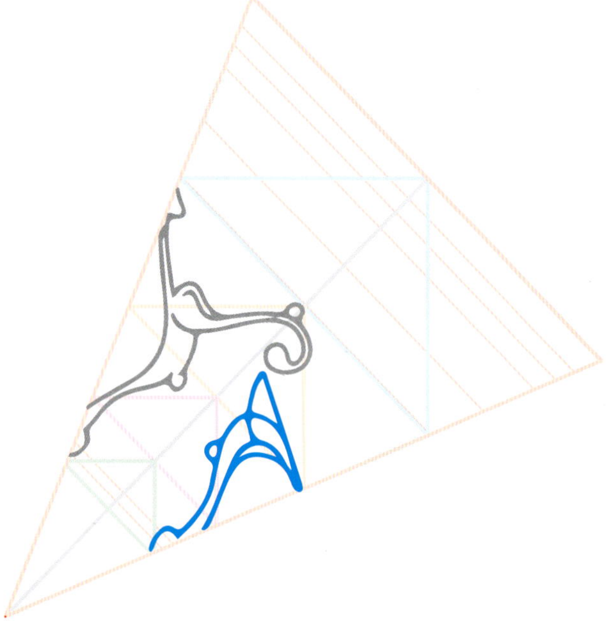

1 Start with the placement of the inorganic shapes on the symmetry lines. First, place half of shape A on the left diagonal line.

2 Second, place half of shape B on the right diagonal line. Both shapes are placed mostly within the three inner eight-pointed stars.

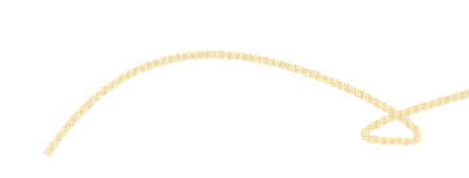

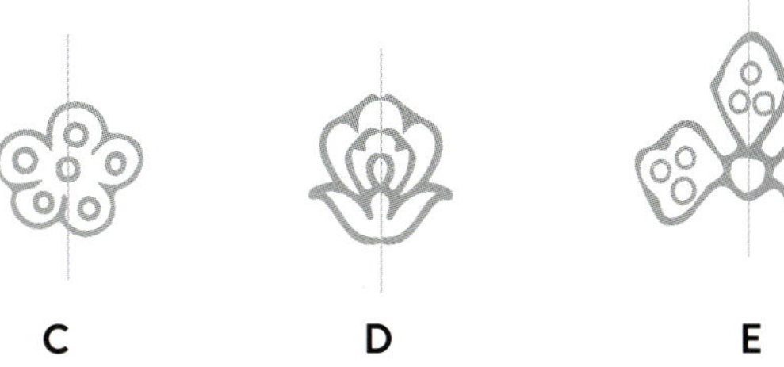

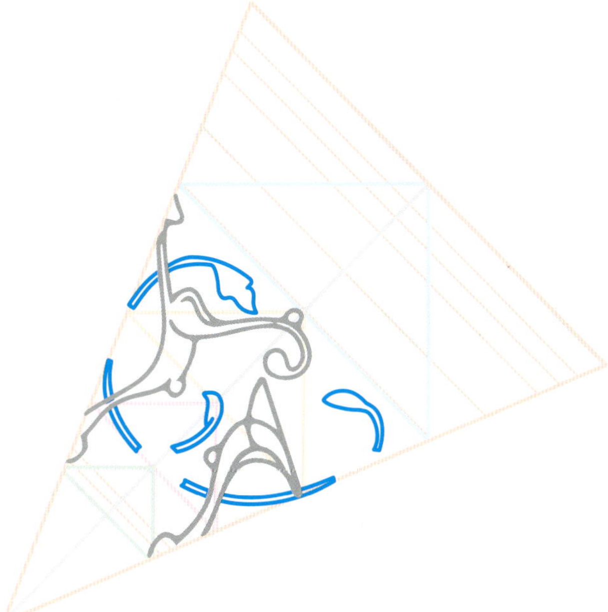

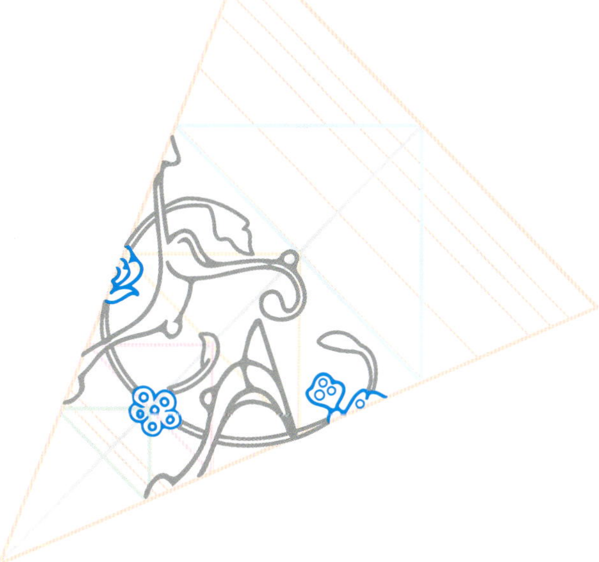

3 It is important to create a connection between the two shapes via branches. The inorganic shapes act as frames to the simple floral motifs that will be drawn in the upcoming steps. Draw simple leaves at the ends of the branches that come from the top and bottom sides of the inorganic shapes.

4 Place flower C in the middle between the two inorganics, flower D inside inorganic shape A and flower E next to inorganic shape B.

5 The design section is now complete. Make sure any additions and alterations are made at this stage, if required.

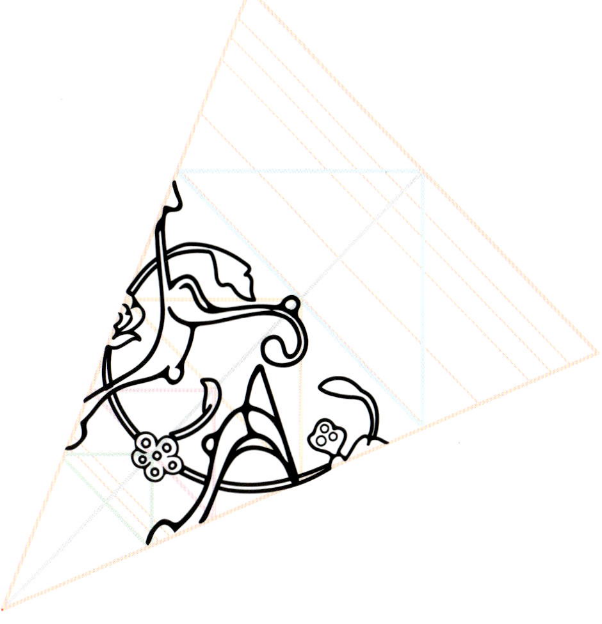

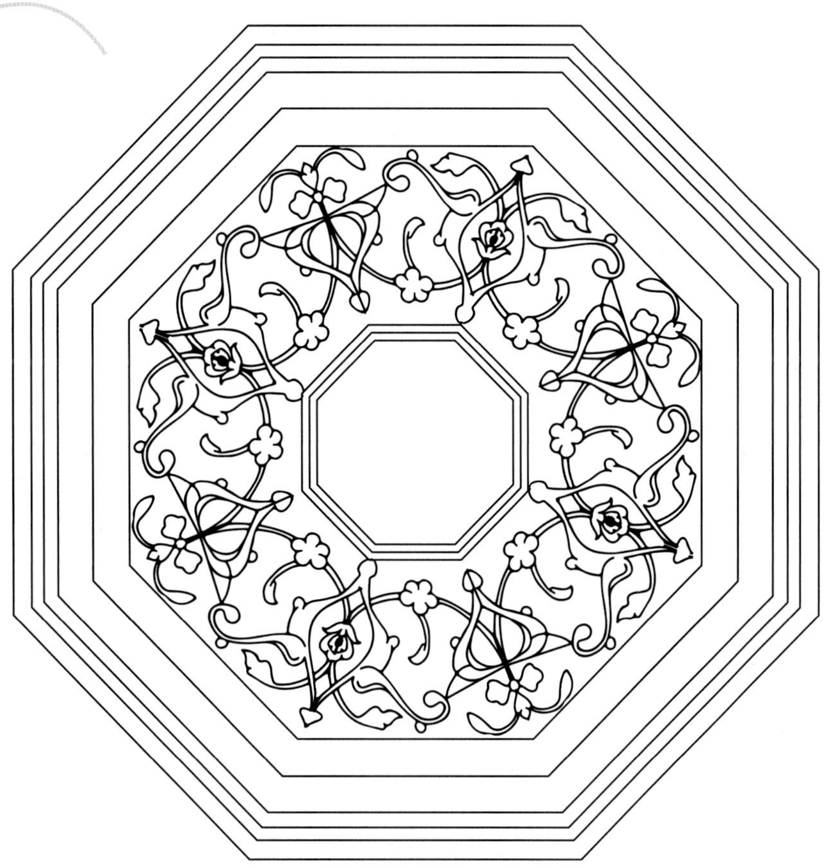

6 Reflect and repeat the section to create the full pattern to be traced and transferred onto watercolour paper, where it can be painted or brought to life with other media.

Tessellating and Finalising the Pattern

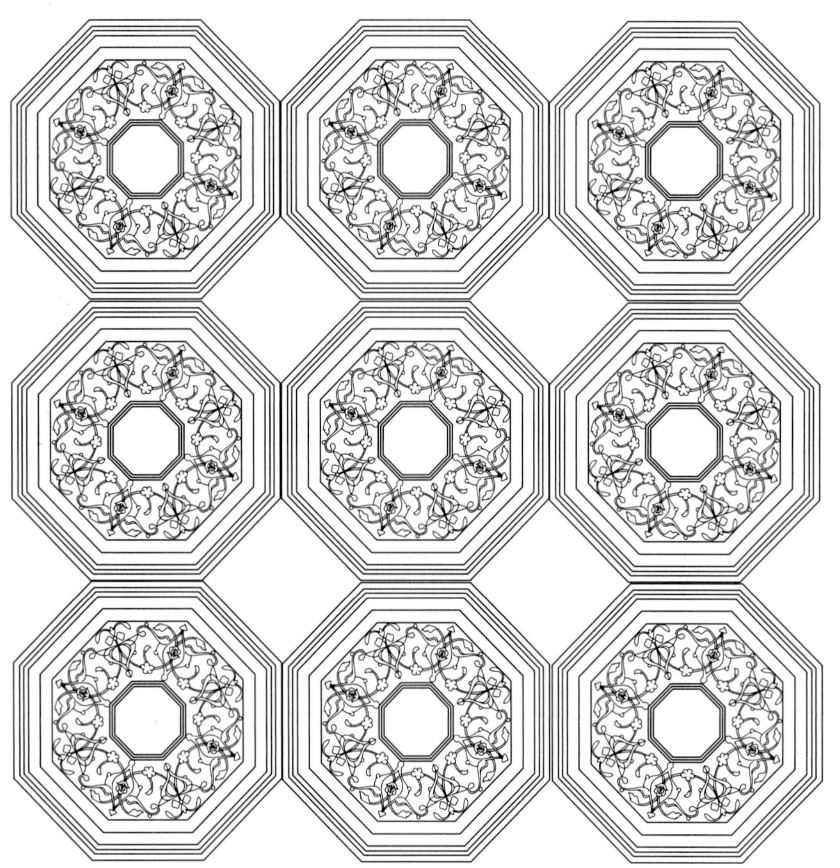

As previously mentioned, tessellating this pattern will give you more painting possibilities, and it's nice to see how this pattern would work in this way. There is a missing design for the dynamic square, which can be left empty, like the central octagon, or you could add Arabic calligraphy or anything else you would like to experiment with. Keep an open mind and try to push your creative limits.

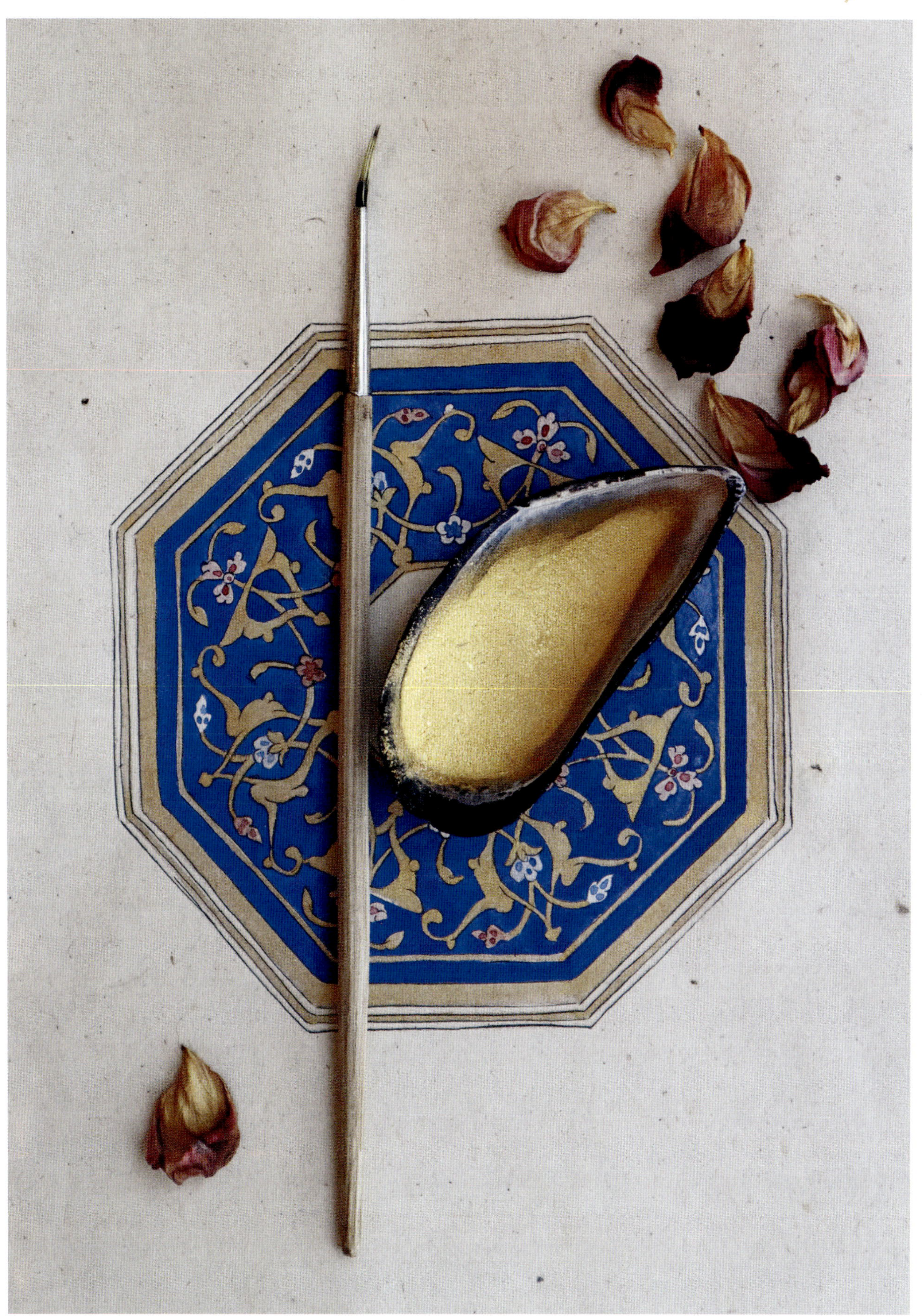

DAMASCUS POTTERY TILE

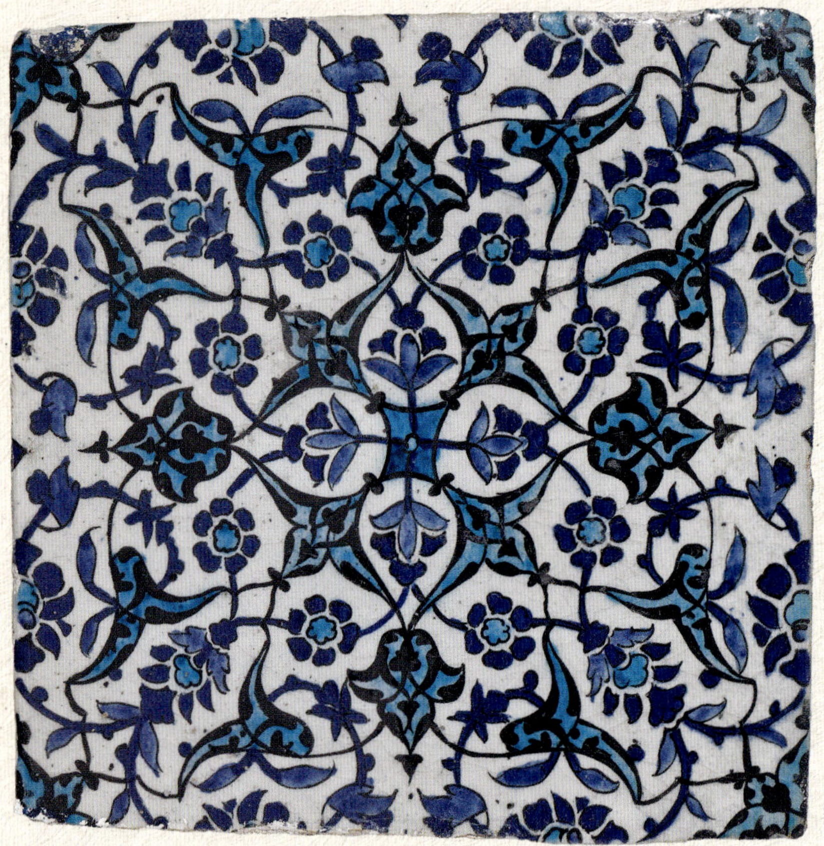

A Damascus pottery tile, Syria, late sixteenth/early
seventeenth century.

The ninth design to study is slightly more detailed than the previous ones. It is a tile
from Damascus that was produced in Syria during the Ottoman period in either the
late sixteenth or early seventeenth century. The design of this tile is similar to tiles in
the Arab Hall at Leighton House Museum in London, which were brought back from
Damascus in the late nineteenth century (1864–79).

Looking at the Geometric Structure

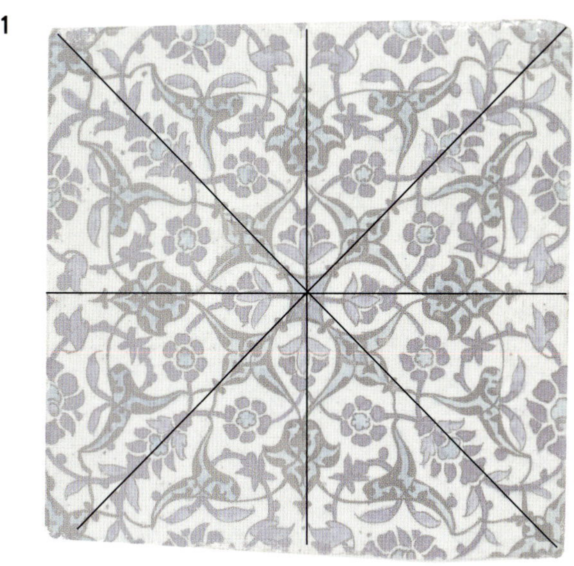

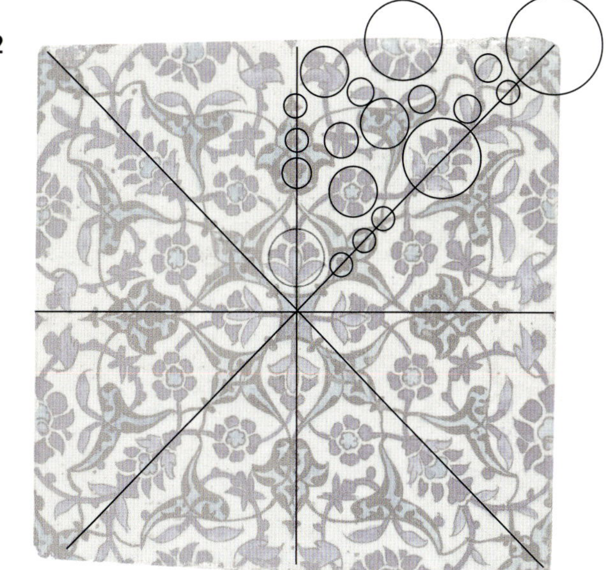

When analysing a pattern on a tile, it is important to really look at the design within it and count how many times motifs are repeated and how the centre of the tile looks. These elements give us an indication of the type of grid we will be working on (1). It is also useful to circle the flowers on a printout of the tile image to get an idea of how the motifs are displayed (2).

Counting the motifs tells us that some of the elements are either repeated as fours or eights and the centre is a dynamic square; therefore, this pattern is based on an eight-pointed star grid (see p.99). The design is drawn in one section (3) and reflected to complete a quarter (4).

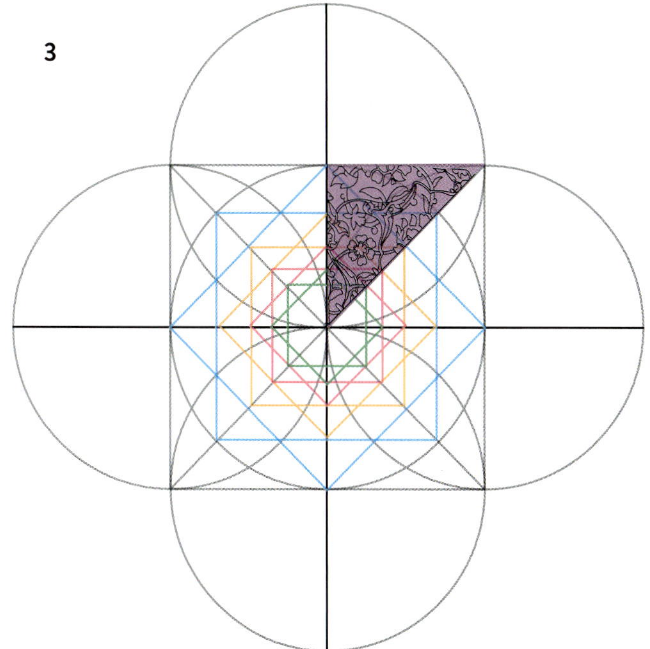

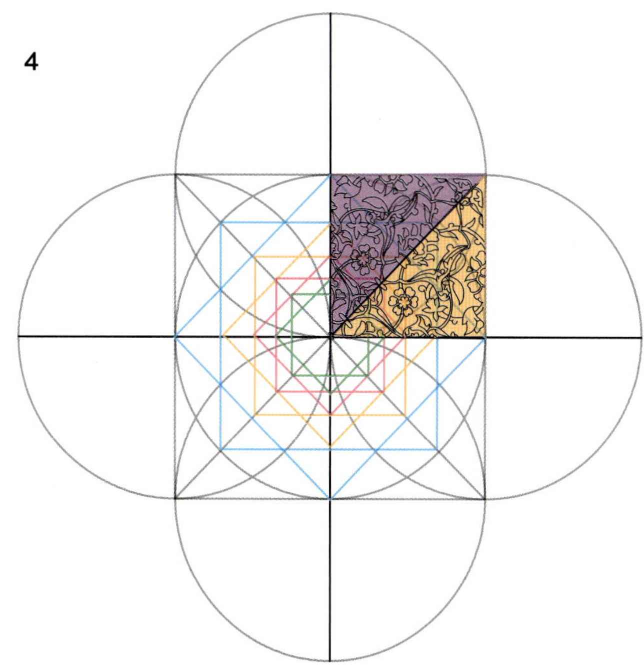

Drawing the Pattern

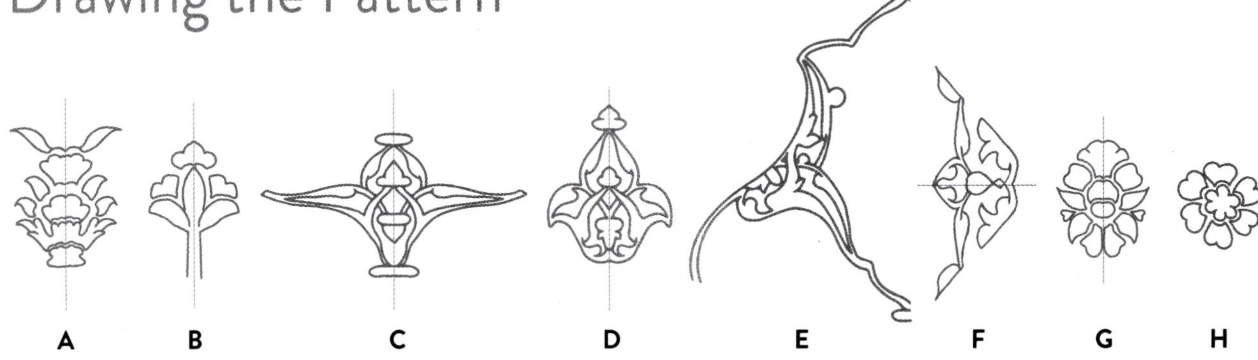

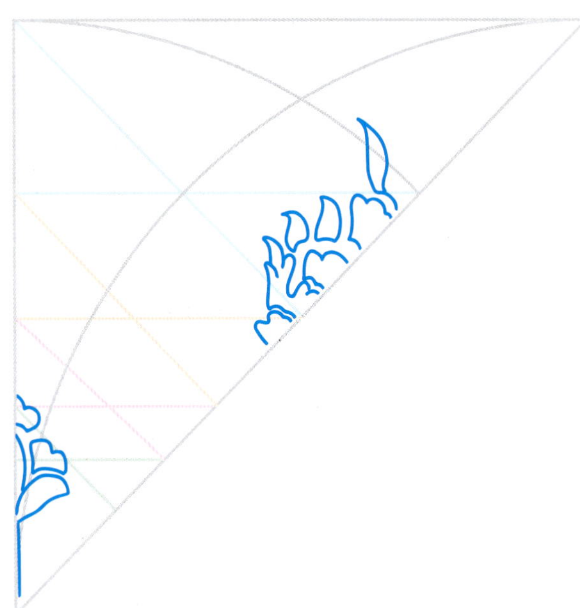

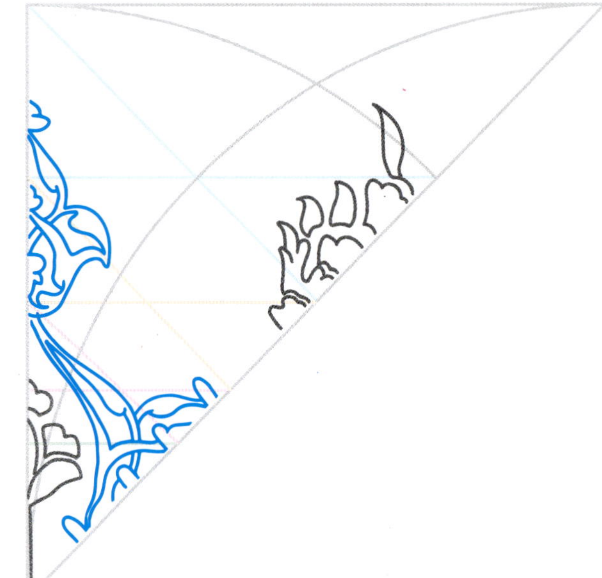

1 The first step is to identify the vertical and diagonal lines of symmetry. Place half of flower A inside the largest (blue) eight-pointed star and half of flower B on the vertical line inside the smallest (green) eight-pointed star.

2 Place half of the ornate inorganic shape C on the diagonal line inside the second (pink) eight-pointed star. It will extend to the vertical line near flower B. Above it, place half of shape D.

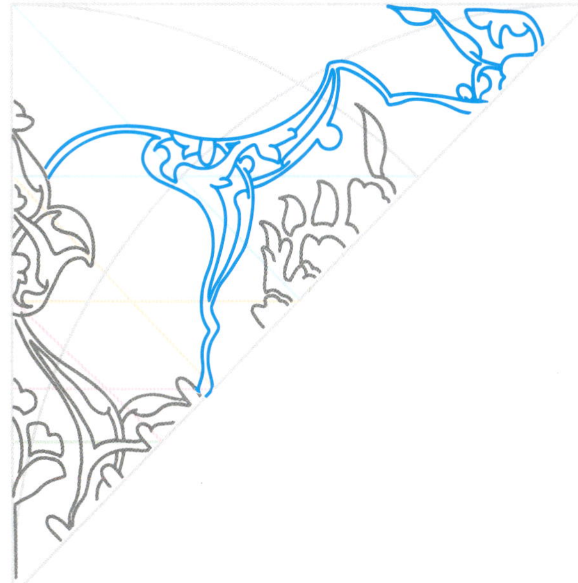

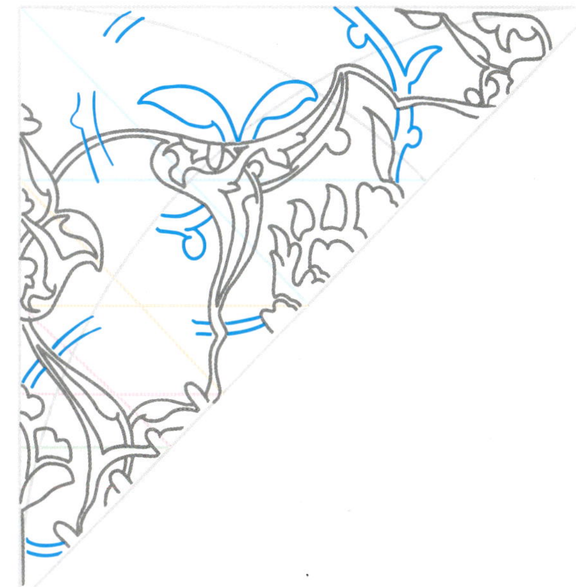

3 Draw shape E with two starting points on each of the symmetry lines: one that comes from the top of shape C and another from the side of shape D coming down to frame flower A. These inorganic shapes act like small frames for the flowers to highlight them, and to add another layer of complexity to the design that looks very attractive when painted. Add shape F in the top right corner, above shape E.

4 Even though the flowers are framed, they are still floating within the space without a connection, so extend a branch from flowers A and B. The branch extension comes from the top and bottom of each flower.

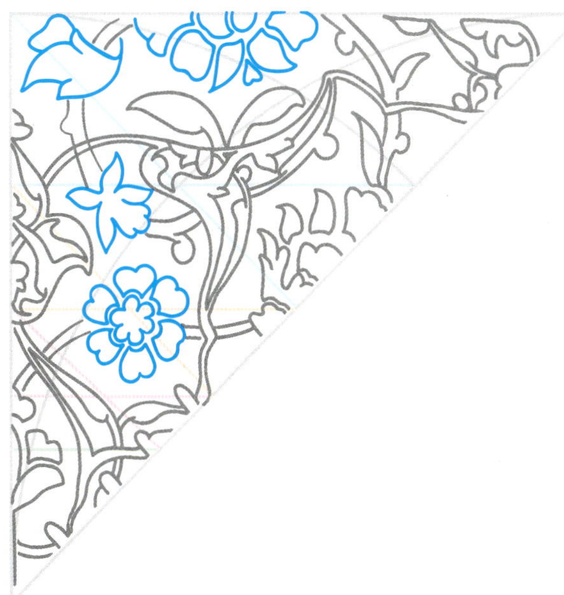

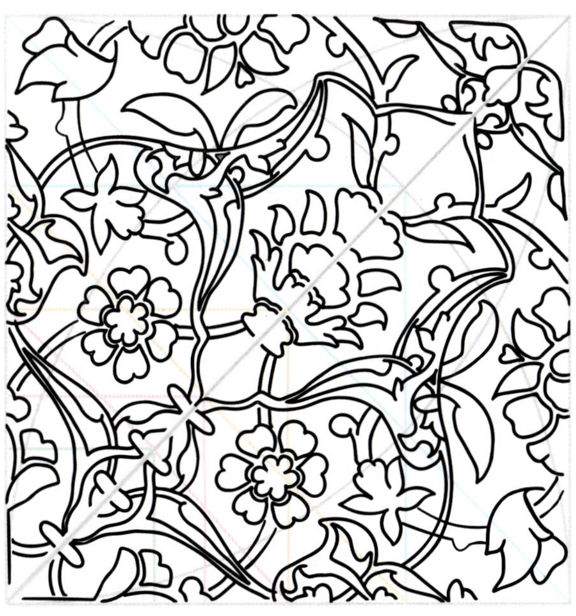

5 Add flower H to the space on the intersecting lines of the second (orange) star. Add half of flower G to the top horizontal line, which will be used for the larger tessellated pattern. Draw in small flowers to fill the other empty spaces along the branches.

6 The design section is now complete. Reflect it to make a quarter and then repeat for the full pattern.

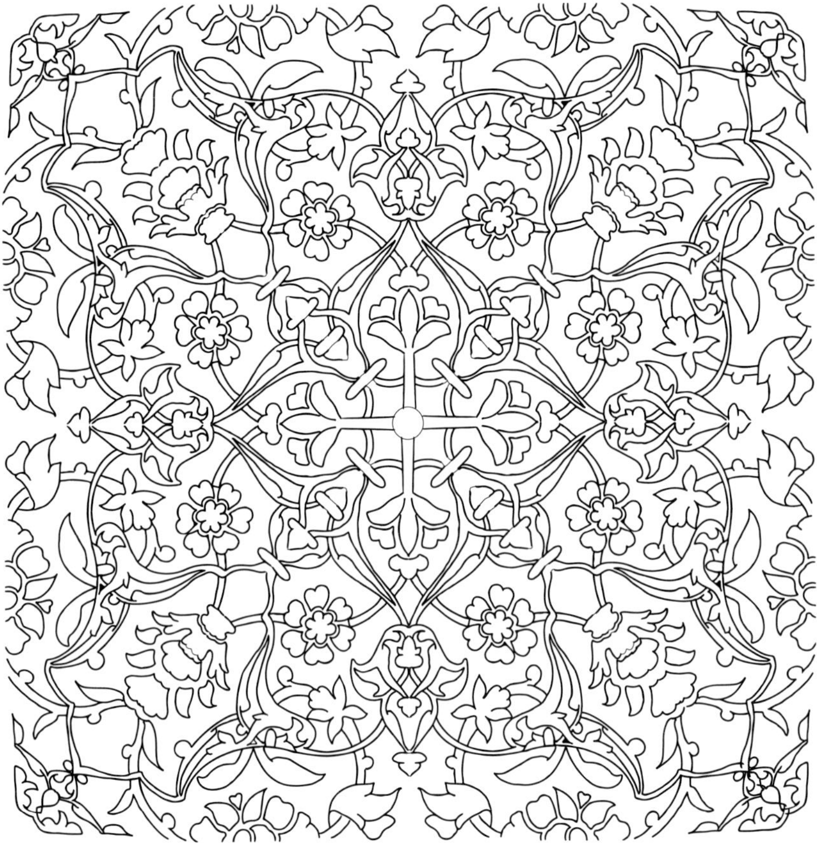

7 This is how the pattern will look when all parts of it are completed. It will be great to paint.

Tessellating the Pattern

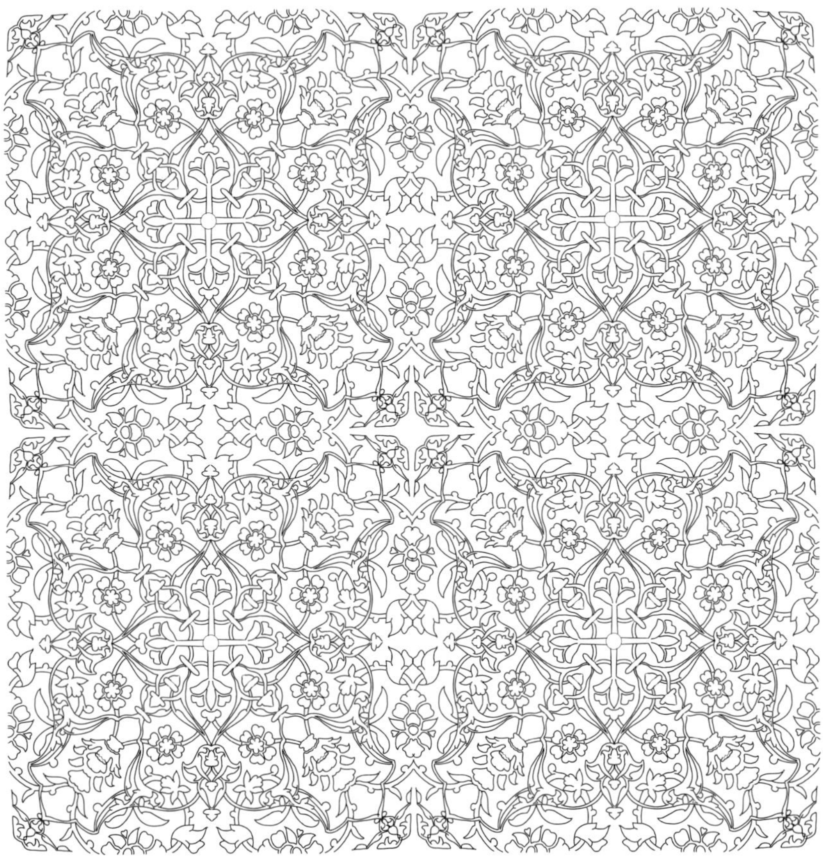

In Steps 3 and 5, shapes F and G were added onto the top horizontal line. Here is how the design will look when tessellated as four tiles. You can see there is a whole new centre and a different feel to the pattern. A painted example of this pattern is included on p.168, with a slightly larger tessellation.

UZBEKISTANI KHIVA PATTERN

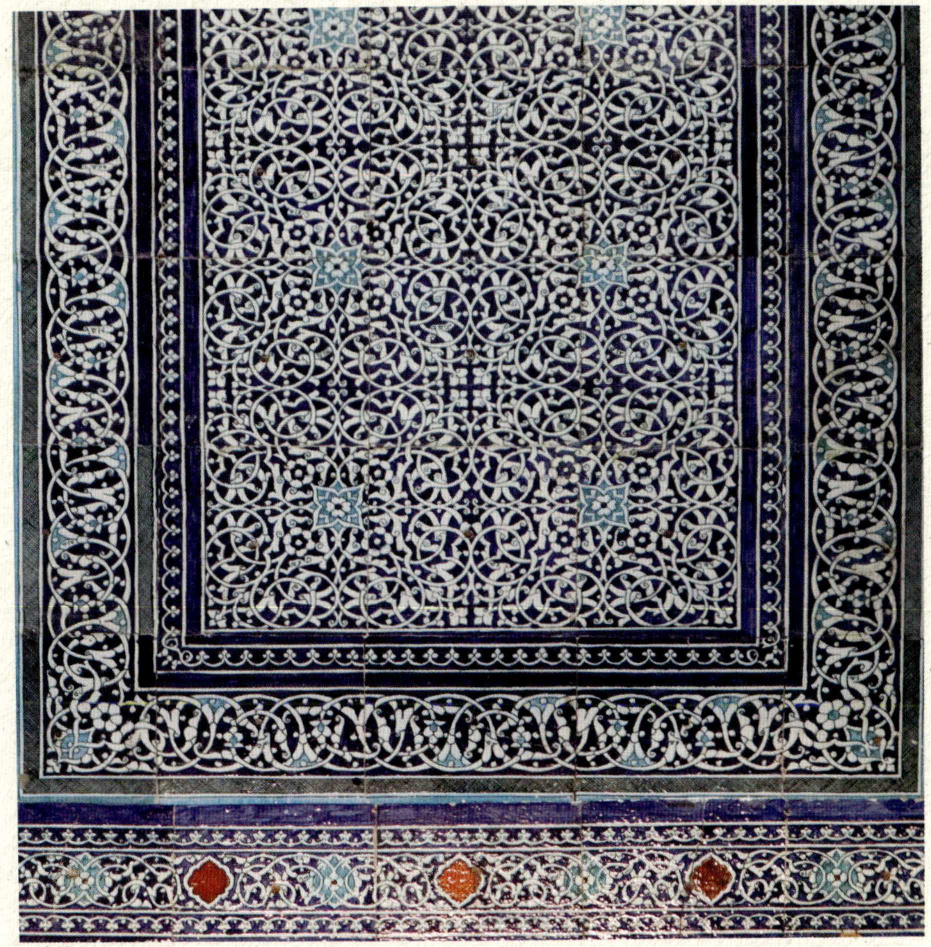

Decoration from a building in Khiva, Uzbekistan.

This is another pattern, also from Khiva, from my trip to Uzbekistan. I find studying patterns that I have seen in person more satisfying because I connected to them on a deeper level. I was so mesmerised by the large scale of these patterns that I would have happily spent days going back to visit them.

Looking at the Geometric Structure

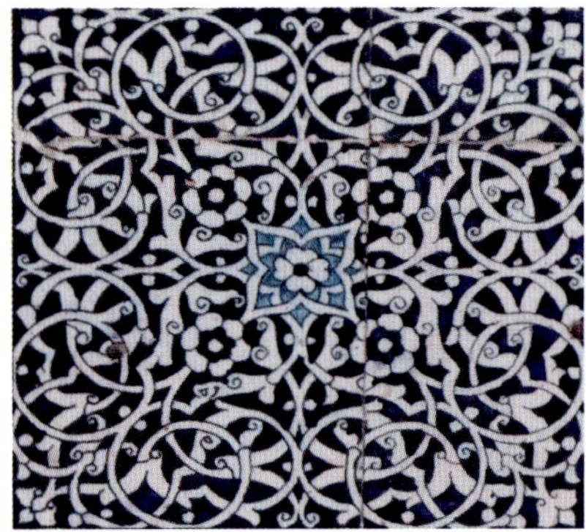

As with the two previous Uzbekistani patterns studied in the six-pointed star section (see pp.72 and 84), the elements here are simple; the complicated appearance comes from the interlacing spirals. It has an eight-pointed star construction that is repeated as a square pattern.

Drawing the Pattern

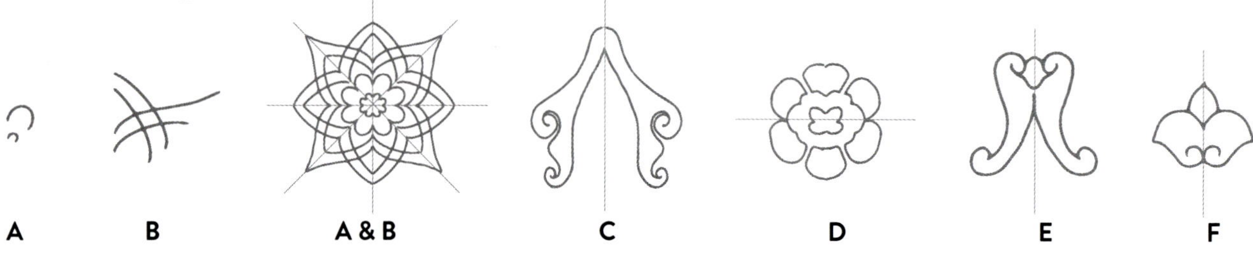

A   B   A & B   C   D   E   F

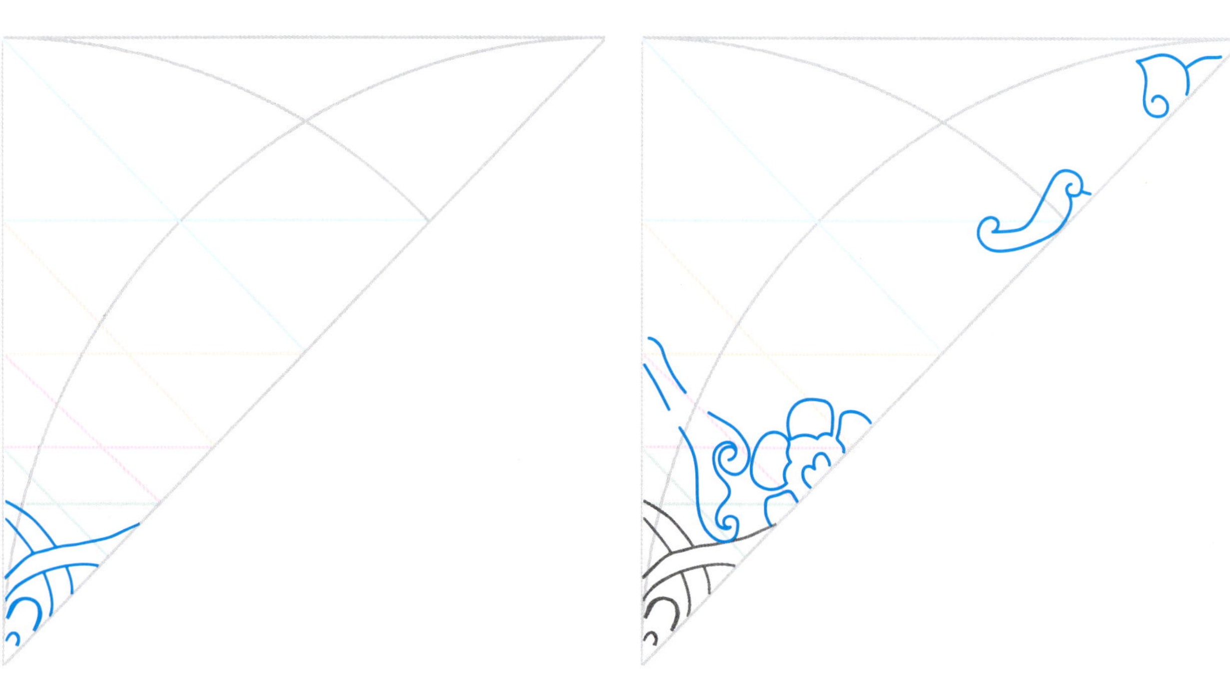

1 The starting point is the centre. Place petal A there and shape B above it, framed by the smallest eight-pointed star. When A and B are combined and completed, they will create a beautiful flower and a curved eight-pointed star (see A & B).

2 We'll now place more shapes on the vertical and diagonal symmetry lines. Place half of shape C on the vertical with a space for a branch to pass through it. On the diagonal line, place half of flower D directly above shape B. On the tip of the largest eight-pointed star, place half of shape E. Lastly, at the end of the diagonal line – in the corner – place half of shape F.

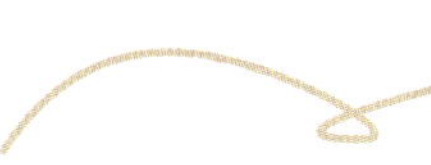

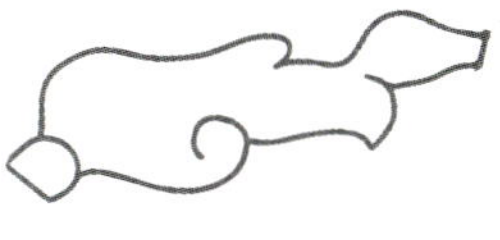

G   **H**

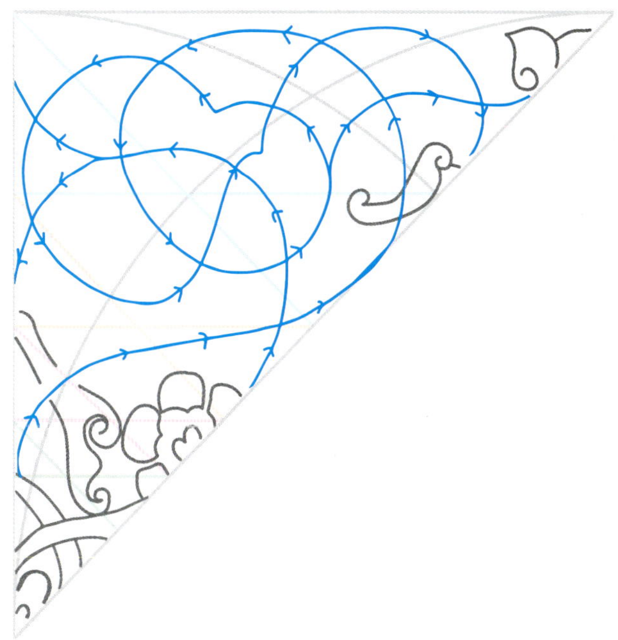

3 The spirals are an essential part of this design. Notice that their direction goes up from both the vertical and diagonal lines. The next steps will look at each spiral and curved line separately.

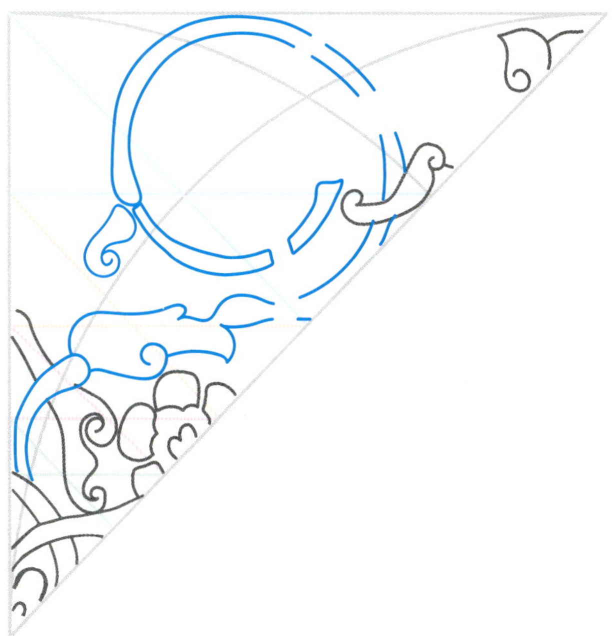

4 For the first spiral, start from the vertical edge of shape B and go upwards into the diagonal line, passing through shape E and into a semi-circle. On the same spiral, add two additional shapes: G and H.

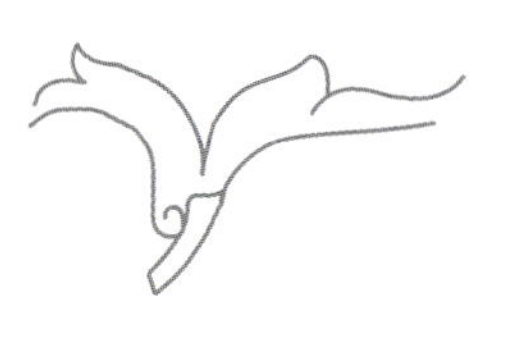

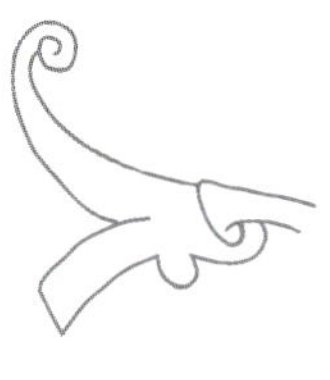

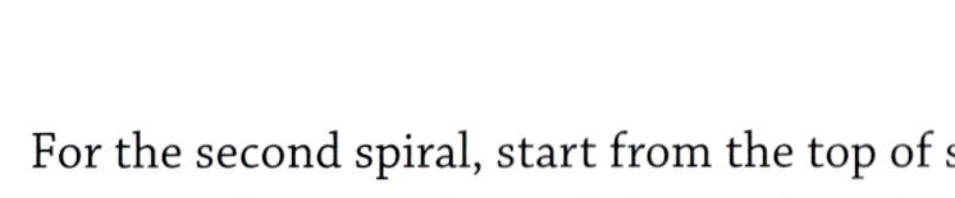

I

J

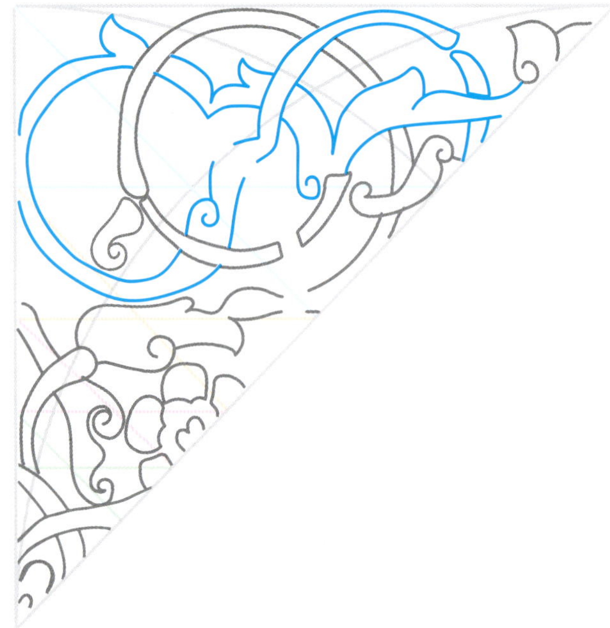

5 For the second spiral, start from the top of shape E. This spiral is not a classical shape. Place shape I at the end of the spiral, touching shape F in the corner.

6 Extend the third curve from the diagonal line to the vertical line. Add shape J at the end of this curve.

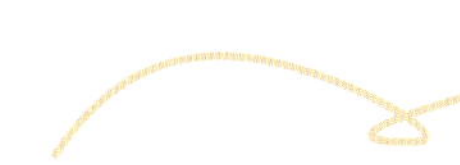

7 Take the completed section and reflect it to give us a quarter. Once that is repeated, we have the full pattern.

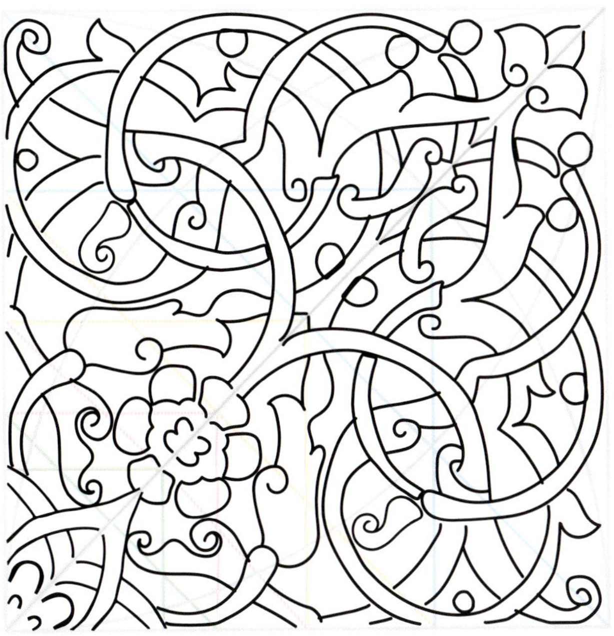

Tessellating the Pattern

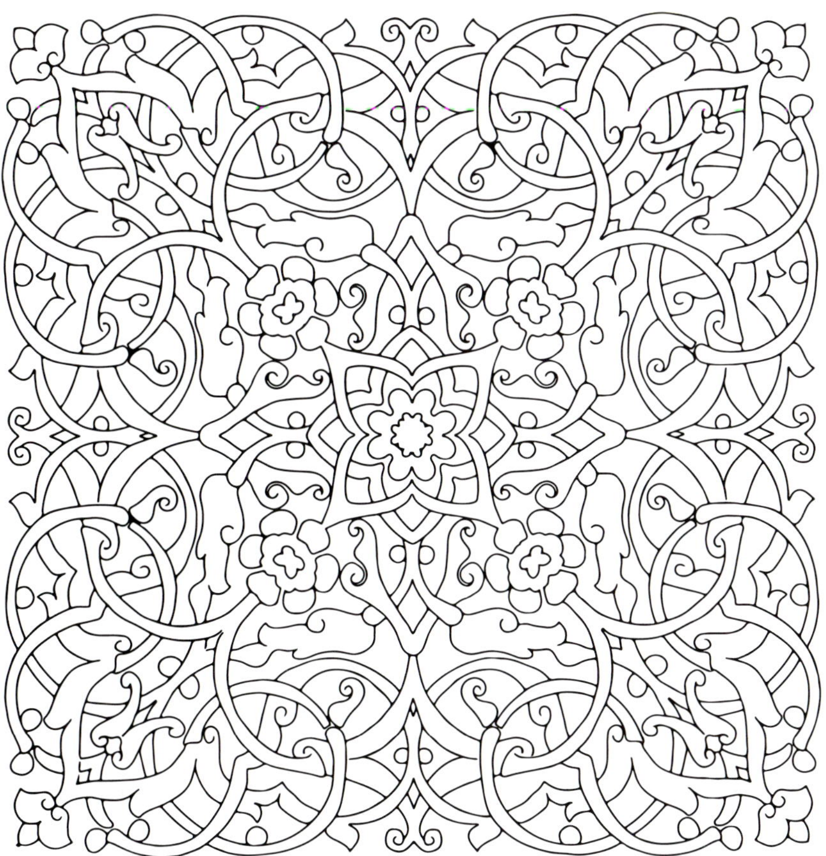

This pattern can be tessellated to give the beautiful repeat that we can see on the original wall from which this pattern is taken.

SIXTEENTH-CENTURY IZNIK TILE PANEL

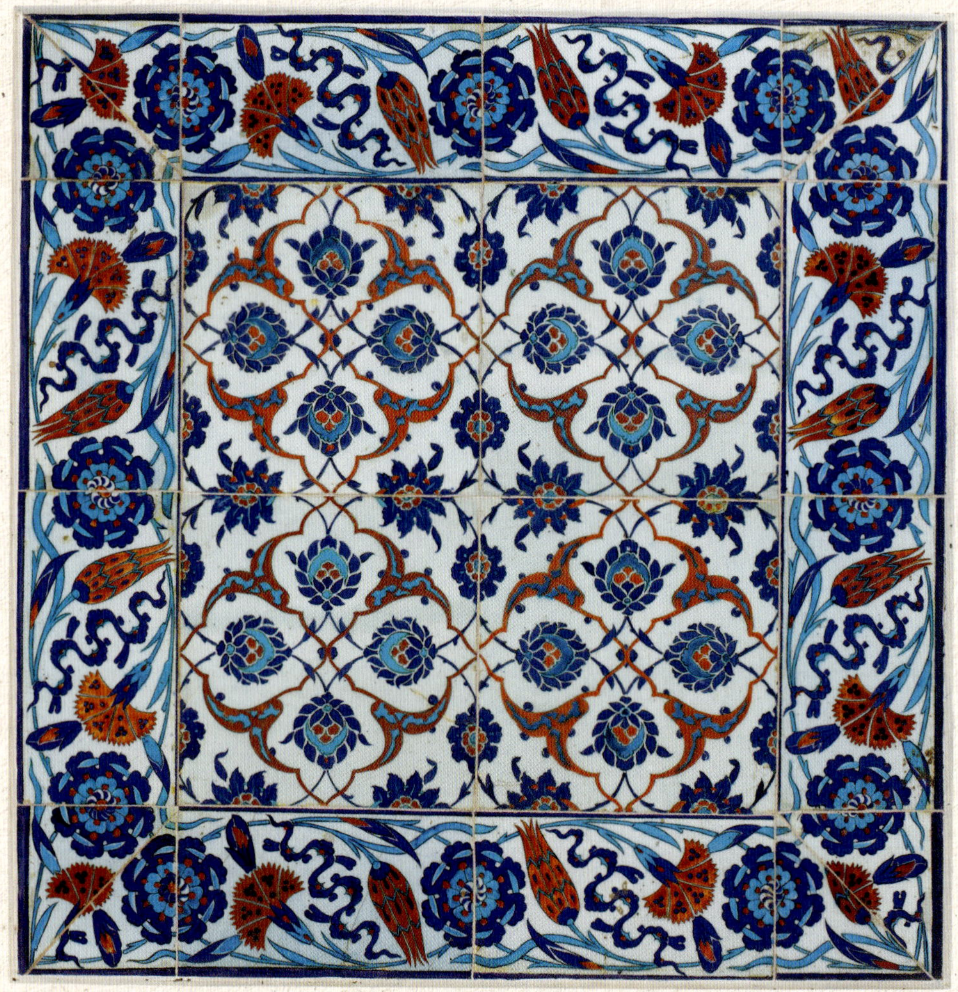

Tile panel, second half of the sixteenth century,
attributed to Iznik, Turkey. It is made of stonepaste
polychrome and painted under transparent glaze;
76.8 × 76.8 × 3.8 cm.

Looking at the Geometric Structure

For the 11th pattern in this section, I have chosen this beautiful tiled panel which dates to the second half of the sixteenth century and is attributed to Iznik, Turkey. This panel is very close in style to the tiles that adorn the Rüstem Paşa Mosque in Istanbul. It can be drawn to the same scale as given here or made bigger or smaller. The flexibility of the tiling here is very satisfying.

There are three parts to this pattern:

Part 1 The one square tile, based on a simple eight-pointed star. This first part follows the same system that has been followed in this chapter – the design section is an eighth that has been reflected to create a quarter. This quarter is then repeated in rotation to create the full pattern.

Part 2 A simple tessellation. Once one full tile is complete, it is repeated three more times to have four tiles next to each other. This can be made bigger by increasing the number of tiles added. Even numbers are necessary for this to work (see p.107).

Part 3 The third part is the border, which is made up of a corner design plus a design of half the border. All of them are then reflected and repeated around the whole tessellated pattern of Part 2 to create the beautiful panel shown on the page opposite.

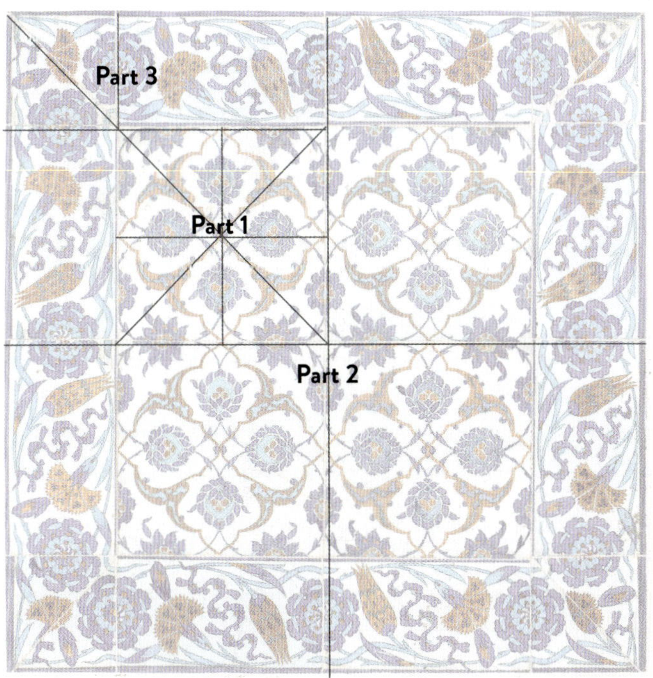

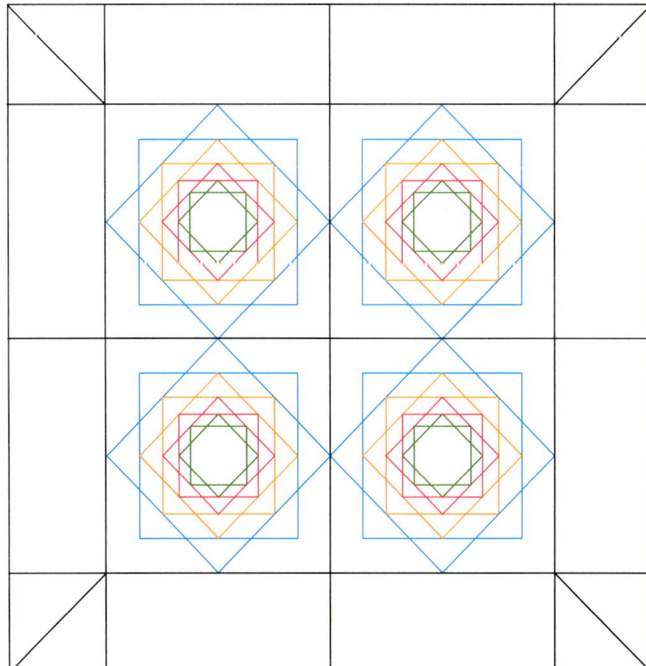

Part 1 Constructing the Square Tile

The design in Part 1 is made of a square tile, based on a simple eight-pointed star (see p.99). It can be designed as quarters, starting with the placement of the flowers and extending the connection between them.

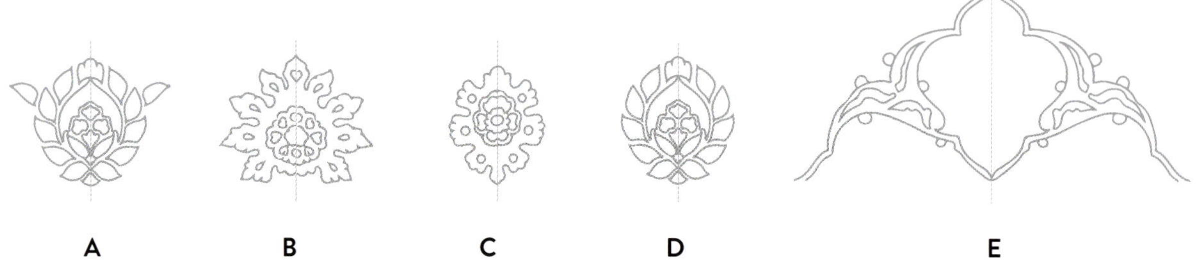

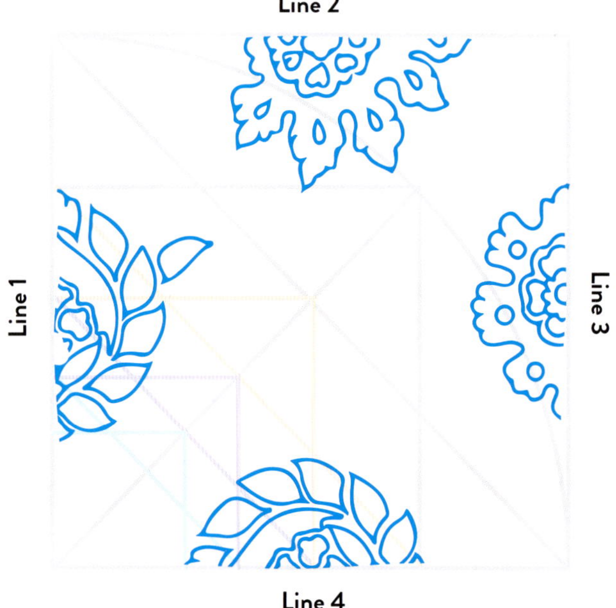

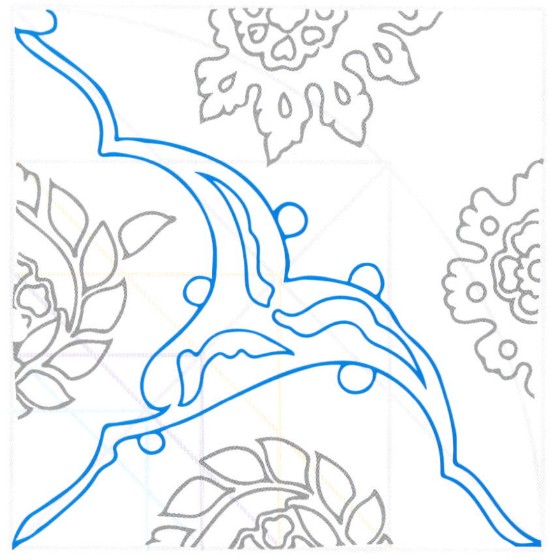

1 There are four flowers: A, B, C and D. Cut each one in in half and add to the middle of lines 1, 2, 3 and 4 consecutively. The placement of the flowers follows a clockwise direction.

2 Place half of inorganic ornate shape E within the square to frame flowers A and D and fill in the square diagonally.

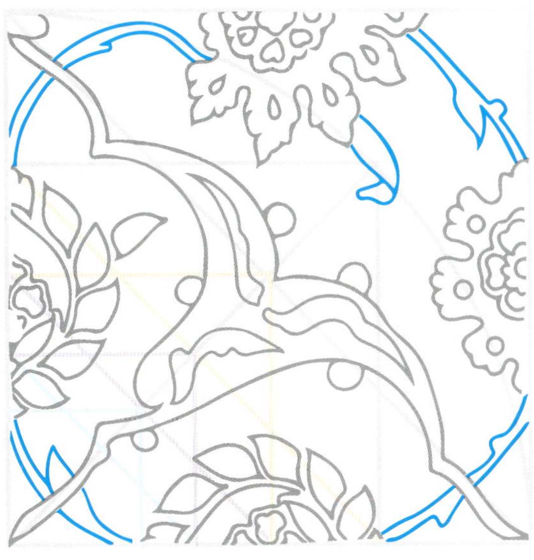

3 Draw a circular branch to connect all flowers to each other. Add small decorative leaves to the branch, which follow the same direction as the flowers. This is all that is needed to complete the design.

4 Reflect the unit to create symmetry.

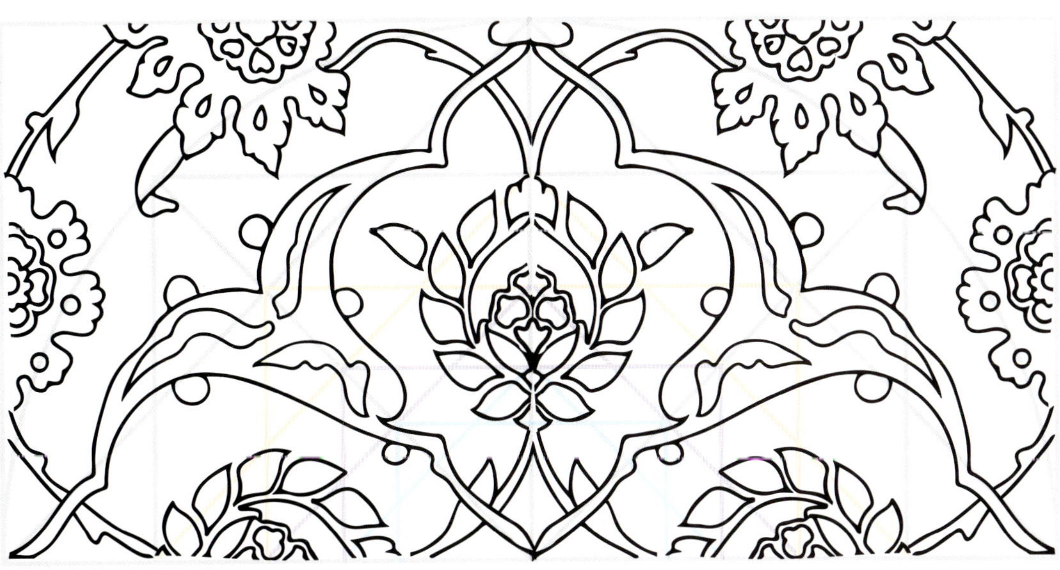

5 Repeat the two-square unit one more time to complete the four-square tile.

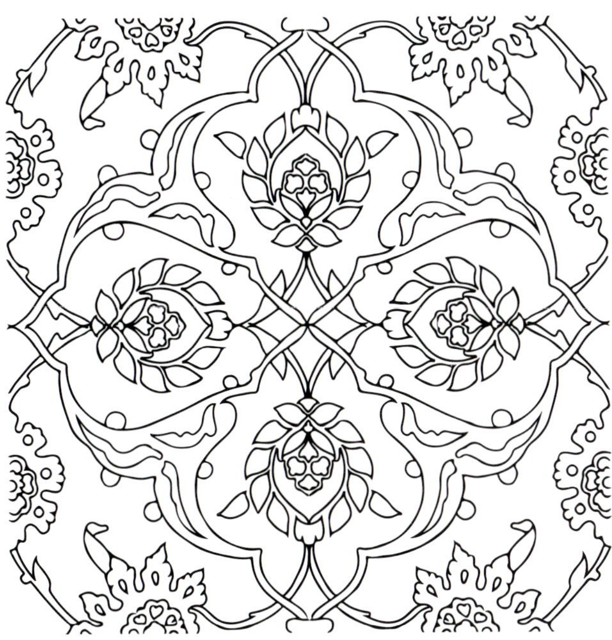

Part 2 Tessellating the Four Tiles

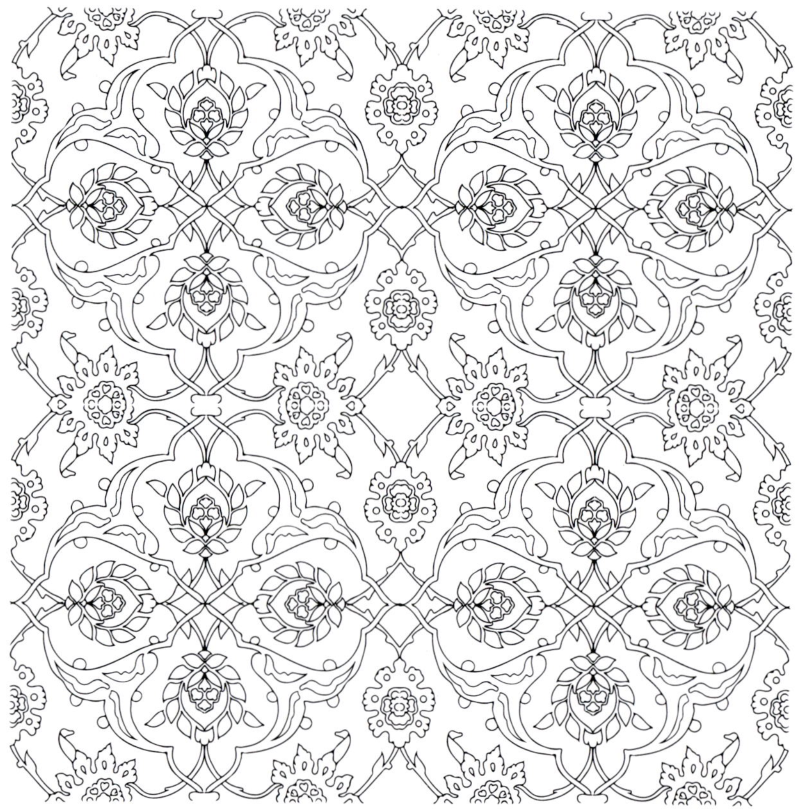

The second part of this design is the tessellation of the four tiles, which creates a much larger pattern. In theory, it can be repeated endlessly and is handy for covering large interior walls.

Part 3 Creating the Border

The third part of this design panel is the border surrounding the four large tiles that were tessellated in the Part 2. There are two components to consider when designing a border: the corner and the repeat within the body of the border. The corner is always unique because it is reflected diagonally, whilst the body of the border is reflected vertically. The body of the border is also dependent on the design. In this particular design, the border follows the geometry of the centres of the four tiles, as illustrated at the start in the geometric structure.

The original design has a few inaccuracies that could have occurred during assembly or when firing the tiles. Ceramic is harder to control compared with paper, so there has been a slight adjustment to place the flowers as exact halves before they are connected with a more consistent branch.

Designing the Border Corners

To start the design of the corner of the border, it is important to highlight the space intended for the design, which is a square shape bisected diagonally.

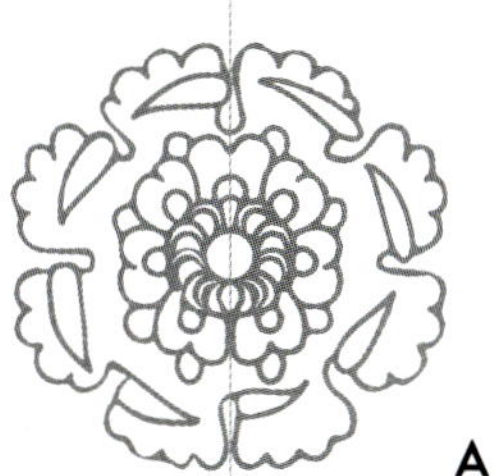

A

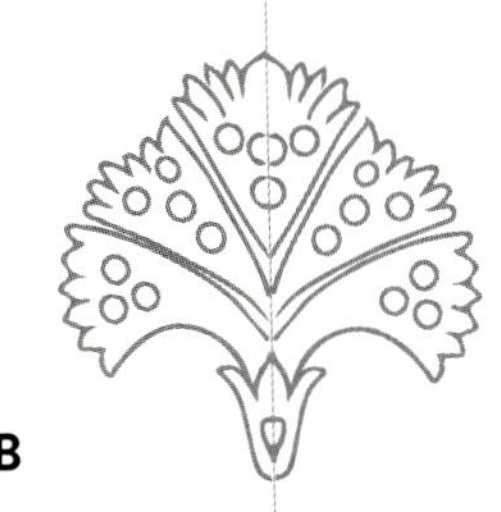

B

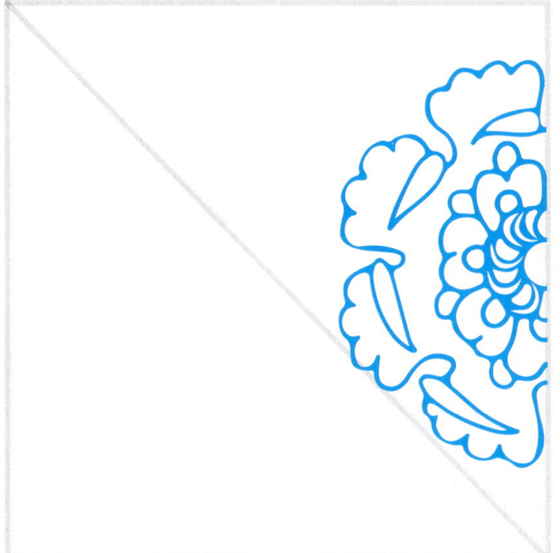

1 Place half of flower A on the vertical line.

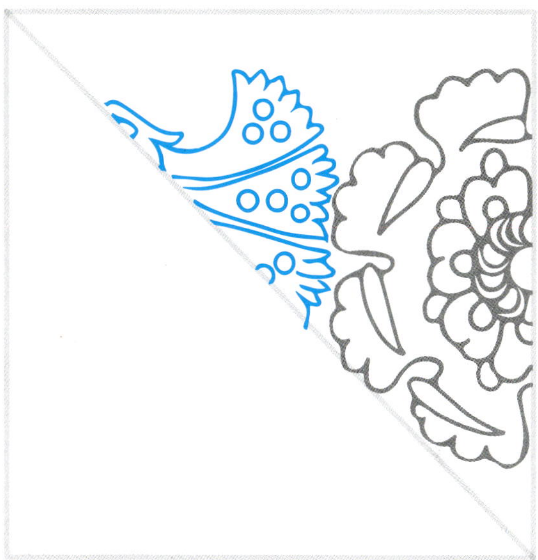

2 Place half of flower B on the diagonal line. Both of the flowers take up a lot of space and do not leave much room for other elements. This follows the simplicity of the design of the tiles.

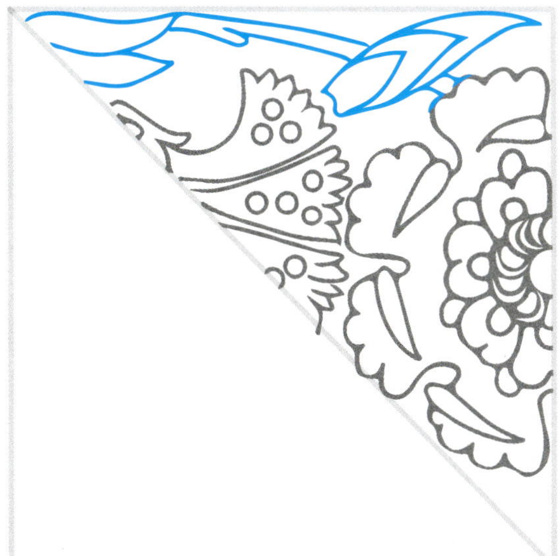

3 Extend a slim branch from the top corner of the section and connect to the top of flower A.

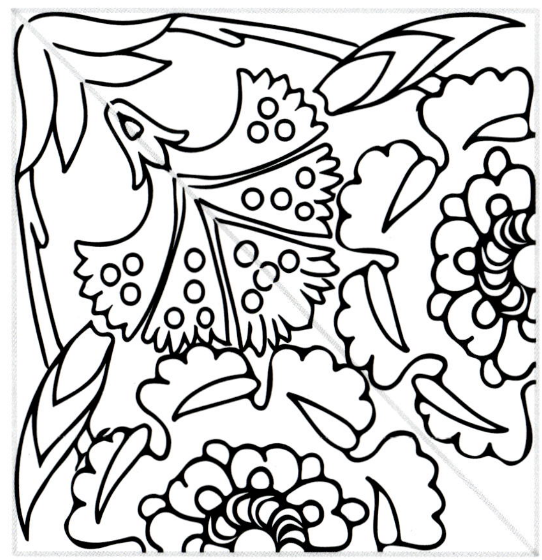

4 Reflect the section diagonally to complete the square corner. This corner will be used four times; however, it will be reflected based on the location in which it is placed. Generally, the direction of the corner changes to face the centre of the design.

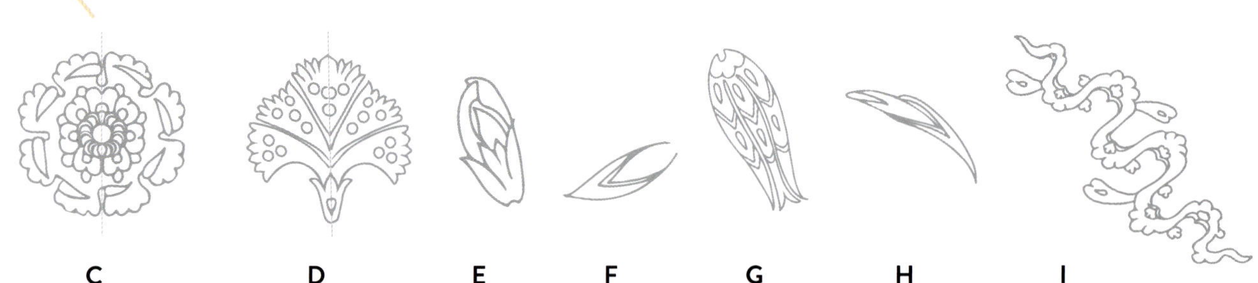

| C | D | E | F | G | H | I |

Designing the Body of the Border

The body of the border is split into two sections and the design is created in
a rectangular unit. There are two vertical lines of symmetry: one at the start,
shared with the corner, and another that runs vertically through the middle
of the border.

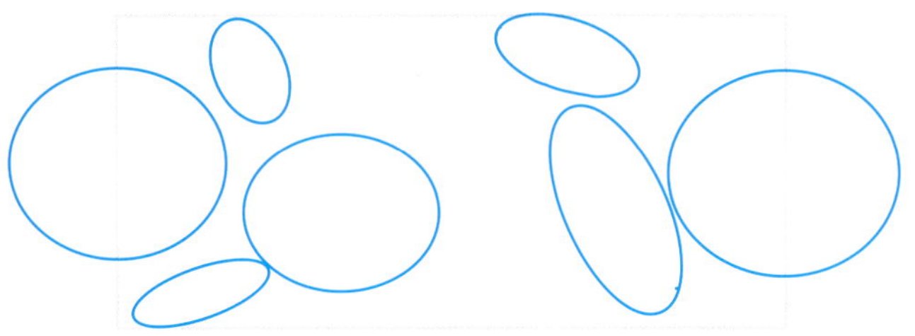

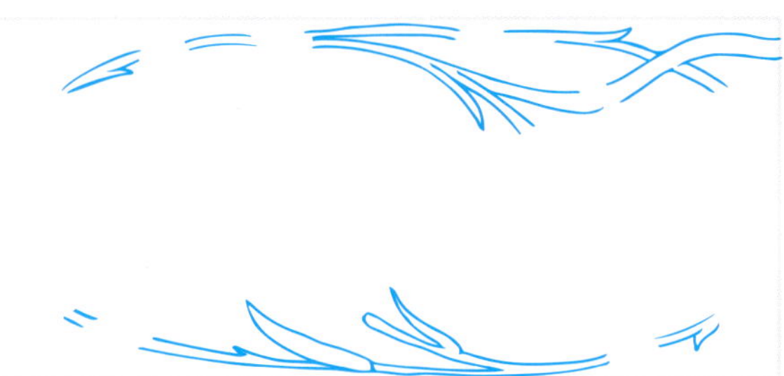

1 The first task is to decide on the placement of the
flowers and branches by circling the appropriate areas.
The two flowers on the vertical lines are pre-decided,
since they are related to the corner design. There does
not seem to be a specific rule to positioning these
flowers, so we can assume it is the personal taste of
the designer who created them. You can adjust the
placement to achieve a design that you prefer.

2 Place the branches at the top and the bottom of the
section; the rest of the space will be populated with
flowers and leaves.

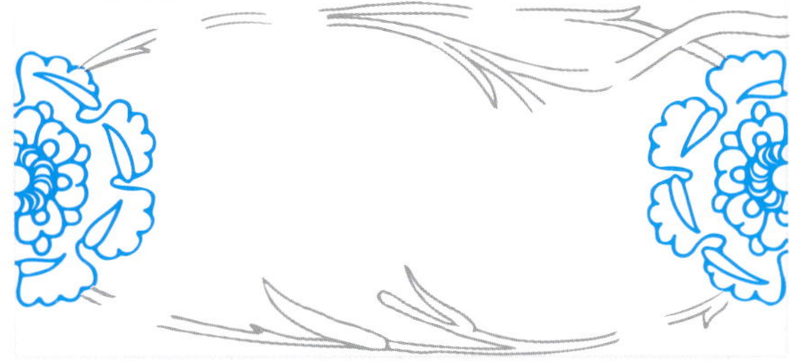

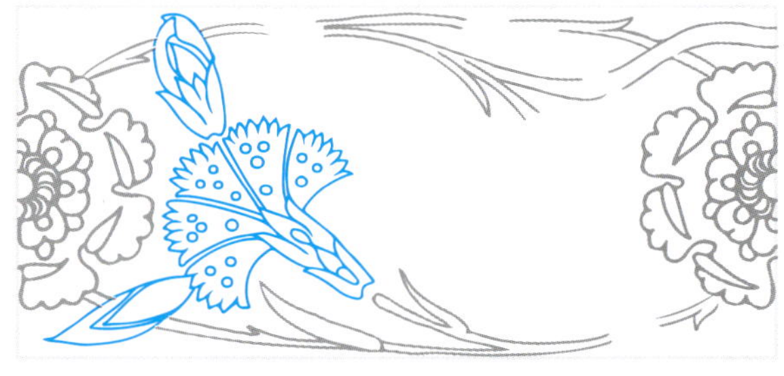

3 Place half of flower C on the symmetry lines. This is
the same flower we used in the border corner. This
technique links the body of the border to the corner.
The original design had a few inaccuracies with this
particular flower because of the moving direction of
the leaves. If you find the changing leaves confusing,
omit these and just use the flower petals.

4 Place flower D diagonally and top with flower E.
Extend leaf F from it, as shown.

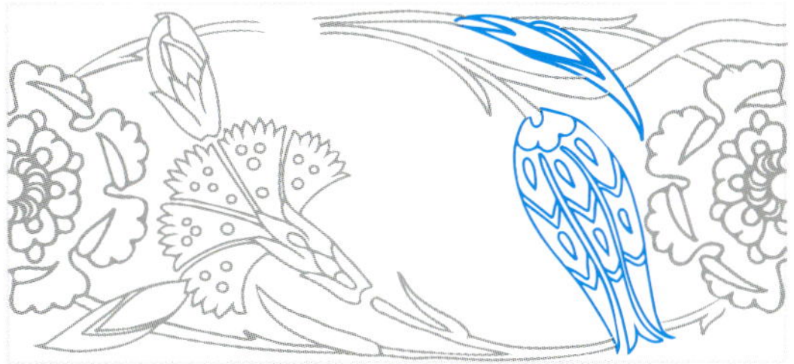
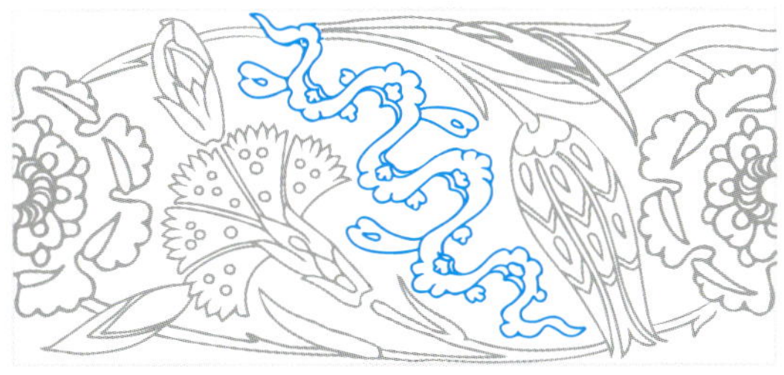

9 Flower G is placed upside down and diagonally on the other side of the section and leaf H is placed on the top horizontal line.

10 Place shape I in the middle of the flowers from steps 8 and 9. With this, the section is complete.

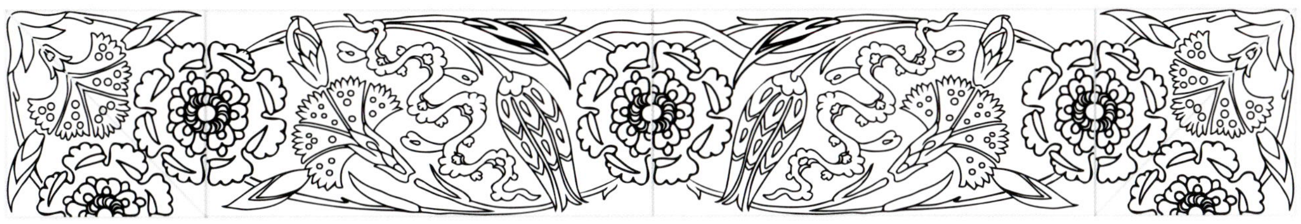

11 Combine the corner and the body of the border to achieve a full top border.

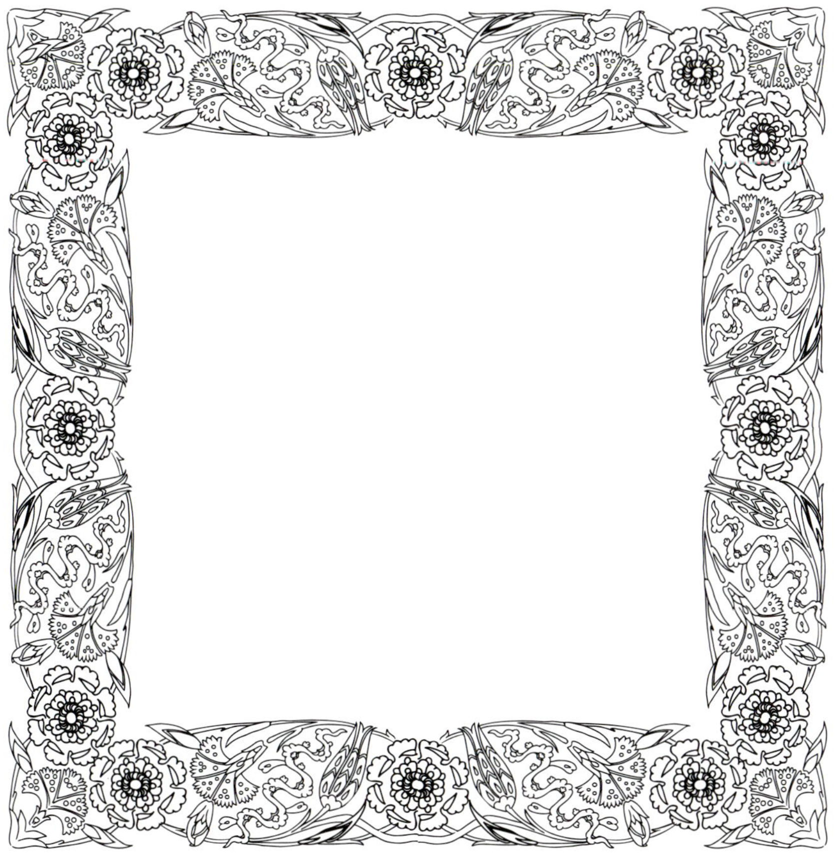

12 The top border is then repeated on the right, bottom and left sides to create a full border to frame the whole pattern. Notice the direction of the border and how the design turns anticlockwise.

Finishing the Design

Now that the pattern is complete, you have the choice to either transfer it to paper or ceramic tile to paint, or to start simply by colouring it with colouring pencils. It will look wonderful whichever way you choose to apply colour.

PERSIAN MANUSCRIPT PATTERN

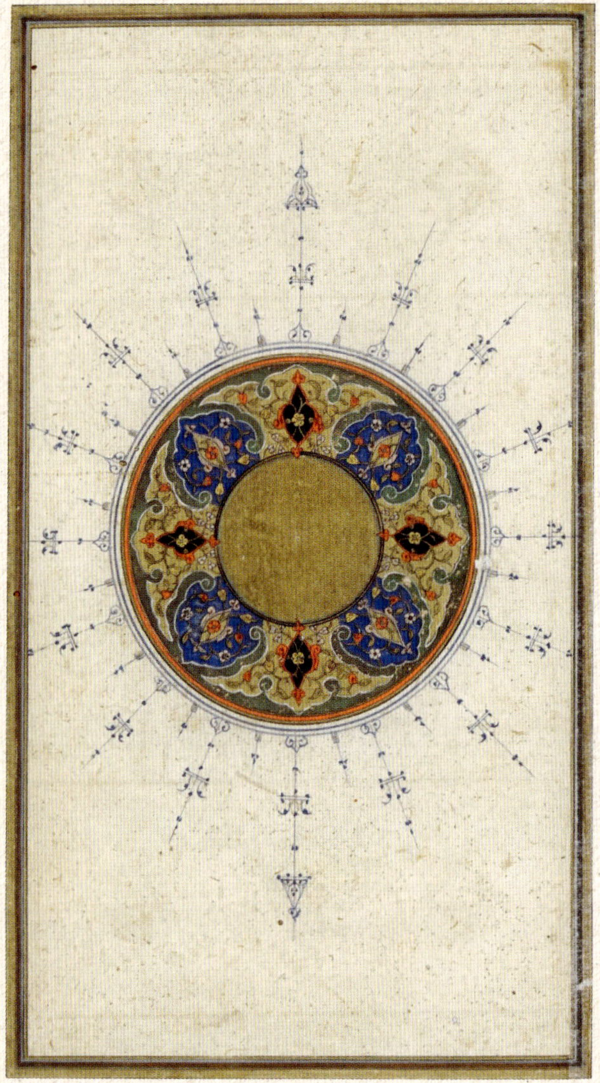

This pattern comes from a Persian manuscript, known as the Nizami Ganjavi (d.1209) Sharafnameh and Makhzan al-Asrar, signed by Shah Mahmud Nishapuri, Persia, Safavid, dated 1533; 29.4 x 18.5 cm.

For the last design, I have chosen another manuscript pattern. As mentioned in Pattern Study 8 (see p.117), finding the right simple manuscript pattern is not an easy task. We are lucky to have access to images from auction houses such as Sotheby's that give us the opportunity to look at and study these patterns further.

Looking at the Geometric Structure

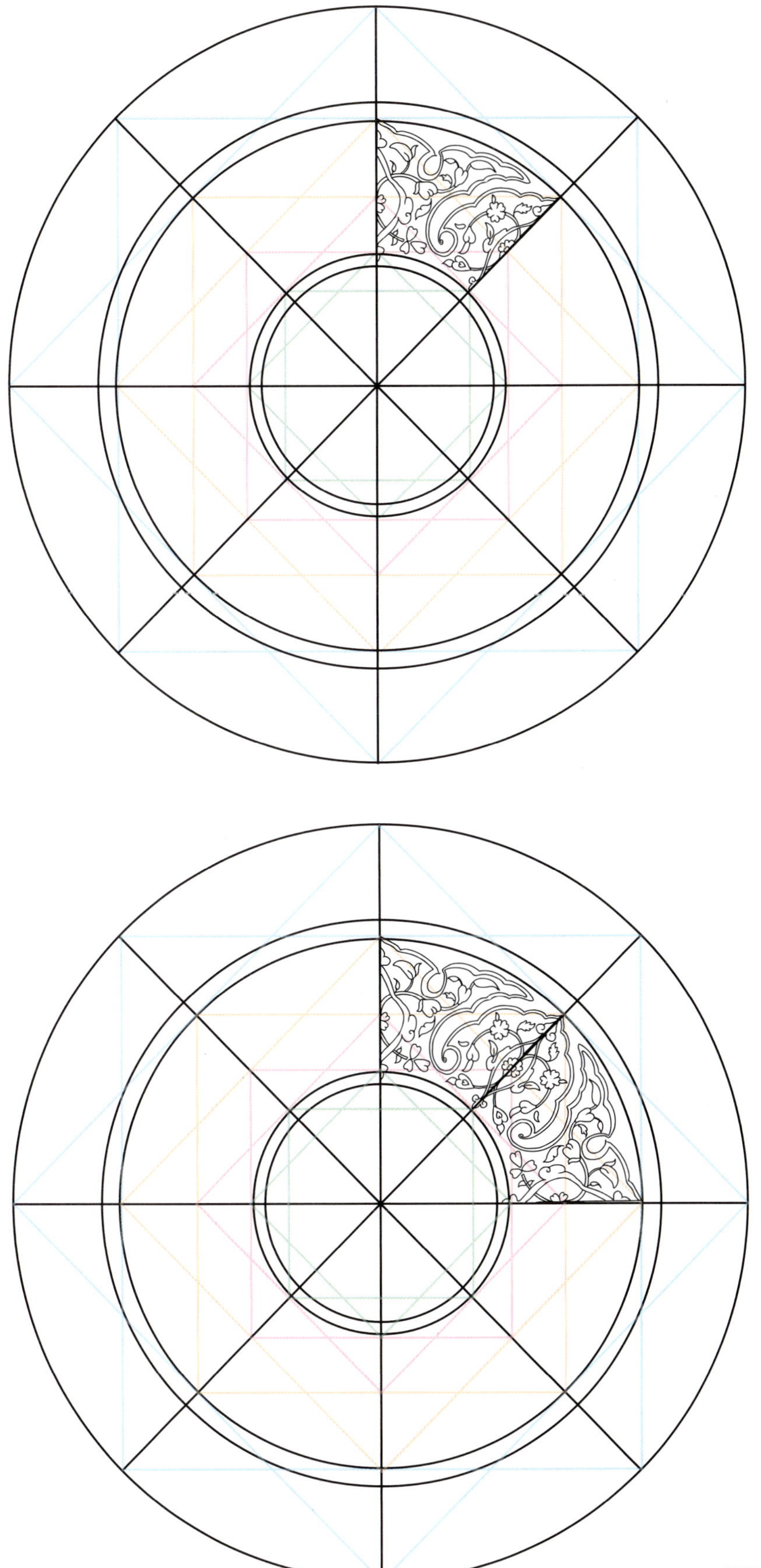

This pattern is also based on the division of the eight-pointed star (see p.99) and its guidelines. However, the final design takes place in the central circle. The design itself is simple and it is interesting to see that the centre was painted in solid gold rather than covered with Arabic calligraphy. It is good to have multiple options.

Drawing the Pattern

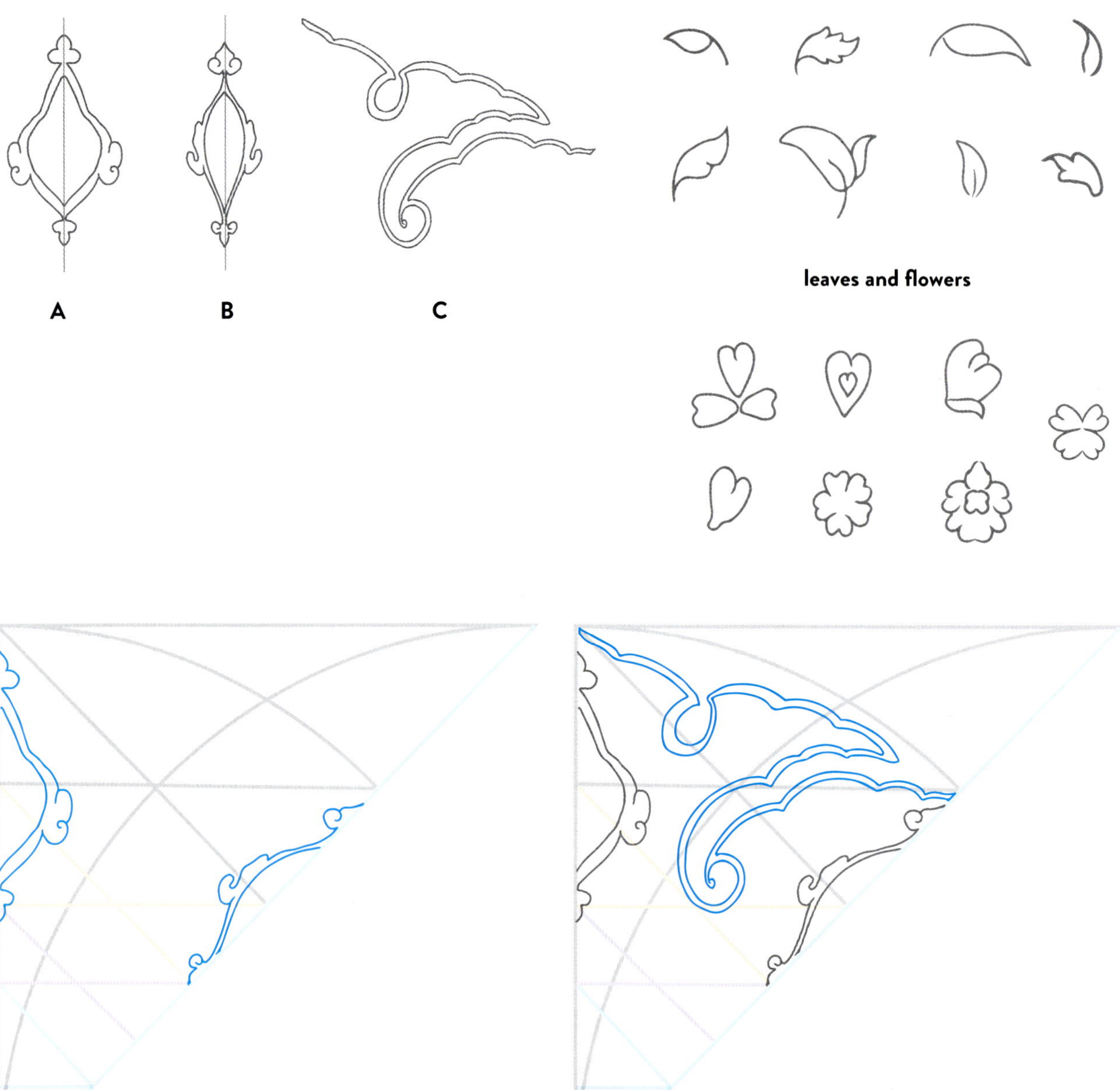

1 When the section is determined, the symmetry lines are also determined. In the case of this pattern, the design is within the circle rather than within the eight-pointed star. Place half of shape A on the vertical line and half of shape B on the diagonal line.

2 Add shape C in between A and B. This shape is sometimes referred to as a 'collar design' because it looks similar to the collars that men wore on their clothing during the sixteenth century. This shape is interesting because it acts like a frame within the circle, giving the whole design a new shape.

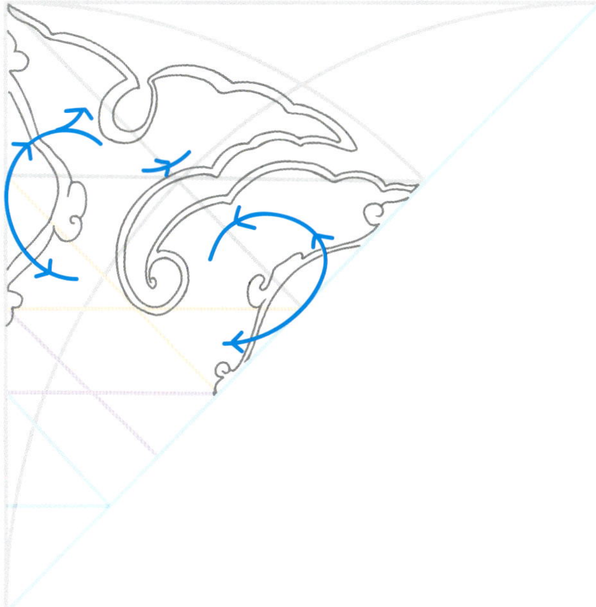

3 The design includes a number of floral motifs and leaves, so it is important to determine the placement of the branches. Position the branches from shapes A and B and spring them from the middle point, going upwards and downwards.

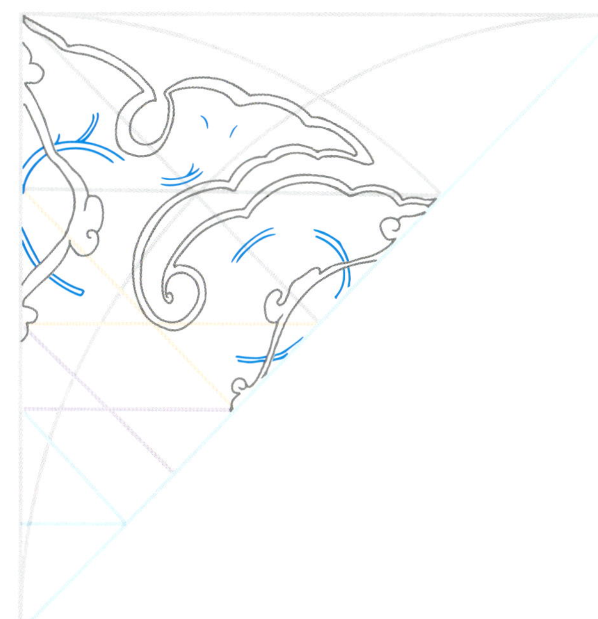

4 Double the lines for the branches to make the painting and outlining stages easier, otherwise, you will end up with very thin lines that are challenging to paint.

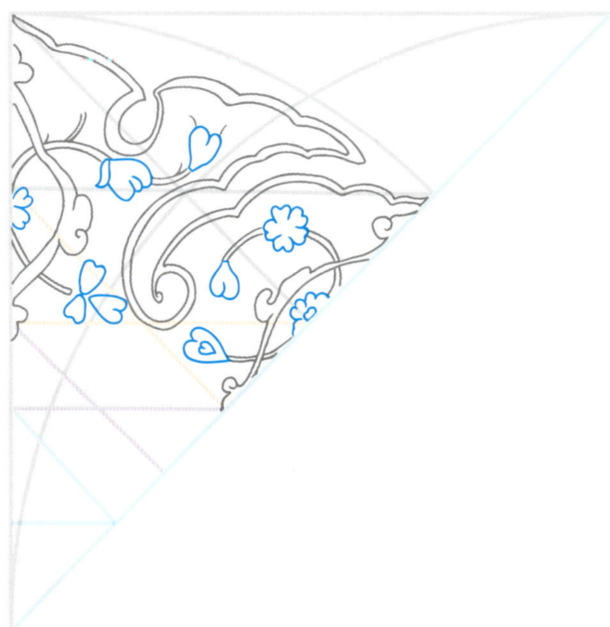

5 Place the flowers on the branches within the design. They are relatively simple because they are very small.

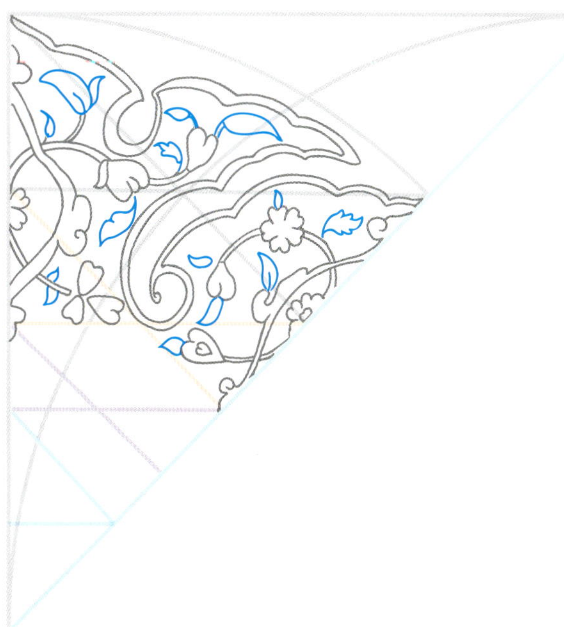

6 Draw leaves in the remaining empty spaces.

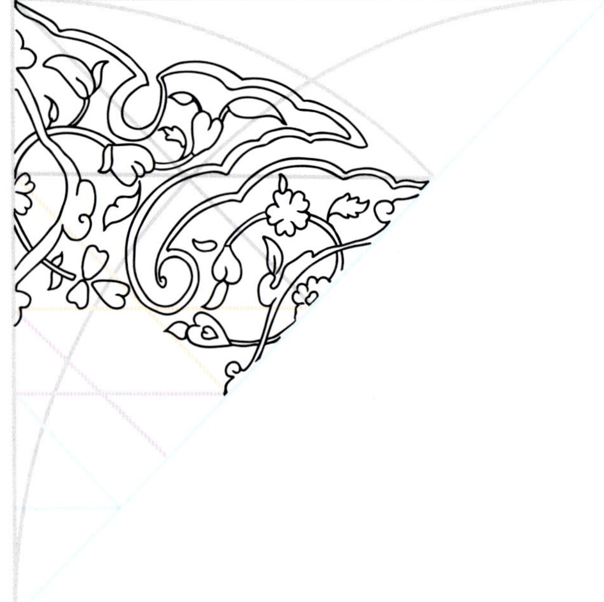

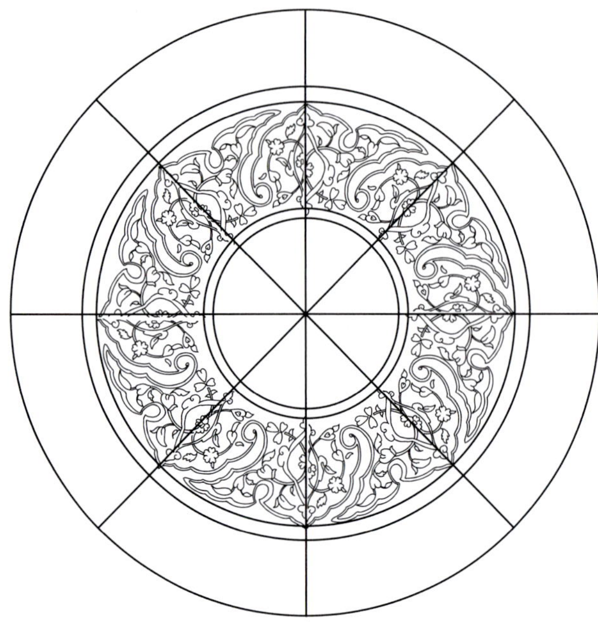

7 The design is now complete. The lines illustrate the reflected section and the repeat.

When you transfer the design for painting, you should remove the division lines.

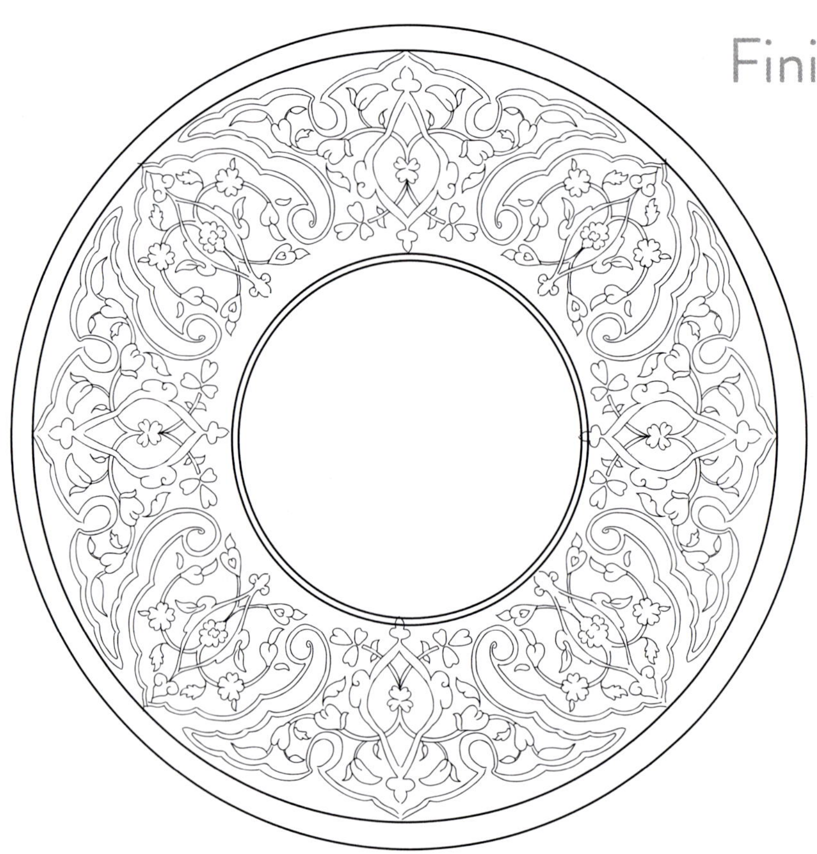

Finishing the Design

This pattern has a number of possibilities. It can be painted as it is or used as a frame for another pattern or calligraphy. The flowers and leaves are drawn in a simple style due to the small size it is drawn, but if you scale this design up you can experiment with making the design more complicated or painting them in a more complex way.

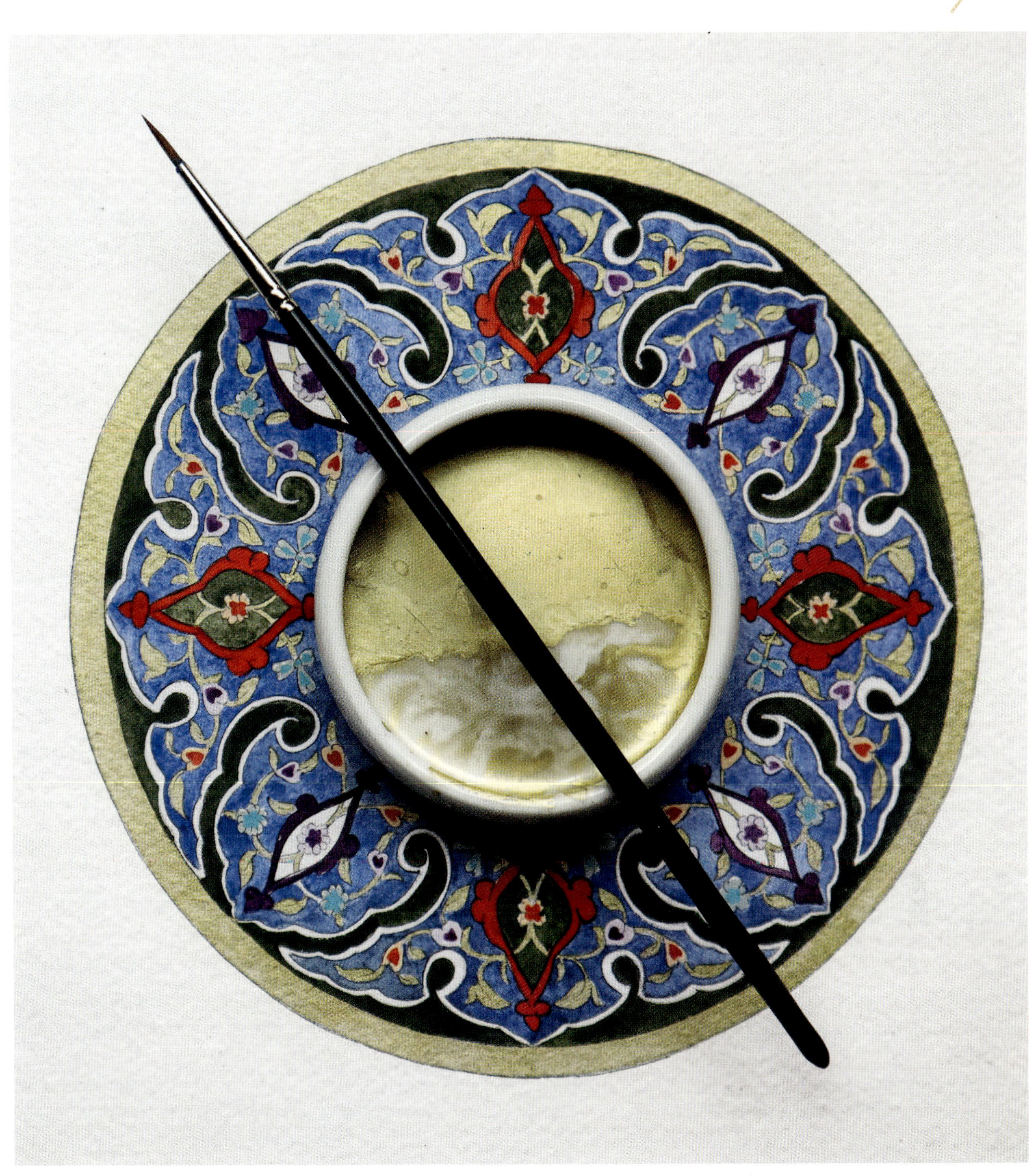

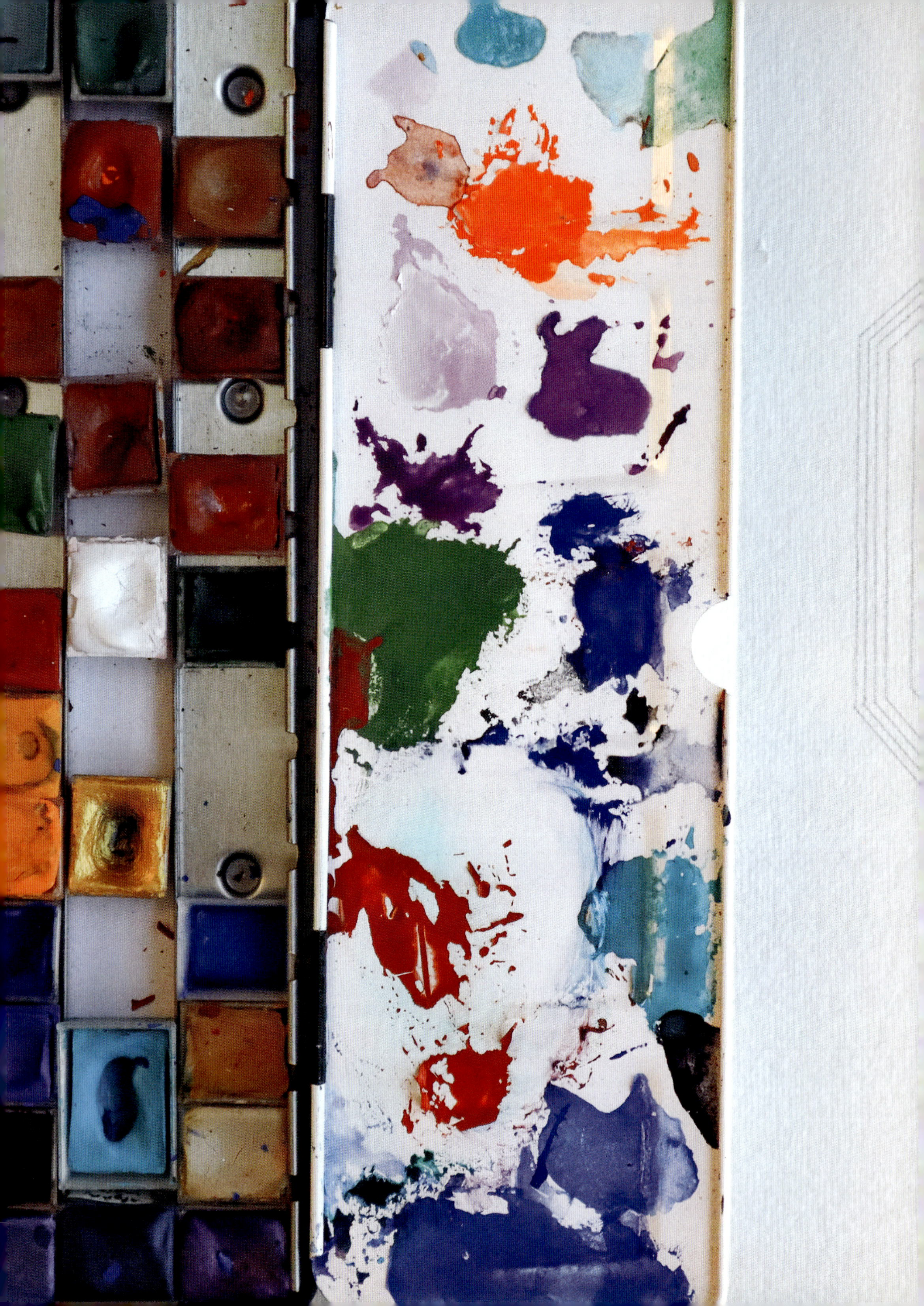

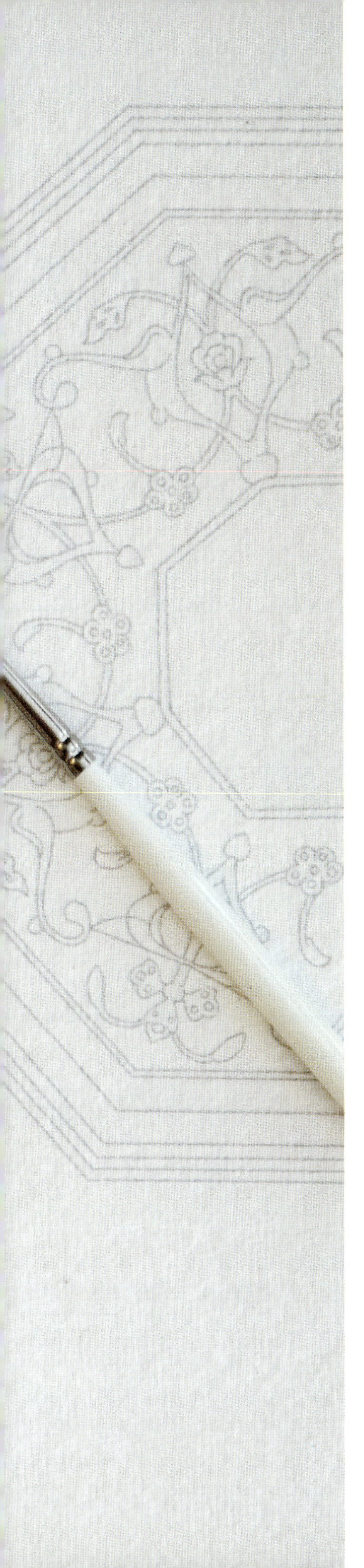

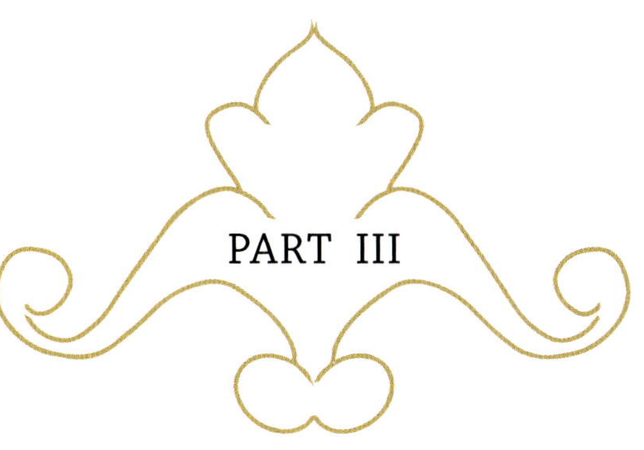

PAINTING PATTERNS

There are many ways you can bring a pattern to life with colour. As seen in museums and galleries, these patterns are applied to a number of media including wooden and metal objects, paper, ceramics and textiles; therefore, there are endless possibilities. Here, you will learn about painting patterns on two main media: paper and ceramics.

When it comes to painting a pattern on paper, I usually limit myself to two painting styles. The first is a contemporary painting style which uses watercolour or gouache following the original colour scheme. The second follows the classical style of Turkish/Persian illumination known as Tezhip in Turkish and Farsi or Tathhib in Arabic, meaning 'ornamenting with gold'. The latter has a specific method and order and is only painted on paper.

As an alternative to paper, ceramic can also be used, but the painting method changes to adapt it to the ceramic surface and this requires more tools, such as access to a kiln. Although painting on ceramic can be considered harder, it gives us the ability to transform objects into functional pieces of art, which can be a practical gift.

CONTEMPORARY PAINTING STYLES

For the contemporary style, there are a few tools that you will require, which are all listed here. In a nutshell, you will need: tracing paper, an HB pencil, watercolour paper, watercolour brushes and watercolour or gouache paints. You can extend this list and add many more art supplies to it, but it is wise to start with a limited number of tools and materials and add to that with your growing interest and artistic practice.

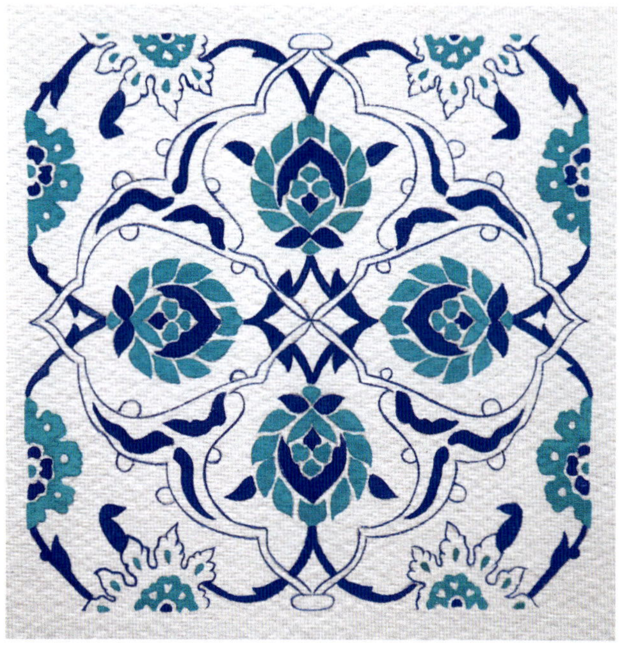

↑ One way of painting Pattern Study 10: Uzbekistani Khiva Pattern (for another, see p.157)

TOOLS AND EQUIPMENT

TRACING PAPER

Tracing paper is essential in transferring the designs that you have developed in the Pattern Study sections. Any type of tracing paper is suitable – the brand names will differ depending on your country.

In the UK, you can use tracing paper from Cass Art, which is either A4 or A3 in size and 90gsm in thickness. Daler-Rowney is another brand that offers tracing paper in various sizes with 60gsm thickness. I have found many brandless packs when I have travelled around, so try any local brand that you find.

HB PENCILS

For the tracing process, you will need an HB pencil, which is the most common pencil type used in schools and can be found everywhere. You can be 'old school' and use a regular one, which will require sharpening, or you can use an 0.5mm thickness automatic pencil with an HB lead. The latter is handy because you want your pencil to be sharp to keep the thickness of the original drawing consistent.

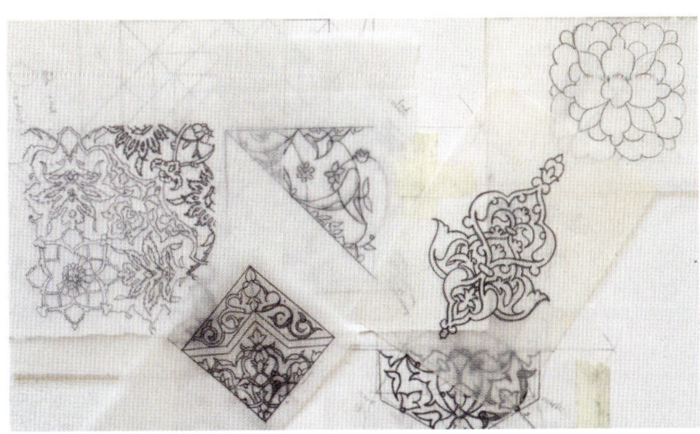

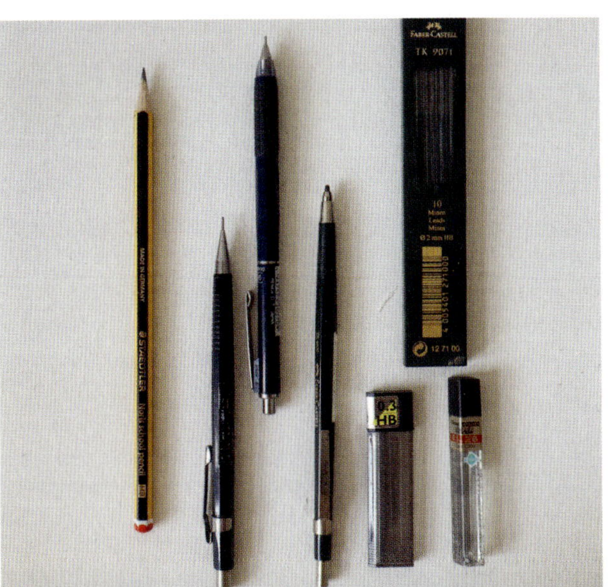

TRACING TECHNIQUE

Once a design is traced with pencil, take the tracing paper and flip it so the pencil side will be facing the watercolour paper. Draw the design again on the other side, following the exact lines that were drawn. This is the best way to transfer all designs from the light tracing paper onto heavyweight watercolour paper.

The same type of tracing paper and transfer technique can be used in the Islamic illumination style discussed later (see p.159).

WATERCOLOUR PAPER

Watercolour paper comes in two main types: hot pressed (HP) and soft pressed (SP). The HP has a smooth surface, whereas the SP has a rough, textured surface and is the most commonly used paper. I use both types, depending on the availability and the look I desire.

The main thing that should be considered is the thickness of the paper. The thicker the paper, the better (use thicker paper that starts at 300gsm and can go up to 640gsm), as it will absorb the watercolour paint and added water so that the paper does not wrinkle or buckle.

There are many other types of coloured paper. Handmade papers are fun to play and experiment with, along with papers made from different types of materials such as cotton and hemp. When the style is contemporary, I am much more relaxed in my approach. It will be good for you to start with the type of paper that you prefer and have access to.

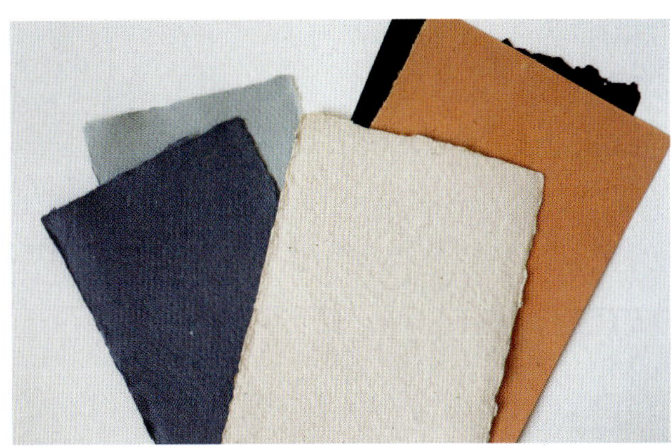

WATERCOLOUR BRUSHES

Brushes are the real stars of painting in watercolour because a good brush can make or break a painting. I know artists should not blame their tools, but a decent paintbrush really makes a difference, and which brush to buy is one of the most popular questions I receive. There is not one answer, though, since there are many good brands around – even new brands can be surprisingly good.

Choice of brush is very personal, but here are a few options to get you started:

- Winsor & Newton Series 7 – the classic choice, which many people recommend and enjoy.
- Da Vinci fine brushes – they are not my preferred choice but many people love them.
- Rosemary & Co handmade brushes – based in York, UK, this brand makes the most beautiful brushes. I have tried most of their natural, blend and synthetic series and they all work really nicely.
- Handmade, ethical squirrel-hair brushes made in India, or handmade, ethical cat-hair brushes made in Iran – both are suitable to use and they can vary depending on the maker.

There are many brands that I am yet to encounter, so be open to trying brushes that are not listed here. The brush is the most important tool, so get a few and see which one you enjoy working with the most.

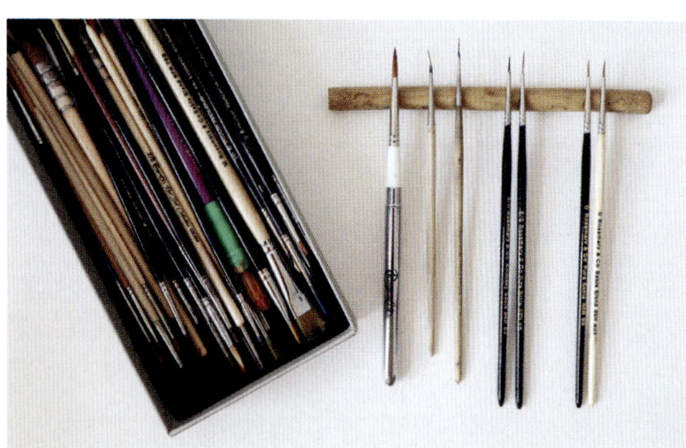

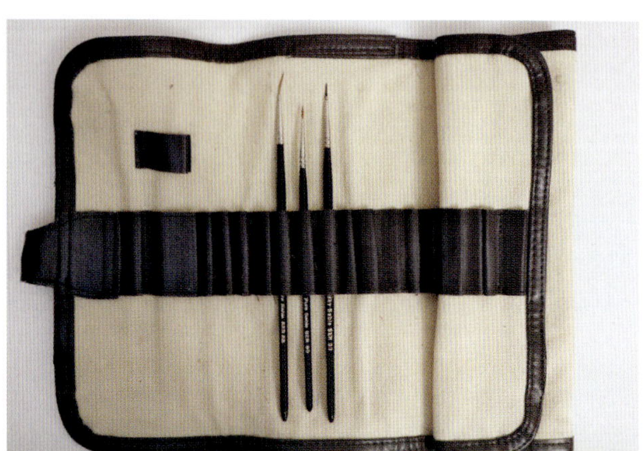

LOOKING AFTER AND STORING YOUR BRUSHES

Since the brush is a vital tool, make sure you take care of it well. Do not leave it dunked in water as this ruins the bristles; clean it with water as soon as you have finished. You can also give the brush a mini spa treatment by rubbing the tip gently with soap every few weeks.

Storing your brush is also important, especially if you are on the move. A brush box is ideal to prevent the tips of your brushes from bending and frizzing. This can be any rectangular-shaped box. There are cloth bags as well, but I find those better for keeping your tools in the house. Getting art accessories is a joy, so you will enjoy the process of acquiring storage for your brushes, and brush rests for while you work.

WATERCOLOUR AND GOUACHE PAINTS

The amazing thing about painting on paper using watercolour or gouache is how accessible and affordable it is. It is best to use paints that you already own when you are starting your practice, but as you are improving your skills you can invest in high-quality watercolours, such as highly pigmented handmade watercolour paints or the classic options of Winsor & Newton and Schmincke.

A lot of students ask about the differences between watercolour and gouache paints and if one is better than the other. The answer is that it depends on your own personal preferences, which you will develop during your practice. I started using gouache first and I love the ease of using it and the coverage it provides in creating opaque backgrounds, but after a few years I felt that it was too flat on the paper and lacked depth, and I then started using watercolours, which were harder to control. I am at a point now where I enjoy both and change my selection based on the project I am painting.

Whether you choose watercolour or gouache paints, make sure that the use of water is controlled. I use a dropper or pipette for adding very small quantities of water – one or two drops at a time. The great thing about both is that they can be kept once they dry and reused indefinitely with the addition of water.

WATERCOLOUR PAINTS

Watercolour paint usually comes in dry blocks. I
tend to use those directly, adding water to the blocks
themselves. Other artists like to use their brush to take
a few washes of that block into a palette so they can
change the shades and mix a few colours before starting.
This is very popular with contemporary watercolourists,
especially those that work on botanical art, since they
may need a specific shade to match the plant or flower
that they are painting. However, when painting the
abstract shapes in Islamic biomorphic patterns, most
colours would be suitable, so using paint directly from
the block is sufficient.

The nice thing about watercolour is the ability to change
the colour tone, depending on the amount of water you
add, and to create depth and motion. This skill comes
with practice and experimentation.

GOUACHE PAINTS

The consistency of gouache and watercolour paint differs
due to the varying quantities of the glue-like substance,
gum arabic, they contain – in gouache paints the amount
is increased slightly to keep the paint as a paste to
prevent it from drying out. Gouache paint comes in tubes
or, sometimes, in small lidded glass jars. To use the paint,
I usually take a very small amount with my brush – you
will be surprised by how the tiniest bit goes a long way.

Try to avoid squeezing a huge amount of gouache onto
your palette. It can be saved by leaving it to dry after
use and wetting again, but it is nicer to use the correct
amount so you do not end up with too many filled
palettes.

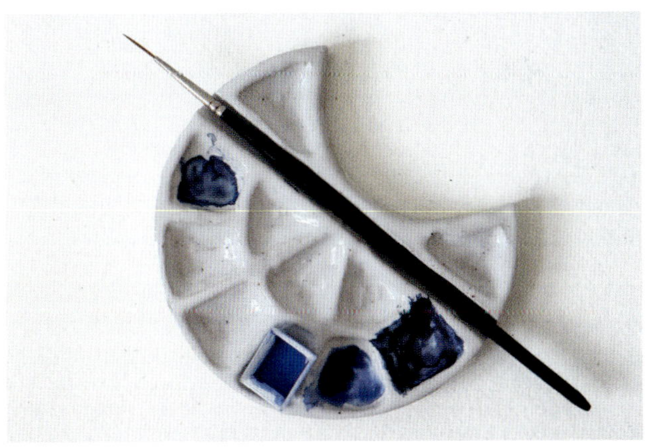

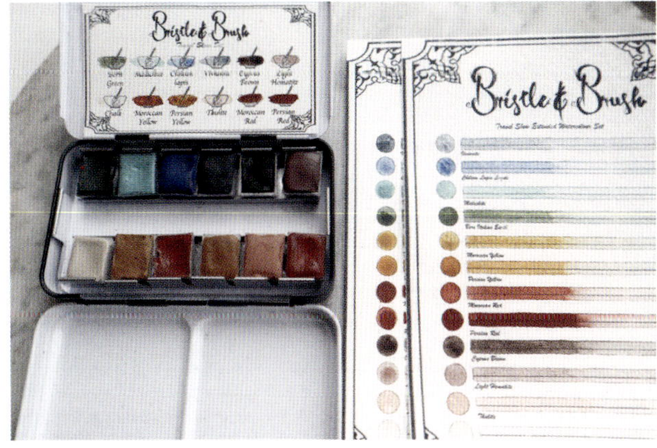

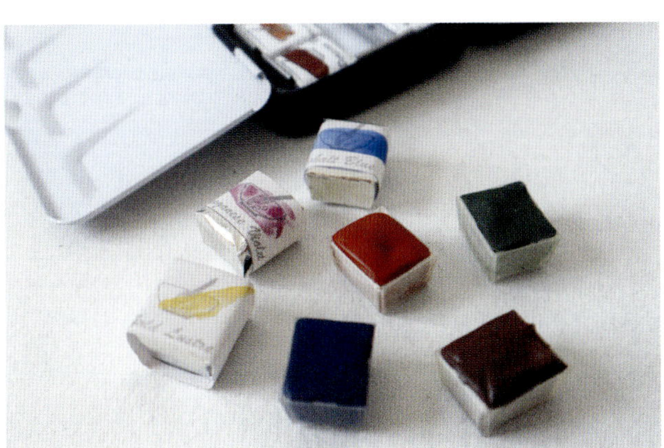

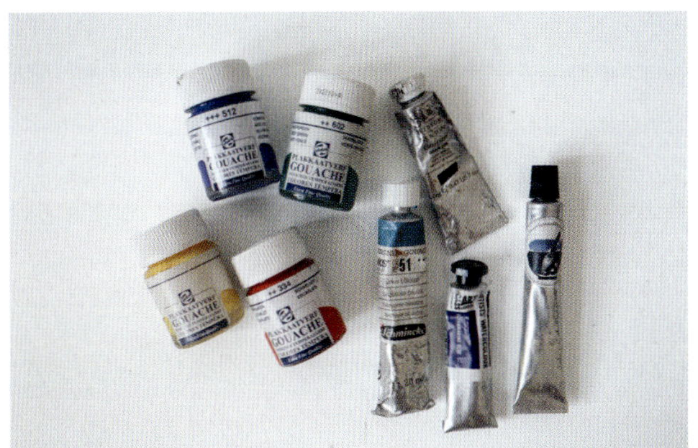

Again, water use is minimal with gouache – you want your paint to be a creamy consistency, not watery. You also do not want clumps, so if you have any, make sure you mix the colours well. It might be a good idea to dedicate a brush to mixing, since this can be too rigorous for fine sable brushes.

Gouache paint is thicker and more opaque than watercolour and it gives a flat finish. These paints were called poster paints as they were used in making posters before it was possible to print high-quality posters in colour. Some gouache paints are not designed to last very long, so you need to check the rate of lightfastness (how long a colour would last if exposed to direct sunlight), which is usually written on the packaging.

Most colours should be fine, but certain shades of orange or paints that were developed from dyes can become fugitive, meaning they will fade away if they are exposed to the sun for too long. This also applies to manufactured and handmade watercolours. You can either trust the rate written on the packaging or carry out the easy test of painting swatches, exposing them to the sunlight and leaving them there for a few months while tracking their brightness, but you only need to do such things if you intend to sell and exhibit your work. There are many artists who have shared their test results with the world and saved us a lot of time.

THE CONTEMPORARY PAINTING PROCESS

Since this is a contemporary style and you are not bound to any specific tradition, I would advise you to paint your patterns in the way you find most comfortable. It is also a good opportunity to replicate the colour palette of the tile you have chosen to paint. Take this as a fun exercise to enjoy painting with watercolour or gouache. The process will feel meditative and slow, which is what you want to feel when painting patterns.

There are three examples below for this process: two that are experimental, with colours that are different to those found in the original tile, and one that closely follows the colour palette of the original.

EXAMPLE 1:
TWO-COLOUR HEXAGONAL TILE

For the first example, I have chosen to paint Pattern Study 1: One-colour Hexagonal Tile (see p.48), which is the least complicated pattern, in a very simple way. On p.53 I shared a few possible colourways if only one colour is chosen, but here two colours are applied.

First, choose the type of watercolour paper you want to paint on. You should be working with a minimum weight of 300gsm. Always experiment with paper because some stock might surprise you. Here, cotton paper with medium roughness from Khadi Papers was selected for its texture. Transfer the design on to the paper.

Second, decide on the colours you would like to use. As mentioned, I planned to paint this design with two

colours, but if you want more or fewer, make sure you determine this first. I would only apply a minimal amount of colour to this design, since it is a simple one. I painted the branches in cobalt turquoise watercolour to begin.

Combining two colours is interesting because you are giving the viewer a visual experience. You can choose any complementary colour, and in this example I chose forest green to tone down the brightness of the turquoise. If you want to brighten up the design instead, you can choose a brighter, warmer colour such as red or orange. You can start painting the areas, or make it easy on yourself by outlining what needs to be painted first then fully painting it. Here I used my favourite size of brush, size 0.

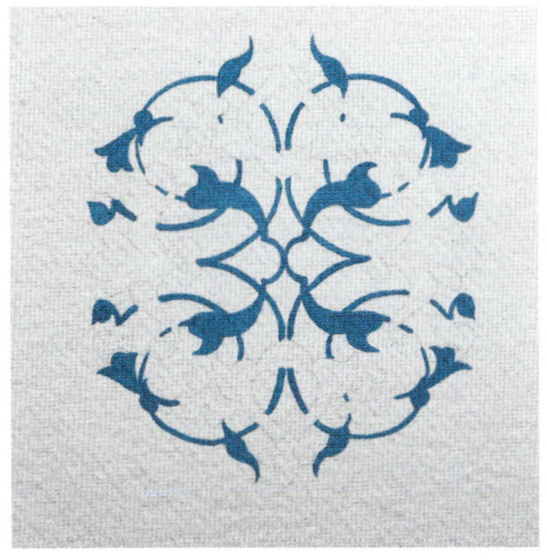 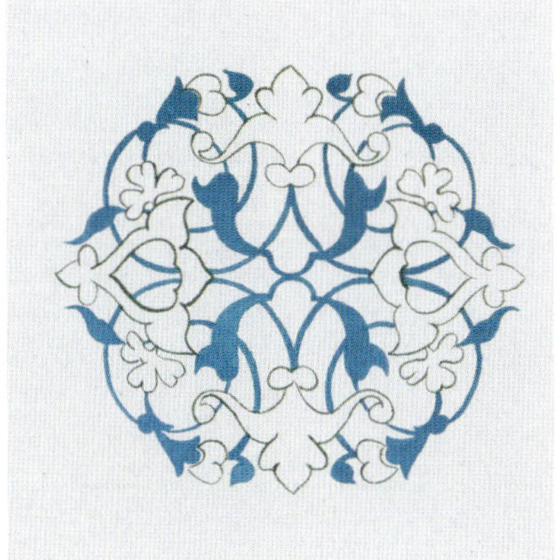 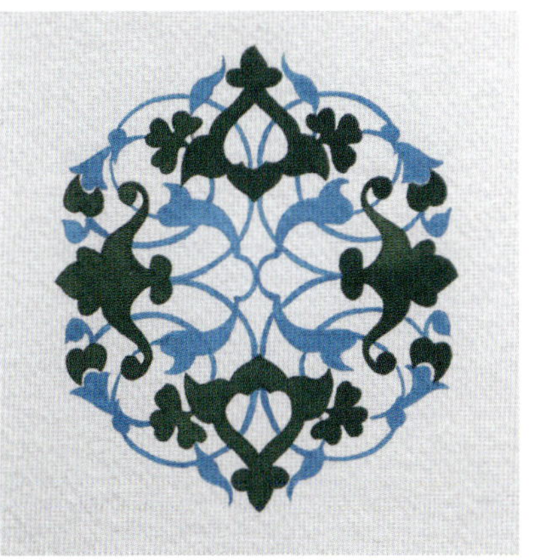

EXAMPLE 2:
UZBEKISTANI KHIVA PATTERN

In the second example, I have painted Pattern Study 10: Uzbekistani Khiva Pattern (see p.131) in a slightly different way. The paper type was the same as for Example 1 (300gsm rough natural cotton paper).

Again, I'm using my favourite size of brush, size 0. I also keep size 1 and size 2/0 in case I need something slightly bigger or smaller. Sometimes, I use a combination of brushes depending on the exact motif I will be painting.

You can follow the same steps or choose a completely different range of colour – it is important that you enjoy this process and make it your own. I started by painting the branches in genuine malachite green, followed by parts of the flowers in genuine carmine. I used natural watercolours, but you can use any brand you like or have available to you.

The remaining inorganic shapes in the middle were painted in gold lustre, a sparkly imitation gold. There are many watercolour gold imitations out there – if you are comfortable using shell gold, you can also use that, but more on that later (see p.160).

I left the rest of the flower parts unpainted and instead outlined them with the same gold to achieve simplicity within the design. When it comes to painting with a lustre paint, you have to angle it in a specific way to see the shimmer sparkling through. The background is also left unpainted, but you can paint it afterwards if you like. I would encourage you to experiment as much as possible when painting it to see the visual impact.

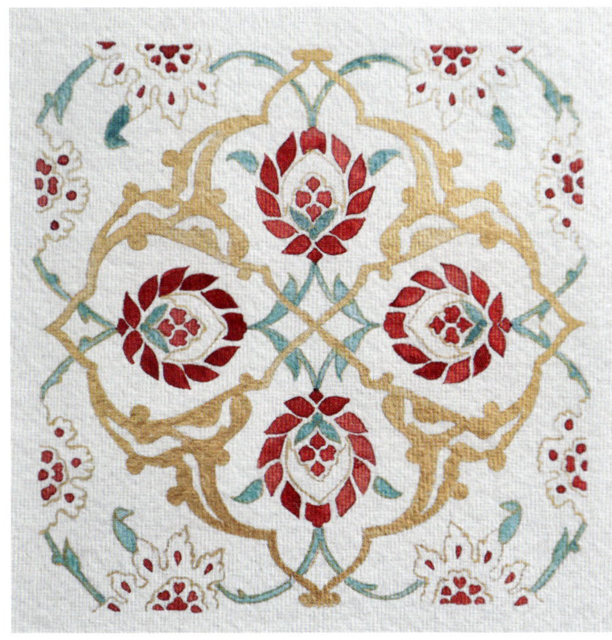

EXAMPLE 3:
UZBEKISTANI PANEL HEXAGON

For the third example, I am using Pattern Study 5: Uzbekistani Panel Hexagon (see p.84). The painting style is reversed when compared with the previous two examples – here the background is painted instead of the foreground.

The benefit of using this style of painting is to highlight the motifs themselves. Of course, white – or even gold – can be used to paint the shapes, but since the paper I am using is white, I have left it without additional paint. It is also nice seeing how the background colour fills the space and creates a shape of its own.

Another way to start painting the background is to outline all the shapes first and then apply the background colour. This makes it a little easier to see the shapes, if needed. You can paint the whole background or leave some parts out. There is so much room to play with.

The contemporary painting style is generally flexible – in essence it is anything you would like to try. Starting with watercolour and gouache is easiest, but you can also begin with colouring pencils or oil paint and then progress to other types of media, depending on what you would like to try next. These patterns can be adapted to most other hobbies and you can combine your various interests if you wish to do so.

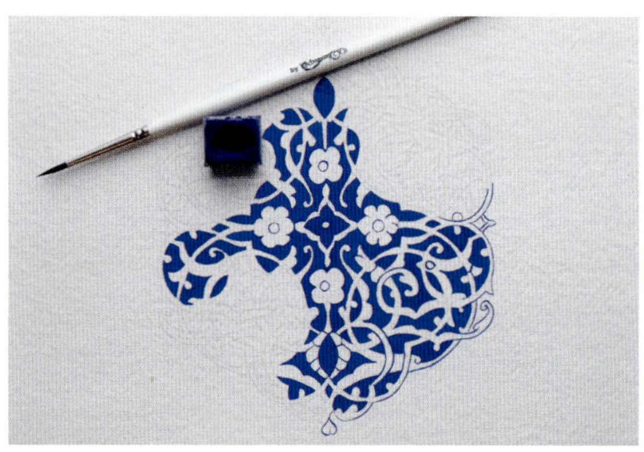

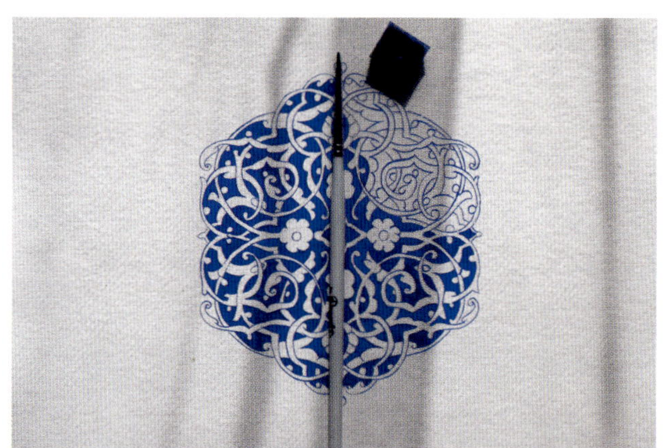

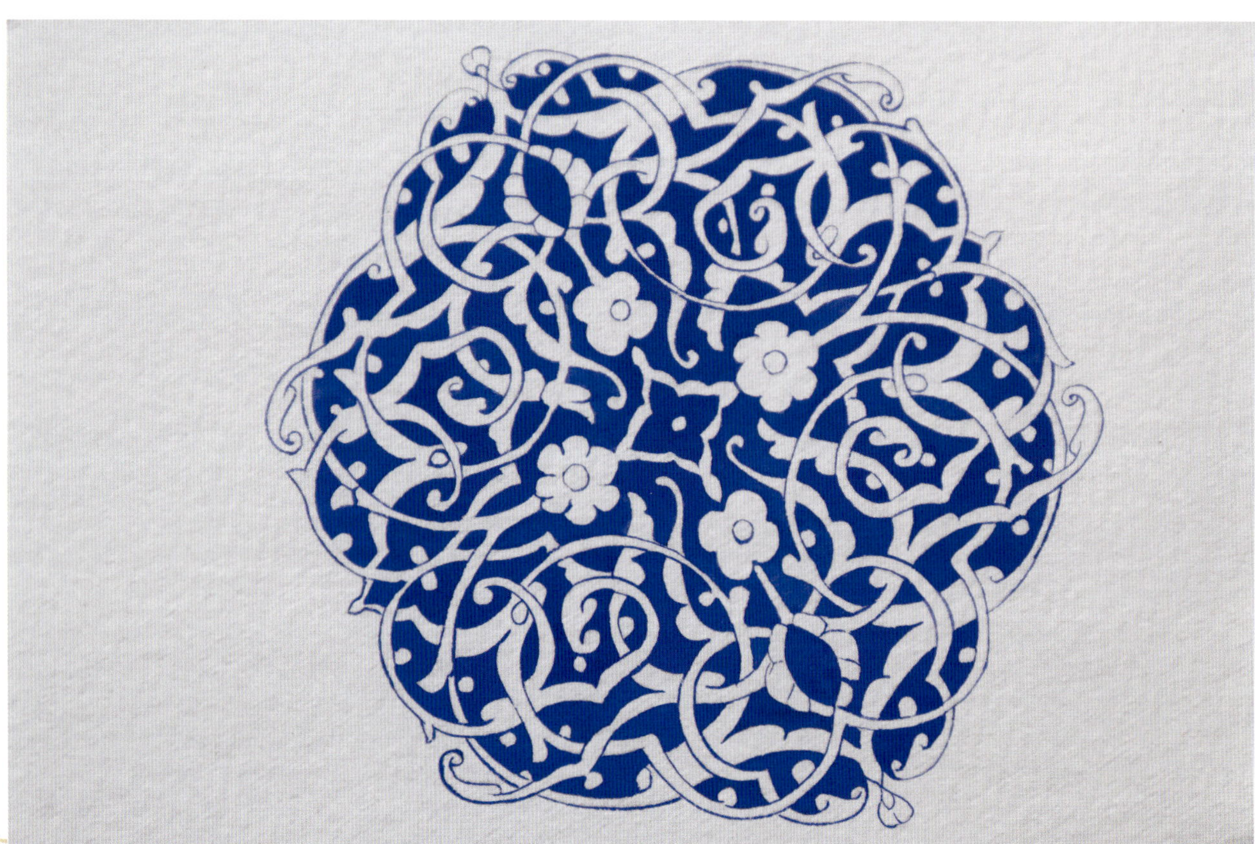

ISLAMIC ILLUMINATION PAINTING STYLES

I have been in love with this style for years. In a way, it is also a contemporary style, but it is influenced heavily by traditions seen in painted and illuminated manuscripts from Islamic countries from the sixteenth to the nineteenth centuries. The practice of this style is commonly taught and continues to be used in Turkey and Iran – their practice might be slightly different to the style I have adopted, so it is always a great idea to learn from several teachers when it comes to traditional practices.

As with the previous style, there are a few tools to be considered before you begin the painting process. There are similarities to the list of tools and equipment on p.153, such as tracing paper and watercolour brushes, and I use the exact same ones for the two methods. The other tools needed are: treated watercolour paper, shell gold and burnisher, black ink and handmade watercolours.

TREATED WATERCOLOUR PAPER

Paper is an essential part of painting, and choosing the right surface eases the process. There are many choices out there, and sometimes even conflicted advice, so it is best to personally test the paper and discover how it feels to you. Be open to changing your mind and trying different surfaces beyond the advice given in this section.

We do not have enough supporting evidence to know if the methods described here were actually used in the sixteenth century, since we do not have documentation or a clear line of transmission, so it is believed that these methods were introduced between the eighteenth and twentieth centuries. Regardless of how old the methods are, they still give a nice finish to the work that makes it look close to an old illuminated manuscript piece.

Hot pressed 300gsm watercolour paper is my usual choice – I love the smooth surface; however, I treat my paper further with dye, sizing and burnishing to make it even smoother and easier to work with.

DYEING THE PAPER

Some artists I have met in Turkey work on paper that has been previously treated or they work directly onto cardboard without changing its surface, especially when using gouache paints, which look nice on this surface. Keep in mind that you can work without this dyeing stage, although it would be nice for you to try it.

The dye is usually natural and is often something that I already have at home. Tea staining works best for my purposes; however, dyeing with onion or pomegranate skins can also provide interesting results. Using tea to stain the paper is easy and requires minimal effort. All you need is a cup of strong black tea and a brush to apply it gently onto the paper. The darker you want your paper, the more layers of tea you will need to add.

The process of using fruit and vegetable skins can vary and may require a mordant. When it comes to onion skin, you can boil it to extract the colours and then apply it gently to the paper after the liquid cools down. Using any plant-based material is usually not very lightfast – the paper's colour can change and fade over time depending on its exposure to the sun.

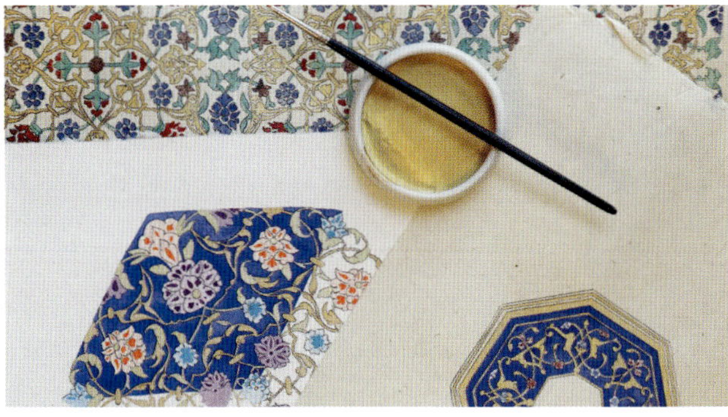

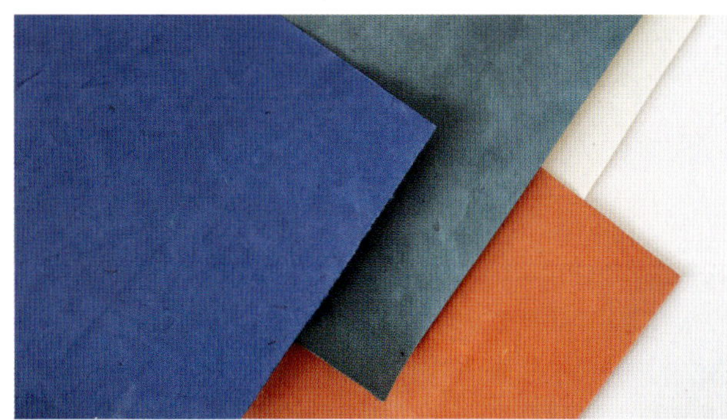

THE SIZING PROCESS

Once the dye is dry, then comes the sizing process, which amounts to closing the pores of the paper and further smoothing the surface. There are many recipes for this, but I will share with you the two easiest ones that I usually use.

The first sizing method is to gently apply an even layer or two of egg white the paper with a sponge or brush. The second is to mix two tablespoons of cornflour with cold water – add one tablespoon of water at a time to make a consistent paste – then add boiling water in small amounts to attain a glue-like consistency. Try to make small quantities of the cornflour mixture because it spoils easily – it's better to prepare it as you need it. Once the liquid cools down, you can apply it as an even layer or two. I personally use the first method, but have included the second one in case you are vegan.

The size of the paper is relevant to the way an artist intends to use the paper and their desired style. For example, an egg size makes the paper shiny. This type of knowledge can be developed with practice and further research.

BURNISHING THE PAPER

Once the paper is dry after the dye and the sizing, it then needs to be burnished because these layers usually change the smoothness of the paper. In summary, burnishing is rubbing the paper with a smooth stone until it becomes smooth and very soft; however, there are many ways to do the same thing.

The easiest method is to get a polished stone like agate that is about half the size of your hand and rub it over the paper in one direction at a time, horizontally, vertically and diagonally. An A3 paper could take half an hour to an hour to become very smooth. The smoothness helps with the outlining stage and the flow of the ink.

Another method is to turn the paper over, place it on a big smooth marble surface and burnish it from the back, so the friction between the marble, paper and stone is like a triple power to get that paper smooth. If a polished stone is hard to get, you can use any smooth surface to go over the paper.

SHELL GOLD AND BURNISHER

Shell gold is the main component of Islamic illumination – it is what turns a painting into an illumination. The addition of the gold is vital and expensive, but it feels incredible painting with it. If you are not able to afford or justify the use of genuine gold, you can use imitation watercolour gold, which will be applied like any other watercolour and would not need burnishing and so on. If you intend to work with genuine gold, there are a few things that you need to do.

USING READY-MADE SHELL GOLD

First, you need to decide if you want to use ready-made shell gold or prepare your own. The ready-made option makes your starting point much easier. Good-quality ready-made golds are found in Turkey and Japan; however, their availability changes based on the suppliers and they are not always easy to find online. Try looking at speciality arts or calligraphy stores in Turkey or Japan, but be aware that importing more than one pot of gold is usually taxed. The price of ready-made gold changes daily, following the gold market; over the years, I have purchased ready-made gold for between £30 and £60 per pot. If you have the budget, you can buy a few and stock up, since genuine gold does not spoil.

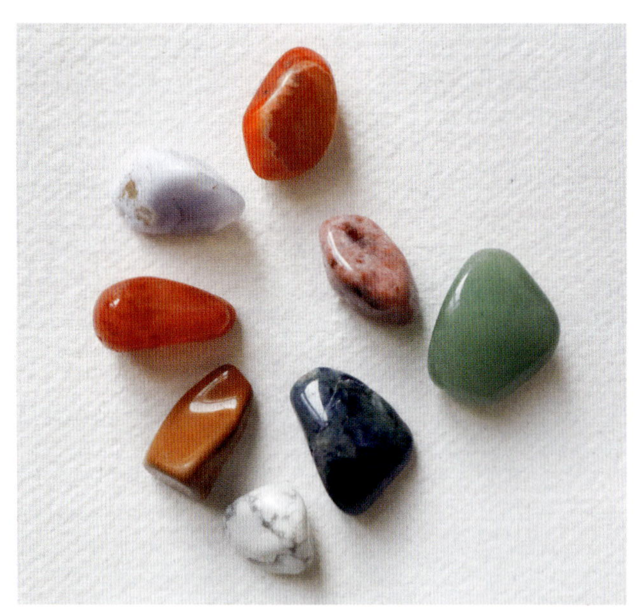

MAKING SHELL GOLD FROM GOLD LEAF

The second option is to make your own shell gold from genuine gold leaf. Some of my students tried to make shell gold from imitation gold leaf, but it did not work for them, so if you are using imitation gold go for the watercolour option or the powder in a jar, rather than going through the lengthy process that is only suitable for genuine gold.

The first time I learnt to make shell gold was with my teacher, Farkhondeh Ahmadzadeh. I found it enchanting – a lengthy but magical process. It is called 'shell gold' in reference to how the gold was stored traditionally in a shell. This method of making shell gold was developed in the Islamic world and it is the most suitable one for hot weather. The European medieval illumination and gilding methods are quite different.

I shared one of my early attempts on YouTube in 2016 (youtu.be/qYMavIeWEWE). The videography is now outdated (I now know that you cannot have nail polish on when you prepare it!); however, it is a useful reference along with the text below.

You will need a book of gold. I usually go for 23.5ct loose gold, which I source from Wrights of Lymm Ltd or Stuart R. Stevenson, but there are many other gilding stores that can provide it too. It is usually half the cost (or less) of ready-made shell-gold. The cheap ones on Amazon are usually not genuine, so I would stick to reputable shops – most of them offer international delivery.

You will need to use an adhesive to allow the gold to stick to the paper – I tend to go for gum arabic. You can prepare it yourself or buy ready-made gum arabic, which is affordable and reliable. For a whole gold book of twenty-five leaves, I use one or two teaspoons of gum arabic. I usually use a small glass bowl, which enables me to move my fingers easily, but most clean kitchenware can be used – find your most comfortable container.

I place the gum arabic I need in a separate palette and start with one teaspoon because the gum tends to dry. I take a tiny drop of gum with the tip of my finger and use it to rub each gold leaf for three to five minutes until the particles become much smaller. The friction of the gold, glass and gum will cause dryness, so have some filtered water next to you. I use a dropper to add a drop or two when my finger can no longer move because of dryness. The process takes an hour or two, but the longer you do it the finer the particles become, and that is the outcome you want for the shell gold.

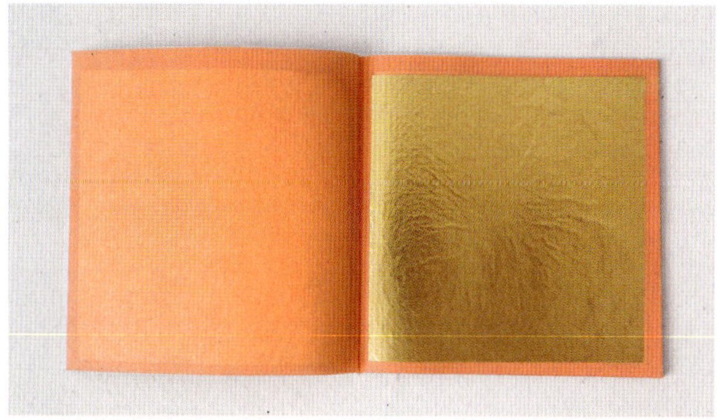

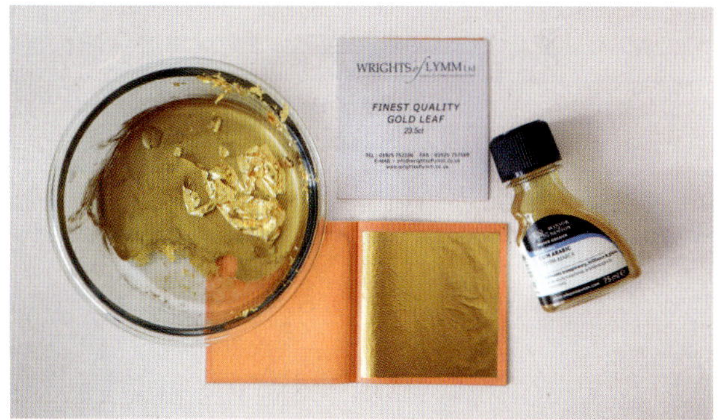

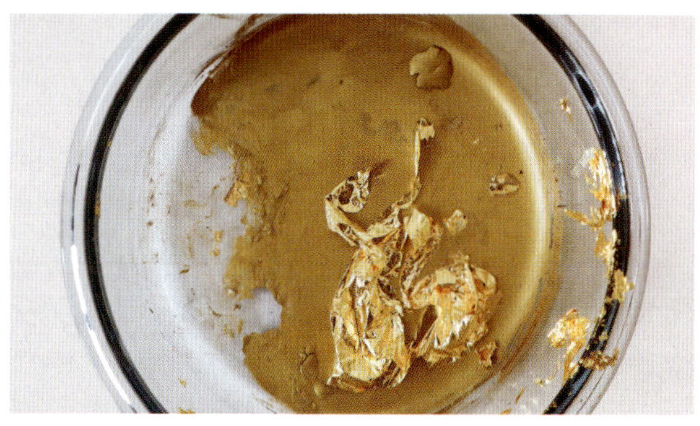

Once you are finished with the gold book, you are ready
to 'wash' the gold, which means pouring filtered water on
top of your dry gold to fill up the little bowl. While you
are doing that, make sure you clean your golden fingers
in the water and that you rub the gold that is stuck to the
bottom and sides of the bowl. Leave for a few hours until
the gold particles go to the bottom of the bowl.

When the gold settles at the bottom and the top half of the
water is clear, it is time to do a second wash. This means
carefully pouring the clear water into a separate container
and adding new filtered water on top of the gold again to
fill the bowl. Wait for another few hours and empty the
second quantity of water into another container.

There will be a small amount of water left in the bowl
covering the gold and you will leave that to dry. Once
it dries, you can carry out your gold test to see if the
process was successful. For this step you will need a
burnisher – a polishing stone for the gold.

The best burnisher to use is agate – either agate with
a wooden handle or a polished agate stone without a
handle (if these are hard to find, in theory any polished
stone or surface will work). The purpose of this is to
apply pressure and friction to the gold to make it shinier.
You can burnish all your gold, or as a styling method just
burnish some of the gold and keep the rest muted. There
is room to play with this.

THE GOLD TEST

The gold test is a simple painting test:
- Add some water to your dropper.
- Drop it onto the dry gold to be mixed with your brush.
- Paint a tiny swatch with it or paint some lines on a
  piece of paper.
- Wait until the gold dries.
- Rub it with a burnisher or a polished stone.
- Rub your finger over it. If the gold is rubbing off, a
  few drops of gum arabic are needed. Do not add the
  gum arabic directly to the gold, but to the water you
  will use for painting with the gold. Redo the test
  using your new water and gum arabic mixture to
  check that you have added enough adhesive.
- If you burnish it and the gold does not shine, then
  you have applied too much gum arabic and it will
  need an additional wash or two.

Knowing the exact consistency of the gold and the best
recipe for you takes a lot of practice and experience, so
whatever the outcome is, keep trying until you get used
to it.

As with everything traditional, there are many recipes for
the same thing and this is only one of them. If you would
like to experiment with a fun way to make gold slightly
differently, another teacher of mine, Anita Chowdry, has
written *The Book of Gold*, which describes the method of
making shell gold in the Indian tradition.

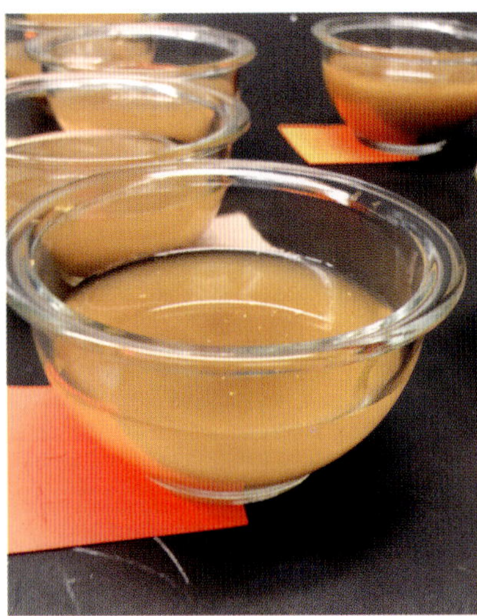

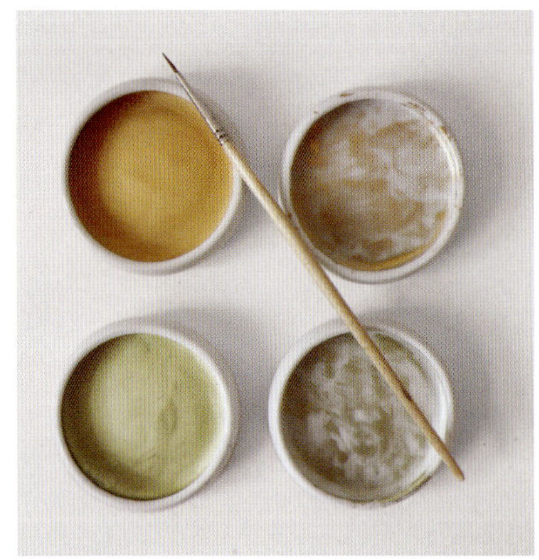

BLACK INK

An additional tool for Islamic illumination is black ink, which is usually used to outline the work, making the shell gold sharper so it stands out from the painting. I enjoy using Winsor & Newton black Indian ink, but a lot of the calligraphy inks are suitable for this; I also like to experiment with locally found ink brands. Some people find the black ink too harsh for their liking, so feel free to try other coloured inks. There is a big range of natural inks now, which opens up a world of possibilities.

Working with ink can be the hardest step to master, so before you use any ink, make sure that you practise with a thin brush (2/0 to 10/0) and ink on a separate paper to get the desired thickness of line. Do not be discouraged if your line is not thin enough, but try to make it consistent at whatever thickness you can manage.

To start the ink practice, take a new piece of paper and draw straight lines with your brush in different directions. You will notice that your hand and brush control changes based on the direction you go in. You might have a directional preference – if that is the case, move your paper around to stick with the most comfortable direction for you.

Try different line thicknesses. In many of the outlined Turkish flowers, you will notice the line going from thin on the side to thicker at the tips and certain turns. This is a more advanced skill to acquire, but keep it in mind. Since you will be outlining curved and circular motifs, include those into your ink practice. Try spirals, the letters S and C, and other shapes that come to mind.

The purpose of this exercise is to warm up your hand to draw shapes that you are not used to. It is important to do this every time before you outline a new painting. Fill one or two A4 sheets with ink lines before outlining your intended design.

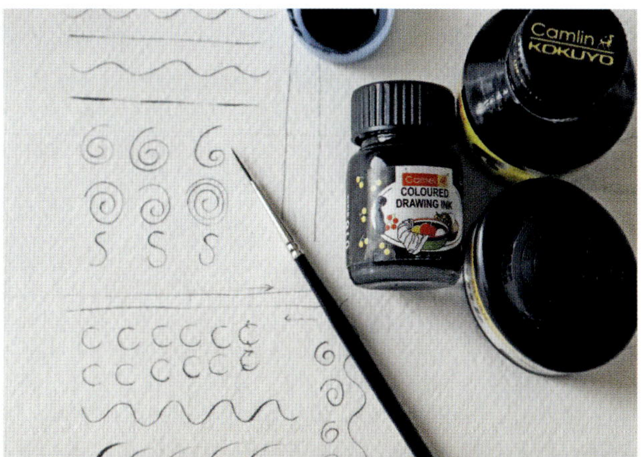

HANDMADE WATERCOLOURS

In the previous section, I told you about watercolour types (see p.154). The ones I mentioned were usually manufactured and there is nothing wrong with that at all – they can give you stunning results. Nonetheless, I wanted to tell you about handmade watercolours and how they can impact your work.

Handmade watercolours can come from two material sources: natural or synthetic. Natural watercolours can be organic or inorganic. Natural organic watercolours have come from a living source such as an insect (carmine), plant (indigo and madder lake) or bone (bone black). Natural inorganic watercolours come from non-living sources such as clay, rock (ochre) and minerals (lapis, malachite, etc.). Synthetic watercolours start with a natural base but need a chemical reaction or a human-made process to achieve the desired colours.

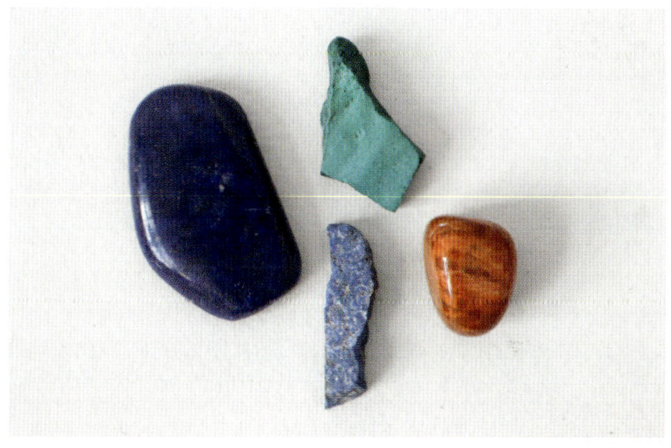

Handmade watercolour makers use a range of these materials in the form of dry pigment that is then mixed with gum arabic, which is the glue that holds the particles together and makes it stick to paper.

You might wonder about the benefit of using these paints and it is honestly a personal preference as to how they look on paper. Natural watercolours are special as they come directly from nature and were used in pre-medieval manuscripts, therefore giving us closer results to the traditional painting method. Synthetic handmade watercolours also vary slightly from store-bought ones because their recipe is different. It is up to you which type of watercolour you end up using, but it is always worth looking deeper into the world of colour to see what possibilities there are.

THE ISLAMIC ILLUMINATION PAINTING PROCESS

EXAMPLE 1:
TURKISH QURAN CARPET PAGE

Now that we have established the required tools, we come to the Islamic illumination painting process. As I mentioned previously, there are no definite sources to confirm that this is the exact process used, but this is the inherited one adopted by many Turkish and Iranian artists who have kept this practice alive for a few centuries.

To demonstrate the process, I have chosen Pattern Study 8: Turkish Quran Carpet Page (see p.117) to paint.

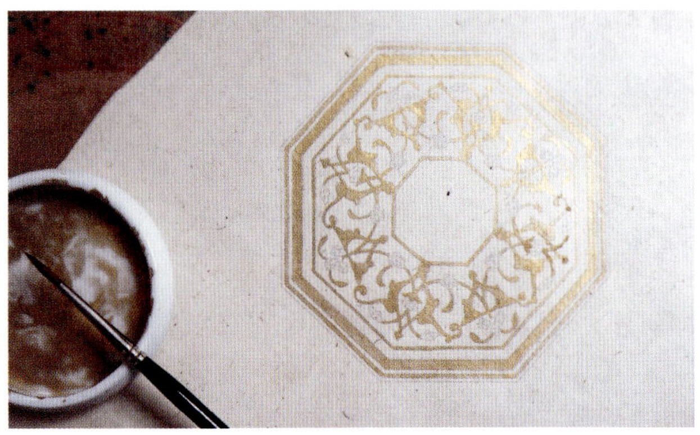

↑ Painting in shell gold.

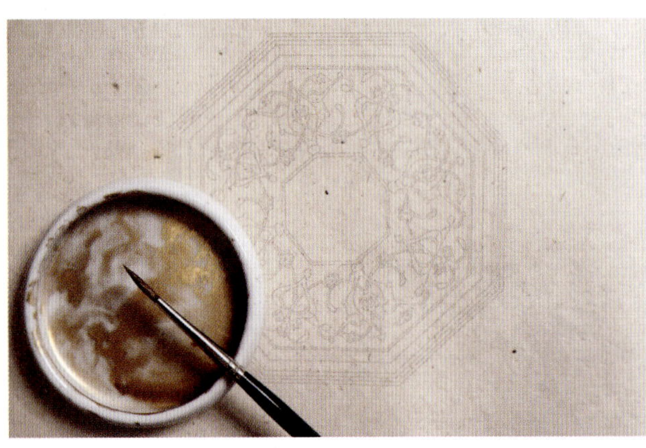

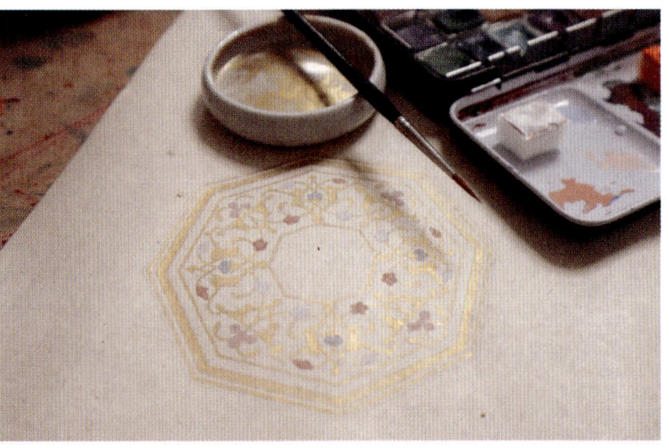

1   Trace your pattern using tracing paper and then transfer it to a treated watercolour paper of your choice. Here I used a pre-treated hemp paper by Khadi Papers. The thickness of this paper is 90gsm, which is thinner than the 300gsm I recommended, so you have to be careful with how much water you are using to make sure the paper is not ruined. You can start with hot pressed 300gsm and then slowly move to thinner paper like this with more practice.

2   Decide how the pattern is going to be painted. Is it all going to be in shell gold? If it contains other floral elements, what colours will they be? Since we are mostly working from patterns found on tiles that are not originally painted in gold, we can be flexible with our choices; however, the colour palette needs to be limited to four colours, otherwise it will look too busy. Here, I painted the inorganic shapes in shell gold and the flowers in white, light pink and light blue watercolour paints.

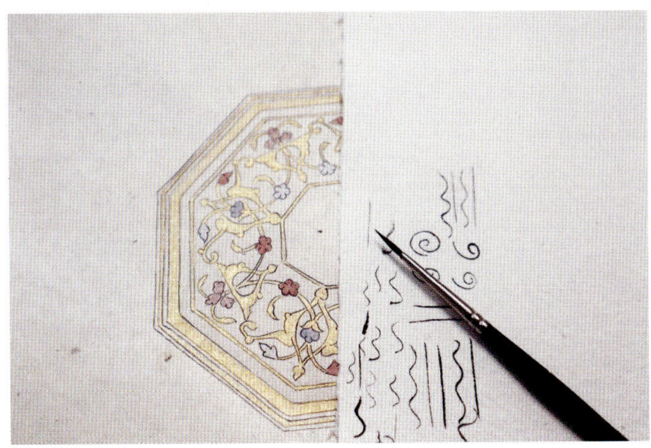

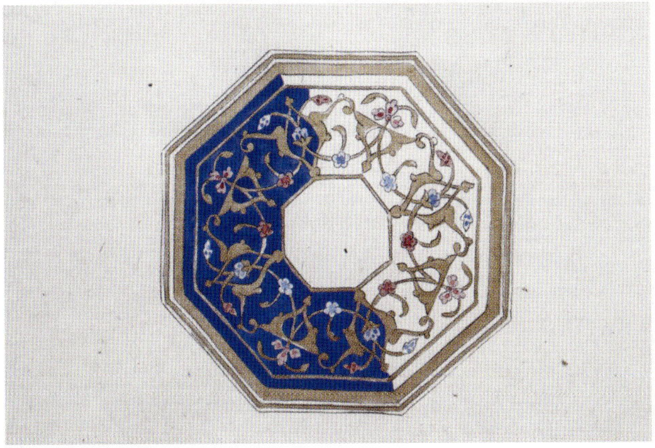

3 Once the colours are blocked on the pattern, it is time to outline the shapes using black ink and a brush. I usually use a thin size 3/0 brush for this step, but try different sizes depending on what you are painting and what you are comfortable using.

It is best to warm up your hand with some practice beforehand – you can trace the design again using the ink and brush on a separate piece of tracing paper. With experience and practice you will be able to better control your brush and ink in order to make decisions about where the line can be thin or thick.

4 Now add a background colour. There is always a debate about whether to leave the background soft and dainty or bold with a darker colour. Here, I have painted one section with a dark background and left the other without, to give you an idea of the two looks.

If you left the flowers in white, like me, you can add some finishing touches to them in this stage, such as a small amount of colour in the centre or any style of shading that you prefer.

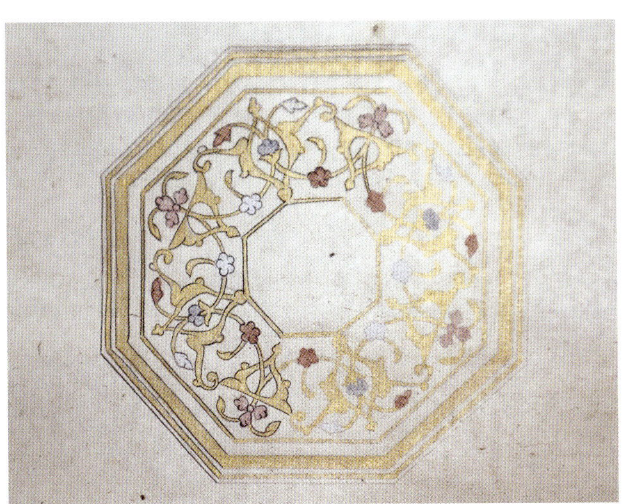

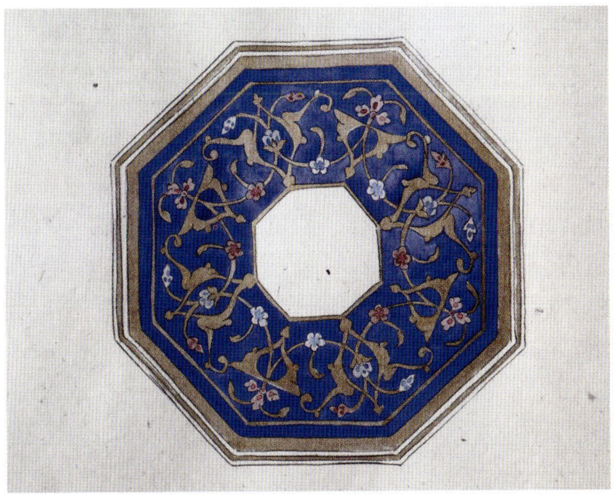

The example above shows how the painting looks with and without outlining. I always love looking at the design when it is half-outlined as it is very satisfying seeing the results. Some people love the sharp finish with the ink that defines every shape, while others prefer a softer finish. If you are struggling with the outlining practice, try painting a few designs without it until you are comfortable enough to tackle it at a later stage.

In the original pattern the full background is painted in blue, the centre is filled with Arabic calligraphy and the remaining spaces are painted in gold. I think that combination is powerful and pleasing to the eye. Above you will see how the pattern looks with a fully painted background. The centre also could have been painted in gold, but I prefer it without.

EXAMPLE 2:
IZNIK HEXAGONAL TILE

For the second example, I have chosen to paint Pattern Study 2: Iznik Hexagonal Tile (see p.54). The painting process follows the same order as in Example 1, although it is executed in a slightly different way to give a traditional look with a contemporary twist. It is good to experiment to find your own style within the vast possibilities of Islamic illumination. It is also enjoyable testing different illuminating metals together, such as different weights of gold or the use of other metals such as silver or white gold.

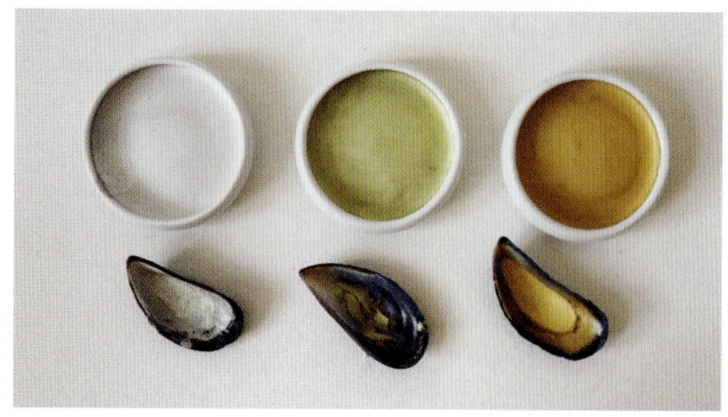

In terms of the paper selection, I started with a cotton paper, handmade in India. I did not apply any treatment, which proved a little difficult while painting and some of the shell gold was absorbed by the paper due to the lack of sizing; however, the results were very appealing to me. You can treat the paper as advised on pp.159–60 or test out the result – the best way to know your personal preference is to try both.

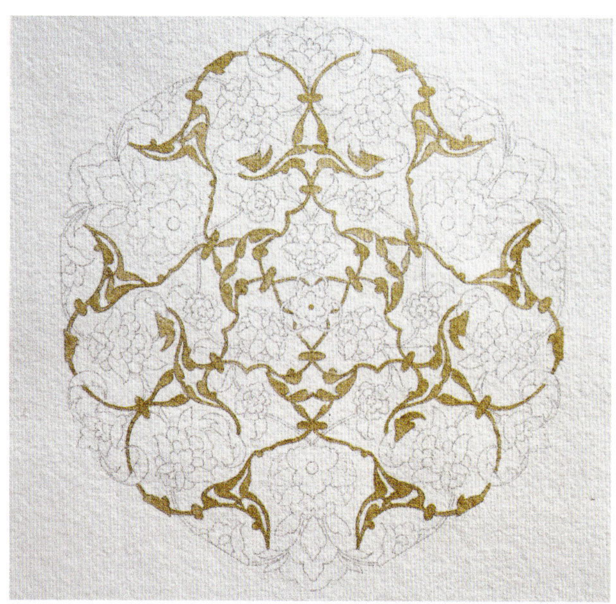

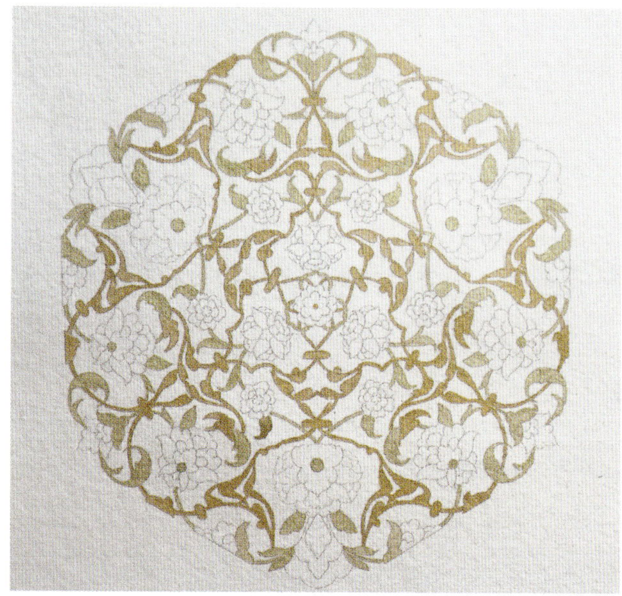

1   I started by painting the inorganic shapes in the classic 24-carat shell gold, which has a beautiful warm, reddish tone. It is interesting what is highlighted when the colour is painted in a symmetrical way.

2   For the branches that connect the flowers, I chose an 18-carat shell gold. Since it is a lower-quality gold it has been mixed with some copper, which gives it a slightly greener tone. Having the two shades of gold is pleasing and gives a unique result to the design.

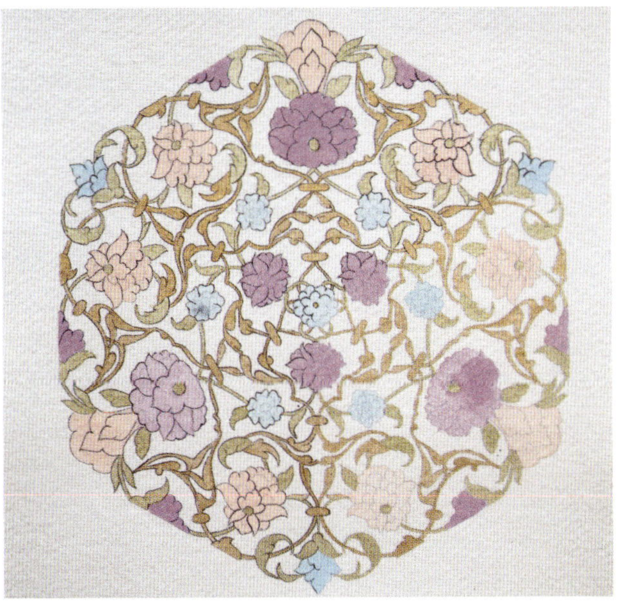

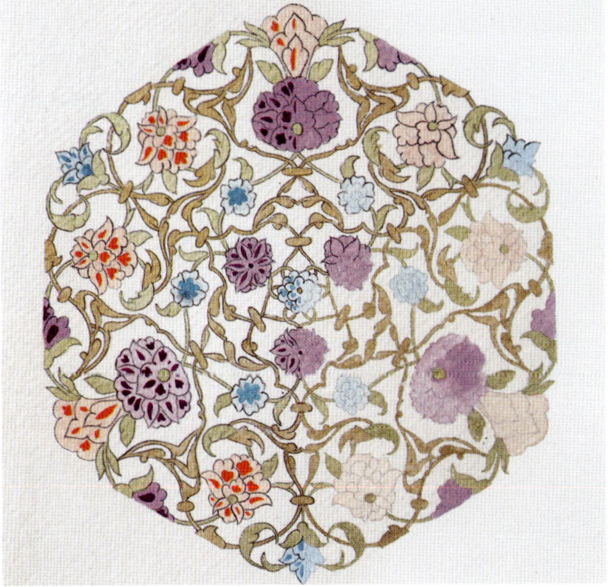

3 I wanted the flowers to be lively to resemble the spring season, so I chose pastel shades for the first painting layer. It is important to keep the exact colour choices consistent for each section and to keep the palette limited for the flowers – I would usually stick to three colours in a small design like this. Having the same colours woven within the design gives the pattern an additional quality of balance. For emphasis, each colour has been used twice throughout the design.

4 Outlining with ink comes next. Again, this image demonstrates how the design looks when three-quarters are outlined and the remaining quarter is left without ink.

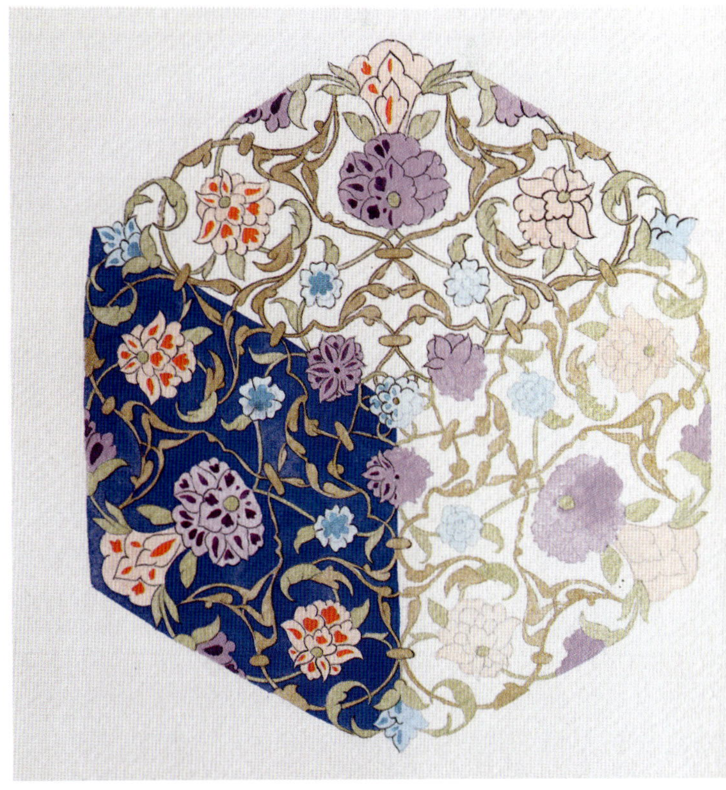

5 The last step could either involve shading the flowers with a slightly darker colour or painting the background. I tend to make a decision based on the painting itself – after all, this is a personal painting and the outcome should also be personal. In the traditional examples, it is uncommon to leave backgrounds unpainted, especially in a geometrically closed design like this. The image here illustrates the difference between having a background and omitting one.

EXAMPLE 3:
DAMASCUS POTTERY TILE

The third example is another mixture of tradition and contemporary practice. It is the tessellated pattern from Pattern Study 9: Damascus Pottery Tile (see p.126). Having a tessellated pattern results in a much prettier composition and the result feels more satisfying and complete.

First, choose the materials. Here I chose the polished smooth paper from Example 1 (see p.164) as there is a large amount of shell gold in this design and I did not want the cotton paper to absorb it. I decided to use natural watercolours, which go well with the genuine shell gold.

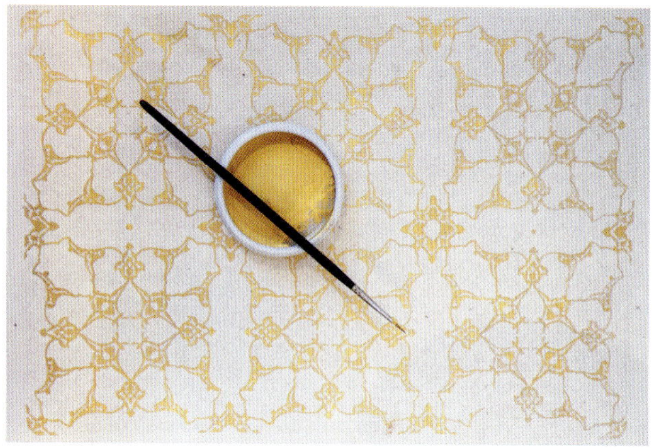

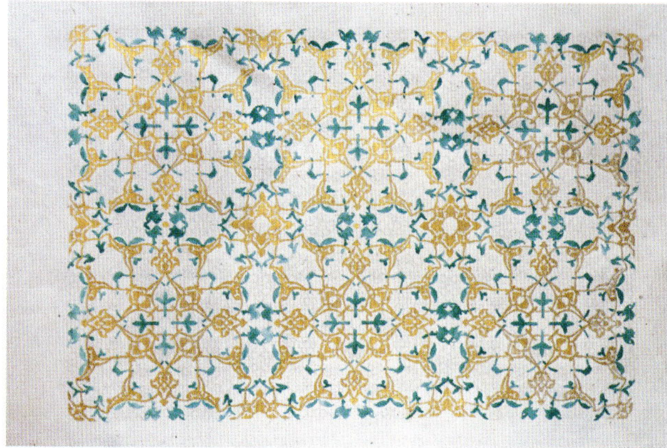

1 Next, decide where the gold and the colours will be placed. As always, gold will be used first to show our respect to this beautiful, precious material. In traditional manuscripts, gold is usually used on inorganic shapes, so I will follow the same order with this example.

2 Continuing with the colour decision, I decided to follow the colours that are usually seen in nature for the botanical design of the remaining floral shapes. Therefore, all the branches and leaves are painted in malachite – the soft, bright green complements the gold nicely.

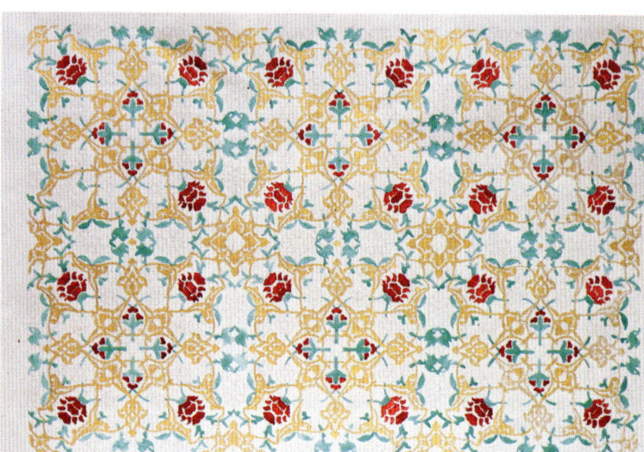

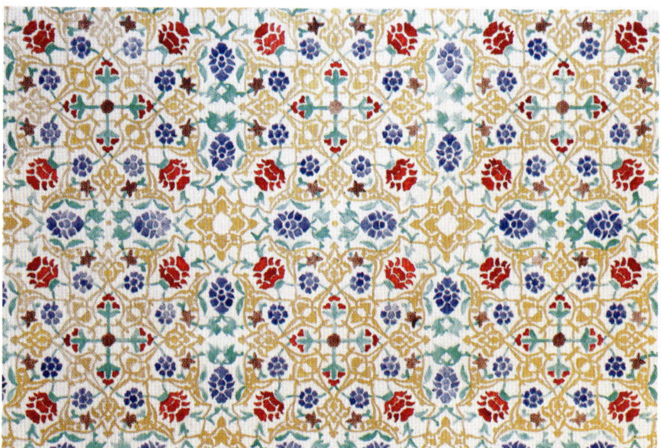

3 There are four types of flowers and as I wanted to limit the colour palette, I alternated between them to paint two types in genuine carmine and the other two in lapis lazuli. It is better to start with one colour and paint it fully before moving on to the next.

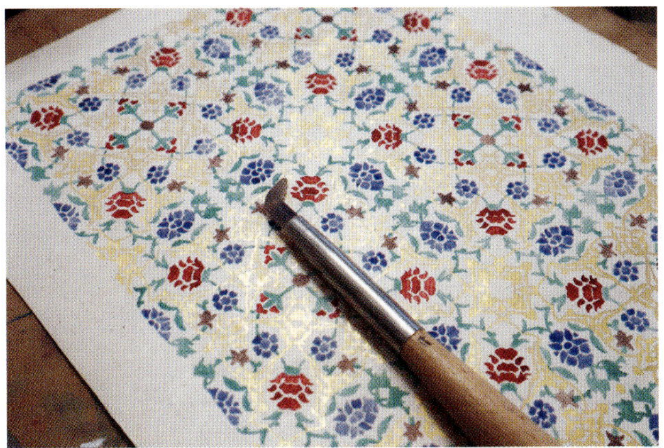 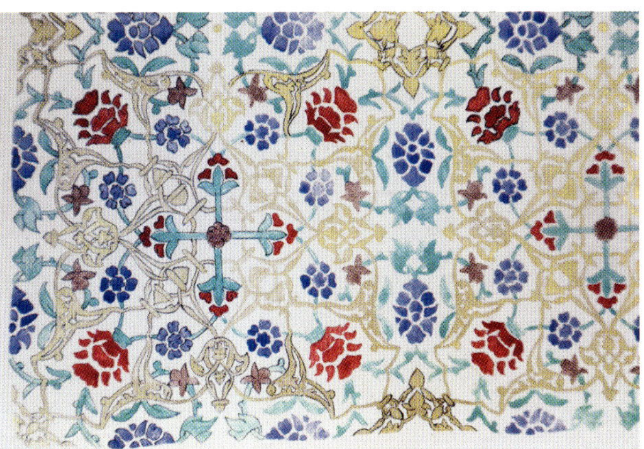

4 Burnishing can be done right after painting the shell gold or after painting all the foreground colour. A burnishing tool or burnishing stone can be used. Both are equally good, so use whichever is accessible to you.

5 The last step in this example is the outlining. This is very time-consuming, especially with a tessellated design, and it can take a few days. Make sure you do some external practice before you begin to outline this design. Be prepared to take it very slow – this step requires an immense amount of patience and hand control.

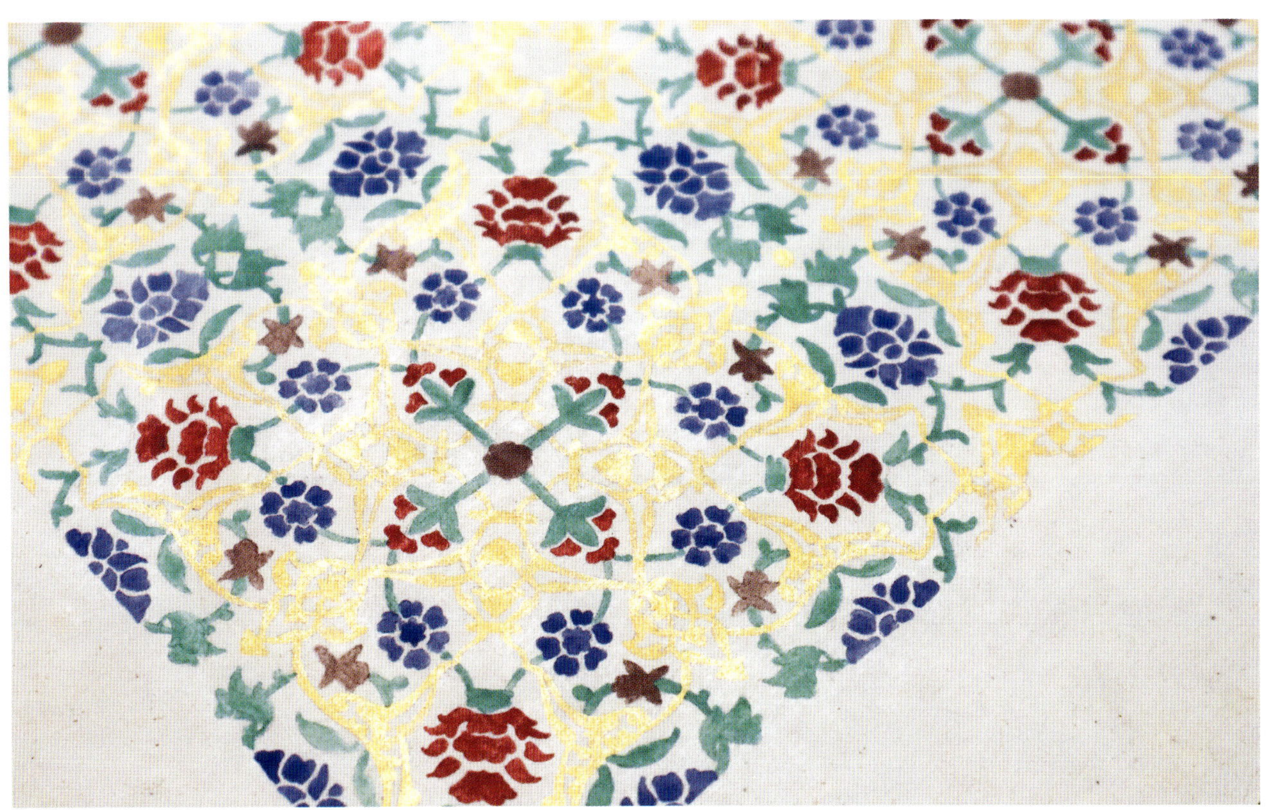

The painting process is complete. Traditionally the background is painted, but I loved the natural colour of the paper so I left it without additional painting. Feel free to paint it to see how much the appearance and feel of the pattern changes.

CONCLUSION

I hope this book will help you to understand the existing visual language of botanical biomorphic and inorganic motifs found in the Islamic world.

Part I briefly discussed pattern development to pique your curiosity. It will be fantastic if you carry on with that line of research and connect the dots between the patterns and their context and history to see the commonalities. Each dynasty brought with it a fresh outlook to the art of patterns, and the changing surroundings, circumstances and patrons each impacted the patterns.

Part II explored the heart of patterns and we went on a small journey to study 12 patterns from various parts of the Islamic world. Some of these objects are now placed in auction houses, such as Sotheby's and Christie's, to make their way to private or public collections. Other patterns, such as those from the Metropolitan Museum in New York, are in accessible public museums for us all to study and enjoy. Other tiles reside in their original habitats in beautiful monuments that you have to travel to see and appreciate.

The pattern choices were varied, but the basis of all patterns was similar. Most biomorphic patterns are based on geometric grids that are either six- or eight-pointed stars. There are more complicated grids that are beyond the scope of this book; however, I would recommend that you take your time to learn each geometric grid and the possibilities they offer. As demonstrated, one grid can give us a number of patterns and there are many more to explore.

Part III was about painting styles, which are split into two areas: contemporary painting and Islamic illumination. The beauty of these patterns is that they can adapt to the paint and tend to keep their beautiful quality, whether painted in gold or watercolours. It is a good idea to experiment with both to find the style that resonates most with you. Learning to paint in the illumination style is a living tradition in Turkey and Iran, and it takes years for practitioners to reach a professional level. It is a true passion to follow the rules of this sixteenth-century painting style. This can be something you aim for or you can follow your own intuition to paint without rules and enjoy the process.

There are more wonderful books that would support your learning of this subject, including those I have listed in the Bibliography. This book is only the beginning of your journey into the world of patterns – there is still so much to study and uncover.

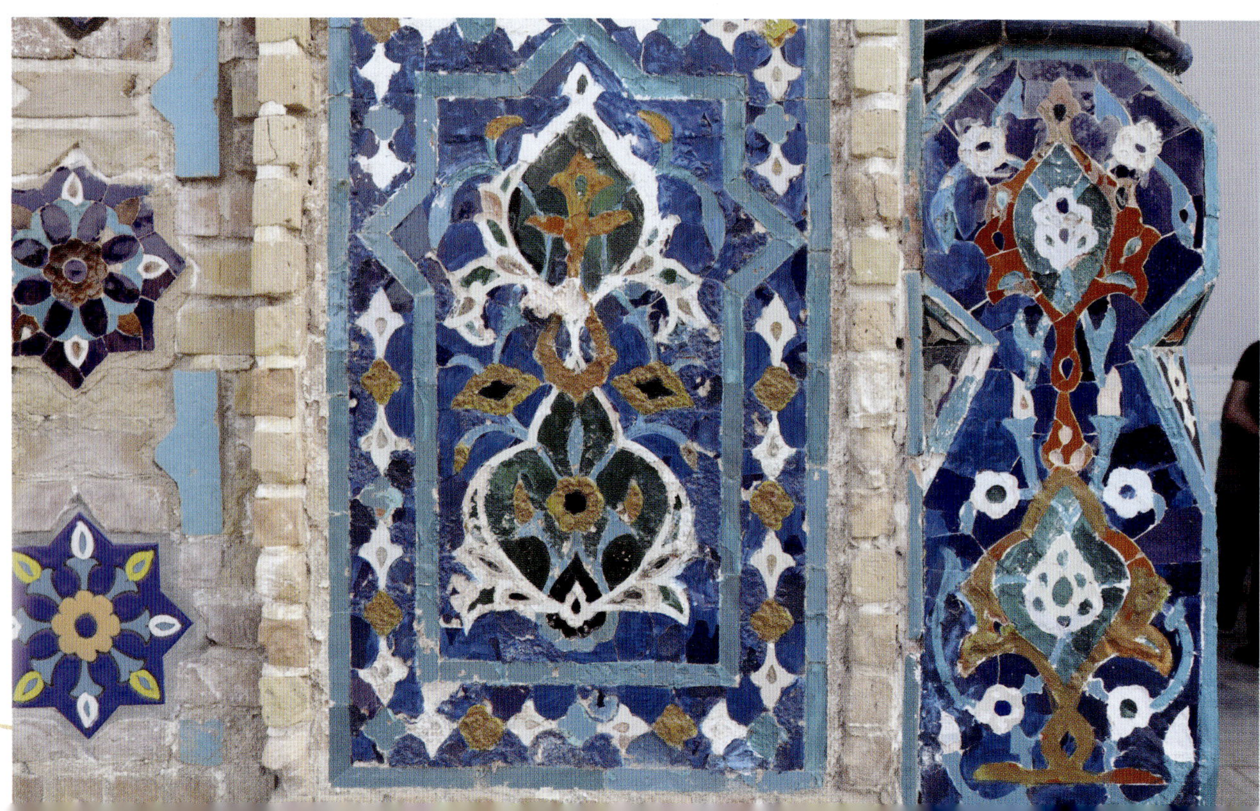

SUPPLIERS

Cass Art
www.cassart.co.uk

Daler-Rowney
www.daler-rowney.com

Da Vinci
www.davinci-defet.com/en

Karin Sanat
www.karinsanat.com/en

Khadi Papers
www.khadi.com

Rosemary & Co
www.rosemaryandco.com

Schmincke
www.schmincke.de/en

Stuart R. Stevenson
www.stuartstevenson.co.uk

Winsor & Newton
www.winsornewton.com

Wrights of Lymm Ltd
www.stonehouses.co.uk

BIBLIOGRAPHY

BOOKS

Azzam, Khaled, *Arts & Crafts of the Islamic Lands, Principles, Materials, Practice* (2021)

Birol, Inci A., *Motifs in Turkish Decorative Arts* (1991)

Blair, Sheila S., *The Art and Architecture of Islam, 1250-1800* (1996)

Canby, Sheila R., *Masterpieces from the Department of Islamic Art in the Metropolitan Museum of Art* (2011)

Chowdry, Anita, *The Book of Gold: Making and Using Shell Gold* (2017)

Critchlow, Keith, *Islamic Patterns: An Analytical and Cosmological Approach* (1983)

Henry, Richard, *Islamic Geometry Journal* (2019)

Medlej, Joumana, *Inks & Paints of the Middle-East: A Handbook of Abbasid Art Technology* (2021)

Onat, Sema, *Islamic Art of Illumination: Classical Tazhib from Ottoman to Contemporary Times* (2015)

Shaw, Wendy M. K., *What is 'Islamic' Art?: Between Religion and Perception* (2019)

Sutton, Daud, *Islamic Design: A Genius for Geometry* (2007)

Williamson, Adam, *Profound Patterns: Islamic Art at Home* (2022)

Wright, Elaine, *Lapis and Gold: Exploring Chester Beatty's Ruzbihan Qur'an* (2018)

WEBSITES

Alhamal, Dr. Esra
Art Illuminated Podcast:
www.islamicillumination.com/podcast

Alhamal, Dr. Esra
Patterns & Illumination, 'Golden Flower Art Challenge March 2021'
www.islamicillumination.com/blog/golden-flower-art-challenge-march-2021

The Met, 'Chronology of Major Empires and Dynasties in the Islamic World' (2023)
www.metmuseum.org/learn/educators/curriculum-resources/art-of-the-islamic-world/introduction/chronology

www.artofislamicpattern.com

www.samiramian.uk

socofujairah.ae

ACKNOWLEDGEMENTS

Thank you to my mother, Najat, for giving me this drive to succeed; the thirst to enquire, read and explore; and for always proofreading my work and endlessly brainstorming and planning with me.

Thank you to my husband Bryan for pushing me forward, talking over countless ideas with me and supporting me every step of the way.

Thank you to my dear friend Samira Mian for always giving me the positive boost I need, chatting with me whenever there is overwhelm or underwhelm and, of course, for helping me with the geometry!

Thank you to the talented Joumana Medlej for our creative chats and for her amazing contributions to the world of calligraphy and pigments.

Thank you to my generous teachers, Anita Chowdry, Farkhondeh Ahmadzadeh, Adam Williamson and Richard Henry, who shared many wonderful lessons with me.

Thank you to the rest of my family and friends for being so supportive and kind.

Thank you to my creative community on Instagram, who have followed Islamic Illumination since day one. They have been a massive support system and an encouraging force to get me where I am today. Their interest and enrolment in my courses have been life changing and I am so grateful to them.

My students on the Domestika course also deserve a big thank you for proving to the world that Islamic biomorphic patterns are so admired and that there is a desire for them to be studied.

Thank you to the Herbert Press team, Clare Sara and Tash, and Bloomsbury Publishing for offering me this wonderful opportunity, for supporting me throughout and for their tremendous effort in bringing this idea to life.

CREDITS

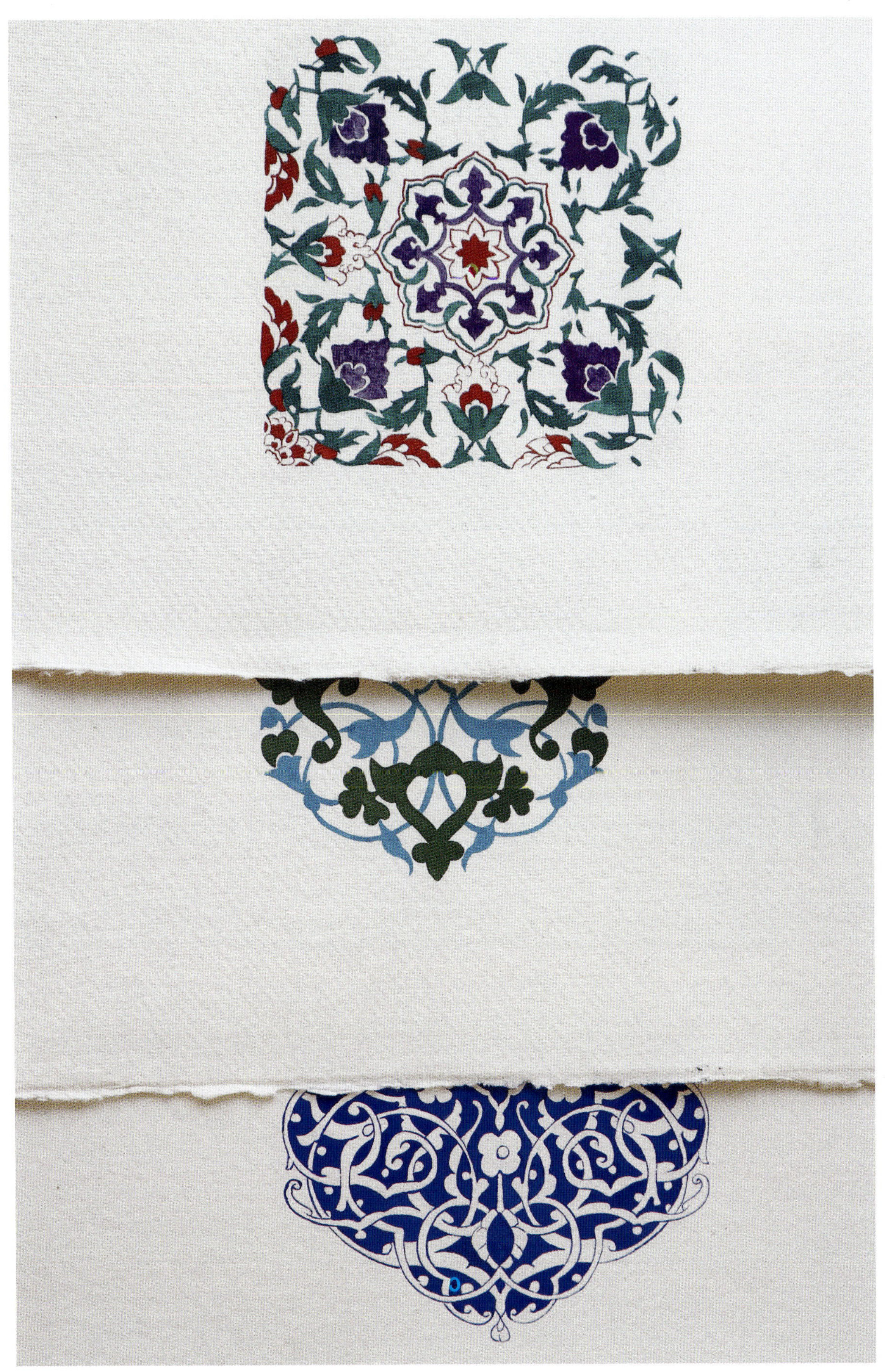

APPENDIX: MOTIF DATABASE

Throughout this book, you have been learning about various motifs, both inorganic and plant based. To help you with your future designs, all these motifs have been collected and grouped in this appendix as three sections: inorganic shapes, florals and leaves.

This appendix is a great resource for you to refer to whenever you want to create your own designs inspired by the classical Islamic biomorphic visual language. There are more motifs throughout the Islamic world, and the more you study patterns, the more you can expand upon this list.

FLORAL MOTIFS

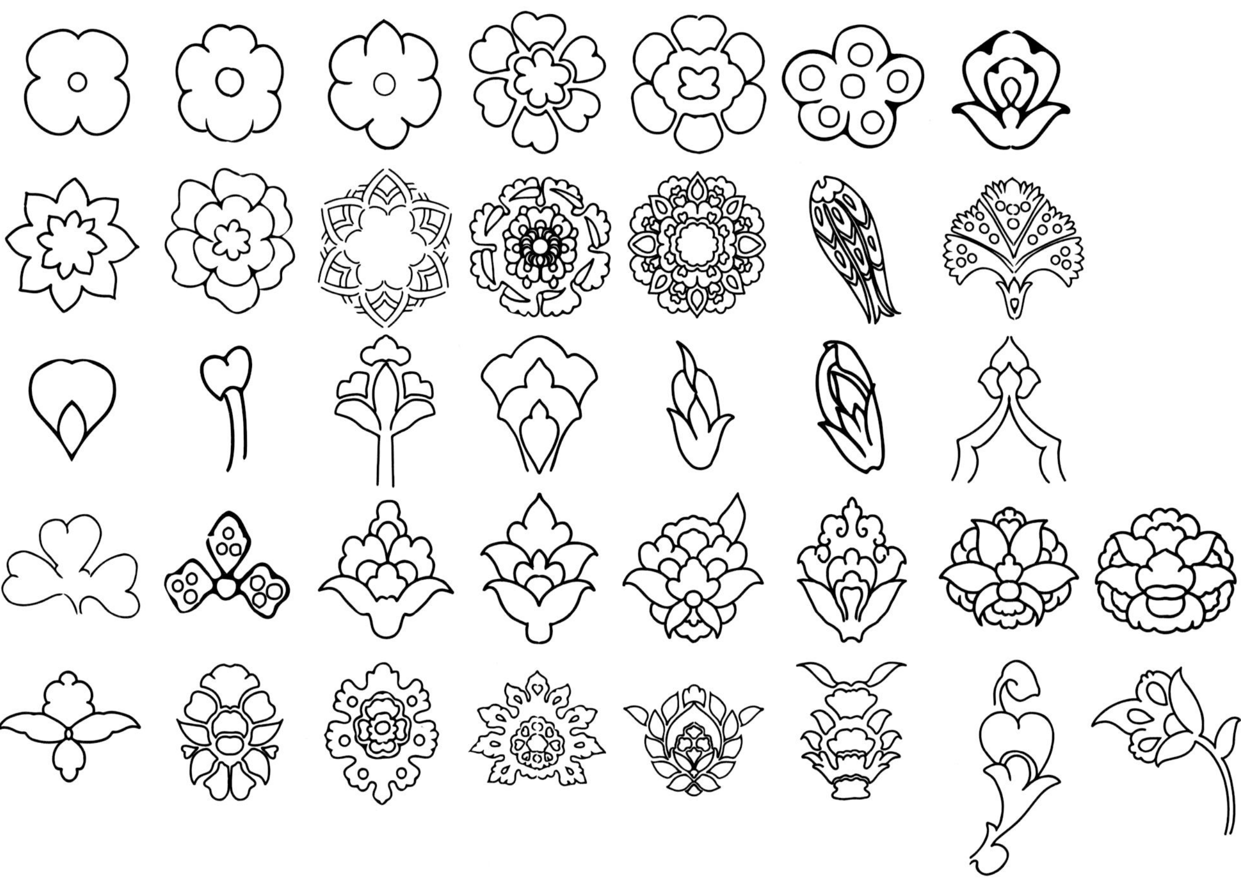

LEAF MOTIFS

INORGANIC SHAPES

These shapes are mostly used as halves on the vertical, diagonal and horizontal lines and as starting points to spirals and other connections.

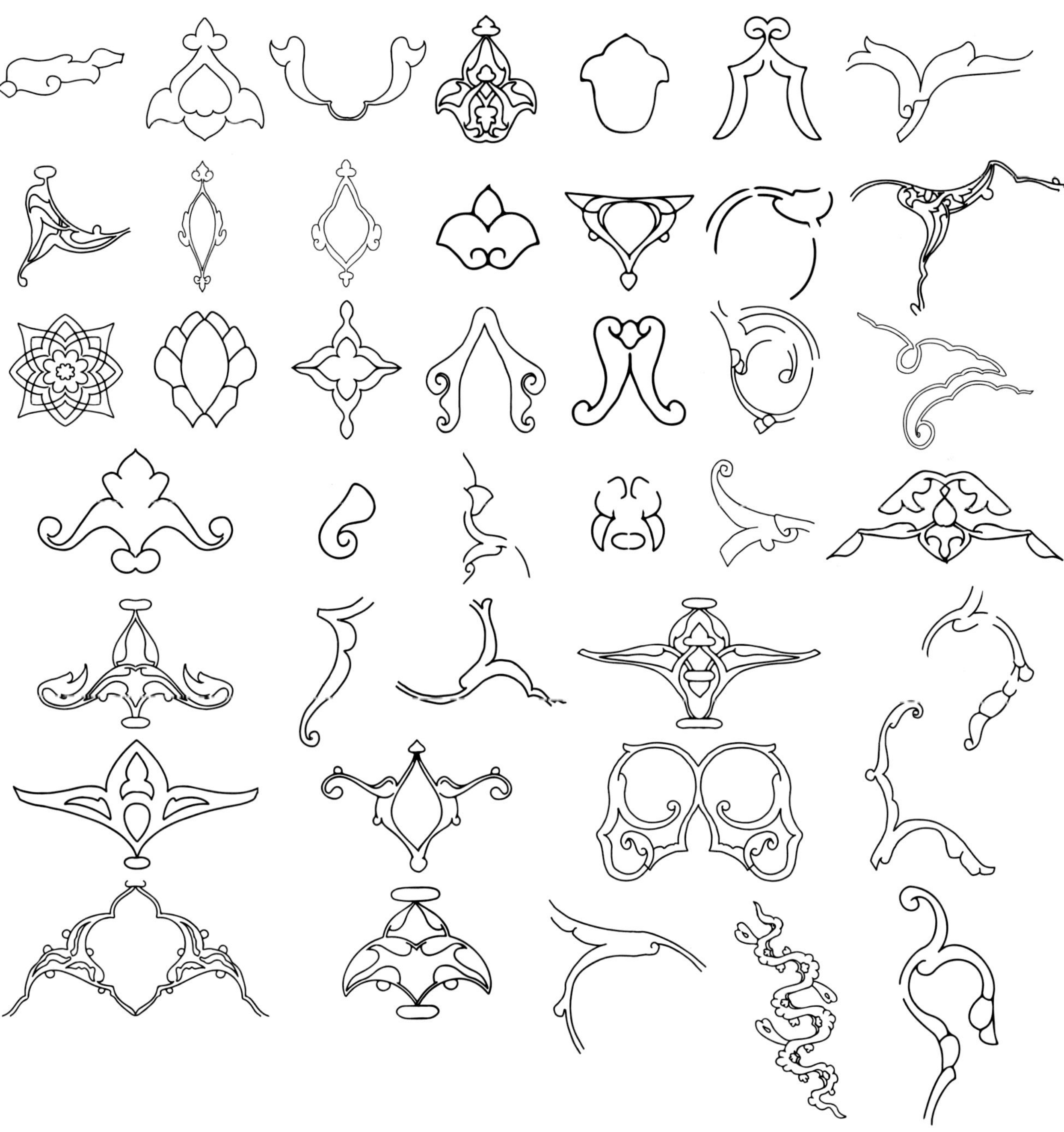

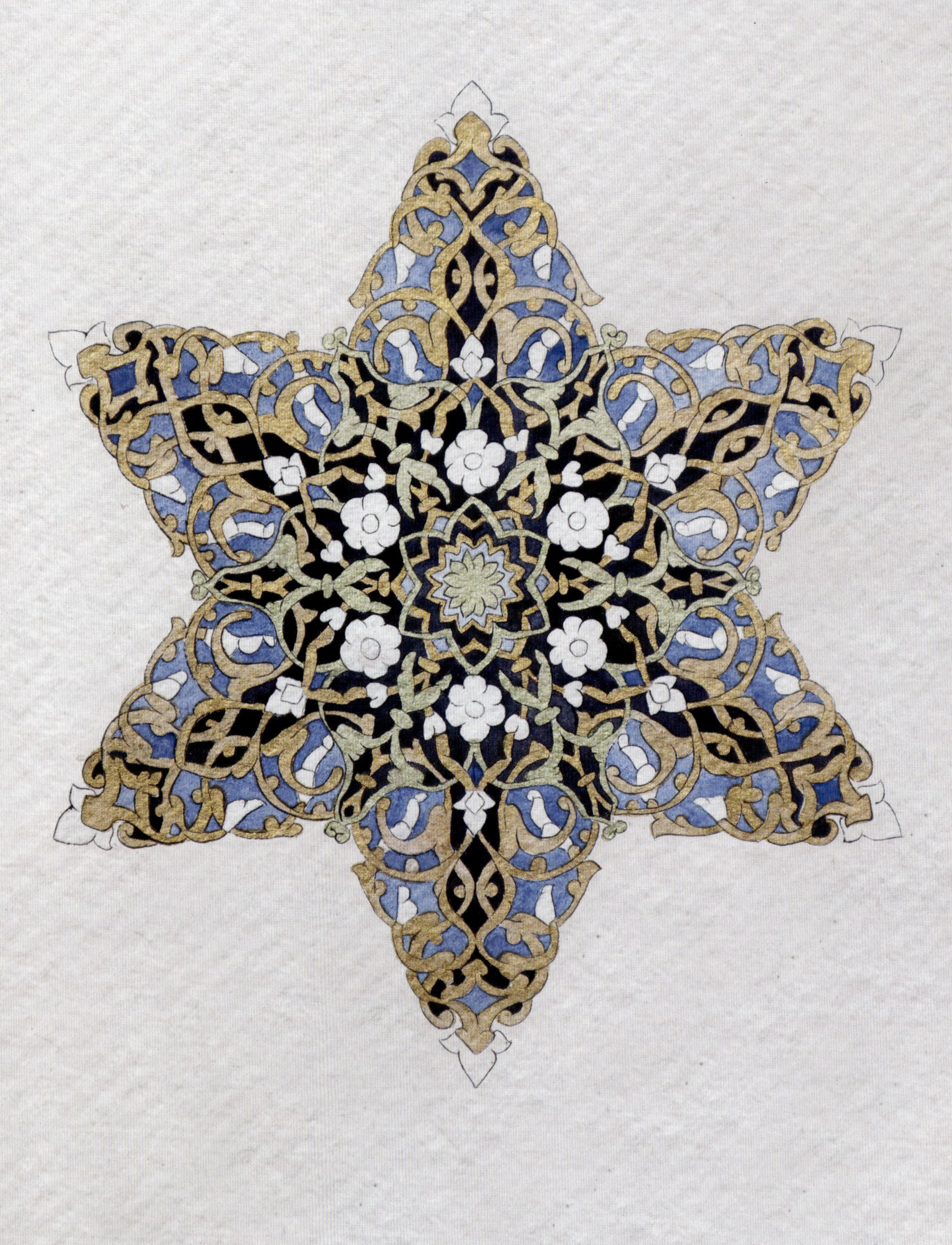